The Possible South

The Possible South

Documentary Film and
the Limitations of Biraciality

R. Bruce Brasell

University Press of Mississippi / Jackson

www.upress.state.ms.us

The University Press of Mississippi is a member
of the Association of American University Presses.

Copyright © 2015 by University Press of Mississippi
All rights reserved

First printing 2015
∞
Library of Congress Cataloging-in-Publication Data

Brasell, R. Bruce.
  The possible South : documentary film and the limitations of
biraciality / R. Bruce Brasell.
      pages cm
  Includes bibliographical references and index.
  ISBN 978-1-4968-0408-2 (hardback) — ISBN 978-1-4968-0409-9
(ebook) 1. Cultural pluralism—Southern States.
2. Documentary films—United States—History and criticism. I.
Title.
  HM1271.B737 2015
  305.800975—dc23   2015019117

British Library Cataloging-in-Publication Data available

For my sisters, Beverly and Patricia

Contents

ix   Acknowledgments

3   Introduction—Southern Discourse, Mediated Distinctiveness, and the Devaluation of the Audiovisual

Part I: Biraciality and Southern Discourse

39   Chapter One—"Experience our past as part of your future": Biraciality and *Tell About the South*, Cultural Citizenship, and Bi-Civic Heritage

69   Chapter Two—"God-created difference": Racial Performance, Regional Exceptionalism, and *bro•ken/ground*

Part II: Biracial Denial One—Miscegenation

99   Chapter Three—"In slave time you know everything happened": The Racial Closet, Southeastern Expatriate Road Film, and *Family Name*

125   Chapter Four—Praying Pigs and Wooden Peg Legs: Racial Poaching, Redemptive Ethnography, and 1970s Southeastern Documentaries

Part III: Biracial Denial Two—Existence of Other Races and Ethnicities

155   Chapter Five—"Wonder if our culture will survive": Racial In-Betweenness, Cultural Preservation, and the Sound of Ethnicity in *Mosquitoes and High Water*, *Living in America*, and *Nuestra Communidad*

179   Chapter Six—"So that we have our own color": Racial Negotiation, Textual Posturing, and *Mississippi Triangle*

197 Chapter Seven—"Too much bad blood": Racial Legitimacy, Representational Strategies, and *Real Indian*

217 Conclusion

223 Notes

271 Bibliography

293 Index

Acknowledgments

This project has been long in the making, over a decade and a half. After the initial draft, I shelved it until two conversations led me to reconsider the decision, one with Jon Smith over lunch when he lived in Birmingham, Alabama, and the other with Jane Gaines over drinks in New York City after a Columbia University film seminar. Without their encouragement this project would continue to lay dormant. The disciplines of these two individuals (new southern studies and cinema studies, respectively) and the locations of the conversations are telling. While the project's combination of cinema studies with cultural studies (as well as race and ethnic studies) is a commonly accepted practice, its blending of cinema studies with southern studies is as incongruent as the common perceptions about the two locations where the conversations occurred. And I have spent the last decade alternating between teaching in the New York City metro area and writing in Alabama; that writing transpired not only over many years but many tables—no desks that I can remember. I wrote on public tables in cozy corners of the Vestavia Hills Library in the Forest and the Hoover Public Library, a patio table on my sister Beverly's back deck, a makeshift table on the front porch of my sister Patricia and brother-in-law Alan's beach house, a tray table at my parents' house while I took care of my father with Alzheimer's disease, and a kitchen table at my niece Tiffany's house while I looked after her son Chance after school. I could not have completed this project without the help of a lot of people. My family provided me with support so I could write full-time in Alabama, and my friends from graduate school (both faculty and former students) provided me with job contacts so I could teach film and media studies in New York City—sometimes visiting positions but more often adjunct ones at multiple colleges in a semester.

    Since this is my first book, I have numerous people to thank for helping me over the years. In addition to Jon Smith and Jane Gaines, mentioned earlier, I am indebted to Chris Straayer, Toby Miller, Charles Reagan Wilson, Tara McPherson, and Robert Stam for their support of the project since its inception. During the past trying decade, Chris Straayer has been a constant source of sanity. Because most of this book was written (and rewritten and then rewritten again) in isolation, the comments by the readers for the University

Press of Mississippi were invaluable. While I take responsibility for all of the flaws, their fierce critiques enabled me to strengthen the manuscript in ways I could not have done without them. If I knew their names, I would shout them from the mountain ridge of Birmingham, Alabama, where I presently live.

The outstanding documentary collections at three particular institutions made the task of accessing documentaries a manageable endeavor: the Media Center of the Center for the Study of Southern Culture at the University of Mississippi, the Media Arts Center of the South Carolina Arts Commission (with the invaluable Susan Leonard), and the Donnell Media Center of the New York Public Library. (None of these centers exist in the same form as when I visited them—some no longer exist at all, and the collections of others no longer reside with them.) While I was able to obtain access to many documentaries through these collections, I was unable to access others, so I am thankful to the following filmmakers and organizations for providing me with such access: Macky Alston for *Family Name* (1997), Louis Alvarez and Andrew Kolker for *Mosquitoes and High Water* (1983), the Tourism Division of the Selma and Dallas County Chamber of Commerce for the Selma television ad, Third World Newsreel for *Mississippi Triangle*, and Women Make Movies for *Real Indian*. I am also thankful to filmmakers Gayla Jamison, Margaret Wrinkle, Chris Lawson, Tim Kirkman, Ellen Spiro, Bill Ferris, Tom Davenport, and Julie Williams Dixon for their conversations and/or e-mails. This project has been so long in the making that over the years I have lost track of who has assisted me. If I have forgotten anyone, my apologies.

I owe thanks to the excellent staff at the University Press of Mississippi, in particular Leila Salisbury for her unflagging support for this project and patience guiding me (and the manuscript) through the process. I am also thankful to Peter Tonguette, whose skillful copyediting greatly improved the final manuscript.

In conclusion, I am grateful for the support and friendship of my professional colleagues: Cynthia Lucia, David Lugowski, Paula Massood, Roy Grundmann, Kirsten Thompson, Antje Ascheid, Alex Keller, Marcos Becquer (deceased), Vinicius Navarro, Federico Windhausen, and Rebecca Bachman. I am also grateful to my non-academic friends: Debra Hunt and Kim Beckham, Patricia Leonardi and Linda McAfee, Janette Curry and Diane Hampton (deceased), Richard Williams and Terry Sneed, Harry Tarver, John and Tanya Morrow, and Mon Ching Mok. And finally, I am grateful to my family: Beverly Brasell, Alan and Patricia Murray, and Marie Brasell. Although our encounters may often be sporadic, their presence has been felt in my life.

The Possible South

Introduction

Southern Discourse, Mediated Distinctiveness,
and the Devaluation of the Audiovisual

With the amplification of capitalism as an international mechanism, the theoretical problems inherent in a restricted focus on the national have become apparent.[1] The primary theoretical paradigm that has emerged to challenge the national as the loci of engagement has been that of the global and more narrow concepts such as diaspora and transnational. But the global is not the only direction that can be taken to bypass the national. I believe an equally appealing move for many people is a turn inward rather than outward. Partha Chatterjee goes so far as to claim that "we should look within the nation rather than beyond it" because "the journey that might take us beyond the nation must first pass through the currently disturbed zones within the nation-state, and that in fact a more satisfactory resolution of the problems within could give us some of the theoretical instruments we are looking for to tackle the questions beyond."[2] The purpose of this book is just such an inward move.

As academicians such as Michael Bradshaw and Richard Maxwell Brown have highlighted, scholars of United States regionalism cannot agree on just how many regions exist in the country, a matter both men vividly illustrate by contrasting a variety of divisions proposed by various authors.[3] This lack of precision, however, they argue does not negate the region as a productive endeavor, its fluidity contributing to its flexibility. After all, boundaries, as Donna Haraway reminds us, only "materialize in social interaction" and "are drawn by mapping practices; 'objects' do not pre-exist as such."[4] And this includes the region too. Numerous approaches have been used over the years to define the region—history, culture, geography, economics, and politics. Although the concept of regionalism is acknowledged to cross over disciplinary boundaries, until recently it was not typically theorized through an interdisciplinary concept, although the region discursively known as "the South" has been approached through the paradigms of myth and an idea and the residents of that region from the perspective of ethnicity.[5] As scholarship of the past two decades attest, these approaches have outlived their usefulness as academics have embraced instead approaching the region through the concepts of invented traditions and imagined communities and the region's residents through consumerism.[6] This introduction offers an interdisciplinary theoretical approach to the region that does not align with any particular academic discipline, that of the region as a discursive practice.[7] While anti-essentialist conceptualizations of the region are now routine, and a shift is occurring toward approaching the region discursively (as represented by the work of Tara McPherson, Leigh Anne Duck, Jon Smith, Scott Romine, and Jennifer Greeson), my aim in the first half of this introduction is to directly explicate what such a conceptual approach might look like from a Foucauldian perspective and to demonstrate how discursive practices are not equivalent to either narrative or representation nor the cultural or the ideological.[8] The second half of this introduction explores the relationship of the region and documentary film, separately and collectively, through the concept of the possible as opposed to the more common approach to both terrains through the real. I prefer to frame the discussion in terms of "southern discourse," rather than "the South," to emphasize this particular approach. Although I have tried to limit the latter phrase's appearance to quotations from other's work, at times I have found myself incapable of evading the grip of such language and have availed myself (in defeat and shame) of it, the most egregious example being the section of this introduction on the possible South. My use of the word "southeastern" throughout this book is meant as a shorthand reference to a geographical area of the continental United States devoid of any evaluative associations. I considered using the phrase "the possible southeast" but rather than geography, "the possible" refers to the discursive practice that is southern discourse, thereby making the phrase inappropriate.

The Region as an Imagined Community

Today, approaching the region through Benedict Anderson's concept of imagined community has become standard practice. He developed the framework to shift the focus through which the nation was conceptually negotiated, defining the nation as "an imagined political community—and imagined as both inherently limited and sovereign."[9] This definition highlights four of the key elements of Anderson's concept: imagined, community, limited, and sovereign. While the region has been argued to share affinity with the first three characteristics, it does not have an affinity with the last one because when sovereignty arises the discussion is considered to have left the purview of regionalism proper and entered that of sectionalism with its nationalistic aspiration.[10] If sovereignty is removed from Anderson's definition, do the remaining elements apply to the region?

For Anderson, the nation is not a product of sociological conditions such as language or religion but has been imagined into existence. As Homi Bhabha attests, Anderson defines the nation "as a system of cultural signification, as the representation of social *life* rather than the discipline of social *polity*."[11] To define the nation as imagined invalidates efforts to differentiate between true and false nations. Under Anderson's theory, nations are to be judged, not by their truthfulness or falsity, but rather by how they are imagined, a concept meant to be very different from imaginary or fictive. Their imagining is not a fabrication created to cover up the true nation because no "'true' communities exist which can be advantageously juxtaposed to nations."[12] By theorizing the nation as imagined, Anderson attempts to move it from the terrain of ideology and false consciousness to that of "a variable cultural artifact that is neither reactionary nor progressive in itself."[13] Like the nation, residents of a region do not know each other although some claim they hold an "image of their communion" as a community, "conceived as a deep, horizontal comradeship," "regardless of the actual inequality and exploitation that may prevail." Similarly, just as the nation "has finite, if elastic, boundaries, beyond which lie other nations" and therefore is not "coterminous with mankind," so too claims of the region (even if deterritorialized) as having finite boundaries beyond which lie other regions and therefore is not coterminous with the nation.[14]

Anderson's concept of imagined community is attractive to scholars who study popular culture and mass media because of how he theorizes its formation and circulation. He holds that individuals dispersed over a wide geographical area begin to perceive of themselves as an imagined community through "the convergence of capitalism and print technology."[15] Print-capitalism provided "the conditions where people could begin to think of themselves as a nation."[16] In other words, an imagined community acquires form through the technical means of mass communication technologies. Today, this technology would include not only earlier forms of print media, such as newspapers, magazines, and books, but also twentieth-century forms such as film, radio, television, video, the Internet, and more frequently today the cell phone and digital platforms, these formerly distinct mediums converging (as well as diverging) today. All of these technologies contain the capacity to nurture the formation of imagined communities.

Anderson's concept was an intervention into the dominant perspective at the time of viewing the nation as a political entity, moving the focus from nationalism as "self-consciously held political ideologies" to "the large cultural systems that preceded it, out of which—as well as against which—it came into being."[17] He shifted the focus from political beliefs to cultural practices. This shift, however, did not negate institutional structures underlying both of these aspects of the nation; it only expanded the intellectual terrain upon which the nation could be engaged to include the sociocultural as well as the geopolitical. While the region, like the nation, has certain conceptual baggage accompanying it, this was not among it.

In addition to these four components of imagined, community, limited, and sovereign (of which the region definitely lacks the latter), Anderson's conceptualization of an imagined community contains two other important elements: culture and institutional structures. To justify use of Anderson's theory, one must believe in a regional culture or a variety of cultures that are interconnected in some manner to justify collecting them under the same rubric of the region.[18] In other words, to pluralize the word "culture" does not resolve this matter since the adjective "southern" continues to persist unaffected. Of course, this raises the larger issue of what one means by the term "culture." Similar to Scott Romine's position that "South is a noun that behaves like a verb," Arjun Appadurai is "troubled by the word *culture* as a noun but centrally attached to the adjectival form of the word, that is *cultural*."[19] Both seek to move beyond a noun that implies an easily classifiable solid object of analysis, an object often reified as static, coherent, bounded, and distinct, be it region, culture, or their combination, regional culture/cultural region. Although there are a number of competing definitions of the word "culture," within the context of this book two particular ones surface: those of anthropology and the arts.[20] While the former field often defines culture broadly as a way of life, the latter uses a narrow definition of artistic practices. As a result of the popularity of the former definition beyond the discipline of anthropology, culture has become everything and everywhere. Although over the past few decades the term has received critical scrutiny, it continues to persist, albeit often redefined as dynamic, contested, fluid, and plural.[21] While the concepts of the social and culture are intricately interrelated, they are not synonymous. Yet the word "culture" often functions as just a substitute for what earlier would have been called "society." A diversity of cultures exists in southeastern states, both in the past and in the present, and scholars who believe in the existence of a southern culture typically acknowledge the existence of this diversity. This issue raises the matter of what the relationship is of the local to the regional. I hold these diverse cultures do not synthesize into a larger regional culture; that regions are not cultural artifacts similar to Anderson's nations because any presumed regional-level culture, as will be explained below, results from the supplemental nature of southern discourse.

While some regional institutional structures do exist, I hold they are too weak to sustain the formation of the region as an imagined community (or social formation), hence its circulation is dependent upon poaching local, national, and global ones as a discursive supplement. Although the discursive is not the same as the cultural, social, economical, legal, political, emotional, geographical, and psychological, southern discourse can embed itself in these other fields, implicating them in the genesis of the regional. Because of southern discourse's elasticity and ability to naturalize its presence, many of the traits that people use to describe what they mean by the word "southern" can typically be said to exist elsewhere in the United States and the world. Although the concept of an imagined community has in the past few decades been applied to a diversity of situations including the "imagined South," given the lingering memories within the United States of the attempted nationhood by eleven southeastern states, the phrase "imagined South" risks awakening the concept's origins in the conceptualization of nationalism. But more importantly, a tendency exists among many users of the phrase to equate it with "representations of the South," which implies a separate external region to which these representations can be compared, thereby inadvertently reinscribing the old truthfulness/fictitiousness dichotomies that the concept was intended to eliminate. To refer to representations as "fabrications" exemplifies the linguistic slippage such phrases as "imagined South" perpetuate, the word simultaneously meaning "to construct" and "to pretend." As a result, I prefer to avoid referring to the region with phrases that include words (or derivatives of them) such as "invented," "imagined," or "fictive," all of which linguistically enable such slippages, even when that is not the aim of the user.[22] One way to avoid such linguistic slippages, as I discuss in the next section, is to approach the region not as represented but as presented.

The Region as a Discursive Practice

While it has become common in the twenty-first century for academic scholars to assume an anti-essentialist perspective toward the region, the conceptual ramifications of what such an approach entails are often under-theorized. I hold the region is a discursive practice enacted through oral and mass communication processes and disseminated as a supplement to local, national, and global institutional structures and/or social formations. This section considers the first half of this claim while the next section explores the latter half. Numerous strains within what I call "southern discourse" can be identified, with certain ones more hegemonic at particular historical moments than others. Some of its past and present components include nostalgia/melancholy, thickness of history, peculiarity/eccentricity, sense of place, backwardness, religiosity, and the civil, and these are intricately woven as I will discuss later with race, ethnicity, gender, sex, sexuality, physical and mental ability, and class.[23] As a discourse, the region is dependent upon a body of rules and structures that regulate its formation as an object of knowledge and thus constitute the conditions of its historical appearance. As Sara Mills notes: "Discursive rules and structures do not originate from socio-economic or cultural factors as such, although they may be shaped to an extent by these factors; rather, they are a feature of discourse itself and are shaped by the internal mechanisms of discourse alone."[24] Discourses are different from economic, political, and social structures although they interact in complex, nonhierarchical ways. The region is not a sociocultural or geopolitical structure but rather a discursive practice. As a discursive practice, it is formed through utterances—be they written or spoken words, visual or aural presentations, historical or fictive narratives, or rhetorical or associative logic—and their sensorial perceptions and emotional affects. This perspective means the region exists through temporal actions, not spatial locations.[25] As long as this discursive practice persists, so too does the region.

Such an approach is not the same as claiming the region is a sign whose meaning individuals struggle to control.[26] Although "discourses are composed of signs," "what they do is more than use these signs to designate things." Rather than "groups of signs (signifying elements referring to contents or representations)," discourses, per Michel Foucault, are "practices that systematically form the objects of which they speak."[27] Transmission mechanisms, be they oral or mass, be they intellectual, perceptive, or affective, do not re-present various representations of the region. The issue is *not* one of representations (or narratives) of the region, whether positive or negative, authentic or fake, real or imagined, but rather one of a discourse that *forms* the region. The region is never represented, but always presented. Just as certain speech acts do not represent that of which they speak but perform it or enact it (such as the "I do" of marriage vows), such is the case with southern discourse as a practice. (While some scholars use the word "discourse" to refer to linguistic discussions or language use, from a Foucauldian perspective, "discourse" is a more expansive concept.) Transmission processes are not channels that relay words, sounds, or images *about* the region but rather they are the means through which the region achieves actualization. No South exists beyond or outside of southern discourse. Any mechanism capable of disseminating knowledge is a potential contributor to the region's continual genesis, every enunciation creating it anew. Some of these means include Hollywood films, television commercials, popular songs, radio talk shows, fictional novels, roadside signs, illustrated travel brochures, broadcast news reports, academic journals, newspaper articles, magazine photography spreads, commodity labels, museum exhibits, store window displays, text messages, historical markers, and heritage tourist attractions. In addition, some oral practices are classroom discussions, telephone conversations, dinner-party banter, church sermons, political-rally speeches, and shopping-mall gossip. Although the broad dissemination of southern discourse typically transpires through mass communication technologies, it is not limited to that terrain because traditions such as visiting relatives and friends in other towns enable an oral mechanism for broad circulation of such knowledge.

John Tomlinson argues that even in today's media-saturated society, the media does not determine our experience of culture but rather mediates it because the relationship between culture and media is one of "a subtle *interplay of mediations*" and "the constant mediation of one aspect of cultural experience by another." In other words, our lived experience of culture includes not only the media but also "the discursive interaction of families and friends, and the material-existential experience of routine life," that is, the social.[28] Our everyday social encounters with other people influence our experience of the media, neither occurs in a vacuum, separate from the other. Oral forms of transmission continue to play a role in the formation of southern discourse today. Certain forms of mass media, however, leave a material residue that can be easily accessed retrospectively for analysis. Face-to-face interpersonal processes and technology-mediated mass processes (and those many intermediate processes between these two) are not mutually exclusive but each impacts and shapes the other.

According to Michel Foucault: "Each society has its régime of truth, its 'general politics' of truth: that is, the types of discourse which it accepts and makes function as true." Like all discursive practices approached from a Foucauldian perspective, southern discourse is regulated by a régime of truth, "the mechanisms and instances which enable one to distinguish true and false statements, the means by which each is sanctioned; the techniques and procedures accorded value in the acquisition of truth."[29] Discursive practices establish norms. This framework means that the classification of certain configurations of the region as truth or false, as authentic or fake, as real or fictional is an act of power that transpires through policing the limits of the permissible within the current régime of truth, not the result of a comparison to a supposedly external region beyond discursive practices. Such designators function to marginalize competing frameworks through processes of normalization, a matter discussed further in chapter three. The region formed through discursive practices is never false, fake, or fictive because it *is* the region. Any South that exists is always an actual one, regardless of which of these designations are used to describe it. Not only does no original South exist for comparison but neither does an external one outside of discursive practices.[30] While the local, national, and global exist spatially, the regional does not, for although it is about spatiality it exists only temporally; any appearance of substance is the result of repetitive action.

Southern discourse is multi-perspectival, control residing neither with residents of southeastern states nor nonresidents. As a result, exactly what constitutes self-presentation is often hard to determine because of the intertwining of southern discourse in national (and global) apparatuses.[31] For example, although literature may be written in isolation, in order to enter mainstream culture, whether popular or elite, it typically must pass through a literary establishment disproportionately located in the New York City metro area. Similarly, for a film to enter mainstream culture, it typically must pass through a Hollywood establishment disproportionately located in the Los Angeles metro area. Regional publishers as well as independent filmmakers do exist, so sometimes the work may be self-presented and not authorized by a national institution. But many independent writers, artists, and filmmakers are only able to create their work because of grants from national not-for-profit foundations, so the judgments of a selection committee from other regions must approve the project. And sometimes those involved in the creation of such works are not even from the region at all. In other words, no group has claims of exclusivity on the production of southern discourse. Just because a text is identified by producers or users as regional self-presentation does not mean that institutional constraints that are not regional impacted its creation. As a result, one could argue that regional self-presentation is inherently duplicitous.

Attempts to exclude certain elements from the definition of the region through claims of inauthenticity or fictiveness are acts of power enabled within the current régime of truth. For Foucault, power can function not only in a hierarchical and repressive manner but also a diffused one, "net-like," with individuals "always in the position of simultaneously undergoing and exercising" power, power producing effects, constituting subjectivities.[32] The current régime of truth frames certain configurations of the region as more truthful than others and some as questionable. But because southern discourse is a contradictory and contested site, it is open to change. Numerous configurations of the region exist simultaneously in struggle for prevalence. Change occurs not through individual unilateral action but collective negotiation. Unlike the concept of ideology, where people need to be liberated from their false consciousness in order for society to change, from a Foucauldian perspective it is the régime of truth that needs to be changed. As Foucault emphasizes: "The problem is not changing people's consciousnesses—or what's in their heads—but the political, economic, institutional régime of the production of truth.... The political question, to sum up, is not error, illusion, alienated consciousness or ideology: it is truth itself."[33] In other words, the concepts of discourse and ideology exist in an either/or relationship, mutually exclusive. Southern discourse operates within a field of power dynamics, and power produces effects in social reality, but as discussed below, I hold those effects are inconsequential in comparison to other discourses more closely tied to social and/or bodily formations.

The perception of authenticity or fakery ultimately depends on the reaction of the reader/listener/viewer to the sensory material s/he encounters, not inherent in the material itself. From the perspective of the region as a discursive practice, such differentiations are not innate but receptional because southern discourse is not cohesive or static but contradictory and regenerative, although at certain moments in time dominants may appear, enabled by the current régime of truth. In other words, not only do numerous presentations of the region exist simultaneously but they can be incompatible, which means the phrase "southern discourse" as I am using it is inherently plural like the word "media"—thus no "s" is needed to pluralize it. Because the region is receptional, people may self-consciously embrace that which has been labeled fake not just out of irony but creative bricolage, using it as a means of resistance to challenge prevalent discursive configurations of the region, utilizing an inauthentic authenticity (or authentic inauthenticity) that one day could itself become an influential force.[34] Along similar lines, sometimes southern discourse coveys meaning impressionistically; percept and affect are periodically even more important than intellectual understanding.

To claim the region is a discursive practice means, first, it is constructed and, second, mediated, the two elements being interconnected. Because the region is a construction, no distinguishing characteristic exists waiting to be discovered through implementation of scientific techniques but rather any claim of distinctiveness is formed through discursive operations, dependent upon repetitive expression for continuance. As a result, no characteristic can be proposed as *the* distinguishing element of the region because any such claim of uniqueness is always a mediated one, formed through the productive constraints of the current reigning politics of truth. A discursive approach shifts concern away from identifying the particular element that makes the region distinct, or whether particular configurations of the region are truth or false, authentic or fake, real or fictive, to analyzing the operation of distinctiveness as a component of southern discourse and how various configurations function within society and their societal effects. While the claim that any defining characteristic(s) attributed to the region is a mediated distinctiveness refers primarily to the way discursive practices operate in general, on a secondary level it also incorporates the mediation of knowledge through communicative technologies and the inter-mediation of these technologies with everyday practices.

The Region as a Discursive Supplement

Writing in the 1970s, when the issue was hotly debated whether "the distinctiveness of the South" would endure or disappear, Carl Degler claims: "Too often in generalizing about Americans, . . . the South as a part of America is somehow ignored. . . . The South's distinctiveness presents a problem to those who would talk about national character, for southerners indubitably live in America; but, equally indubitably, they are not like other Americans."[35] His argument implies that the national does not incorporate the regional but it should. If his accumulative-oriented position is extended to its logical conclusion, then one can similarly argue that the regional likewise should incorporate the local but ignores it too. The complaint that the regional ignores the local only holds if one believes the local, regional, and national *are* accumulative formations. What is the relationship between the regional and the local if one believes the region is a discursive practice? Is it accumulative? How does one move, after all, from the level of the local to the regional? Is the regional a mathematical accumulation of all of the locales within its purview? Such statistical accumulations raise numerous technical questions regarding methodological validity, as noted by scholars such as Paul Claval. The statistical process of regionalization, he argues, "is never a perfect superimposition of boundaries: the assemblages identified by this procedure depend on the criteria used."[36] In other words, the selection of different criteria produces different regions. Even if one desired to define the region through a primary characteristic, the question would still arise as to which criterion should be used? Such a choice always entails personal preferences.

When conceptualizing the relationship between the local and the regional, three possibilities immediately surface. Does the local *determine* the shape of the regional? Or, does the local influence the regional but *relative autonomy* exists between the two, with some locales incorporated while others are ignored? Or, does *no necessary correlation* exist between the two, the local being a sociocultural and geopolitical formation as well as a discursive one, with the regional being only a discursive one? No correct answer exists because one must always make a theoretical assumption in order to connect the two. I believe the local, regional, and national are not part of an accumulative system that is hierarchical based on ascending size because they have different bases of formation—the local and national being sociocultural, geopolitical (as municipalities, states, and nations), and/or discursive, while the regional is only discursive.[37] After all, the states are united into America, not the regions. Although some regional institutional structures do exist, they are weak in comparison to those at these other levels. (Not only do regional institutions often configure the region differently but so do national entities with regional divisions. For example, the Southern Governors' Association includes many states not included in the typical definition of the southeast United States used by political scientists, while the Southern Poverty Law Center focuses on hate groups all over the country, not just in the region.) Although he approaches the region from a different theoretical perspective, John Shelton Reed previously noted this institutional deficiency when he surmised that not only does "the role of most regional organizations in the group life of American regional groups seems to be minimal" but "the major agencies for transmitting the self-images and subcultures of American regional groups are not themselves regional or quasi-regional but exist instead at the level of local communities."[38] Because insufficient institutional support exists, the region must poach on local and national formations and structures—be they commercial, not-for-profit, or governmental, be they social, cultural, educational, political, or religious—through a discursive supplement.[39] While these formations and structures are *not* the region, they enable its enunciation and circulation through this discursive supplement that saturates everyday practices, bequeathing a southern supplement to commonplace activities such as eating and visiting, to basic social organisms such as the family and the church, and to sociocultural and geopolitical institutions at the local, national, and global levels.[40]

I am, obviously, not the first scholar to propose that the region functions as a supplement. Leigh Anne Duck, in her book *The Nation's Region: Southern Modernism, Segregation, and U.S. Nationalism*, has previously done so from the perspective of the region as a cultural discourse.[41] But I want to flesh out what this means within the context of the region as a discursive practice, a much broader terrain than the cultural. The concept of the supplement is borrowed from Jacques Derrida and his reading of Rousseau. The word has two meanings: first, to add something extra, adjoin, and, second, to substitute, replace. I use the word primarily in terms of its first meaning, but as Derrida argues the two meanings are intricately intertwined and can never be completely separated. Jonathan Culler succinctly summarizes the connection: "The supplement is an inessential extra, added to something complete in itself, but the supplement is added in order to complete, to compensate for a lack in what was supposed to be complete in itself."[42] Two of the most famous applications of the concept are writing as a supplement to speech and masturbation as a supplement to sex. Per Derrida,

> The supplement is maddening because it is neither presence nor absence and because it consequently breaches both our pleasure and our virginity.... The supplement has not only the power of *procuring* an absent presence through its image; procuring it for us through the proxy [*procuration*] of the sign, it holds it at a distance and masters it.... The supplement transgresses and at the same time respects the interdict. This is what also permits writing as the supplement of speech; but already also the spoken word as writing in general.[43]

The presence of an absence that the supplement replaces enables its attachment. On a pragmatic level, southern discourse circulates as a discursive supplement to local and national institutional structures because regional ones are too scarce and/or too weak to sustain its formation. While these institutions do not need southern discourse for their existence and the discourses of these institutions are not supplanted by southern discourse, their amenability to its addition (using Derrida's conceptualization) indicates the presence of a lack within them which is satisfied by the regional.[44] This means that while no particular region of the country is exceptional, the concept of regionalism itself is because, first, it is a discursive practice rather than a social, cultural, geographical, political, psychological, or economical formation similar to the local and national, and second, it is a discursive supplement that circulates through local, national, and global institutional structures and formations. In practice, unfortunately, the exceptionalism of regionalism is routinely collapsed onto "the South." While I have used the word "supplement" to describe the regional, other terminology exists to convey the same framework such as "poaching" and "parasite." The regional is a discursive parasite because it depends on local and national formations and institutional structures for its enunciation and circulation, feeding on them to sustain its existence because regional ones are not substantial enough for such purposes. Similarly, the regional poaches on local and national formations and institutional structures that are not its own for existence.

Subjectivity and the Region as a Discursive Practice

Rather than "identity," in her book *The Nation's Region* Leigh Anne Duck refers to the southerner as an "affiliation." Her avoidance of the word "identity" seems to be intentional, a preference subsequently confirmed in her article "Southern Nonidentity," in which, after raising the specter that "the concept of 'Southern identity' might be inherently treacherous," she argues that the articles she is responding to in a special issue of *Safundi* repeatedly, "in articulating identity, uncover nonidentity" and proposes that southern studies "imagine what it would mean to do without such notions" as identity. In other words, she advocates a "Southern studies without 'The South.'"[45] This book is an attempt at just such an approach. From a Foucauldian perspective, discourses form subjectivities, not identities. Does southern discourse form a southern subjectivity (or even a variety of southern subjectivities, given that it is inherently plural, although often with a dominant)? While race, sex, gender, sexual orientation, and class (and many others that I have not specifically listed, such as physical and mental ability) transpire within everyday social life, the regional is usually inconsequential on that terrain. And when it does come into play, the incident typically occurs because it has been attached to one of these bodily/social manifestations. Unlike them, the regional lacks direct bodily/social manifestation except in a few situations. Because the region is a discursive practice, it has to poach on one of these bodily/social manifestations in order to achieve concrete materialization within everyday social experience. Just as the region sustains its existence through a discursive supplement to local, national, and global institutional structures because insufficient regional structures exist to do so, so does the southerner in relationship to bodily/social manifestations because specific regional manifestations are rare. This results in differentiating the regional as a bodily/social category from these other ones and helps to explain its inconsequentialness within everyday lived experience (except when it threatens to assume national form). Although discourses produce subjectivities, because southern discourse is supplemental it lacks the effective means to maintain a sustainable, everyday southern subjectivity, unlike those of race, sex, gender, sexual orientation, and so forth. In other words, regional affiliation is fleeting, immaterial in both senses of the word. While I do not want to go so far as to claim southern discourse is completely incapable of forming southern subjects, its subjectivities are typically so ethereal that they appear nonexistent in everyday social life.

Another way of framing this phenomenon is through Michel Foucault's concept of governmentality, which approaches governance not in terms of territory but of population, both as individuals and as a collective, and is thus concerned with governance of the self as well as the social.[46] The nation, the state, and the municipality all have populations for which they are responsible to varying degrees and whose welfare in certain areas accrues to them. (One might also add the county but it is an association rarely invoked as an affiliation similar to one's country, state, or city.) The power accompanying the governance of a population enables these associations to form subjectivities. The region not only has insufficient power but no such population for which it is obligated. In other words, regional subjectification (to use Gilles Deleuze's preferred term for Michel Foucault's subject) is at worst an oxymoron, and at best a paradox. As a result, unlike these other affiliations, the region attempts to form subjects without power, whether disciplinary or coercive, and is thereby unable to sustain a viable subjectivity but is able to maintain an immaterial affiliation. (Of course, the historical period of the Confederate States of America had a population to govern. One could counterargue that the memory of this occurrence sustained through certain strains of southern discourse enables the formation of a southern subjectivity today. But such memory rarely shapes everyday social life; in other words, at best such subjectivity would be tenuous as well as fleeting.)

Another way to frame this phenomenon is Pierre Bourdieu's approach to the family. He holds that "the family as an objective social category (a structuring structure) is the basis of the family as a subjective social category (a structured structure), a mental category which is the matrix of countless representations and actions (e.g. marriages) which help to reproduce the objective social category. The circle is that of reproduction of the social order."[47] In other words, our perception of the family as a social formation is impacted by our understanding of the family as a discursive formation. So the family is simultaneously a societal structure and a discursive category. While I hold the region to be a discursive practice, because sufficient structures do not accompany its discursive formation, it is not a social formation as well. As a result, the regional is a social category without a corresponding social structure. It is only a discursive formation and thereby unable to function on the everyday level, as does the family, which includes both types of formations. Bourdieu's argument about the family is descriptive of most social formations, especially those tied closely to the body. But, if one accepts that the region is a discursive supplement, it does not apply to the regional.

While the southerner typically assumes bodily/social form through poaching on forms already existing, an area where it does not is the aural. Accents are bodily, formed through the vocal cords. While accents can have racial, gender, class, and other inflections, the aural is the one bodily manifestation where the southerner is not dependent upon such inflections for physical materialization. Within certain social terrains, only aural differences of class, race, gender, and so forth are noticed, not any local (or regional) inflection. But outside of those terrains, the local (or regional) inflection becomes noticeable. Of course, *a* southern accent does not exist. Many different accents exist across southeastern states but while some remain local, others have been incorporated into southern discourse as "southern." Good examples of the former are some of the various New Orleans accents captured by Louis Alvarez and Andrew Kolker in their 1985 documentary *Yeah You Rite! The Way They Talk in New Orleans*. In other words, even at the level of accents, mediated distinctiveness operates; some accents are accompanied by a discursive supplement while others are not. Accents tend to function as bodily/social manifestations of regional affiliation primarily on terrains where such accents are not the norm; in other words, it depends on difference in order to be noticed. Because the regional is a discursive supplement with rare direct bodily/social manifestations, it is easily discarded within the everyday in a way not typically available to race, sex/gender, and other bodily/social formations.

History and the Region as a Discursive Practice

An objection might be raised that approaching the region as a discursive practice ruptures this particular region's intimate confederacy with history, making history irrelevant to an understanding of it because it is, after all, only discourse. Such a view rests on certain conceptions of history and discourse, conceptions that frame the two as antagonistic. History, however, is discursive as conceptualized by Hayden White (by way of Michel Foucault). History is typically thought of as the reconstruction of the past as it actually happened. Such a view, according to Alan Munslow, is based on a "belief in some reasonably accurate correspondence between the past, its interpretation and its narrative representation."[48] In other words, the historian can know the past as it actually was, directly access it through historical evidence, and thereby objectively reconstruct it in his or her written narrative re-presentation. Such a view assumes an "unmediated correspondence between language and the world as a discoverable reality."[49] White argues that the writing of history is a linguistic act and that written descriptions cannot reflect past events because language is not a transparent medium of representation. As he phrases it, "there is no value-neutral mode of emplotment, explanation, or even description of any field of events, whether imaginary or real," because, "not only all interpretation, but also all language is politically contaminated."⁵⁰ According to him, interpretation moves beyond just the historian's selection of events used in the historical narrative to include the very act of describing those events selected. In other words, "descriptions of events *already* constitute interpretations," so rather than finding "the form of his [sic] narrative in the events themselves," the historian imposes it upon the events through "the very *act of identifying and describing* the objects that he [sic] finds there. The implication is that historians *constitute* their subjects as possible objects of narrative representation by the very language they use to *describe* them."⁵¹ From this perspective, the very act of writing is itself a form of interpretation because of the nature of language. Acknowledging this linguistic element means accepting that "the facts do not speak for themselves," but "the historian speaks for them, speaks on their behalf, and fashions the fragments of the past into a whole whose integrity is—in its *r*epresentation—a purely discursive one."⁵² Because the past can only be approached through the present, history becomes not the discovery or recovery of the past but rather the production of a past through the act of narrativization in the present. History is an act of production not only through the process of collecting, selecting, and emploting the facts to be included in the story being told but also through the very language used to tell that story. (The same can be said of documentary film if one considers film form a language.)⁵³ Like literature, history is also wedded to language, a similarity that some historians find uncomfortable to acknowledge. History is a form of storytelling about the past.

A discursive approach, such as Ella Shohat and Robert Stam highlight in their 1990s groundbreaking book *Unthinking Eurocentrism: Multiculturalism and the Media*, "disputes the hegemony of the visual and of the image-track by calling attention to its complication with sound, voice, dialog, language."⁵⁴ As cinema and media studies scholars, Shohat and Stam are part of a field that historically privileged the visual over the aural. In contrast, the hegemony that exists in southern studies is of the written (whether literature or historical evidence) at the expense of a serious engagement with the audiovisual, as evidenced by the disciplines of English and History with their literary analysis and historical emplotments dominating the field.⁵⁵ These two disciplines are typically perceived to align along a fictional/factual divide, with one focusing on the imaginary and the other the real. A discursive approach offers a way to circumvent not only the domination of the written over the visual but this artificial disciplinary divide as well. To reposition the conversation about the regional around its status as a discursive practice is not an anti-history move but it does position history on an equal plane with literature (and literary criticism) in terms of truth claims, thus denying both their privileged positions within academia for the production of southern discourse. Just because the publications and classroom discussions of academia may have limited circulation compared to popular culture as discursive practices that form the region, they are still a part of the process, not outside it. In other words, scholars are intimately implicated in the formation of the very thing that they are attempting to analyze. As a result, the writing of critical analysis and the writing of history become just two practices among many others that contribute to the discursive formation of the region. Although southern studies has been slow to engage with sites beyond the traditional purview of these two disciplines, a change is beginning to occur, as represented by the work of scholars such as Tara McPherson, Jon Smith, Riché Richardson, Grace Elizabeth Hale, and Jessica Adams, all of whom engage with material beyond just the written. The discursive perspective ruptures the hegemony of the word (whether oral or written, literary or historical) that dominates southern studies, opening up a lacuna where a serious negotiation can finally begin of the audiovisual (as well as the three-dimensional) in relationship to the regional.[56]

The Possible and the Region as a Discursive Practice

In a review of Tara McPherson's book *Reconstructing Dixie: Race, Gender, and Nostalgia in the Imagined South*, Jon Smith notes that, while she states that her "purpose is not to fault these various representations of the Civil War for failing to match some (imagined) utopian image," nonetheless "that imagined utopian image of the non-lenticular does exist as a goal in nearly every one of her chapters, sometimes operating structurally as a 'real' South which the 'imagined' Souths fail to represent honestly, and looking forward to that ideal/real is part of what makes this an important book."[57] Scott Romine, in *The Real South: Southern Narrative in the Age of Cultural Reproduction*, while concurring with Smith's critique, reframes the issue, seeing the deficiency "less as a matter of *distorting* the South than of *deploying* a South that ought not to be." Instead of the distinction between a real and imagined South that Smith observes operating in McPherson's book, Romine focuses on the discrimination "between desirable and undesirable ways of using the South."[58] Smith's critique of McPherson is one common to most usages of the concept "imagined South." But what Smith identifies as an implied real South that the imagined South fails to represent, I read as the presence of a possible South, not a real South, because from a discursive perspective the distinction between an imagined South and real South is moot because any South presented is an actual South (regardless of how it is labeled under the current régime of truth). That Smith places both words in quotation marks indicates his perceiving them as equivalences, and he even invokes that this is a possible South rather than a real South when he comments that he is "looking forward to that ideal/real"—in other words, the realization of this possible South that moves beyond lenticular logic. Romine also alludes to the possible that always accompanies the real with his reference about "a South that ought not to be"—in other words, the realization of a possible South that is viewed by someone as socially detrimental. Although scholars are invoking Benedict Anderson when they refer to "imagined South," the colliery of the real looms large over the framework because of the dominance in academia of Lacanian psychoanalysis within most of the humanities and its strong presence in some manifestations of the social sciences.[59] Romine's book is a critical intervention into this implied real South that routinely accompanies discussions of the imagined South. As a result of the Lacanian specter that typically accompanies such discussions (which Romine's framework moves beyond), one easily becomes ensnared within the language of the imaginary, real, and symbolic, thereby inhibiting access to the alternative framework of the real and possible. Even though Jon Smith and Scott Romine do not openly acknowledge the possible, its presence haunts their references to the real. My aim is not to propose "the possible South" as a replacement for "the imagined South"—which continues to be a popular expression—as a means to eliminate the potential of an implied real South that may accompany the phrase. Instead, I want to explore the alternative terrain of the possible that arises when the popular language of the real and imagined in relationship to the regional are discarded.

As discussed earlier, a discursive practice for Michel Foucault "is a body of anonymous, historical rules, always determined in the time and space that have defined a given period, and for a given social, economic, geographical, or linguistic area, the conditions of operation of the enunciative function."[60] These rules form the body of knowledge that constitutes the current régime of truth determining the field of possibilities. For Foucault, they set the "limits and forms of the *sayable*. What is it possible to speak of?"[61] This situation is why Foucault holds that in order to create social change, the conditions of possibilities—the current reigning régime of the production of truth—needs to be changed, not the individual's consciousnesses. Rudi Visker notes: "Discourse is a *practice* which cannot be reduced to a function of reference or expression. Rather than refer to pre-given objects, it brings its own object into being. Rather than document the originality of thinking subjects, it binds them to a set of rules which makes their thought and their originality possible."[62] In other words, the set of rules determine the contours of the body of knowledge constituting the current régime of truth, which delimits the field of possibilities permissible and expressible through discursive practices.

The possible is not desire, fantasy, or the imaginary—but it also is not hope. Giorgio Agamben, referencing Aristotle, distinguishes between a generic potentiality and an existing one. The former is generalized such as "a child has the potential to know, or that he or she can potentially become the head of State," while the latter refers to having a "knowledge or an ability" that can be brought into actuality. Agamben uses the example of the architect who "has the *potential* to build" or "to not-build."[63] While some scholars call the former "possibility" and the latter "potentiality," I am using the concept of the possible in this latter sense, which, as Agamben highlights, is concerned with "not simple the potential to do this or that thing but potential to not-do."[64] The possible is not wishful thinking but the range of options present that can be realized, of which only one or a few are realized. Although Agamben's example implies individual agency, I am using the possible in an impersonal, anonymous sense as an element present within any discursive practice.

While I am using a Foucauldian approach, Gilles Deleuze and Félix Guattari offer a means to engage further the concept of the possible inherent within Foucault's conceptualization of discursive practices, which he does not expand upon further.[65] Within cinema studies, Saussurian semiotics and Lacanian psychoanalysis dominates, which is one explanation frequently offered for why Deleuze and Guattari, although routinely celebrated, have not been widely integrated into the field. Instead of the Saussurian signifier, signified, and referent, they offer Louis Hjelmslev's content and expression, each with its own form and substance. And instead of the Lacanian triad of the real, imaginary, and symbolic, they offer two couplets, the virtual and actual, and, the possible and real. Deleuze explicitly asserts that theory is "like a box of tools" and "must be useful."[66] Deterritorization is one of his and Guattari's theoretical concepts that has been widely embraced and easily grafted onto film and social theory. But because their theories begin from a different baseline than that commonly used in these fields, at a certain point of engagement with their concepts one must embrace their overall theoretical framework due to their esoteric terminology and the embedded assumptions within them. I am, however, going to run the risk and toolbox their engagement with the possible.[67]

The concept of the possible runs throughout Gilles Deleuze and Félix Guattari's work, both individually and collaboratively. While Deleuze's two cinema books argue "that cinema has a special relation to duration" that offer new perceptions not previously available to the human eye, when it comes to the possible I found his concept of the time-image to be unhelpful.[68] However, two sites where, either individually or jointly, they explicitly explore the possible that I find helpful are Deleuze's *Bergsonism* and Deleuze and Guattari's *What is Philosophy?* While the condensed summations of these works to follow are overly dense, and at times rather opaque, hopefully by the end of this section their important elements relevant to my main argument will become perceivable. As many scholars have highlighted, when reading *Bergsonism* it often becomes difficult to distinguish between where Bergson ends and Deleuze begins. He argues Bergson privileges the virtual/actual couplet over the possible/real couplet, with which he concurs, offering a critique of the concept of the possible. The concepts of realization and actualization are integral to these couplets; realization is based on resemblance and limitation while actualization on difference and divergence. As a result, only the process of actualization is an act of creation. While the possible and the real are both actual, the possible is not real and only through a process of realization becomes real. In contrast, while the virtual and actual are both real, the virtual must be actualized to become actual. In the former case, the real is already contained within the field of the possible; therefore, the two resemble each other and realization occurs through the delimitation of the field of the possible, with only selected possibles realized as real. So no difference exists between the possible and the real; the latter is just a subset of the former. This means the real is preformed. As a result, the real preexists itself: "[e]verything is already *completely given*: all of the real in the image, in the pseudo-actuality of the possible."[69] Per Deleuze, "While the real is in the image and likeness of the possible that it realizes, the actual, on the other hand does *not* resemble the virtuality that it embodies."[70] In the latter case, because the actual diverges from the virtual, the two are different, thereby making the process of actualizing the virtual an act of creation. Because the virtual/actual framework entails a movement of positive creation unlike the negation of the possible/real, he prefers the former.[71] Of course, because each book by Deleuze is an investigation of a particular problem and not the further elaboration of a grand scheme (although ultimately he and Guattari do offer an overarching theoretical framework even if it is not a master narrative), his later engagement with the possible shifts.

Rather than maintain the ontological separation of the two couplets, *What is Philosophy?*—his final collaborative work with Guattari—offers an interstitial. Deleuze and Guattari differentiate between philosophy, science, and art as forms of thought by aligning each with the creation of, respectively, concepts, functions (also called propositions), and sensations (broken down into precepts and affects). Philosophy creates the form of concepts on a plane of immanence associated with the virtual and the event; science creates functions of knowledge on a plan of reference associated with the actual and states of affairs; and art creates the force of sensations (precepts and affects) on a plane of composition associated with the possible and the monument. While philosophy and science are aligned along the virtual/actual couplet, respectively (philosophy "giving the virtual a consistency specific to it" and science actualizing the virtual, thereby making philosophy's plan of immanence the virtual and science's plan of reference the actual), art is not.[72] When discussing the work of art as a monument, a monument not because of physical size but blocs of sensations, Deleuze and Guattari observe: "The monument does not actualize the virtual event but incorporates or embodies it: it gives it a body, a life, a universe. . . . These universes are neither virtual nor actual: they are possibles, the possible as aesthetic category . . . , the existence of the possible, whereas events are the reality of the virtual forms of a thought-Nature that survey every possible universe."[73] While the artistic plane of composition is that of sensation and the possible, the possible monument of art (erected with its sensations) incorporates the virtual event of the philosophical plan of immanence that flies over all possible universes.[74] As Ronald Bogue notes: "Philosophy's domain is virtual; art's domain is possible—but finally this opposition of virtual and possible is not absolute, for the possible is the embodied virtual."[75] Unlike earlier, when the two couplets of the possible/real and the virtual/actual were approached as ontologically competing frameworks, here they are connected through the establishment of a relationship between the possible and the virtual.[76] Although Deleuze preferred the virtual/actual couplet over the possible/real couplet, he ultimately could not forsake the possible, and even suggests the virtual is actualized through the possible.[77]

Prior to *What is Philosophy?* Deleuze and Guattari explore in "May '68 Did Not Take Place" the relationship of the possible to the event without the burden of the regimented distinctions drawn in that later work between philosophy, science, and art. They argue that the event is a bifurcation, "a splitting off from, or a breaking with causality" that forms "an unstable condition which opens up a new field of the possible" that "passes as much into the interior of individuals as into the depths of a society."[78] The possible does not preexist the event but rather the event creates the possibility of a new existence. The tinge of mysticism that lingers over their definition of art as the creation of sensations on a plane of composition also surfaces with the event, which they maintain is "a visionary phenomenon, as if a society suddenly saw what was intolerable in it and also saw the possibility for something else."[79] If expressed in terms of their later formulation, this means the event of the philosophical plan of immanence flies over the possible of the artistic plane of composition. As a result, the possible is aligned simultaneously with art and the event, two arenas, as will be discussed in the next section, relevant to the conceptualization of documentary film.[80]

My aim is not to overlay Gilles Deleuze and Félix Guattari's couplets onto my Foucauldian approach to the region as a discursive practice—although, in a rather Deleuzian-sounding moment, Michel Foucault did assert: "Popular struggles have become for our society, not part of the actual, but part of the possible."[81] Although Foucault and Deleuze and Guattari continually adjusted and adapted their intellectual positions, regardless of which points in their thinking one uses to compare them, significant conceptual differences exist. My main point is that all presentations of the region are actual (whether labeled "real" or "imagined," "authentic" or "fake"), with the possible an integral component of it. My configuration of the possible South, however, plays fast and loose with Deleuze and Guattari's two couplets through a linguistic (and philosophical) sleight of hand. While based on Deleuze's original formulation, a possible South would already be actual but would need to be realized, taking a lead from Deleuze and Guattari's linking of the possible to the virtual as its embodiment and the suggestion that the possible has the ability to actualize the virtual, I will be referring to the actualization of the possible South, not its realization, thereby eliminating the real from the formulation. The possible South is not a standard for judging the objectivity of a presented South but rather the manifestation of a becoming that can create—actualize—something new.[82] The possible is not inherently progressive and can just as easily be regressive, although my goal is to enact discourse that actualizes the former type. From such a perspective, the possible becomes the site for change. While no guarantees exist, the site of the possible invokes what Giorgio Agamben calls "the coming community" that emerges from "the possibility of the whatever," which "is a threat the State cannot come to terms with."[83] Of course, within an American context the word "whatever" conjures teen-movie slang and an attitude of disregard (and sometimes disdain). But, for Agamben, "whatever" is the terrain of the possible.

The Possible and Documentary Film

Independent documentary filmmakers—and the scholars, critics, and cinephiles who consume their media products—routinely express an expectation that documentary film should help change the world for the better. But as numerous scholars point out, when asked, people can identify very few documentaries that have such an effect. If documentary film is a discursive practice, as argued by Elizabeth Cowie, then this expectation can be read as a response to the possible contained within that discursive expression.[84] Per Cowie, "by narrating its images of the specific, of reality, in relations of causality, documentary also narrates an envisioned possibility of other outcomes and other narrations of causality."[85] For her, the possible arises from the emplotment that is applicable to documentary film, just as it is to fictional film.[86] But another type of the possible accompanies documentary film; this possible rises not from the process of constructing the text, but from the percepts and affects sensed by the audience. As noted earlier, for Gilles Deleuze and Félix Guattari, art gives life to a universe that is neither the virtual nor the actual but the possible. While concepts, functions, and sensations within Deleuze and Guattari's framework are all means of thinking—thought-forms—they also enable becoming, each offering a different kind of becoming. Art enables sensory becoming. (I use the word "art" in the broadest sense of cultural expression, thereby incorporating works that are nonfiction as well as fiction, mass manufactured as well as individually crafted, popular culture as well as high art, and commercial products as well as nonprofit commissions.)[87] So, documentary film as an art form offers a sensory becoming to spectators. Jane Gaines critically interrogates the association of documentary film with social change through this issue of sensations, labeling it "political mimesis." She aligns the sensational bodies on the screen in sensual struggle with the bodies in the theater audience, where documentaries seek to engage "audiences to carry on that same struggle."[88] After differentiating between the concepts of mimesis and mimicry (the later she associates with "mindless imitation" and "mechanical copying"), she defines political mimesis as "a use of mimesis that assumes a mimetic faculty on the part of its audience—the ability to 'body back,' to carry on the same struggle."[89] In other words, documentary film's realist aesthetics produce affects in the viewer to carry on in the world the struggle viscerally presented on the screen. Gaines's concern is with affect, not effects. According to Gaines, through the use of mimetic sensuous images of struggle, documentaries seek to influence the events of the historical world; in other words, political documentaries use a copy of the world to influence the audience to intervene in that world. Such an approach acknowledges that audiences respond to documentaries on not just an analytical level but also on an emotional level, as they do to fictional films.

From a Deleuzian and Guattarian perspective, a certain irony exists in claiming documentary film is an art form because, as a result, a genre closely associated with the real is aligned instead with the possible. Use of the real to differentiate documentary film from fictional film typically focuses on the ontological status of the world within the frame (the image) to the pro-filmic event captured. As Brian Winston demonstrates, such claims are based on a belief that the camera is "an instrument of scientific inscription producing evidence objective enough to be 'judged' by a spectator."[90] While he believes documentary images can be distinguished from fictional images, he holds this cannot be done by "merely reading authenticity off the screen."[91] Rather, similar to Bill Nichols, he contends the distinction must be based on reception, not representation, on "the audience's relation to the screen," not the "qualities of the image."[92] From such a perspective, "documentary legitimacy" depends on the audience acknowledging "that the relation of image to imaged depends not on the image's intrinsic quality guaranteed by science but on our 'caveat emptor' reception of it, pixels and all," a process that includes intertextual and experiential knowledge "to determine the 'documentary value' of the accounts of 'the' world the films give."[93] Unlike the claim of the real, the possible informs simultaneously the textual world, the pro-filmic world, and the spectatorial world and is thereby compatible with the differentiation of documentary from fiction based on audience reception rather than the ontological status of the image.[94] But if documentary film is an art form, and art creates sensations, then is not the differentiation between documentary and fiction eliminated? As mentioned earlier, Deleuze and Guattari view the event as a splitting in time that "opens up a new field of the possible." This means that the possible arises within documentary film not only through its status as an art form but also through the captured pro-filmic event, which it takes unto itself. This latter situation differentiates the documentary from the fictional film, this double dose of the possible resulting in greater expectations by audiences for the medium to change the world.[95] In other words, this expectation arises not from a greater claim to the real than the fictional film but to a greater claim to the possible.

Documentary Film and the Region as a Discursive Practice

Audiovisual technology cannot, of course, directly present the region for two reasons, one related to the medium, the other to the region. First, film as a technology can only directly capture the nano-local, that very narrow slice of pro-filmic actuality present immediately before the camera. The institutions that fund, produce, distribute, and exhibit films may be local, national, or global but from the perspective of the audiovisual these larger territories must be discursively constructed from nano-local manifestations through the techniques of editing, cinematography, mise-en-scène, and sound. Second, even if this technological mediation did not exist, the region could not be directly perceived because it is not a geopolitical or sociocultural formation but a discursive practice that only intersects with social and bodily formations as a discursive supplement that poaches off the subjectification enacted by local, national, and global formations and institutions. In other words, whether technology is involved or not, the regional only exists through discursive mediation; its existence is a temporal duration rather than a spatial corporeality. This situation has an affinity with that of the audiovisual. While the audiovisual exists as a physical object, even if just binary codes of zeros and ones on a digital chip, the perception of this type of audiovisual object is both quantitatively and qualitatively different from that during its transmission, where that documentary object becomes temporarily a spatial one through duration.[96] Of course, the idea that the audiovisual text exists only in time is an old one in film theory. But it shares analogy with the framework of the region as a discursive practice. Without duration, neither exists. Film and the region share another similarity. The documentary presentation of the pro-filmic actual is inherently dependent upon technological mediation. Similarly, the presentation of the region is inherently dependent upon discursive mediation that at times assumes material form as a discursive supplement to corporeal bodies, physical objects, and social practices. Although they differ significantly, they are both dependent upon mediation for their existence.

Documentary film tends to use two strategies in relation to the regional, a direct meta-level enunciation of the region—such as *Tell About the South* (Ross Spears, 1996) and *Greetings from Out Here* (Ellen Spiro, 1993) discussed, respectively, in chapters one and three—or an indirect, additive enunciation that frames the local as an expression of the region—such as *bro•ken/ground* (Margaret Wrinkle and Chris Lawson, 1996) and *Family Name* (Macky Alston, 1997) discussed, respectively, in chapters two and three.[97] These can be thought of as, respectively, macro and micro strategies of expression. When dealing with textual manifestations like documentary film, these strategies may transpire within the text, within the societal reception of the filmmaker and the text, or, as more often the case, both. Because of the nature of audiovisual technology, the pro-filmic, nano-local snatches of spatiotemporal actuality captured by the camera must be constructed into the local, regional, national, and global. Sometimes these fragments are constructed into the local and then framed as manifestations of the regional (or national) while other times they are constructed directly as the regional (or national). In both cases, the mechanisms for connecting the pro-filmic, nano-local fragments of actuality captured by the camera into the region are the same.

In documentary film, this process transpires through two primary means: linguistics and/or audiovisuals. While from a Foucauldian perspective, discourse relates to the societal formation of knowledge and practices, Norman

Fairclough uses discourse in the restricted since of "spoken or written language use," approaching "language use as a form of social practice, rather than a purely individual activity or a reflex of situational variables."[98] Application of this narrower approach discloses a dominant mechanism through which the captured pro-filmic, nano-local actuality is linked to the region. Although banal, use of the words "southern," "southerner," and "the South" is a highly effective means to do so, whether within the text, through verbal statements by a narrator or social actors, written statements on an intertitle or superimposed over the image track, or outside the text, through inclusion in the film title, the production company name or sponsoring and advising organizational names or mention in promotional materials, media articles, and film reviews. Extratextual material circulates around the documentary and is encountered by potential listening viewers, thus guiding them to perceive the documentary as being about the region, thereby making it regional regardless if the text constructs its focus as purely local. The pro-filmic, nano-local actuality becomes regional through such unobtrusive (and often unnoticed) operations. Through the continuous accumulation of these inconspicuous occurrences, impressionistic meaning is attributed to the region. While such linguistic operations are explicit and easier to identify, association also occurs audiovisually, although such connections are more ambiguous and open-ended because of the difference between audiovisuals and linguistics. Certain images and sounds become read as indicative of the region because of the discursive southern supplement that accompanies them. These commonplace operations transform the snippets of nano-local actualities captured by the camera into manifestations of the region, thereby not documenting or representing the region but forming and presenting it.[99]

Documentary Film, Thick and Thin Discursive Supplements, and *Mai's America*

Southern discourse is a potent practice and, although a supplement, can easily overwhelm that which it encounters, like the parasite moss can do to the tree to which it attaches. As discussed, film captures only the sensory perceivable local that must then be framed discursively as the regional, a process that can transpire through a number of means. Although I tend to speak in terms of texts, southern discourse is not a thing but a process and, in terms of textual-based cultural expressions, emerges through the reception process of the texts, although obviously guided (as well as often circumscribed) by the construction of the text and the operative cultural codes of the time. In a rather perverse way, this is what New Criticism was about—the reception of texts—but the movement limited such reception to that of an elite literary clique, discounting that of other textual users. Some scholars are concerned with how discourse circulates and interacts in the lived social world while others focus on its materialization in textual form. A recurring challenge for film, media, and literary scholars is the integration of these two concerns. One of the advantages of focusing on documentary film is that as a medium, the difference easily blurs. Unfortunately, a tendency exists in popular culture to view documentary as audiovisual reproductions of the lived social world, ignoring the textual component it shares with fictional media. Like New Criticism, I too tend to privilege in this book my own reception of the documentaries under consideration, although I do attempt to also historicize them. But one can write about film without recourse to any cinematic texts, relying instead on the extra-cinematic material that surrounds the circulation of films, such as oral conversations and media coverage (within which I include academia because academic journals and books *are* media, and many mediamakers encounter—albeit in a limited way, perhaps—some of this material as college students). While some texts are constructed by the makers to explicitly include a southern supplement (or, from the perspective of documentary film, the texts absorb it from the pro-filmic spaces and events captured by the camera), such is not needed in order for one to emerge. It can emerge through the extra-textual that then becomes a lens through which the text is perceived by other textual users. One documented and easily accessible residue of such reception is media reviews.

An excellent example of the potency of southern discourse to overpower the national is the documentary *Mai's America* (Marlo Poras, 2002), which explores a cross-cultural exchange between the United States and Vietnam. The documentary follows Mai, a Vietnamese exchange student, as she encounters America.[100] The filmmaker initially followed four Vietnamese exchange students, one living with an Iranian woman in the state of Washington, one with a religious family in rural Illinois, one with a white family on a Hopi Indian reservation, and Mai in Mississippi. However, due to the financial and technical difficulties of recording four people scattered across the United States, the filmmaker narrowed her focus to only one exchange student. She chose Mai because of her personality and natural presence before the camera.

Borrowing Clifford Geertz's terms for anthropological writing of "thick description" and "thin description," the ascription of a southern supplement to various formations, institutions, practices, and texts can be thought of as thick or thin, the former dense because explicit, the latter slender because insinuated.[101] Although the documentary was meant to be about experiencing America, because its primary social actor resided in a southeastern state, the majority of media reviewers ascribe a thick southern supplement to it, thereby perceiving the documentary about Mai's experience of an "eccentric Southern-American culture" rather than an American one.[102] While reviewers routinely note that Mia's experience as a foreign exchange student occurs in Mississippi, many reviewers go further and specifically reference the setting as a regional one, this association inflected with a contemptuous tone, sometimes explicitly stated, other times inferred through disparaging descriptions. When screened at the Eleventh Annual Philadelphia Festival of World Cinema, one reviewer described *Mai's America* as "the *Deliverance* tale of a Vietnamese exchange student stranded with a redneck family." *Daughter from Danang* (Gail Dolgin and Vicente Franco, 2002), about an adopted Amer-Asian woman raised in Tennessee who returns to Vietnam to meet her birth mother, was screened at the same festival, leading this reviewer to conclude: "The American South just can't look good, can it? I hate to sound geocentric, but if you watch just two films in this festival—*Daughter from Danang* and *Mai's America*—you'll come away thinking that, all things considered, you'd rather be in Vietnam."[103] One only has to ask the reviewer: Would you rather be in Vietnam than America? The implied answer is "no." In other words, "[t]he American South" does not—and cannot—represent America but is a site unto itself.

A minority of media reviewers, however, take a cue from the documentary's title—*Mai's America*—and attempt to critically engage with how the documentary's chronicle of Mai's time in the United States deconstructs and challenges the American dream and values. One reviewer describes the documentary as a "trip down the rabbit hole of American consumerism, hypocrisy and class warfare" and another as capturing "the self-absorption and emptiness of an aspect of American life."[104] Interestingly, neither of these reviewers specifically mention "the South," only "Mississippi" and "America," but they still ascribe a southern supplement to the documentary, but thin rather than thick, through descriptions of the social actors combined with use of words that connotatively invoke the region, such as "redneck" and "grotesque." A thin southern supplement is similar to a specter—it is elusive, its presence more felt than seen. The audiovisual oftentimes relies to a greater extent on inference and affect rather than linguistics. This haunting audiovisual presence that listening viewers encountered was channeled by media critics into their reviews, even if they did not explicitly reference the region.

Mai is hosted during her senior year by first a working-class white family (called, Mai informs us, "white trash" by a school friend), followed by a religious black family. While on the surface these two families confirm the discursive racial configuration of the region as—to be discussed in the next

Marlo Poras's 2002 documentary *Mai's America* follows Vietnamese exchange student Mai as she attends her senior year of high school in Mississippi, documenting her encounter with a cast of social actors not often associated with the region, including

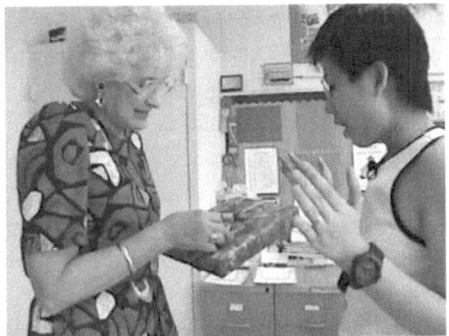
white liberals,

sexual minorities (transgender people), and

non-black-or-white racial minorities (Asian Americas).

section—biracial, the documentary includes a cast of social actors which moves beyond the limitations of this framework. And most media reviewers referenced—in order of frequency—one or more of them: her friendship with a white man, Chris, struggling with his gender identity (referred to variously by reviewers as a "drag queen," "transvestite," and "cross-dresser"); a liberal, white high-school teacher; and a second generation Vietnamese-American youth, Tommy, discovering his ethnic heritage. While this assortment of sexual minorities, white liberals, and non-black-or-white racial minorities have the potential to expand the presentation of the region, most reviewers instead describe them in such a manner as to invoke the characters of a southern gothic short story or novel, thereby reinforcing the association of the region with eccentricity. Given the region's historical association with degeneracy and perversity that continues to circulate within certain strains of southern discourse, use of the region for a negative critique of America allows viewers not affiliated with it to disavow the applicability of that critique to themselves by collapsing the critique onto this familiar regional presentation. This critique of how the region can discursively function is not new and has obviously been noted by many scholars before me. What I find amazing is that it continues to persist.

The media reception of the documentary raises serious questions about the ability of some locales to thwart the poaching of southern discourse as a supplement, which appears to be a prerequisite in order to signify America within the national consciousness. The question arises: do viewers perceive the documentary as a critique of America or just a presentation of an eccentric region? If the *reviewers* are any indication of the general response of viewers—which of course they may not be—then southern discourse overpowers American representativeness for most but not all. Oftentimes claims of southern exceptionalism—a claim that disqualifies the region from representing the country—are not necessarily about the region being distinct from the rest of the country per se but rather the ability of southern discourse to overwhelm that which it supplements. Such a claim grounds the concept of regional exceptionalism not on the basis of any particular characteristic that circulates within the discourses about the region but rather the ability of that discursive practice compared to other ones to dislocate that which it is supposed to supplement.

Biraciality and Its Discontents

Carl Degler claims that "the modern distinctiveness of the South"—though one of degree rather than kind, when compared with the rest of the country—"has its origins in the remote past."[105] Although he acknowledges that white supremacy was a national attitude, he holds in this region it was institutionalized, first through black slavery and later through racial segregation. He never addresses, however, why the institutional changes to the racial landscape as a result of the civil rights movement did not eliminate this distinction. When discussing the present, his argument switches from white supremacy to racial demographics—the region is distinct because of "the homogeneity of its European stock and the duality of its racial makeup."[106] In other words, "the modern distinctiveness of the South" is biraciality, which today dominates the current régime of truth within southern discourse regarding the racial contours of the region. Of course, such a discursive framing ignores the mono-racial and multiracial locales that exist across southeastern states. Some areas in those states are predominately white; others are not. And numerous tri-racial configurations exist, although the components of that trilogy differ from one specific locale to another. For example, in Mississippi a tri-racial configuration in the Delta is black, white, and Chinese, while one in the east central section of the state, around the town of Philadelphia, is black, white, and American Indian. In Alabama, a tri-racial configuration in the area north of the city of Mobile, around the town of McIntosh, is black, white, and American Indian, while one south of the city, around the town of Bayou La Batre, is black, white, and Southeast Asian. Even if one claimed southeastern states were tri-racial rather than biracial, the problem emerges of the groups composing that tri-raciality differing from one locale to another, so the region would not be made up of just three racial groups (as the term implies). At the local level, a diversity of racial configurations exists across most southeastern states. This does not mean, however, that the discursive framing of the region as biracial is false because it ignores such diversity. Because the region is a discursive practice with no necessary correlation to the local, any distinctiveness attributed to it—such as biraciality—is *always* a meditated one, formed by discursive practices within the current reigning politics of truth, and disseminated through a discursive supplement to local, national, and global institutional structures and formations.

This book uses cultural and social theory to explore issues surrounding the articulation of race as biracial within southern discourse.[107] In the aftermath of the civil rights movement, blackness was incorporated into the definition of the region alongside that of the previously existing whiteness, reconfiguring the region as biracial. One result of this change was the emergence of civil rights heritage tourism on a par with that related to the Civil War. Chapters one and two explore this reconfiguration of race as biracial within southern discourse through the concepts of racial symmetry, using the documentary *Tell About the South*; racial citizenry, using civil rights tourism advertisements and attractions; and racial performativity, using the documentary *bro•ken/ground*. The remainder of the book, using documentary films, examines issues associated with this framework. The book is not a history of documentary films about locales within southeastern states related to race but rather a study of how documentaries function as a site where southern discourse assumes material form and is therefore frozen in time, thereby allowing easy access for analysis. Hence, while I will offer detailed readings of particular texts, broader conceptual issues related to the formation of race (in conjunction with class, sex/gender, and sexuality) in southern discourse are my ultimate concern, and the analysis rises to that level through the conduit of film.

Although the framing of the region as biracial within southern discourse is meant to be a progressive allusion to integration, it performs a number of regressive functions. Two of the main problems associated with this discursive framing are: first, it assumes racial purity and, second, it assumes two races exist. In other words, biraciality enacts two denials about the region: (1) the existence of miscegenation, and (2) the existence of other races and ethnicities. While miscegenation is usually thought of as being bodily, it can also be approached as culturally. Chapter three considers bodily miscegenation through a discussion of the closet and one of the few documentary cycles associated with the region based on stylistic features rather than content perspective: the southeastern expatriate road film. While the chapter focuses primarily on *Family Name*, it also considers *Greetings from Out Here* and *Dear Jesse* (Tim Kirkman, 1997). Local documentary filmmaking did not emerge in the region until the 1970s. Chapter four uses 1970s southeastern ethnographic documentaries, which includes films such as *Hush Hoggies Hush: Tom Johnston's Praying Pigs* (Judy Peiser and Bill Ferris, 1978), to explore the issue of cultural miscegenation through the concept of poaching.

The second denial enacted by biraciality is the presence of other races and ethnicities in the region outside of this black/white binary, both in the past and the present.[108] Most documentaries dealing with locales in southeastern states typically focus on blacks and/or whites but I have been fortunate to discover a few that move beyond this discursive confinement. Chapter five considers Spanish-speaking ethnicities and racial in-betweenness by looking at *Mosquitoes and High Water* (Louis Alvarez and Andrew Kolker, 1983), which is about the descendents of eighteenth- and nineteenth-century Carney Islands immigrants to St. Bernard Parish, Louisiana; *Living in America: One Hundred Years of Ybor City* (Gayla K. Jamison, 1987), which is about the Italian, Spanish, and Afro-Cuban immigrants in the Ybor City neighborhood of Tampa, Florida, from the late nineteenth century to the present; and *Nuestra Communidad: Latinos in North Carolina* (Joanne Hershfield and Penny Simpson, 2001), which is about recent Latin American immigrants to the state of North Carolina. Chapter six probes the racial negotiation experienced by Asian

Americans, considering one of the rare documentaries to use a tri-racial perspective, *Mississippi Triangle* (Christine Choy, Worth Long, and Allan Siegel, 1984), which concerns the Chinese community that has existed in the Mississippi Delta since the nineteenth century. Chapter seven engages the problem of racial legitimacy confronted by federally non-recognized Indian groups through an exploration of the short film *Real Indian* (Malinda Maynor, 1996), which takes as its subject the Lumbee Indians of North Carolina. The chapter also considers the borrowing by southeastern Indians of the Hollywood Indian stereotype.

Because southern discourse frames the region as biracial (i.e., black and white), European ethnicities in the first half of the twentieth century were not considered white southerners and therefore occupied a position of racial in-betweenness. As a result of the intersection of white privilege and the discursive presumption of biraciality, racial groups such as the Chinese in the Mississippi Delta had to negotiate a racial position as not-black through coalition politics with whites. In an attempt to survive the onslaught of European invaders, many southeastern Indians adopted strategies of sociogeographical isolation and cultural assimilation. These strategies, however, resulted in the loss of their specific native language and culture, meaning that today they routinely have their racial legitimacy called into question. While the situations of white ethnicities, Asian Americans, and American Indians are very different, each has had to navigate the biracial component of southern discourse. Because their situations were different, they dealt with this presumption differently, as chapters five, six, and seven reveal.

Conclusion

After reading an earlier incarnation of this introduction, my mother responded to it by commenting, "You're saying the South doesn't exist." Although I may have tried to destroy a particular way of understanding the region, I have not tried to destroy the region itself, an act I find both fruitless and meaningless. As Edward Ayers resolves, "There is no essence to be denied, no central theme to violate, no role in the national drama to be betrayed."[109] Rather, I have tried to outline the ramifications of one non-essentialist approach to the region, that of a discursive practice. This theoretical position means that the issue of whether a regional distinctiveness exists—and, if so, will it continue—becomes irrelevant because any distinctiveness that may be claimed on behalf of the region is constructed through discursive practices and circulated through oral and mass communication processes as a supplement to local, national, and global institutional structures and formations—in other words, a mediated distinctiveness. Such a framework circumvents the common divide between history and literature (and parallel divisions such as the factual and the textual, the real and the imagined) routinely found in discussions about the region. But more importantly, this approach circumvents the devaluing of the audiovisual, which results from the hegemony of the written that dominates studies of the region. Rather than obsess over the region's realness or fictitiousness, its truthfulness or falsity, its objectiveness or subjectiveness, its authenticity or fakery, such an approach focuses on how regionalism functions within the local, the national, and the global. Jonathan Dollimore defines "the perverse dynamic" as the "instabilities and contradictions within dominant structures" which, though disavowed or masked, continue to exist and therefore enable "a perverse return, an undoing, a transformation."[110] The hope is that this book will function as such an undoing of the region through the ever-present possible South, encouraging new mediated formations because, as a discursive practice, the region is a site of continual contention, struggle, and negotiation.

Part I

Biraciality and Southern Discourse

Chapter One

"Experience our past as part of your future":
Biraciality and *Tell About the South*, Cultural
Citizenship, and Bi-Civic Heritage

Introduction

Although civic heritage attractions sponsored by cities and states function to preserve local history and develop tourism in their particular area, they are also sites of cultural citizenship. While Civil War battlefields have long been popular tourist attractions, many municipalities and states now market sites of engagement from the civil rights movement as well. A tourist brochure for "Central Alabama's Black Heritage Trail" claims: "Just as there were battlefields for the Civil War, so there were battlefields for Civil Rights."[1] The wide circulation of spectacular media images of violence from the 1950s and '60s to signify entire civil rights movement campaigns justifies positioning the movement on a par with the Civil War.[2] And like Civil War battlefields, the sites where violent civil rights incidents occurred are continually being turned into tourist attractions through historical markers, memorial shrines, and museums. The design of this brochure is telling. The words "Alabama's" and "Heritage" are both in larger and more colorful typeset than the other words in the title and, at first glance, appear to *be* the title. Such a design functions to ensure that, although the brochure's specific focus is on "Black Heritage," "Black" is perceived as an integral part of a larger "Alabama's ... Heritage." In other words, "Black Heritage" is a constitutional component of, not a competing one to, "Alabama's ... Heritage." The brochure describes "central Alabama" as being "like the rest of the South," discursively linking the local to the regional and in the process expanding the old configuration of the region as equivalent to whiteness to also incorporate blackness. Through such discursive supplements, this bifurcated civic heritage becomes an expression of a biracial region, one composed of two races—black and white. Of course, this newer manifestation of cultural citizenship depends upon the prior successful enactment of a political citizenship, which as a result incorporated

The graphics on the cover of this central Alabama tourist brochure for Selma, Montgomery, and Tuskegee is designed such that "Black Heritage" is visually a constitutional, not competing, component of "Alabama's Heritage."

blackness as a constitutional component of the civic and therefore is part of the now-reigning status quo rather than an outside challenger to it. This chapter considers the reconfiguration of race within southern discourse as biracial through the incorporation of blackness, looking at its enunciation in the documentary *Tell About the South* (Ross Spears, 1996) as a structuring principle, followed by an exploration of the formation of racial citizenry in two civil rights heritage tourist attractions—the Birmingham Civil Rights Institute (BCRI) and the Freedom Walk in Kelly Ingram Park, across the street from the BCRI—as illustrative of such incorporation.

Southern Discourse and the Emergence of Biraciality

In his now canonical conceptualization of sociocultural formations, Raymond Williams uses a temporal model of the simultaneous existence of dominant, residual, and emergent formations. In other words, besides its current dominant formation, every culture also contains residual elements "formed in the past, but . . . still active in the cultural process" as well as emergent elements that are new, "continually being created."[3] Although Williams is concerned with sociocultural formations, his three basic temporal categories apply to discursive practices as well because not only does southern discourse change over time but, at any point in time, it also contains numerous strains simultaneously. Subsequent to Reconstruction, the articulation of race within southern discourse was configured as white. One of the most famous (and frequently quoted) expressions of this formation is Ulrich B. Phillips's 1928 contention that "the central theme of southern history" is that "white folk" are resolved that the region "shall be and remain a white man's country."[4] Although his article technically is concerned with nineteenth-century history, it also expresses the tenor of the times in which he wrote, which was the heyday of the racist Dunning school of Reconstruction (of which he was a part). In the aftermath of the civil rights movement and the changes it initiated, the discursive association of the region with whiteness was gradually displaced by one with biraciality, although the former continues to exist in residual form, even today.[5] Historian George Tindall gave expression to this emergent trend in 1960, while simultaneously acknowledging the dominant association at the time, when he noted, "[t]he historian can report, too, that the Negro has been a southerner," although "[t]he point is seldom comprehended in the general usage of the term *southerner*."[6] In a 1982 article, sociologist John Shelton Reed and political scientist Merle Black argued that, between the early 1960s and the 1970s, many blacks residing in southeastern states changed from being unclear "whether the category [southerner] was meant to include them" to considering "themselves to be Southerners."[7] They conclude: "We suspect that 'Southerner' still primarily means *white* Southerner for most of the region's dominant racial group, although many Southern whites would, on second thought, probably allow that Southern blacks are indeed Southerners, too."[8] Although framed in terms of identity, they enunciated this shift underway within southern discourse of incorporating blackness into the definition of the region alongside that of whiteness, thereby reconfiguring it discursively as a biracial region rather than a white supremacy region. This shift was not only gradual but also uneven. Often the phrase "black and white" was used instead of "biracial." But such expressions still convey this shift because the common definition of biracial in relationship to the region is "black and white."⁹

This gradually becoming dominant articulation of race as biracial within southern discourse grounds the basic premise for Joel Williamson's 1980 book *New People: Miscegenation and Mulattoes in the United States*. He argues that the country acquired its understanding of race from the southern states, that "Southern attitudes about race had high power in the North; they were exportable and fully as capable of migration as the Southern Negros who went north during the first decades of the twentieth century."¹⁰ The trajectory of the book's argument starts with the southeast but ends with Harlem in the northeast. He argues that, prior to 1850, race functioned differently in the "upper South" than the "lower South"; free mulattos were considered black in the former but in the latter they were considered a distinct group who occupied "a middle space between black and white."¹¹ According to Williamson, after 1850 a shift occurred in the "lower South," and mulattos began to align *as* black, both politically and culturally, when whites made clear their "determination to have a biracial rather than a tri-racial society."¹² He argues that the Harlem Renaissance signaled the completion of this shift, with blacks now embracing the one-drop rule devised by whites to define who is black. Although Williamson frames the issue as a choice between a biracial or tri-racial society, for him the third component of a tri-racial society is mulatto, not American Indian.¹³ As will be discussed in chapter seven, by focusing on black and white relationships, biraciality allows forgetfulness of the Native American populations within the area and the history of cultural, social, and sexual intercourse both blacks and whites had with them and, more importantly, the near-successful genocide enacted upon them. Williamson claims that, by the 1960s, the "drive for a biracial society had reached its culmination."¹⁴ Although blacks represented 11.7 percent of the United States population, according to the 1980 census when his book was published, he concludes that the United States is "a biracial society." If, instead of narratively moving geographically northward from the southeast United States, Williamson had moved westward he would have confronted a different history of miscegenation than the one he constructed. Latinos, who are missing from his narrative, have sometimes been framed within popular discourses as a "new race" (hence, new people) that resulted from the interaction of the indigenous residents of the Americas and the invading Spaniards. Of course, this omission is justifiable given that his book is about mulattoes (who have historically been defined as a mixture of black and white) and not about miscegenation per se. The book stands as both an example of the influence of this emergent discursive trend at the time of framing the region as biracial while simultaneously contributing to its formation as a dominant understanding. It also illustrates how discursive constructions of the regional routinely inform claims about the nation.

One of the earliest academic treatises on this discursive reshaping of the region within southern discourse, from a white (supremacy) region to a biracial region, was offered by Stephen Smith in his 1985 book *Myth, Media, and the Southern Mind*. He holds that, as a result of the turmoil of the 1950s and 1960s, a "new mythic vision" came into fruition in the 1970s, challenging the old mythologies of the Lost Cause and New South that "could no longer serve to explain the South to itself."[15] Writing in the early 1980s, Smith leaves open the question of whether new media at the time, such as cable and satellite television, "will facilitate stability of the new visions which have replaced the old mythology or merely result in mythic confusion."[16] Although Smith identifies three mythic themes that he believes constitute this new framework, my concern here is only with the one he calls "a biracial egalitarian South" that attempts "to explain the current legal and social status of interracial participation in the regional dream."[17] Taken literally, the term "biracial" is a misnomer because obviously even during the antebellum period, blacks and whites interacted regularly. Hence, Smith qualifies it with the additional word "egalitarian" to signify that the old association with white supremacy is being replaced by one of racial equality where, unlike in the past, the two races cooperate to run politics and society. While today the term "biracial" may not invoke racial egalitarianism, it does signal a discursive shift in conceiving the region as no longer a white society but a white *and* black one. Although Smith approaches the region through the concept of myth and his purpose is to *describe* a new "cultural myth of the contemporary South . . . that both blacks and whites are shaping," his book contributes to the discursive reconfiguration of that region as biracial and assists to define that term as two separate races, black and white, sharing the same territory.[18] (Because the regional is a discursive practice, scholars of the region are intimately implicated in the formation of the very thing that they are attempting to analyze, including the book you are currently reading.)

Today, the dominant—although not the only—articulation of race within southern discourse is biraciality.[19] Its usage typically does not presume the existence of racial harmony between the two groups, only that they struggle to live together in a racial truce that is mutually acceptable in proportion to each groups' political and social power. While previously whites de facto dictated the status quo, now it must be negotiated between whites and blacks in those locales where blacks constitute a significant portion of the populace. In other words, from the perspective of population proportion, while nationally blacks constitute a minority, in numerous locales they are a majority or near-majority, which in the post-civil rights era translates into electoral power.[20] Although biraciality is informed by politics, the term circulates as a descriptive demographic one, its political aspect typically sublimated.

The word "biracial" is used very differently when referring to the regional than when it is used to refer to the individual, where it means a person of mixed race ancestry. For example, if an individual's parents are of different races, he or she is considered biracial. Such individuals are more commonly referred to as mixed race. While the terms "mixed race" and "biracial" are interchangeable when referring to such a person, to refer to the region as mixed race implies something very different than that of an area composed of two races, regardless of whether those two races live in harmony or antagonism. To say that the region is mixed race would be to confirm the worst fears of white supremacists—that it is one mongrel race. Unlike the phrase "mixed race," the dominant discursive application of the word "biraciality" to the region assumes biological separation—and, to a certain degree, cultural separation as well—regardless of whether social segregation or integration exists.

Tara McPherson argues in *Reconstructing Dixie* that a "lenticular logic of racial visibility" informs contemporary understandings of the region. Per McPherson,

> a lenticular logic is a monocular logic, a schema by which histories or images that are actually copresent get presented (structurally, ideologically) so that only one of the images can be seen at a time. Such an arrangement represses connection, allowing whiteness to float free from blackness, denying the long historical imbrications of racial markers and racial meaning in the South.[21]

While the result of lenticular logic may be monocular in that only one image (one race) is seen at a time, from a structural perspective it is a binaristic model (i.e., two races, black and white). This underlying structure finds explicit expression when she describes how the lenticular image that serves as the basis for her metaphor works: "A lenticular image is composed when two separate images are interlaced or combined in a special way. This combined image is then viewed via a unique type of lens, called a lenticular lens, which allows the viewer to see only one of the two views at a time. Rotating the picture slightly brings the second image into focus, displacing the first."[22] The metaphor is inherently binaristic. While McPherson's concern is with the way in which whiteness and blackness are separated by this logic, the structure itself functions discursively within society to restrict the vision of race to that of two. Lenticular logic, as McPherson notes, is "not the only game in town."²³ It is just one particular manifestation of a broader binaristic logic that dominates understandings of race, concretely in the discursive framing of the region and vaguely in the nation as a whole. While the introduction of counter logics that allow for the simultaneous presence of blackness and whiteness would be beneficial, they would still be operating within the binaristic mode that informs lenticular logic. The operation of this broader binarisitc framework needs exposure and analysis (along with an exploration of its limitations), and biraciality is one of its prime expressions today.

While in Joel Williamson's framework, discussed earlier, the nation acquires its understanding of race from the southern region of the country, a more common perspective today is that the nation is "constructed through the abjected regional Other, 'The South.'"²⁴ Given that southern discourse is not controlled by any particular social group or institution (whether local, regional, national, or global), the racial framing of the regional always has national as well as local functions. One common strain within southern discourse is that the articulation of race is more pronounced in that region than the nation as a whole. (One could similarly argue that the locales of Los Angeles and New York City have served a comparable national role at particular historical moments.) As the canon wars of the early 1990s demonstrated, a widely held assumption existed that American culture meant white culture. Shelley Fisher Fishkin argues that the early 1990s was a "defining moment in the study of American culture" because of an explosion of scholarship that investigated the "African-American roots of mainstream (and supposedly 'white') American culture" and vice versa, thereby moving beyond the perspective of America as monocultural to one of multicultural, acknowledging its hybridity.²⁵ In addition to articles and books dealing with specific locales and the nation as a whole, she also mentions a number of publications about "the South." Southern discourse as a practice includes areas of contestation as well as contradiction. One such area is that of regional exceptionalism; the region is routinely framed as an exception, especially in popular cultural expressions related to race. But as Fishkin's argument highlights, the nation has similarly been presumed in the past to be a white society. In other words, regional exceptionalism does not exist from the perspective of race. The title of the article in which Fishkin makes her claim—as well as her basic argument itself—implies a biracial nation; only a footnote disclaimer informs us otherwise that she views American culture as mestiza, not biracial. While the nation may not be routinely framed explicitly as biracial, its binary logic regularly informs discussions of race at the national level, such as Fishkin's American studies article.²⁶ Confrontation with the ramifications of this binaristic tendency at the national level is elided by displacing biraciality discursively onto the region through a southern supplement, where it functions openly as an organizing frame of reference.[27]

Racial Symmetry and *Tell About the South*

Because of the prominent position of biraciality within southern discourse, most documentaries concerned with the region work from this presumption. It permeates their narrative construction and thereby their enunciation of the region. A good example of this phenomenon is Ross Spears's 1996 documentary *Tell About the South*, which presents a history of "modern southern literature" during the first half of the twentieth century. The film is the first in a series of three feature-length documentaries Spears made covering the topic across the twentieth century. Over a sepia-colored photograph of a luxurious plantation house, a voice-over narrator asserts, "The history of the American South has differed radically from that of the rest of the nation"; it is followed by another sepia-colored picture meant to explain that difference—blacks hunched over picking cotton supervised by a white man sitting on a horse.[28] As this additional photograph appears, the narrator continues: "For more than two hundred years, it [the South] relied on an economic system based on African slaves." After noting that the region "lost a devastating Civil War" and "for nearly a century afterward it experienced severe hardship" (this time accompanied by a sepia-colored photograph of building ruins and then one of dead bodies), the narrator divulges that, as a result (now over black-and-white pictures of blacks and whites socializing on town sidewalks), by the beginning of the twentieth century, blacks and whites in the region "lived together in a tense social system of oppressive laws and convoluted customs." While pictures of the nineteenth century are sepia-colored, the collection of street-life depictions from the early part of the twentieth century are all in black-and-white. Ironically, these images of black and white people—sometimes of only one of the two races, other times of both races together in the same frame—are themselves shown in black-and-white, as race and color hue, visual imagery and technological medium, merge in a unified signification. The change from sepia to black-and-white prints visually clues the spectator to read the twentieth century as a time of solidification of the racial division between the black and white races—whereas earlier times may have been tinted, the first half of the twentieth century showed only stark contrast.

The region, as enunciated in the documentary, is distinct, this distinction the result of the region being a biracial society as a result of slavery and the plantation system, a position compatible with that expressed two decades earlier by scholar Carl Degler (mentioned in the introduction). *Tell About the South* uses the articulation of race within southern discourse as biraciality to structure its telling of the story of southern literature. The documentary is composed of an introduction along with four segments, each introduced by intertitles: "Fugitive Poets/Blues Poets," "Harlem Renaissance: Jean Toomer," "Mississippi Mythmaker: William Faulkner," and "Leaving the South: Zora and Tom." For a spectator familiar with the history of American literature, the racial configuration of these groupings quickly becomes apparent: three are black and three are white. The documentary positions the beginning of modern southern literature with two groups of poets. One is high art, the other low; one is made up of white urban males in Nashville, Tennessee, the other rural black males in the Mississippi Delta. Although the idea of treating Delta blues lyrics as poetry is commendable, especially considering that written texts on the history of southern literature ignore them, the usage still strikes a discordant note, an awkwardness accentuated by the very structure of the documentary itself.[29] A filmic dramatization of a short scene from each of the literary groups/writers is included in the segment discussing their lives and work. Such a sequence transpires from John Crowe Ransom's 1924 Fugitive poem "Bells for John Whiteside's Daughter," Jean Toomer's 1923 novel *Cane*, William Faulkner's 1936 novel *Absalom, Absalom!*, Zora Neale Hurston's 1937 novel *Their Eyes Were Watching God*, and Thomas Wolfe's 1929 novel *Look Homeward, Angel*. While all five of the written works receive a dramatic sequence, the lone oral work—blues lyrics—does not, although nothing technically would prevent the filmmaker from doing so. If a poem can be dramatized, then surely song lyrics can too. Instead, blues lyrics are only heard sung on the soundtrack. But even the dramatizations of the poem and the novels include a voice-over narrator reading parts of the written literary text being audiovisually dramatized. Based on the overall content of the documentary, it appears blues lyrics were included to provide racial symmetry for its narrative structure, to make the documentary racially even—evenly biracial. The omission of a dramatized sequence for the blues poets causes them to stand out from the other five groups and individuals covered in the documentary. The documentary reconstructs the southern literary canon to be racially symmetrical. It still remains, however, primarily a male one; only one of the six literary groups/writers is female. The documentary includes a brief interlude on Erskine Caldwell and Margaret Mitchell but the section does not contain an intertitle. This omission can be justified because the section is short, plus a dramatic sequence based on a novel by each writer is not included. Their marginalization may be attributed to their writing "popular" fiction rather than "serious" literature. Although their inclusion would increase the percentage of women from one-sixth to one-fourth, it would destroy the racial symmetry of the documentary because both writers are white.

The two middle sequences of *Tell About the South*, which explore the lives and works of Faulkner and Toomer, explicitly make a connection between the writers' choices of using modernist writing techniques with that style's ability to manifest on a structural level their intellectual perception of race in that region. According to interviewee Thadious Davis, by the end of the 1920s Faulkner began experimenting with various modernist fictional techniques. She observes:

> Faulkner came to understand more about the ways in which the world that he lived in was divided up, fragmented, fractured, not whole, irretrievably broken, racially divided—All these various kinds of tensions inherent within the South that he knew and [I] think made the methodology of high modernist more interesting to him—Putting many voices into the telling of the story. No one perspective from the many voices heard in the text assumes authority.

In other words, the region is a "racially divided" society and, if it is to be discussed, a style is needed that allows for the simultaneous presence of those "many voices." A similar theme emerges in the sequence on Toomer. An off-screen actor reads Toomer's written words: "In my body were many bloods, all blended in the fire of six or more generations. I was either a new type of man or the very oldest. When I live with the blacks, I'm a negro. When I live with the whites, I'm white. As a usual thing, I do not see differences of color. I see differences of life and experience." When analyzing Toomer's novel *Cane* within its historical time period, interviewee Rita Dove states:

> Everything seems to be so absolute in its genres. I mean there were novels, there were short stories, there were poems. But there wasn't anything that kind of mixed them [the way *Cane* does] . . . I realize that he was really bunking all those genres because it didn't fit his experience. He was saying I'm going to create something new because this is the only way to give a sense of the whole, the whole aura of the place, you know of the South.

A mixed style, pieced from many genres, was chosen because it paralleled his experience of race as "many bloods," an experience which included not just racial interaction between blacks and whites, but his own racial identity of being both black and white. It is as though racial mixing necessitated genre mixing, as style mimics content. Although the elements of the documentary

The structure of Ross Spears's 1996 documentary on the history of southern literature during the first half of the twentieth century, *Tell About the South*, is a symmetrical biracial one, as highlighted by its intertitles and dramatization sequences.

Dramatization of scene from Ransom's "Bells for John Whiteside's Daughter."

Sheet music for Johnson's "Hellhound on My Trail."

Dramatization of scene from Toomer's *Cane*.

Dramatization of scene from Faulkner's *Absalom, Absalom!*

Dramatization of scene from Hurston's *Their Eyes Were Watching God*.

Dramatization of scene from Wolfe's *Look Homeward, Angel*.

which present Faulkner and Toomer as being concerned with "many voices" and "many bloods," respectively, have been highlighted here, the black and white grid which structures the overall documentary on multiple levels (i.e., film color, narrative structure, linguistic choices) sutures these textual fissures of a multiracial understanding of the region, guiding the spectator to interpret "many voices" and "many bloods" as biracial, maintaining the black and white binary which informs the documentary.

As mentioned earlier, the documentary maintains a racial symmetry through the selection of writers examined. This overall structure itself tells a story about the relationship between the two races—black and white—chosen for consideration. This critique is not meant to be a statement on the quality of the documentary (which is impressive) but rather an illustration of the pervasiveness of articulating race as biracial within southern discourse. The narration begins with a contemplation of the white Fugitive poets before proceeding to the black blues poets, the black writer Toomer, and then the white writer Faulkner. Even though the first segment is identified by the intertitle as about "Fugitive Poets/Blues Poets," the slash in the title is taken literally and the two groups are discussed in linear succession, maintaining the racial divide on a narrative structural level. But this racial separation changes upon reaching the last segment of the documentary, "Leaving the South: Zora and Tom." Although, as with the very first segment, the intertitle notifies the spectator that the documentary will be exploring the work of a black writer and a white writer, a significant change occurs. Rather than discussing Hurston and Wolfe sequentially—the way the Fugitive poets and blues poets were—the segment intercuts the analysis of them, literally blending the black writer and white writer. This racial movement within the overall structure of the documentary can be read in two very different ways. One interpretation suggests a conceptual movement from racial segregation to one of racial integration, the races being "blended" in a manner similar to Toomer's framing of his racial heritage. The other interpretation is derived from comments made by the voice-over narrator at the end of the documentary: "World War II changed the South forever. And William Faulkner's nostalgia for his black nanny soon seemed naïve. The next generation of southern writers would discover the worlds of black and white to be on a collision course." This second interpretation views the progression from racial separation to racial mixing in the structure of the narrative as representing racial "collision" rather than integration, with racial worlds colliding rather than blending into one another. The timeline implies that collision is the civil rights movement of the 1950s and '60s, which was the big bang that initiated the discursive change from framing the region as a white supremacy society to a biracial society. Ultimately, whether the interaction between blacks and whites is viewed as leading to harmonious integration or clashing antagonism, the end result is still a racially conscious society composed of two races, black and white—that is to say, biracial. Although the structure of the documentary's enunciation of race moves from their segregation to integration, the framework of biraciality remains intact. While the word is often used to signify integration, it can also be used in relation to segregation. In other words, biraciality is neither inherently reactionary nor progressive; its political valance dependent upon context.

The State Apparatus, Civil Rights Heritage, and Black Citizenry

One of the key lessons academics have learned from theorists such as Antonio Gramsci and Michel Foucault is to question ahistorical dominant/subordinate models of state power.[30] Gramsci has taught us that no guarantee exists of the form and distribution that power will assume, while Foucault has taught us that power also operates as a web, social actors simultaneously undergoing and exercising power. Still, the temptation exists to assume that "[d]espite all the forces working at cross-purposes within the state," it "still preserves an overall unity."[31] Writing in the period between the two World Wars, Gramsci was interested in the Italian "southern question," a concern that made him keenly attuned to variations within the nation.[32] When considering the lessons that could be drawn from Gramsci's perspective for the study of race, Gramsci's concern with "regional unevenness" led Stuart Hall to list among his eight insights the need to understand "the tensions and contradictions generated by the uneven tempos and directions of historical development." When applied to the analysis of race, this suggests: "Racism and racist practices and structures frequently occur in some but not all sectors of the social formation; their impact is penetrative but uneven; and their very unevenness of impact may help to deepen and exacerbate these contradictory sectoral antagonisms."[33] In terms of the state apparatus, this means that not only does its formation change over time but meaningful variation exists—first, between the various levels within the state apparatus and, second, between its different locales.

When considering southeastern states such as Alabama, it becomes obvious that the racial characteristics of the state apparatus have changed significantly since the 1970s. As a cursory review of elected official statistics highlights, the number of black elected officials, whether in aggregate or by state, has not obtained proportional representation to the size of the black voting-age population. But the states with the highest such percentages are all located in the eleven former Confederate states. Only the District of Columbia exceeds them, and it is technically not a state. In other words, southeastern states are home to a disproportionately larger share of black elected officials based on the population distribution of blacks in the United States. Thus, not all locales are the same within the country (and, it might be added, not even within southeastern states). The state apparatus is composed of a variety of layers—city, county, state, and federal. While blacks in some locales of southeastern states have achieved close to proportional representation in some levels of government (such as city council and mayor, county commission and sheriff, state congress) they have not in others (such as state governor and federal senator), although exceptions always exist. The general trend—which continues to hold despite the election of Barack Obama as president of the United States and claims of a post-racial or color-blind society—of the majority of whites in these states not voting for black candidates means black political successes typically occur in municipalities and districts where blacks constitute a simple majority.[34] The discussion of race and politics can no longer be framed in blanket terms of the state being a white institution since blacks are power brokers in those portions of the state apparatus where they constitute a majority of the political constituency. This inclusion, however, does not mean that racial parity exists across the complete political landscape. For example, black political power tends to reside primarily at the level of the local. Blackness has been institutionalized as part of the representational apparatus of states like Alabama. After a state law was passed in 1999 that enabled a judge to suspend the driver's license of an individual convicted of gas theft, many gas stations displayed stickers on their pumps of a state trooper holding a driver's license in his extended hand with a written statement next to the photograph warning of the consequence of driving off without paying. The human figure on the decal signifying the power of the state was a black man. As a result of the civil rights movement, blacks are no longer excluded from state representation, both in terms of political power and audiovisual imagery. Around the same time, a similar warning sticker appeared in Mississippi but unlike in Alabama, it exhibited a white law enforcement officer. (Again, it is worth repeating, this does not mean that this inclusion has occurred across all levels of the state apparatus nor evenly in those levels where it has occurred.)

Citizenship contains a cultural component as well as a political component. Toby Miller argues that citizenship has been constructed around three zones that, though overlapping, have distinct histories. These are political citizenship (the right to vote), economic citizenship (the right to work), and cultural citizenship (the right to speak). While the first deals with political rights, the second and third deal with economic welfare and cultural representation, respectively.³⁵ While the goals of the civil rights movement were diverse, one area where it succeeded was in obtaining electoral access for all citizens through such political achievements as the Voting Rights Act of 1965.³⁶ One effect of this electoral accomplishment has been the dispersal of black citizenship into the cultural realm through civic heritage tourism. Besides the traditional judicial and educational means, the governance of racial citizenry also occurs through the popular, its most overt manifestation being municipal- and state-sponsored museums and historical sites. Miller argues that the "public is formed and reformed on a routine basis through technologies of truth—popular logics for establishing fact."³⁷ Heritage institutions and historical locations are sites where "the popular and the civic brush up against one another," "disciplining the citizen 'through a pursuit of the popular.'"³⁸

David Brett defines "heritage" as "a contemporary mode of popular or non-specialist history" which includes "the process of self-definition through historicised self-presentation, and carries with it the signs of contention even when (as is usually the case) those signs have been hidden, ignored, or not noticed."³⁹ The forms of "historicised self-presentation" that this recent addition to civic heritage assumes are diverse, including the designation of certain locations where civil rights incidents occurred as historical sites, the sponsorship of re-enactments of significant civil rights events, and the establishment of museums and memorials. For example, Montgomery, Alabama, has the Civil Rights Memorial, designed by Maya Lin, who also designed the Vietnam War Memorial on the mall in Washington, D.C., and Birmingham turned Kelly Ingram Park into a civil rights memorial.⁴⁰ Citizens in Selma established the National Voting Rights Museum and Institute, and in Birmingham the Birmingham Civil Rights Institute, all further contributing to the reconstruction of civic heritage at the local level to include the movement's history. Most (though not all) of these memorials and museums are the result of city and state polity. Such is the case with the Birmingham Civil Rights Institute and Kelly Ingram Park across the street from the BCRI, which serve as a good example for exploring how civil rights attractions racialize citizenry.

Black Cultural Citizenship and the Birmingham Civil Rights Institute

Today, the histories of the civil rights movement have been commodified not only through an ever-expanding stream of academic publications on its various aspects but also through the packaging of those histories for tourism. Historical tourism, per Valene Smith, emphasizes "the glories of the Past" and typically favors activities such as "guided tours of monuments and ruins, and especially light and sound performances that encapsulate into a brief drama the life-style and key events that textbooks record."[41] Heritage attractions are the embodiment of, to borrow a phrase from John Urry, "'artifactual' history, in which a whole variety of social experiences are necessarily ignored or trivialised."[42] This evasion (and/or minimization) occurs as a result of privileging the presentational mode of spectacle, which according to Barbara Kirshenblatt-Gimblett "by its very nature, displaces analysis and tends to suppress profound issues of conflict and marginalization."[43] Therefore, contentious issues are displaced when civic heritage sites use the presentational style of spectacle to represent history in their attractions. These displacements function to form a unity amidst present-day fragmentation by attributing this presumed present-day solidarity as a continuance from the past.

An example of a civil rights heritage attraction that sutures certain components of the past and offers a popular history that elides discord is the Birmingham Civil Rights Institute in Birmingham, Alabama. The BCRI, which opened in 1992, espouses a mission to offer programs and services "designed to promote research, provide information and encourage discussion on human rights issues locally, nationally and internationally."[44] As part of its efforts to achieve this mission, the BCRI houses a permanent exhibit dedicated to relaying a general history of the civil rights movement and the specific role Birmingham played in it.[45] The exhibit's gallery on Birmingham in 1963, entitled "Birmingham: The World Is Watching," contains no mention of the intra-racial differences that existed within the black community at the time between middle-class blacks and civil rights activists, between local civil rights leaders and national ones, and between civil rights protestors and loitering onlookers.[46]

First, the Birmingham gallery elides the division and conflict that existed at the time within the Birmingham black community over local civil rights initiatives. In his detailed study of the 1963 Birmingham campaign, Glenn Eskew documents that the traditional black leadership class in Birmingham—ministers and business leaders—were openly hostile to the movement and "organized an accommodationist movement to counter the ACMHR-SCLC," while the local black newspaper ignored coverage of the movement's campaigns.[47] Even the arrest of Martin Luther King Jr. on 12 April 1963, which resulted in his penning the now-famous "Letter from Birmingham City Jail" during his incarceration, did not galvanize the local black community to join the movement. It was the lack of widespread black community support and participation that led eventually to the strategy of recruiting black students to march.

Second, the Birmingham gallery elides the division and conflict that existed at the time between local and national civil rights leaders. During the five weeks of protest from 3 April 1963 to 10 May 1963, the campaign developed through trial and error, with local leaders and national leaders clashing, disagreeing on everything from what strategies should be adopted to when the campaign should be halted. The campaign began as lunch counter sit-ins and store boycotts and pickets, progressing to marches in violation of court injunctions which led to jail-ins, kneel-ins at white churches on Easter Sunday, and, eventually, the use of black schoolchildren as marchers. This last strategy resulted in resuscitating the waning campaign, which was in danger of ending in defeat similarly to the one in Albany, Georgia, the year before.

Third, the Birmingham gallery elides the division and conflict that existed at the time between movement protesters and curious onlookers. The use of black students as marchers became dubbed "the children's crusade" by the media; they marched most days from Thursday, 2 May 1963 to Tuesday, 7 May 1963. The bystanders mingling around Kelly Ingram Park during the children's crusade typically outnumbered the student marchers. Eskew argues that these "spectators gave the appearance of mass support" for the movement when in fact "most people in the black community remained apathetic" toward it.[48] Although "unorganized African American spectators had observed each major march, . . . because they were apathetic, irreligious, and alienated, they had refused to join the nonviolent movement. Yet they participated in other ways that expressed the rebellion of black Birmingham."[49] Those "other ways" were through verbally taunting the police and throwing bricks, rocks, bottles, and other such objects at them.

Barbara Kirshenblatt-Gimblett claims that "[d]espite a discourse of conservation, . . . heritage produces something new in the present that has recourse to the past."[50] Similarly, David Brett holds that "the representation of the past has a direct bearing upon political legitimacy in the present."[51] Most civil rights attractions are straightforward about what they desire to produce in the present through their use of the past—the creation of (1) racial reconciliation and healing between whites and blacks for the prior injustices whites inflicted on blacks, and (2) cooperation between the two races to build a better future where race never again serves as a basis for social and political injustice. While these sites do actively contribute toward the achievement of these goals (whose attainment obviously still remains to be actualized), they are also structured to relay a certain racial understanding of the world. In particular, the exhibits in the Birmingham Civil Rights Institute relay to visitors simultaneously a sense of what can be accomplished through collective action and an understanding of the civil rights movement as an instance of unified black collective action (accompanied by a few white participants). These past actions are positioned as the reason why the exercise of civil rights by blacks in the present is possible, implying that the need for collective action has not been eliminated but has shifted from the streets to the voting booth, from civil disobedience to citizenship. The displays elide from the past the divisions and conflicts among local black residents as well as within the movement itself in order to impute to the present an unbroken chain of empowered, cohesive black citizenry. The displays convey a world in which all blacks are civil rights movement participants, bound by a common civic heritage. The movement is framed as a unifying historical experience similar to slavery and segregation before it, even though many blacks did not participate in the movement.[52] Regardless of race, visitors leave with a perception of black cohesion, both in the past and the present, this present cohesion being a continuation of an equally cohesive shared past, the civil rights movement.

Touristic Experiences of Transracial Subjectivity and Civil Rights Heritage Sites

Civil rights museums and historical sites are often structured on the principle of visitor interactivity. The permanent exhibit of the Birmingham Civil Rights Institute begins with a short documentary film about the history of Birmingham from its founding up to the 1920s. The documentary concludes with the now-classic picture of two water fountains standing side by side, a nice modern one labeled "Whites" and to its right a clearly inferior one labeled "Colored." As this frozen image on the wall-sized screen shrinks to life-size, the screen lifts to reveal a proscenium through which a three-dimensional live replica appears of the two water fountains underneath the celluloid image. The overlay film image gradually fades, leaving only the live replica which serves as the entranceway to the galleries that will present a "journey" that "moves from the era of segregation to the birth of the Civil Rights Movement and the worldwide struggle for civil and human rights."[53] A bodiless voice instructs visitors to walk through the screen opening to begin their tour. In other words, visitors must enter the exhibition halls through a framing device that was first a film screen and then a theater proscenium, thereby becoming placed as, if not actors, then re-enactors in the drama of racial interaction that will unfold before them. They are encouraged from the beginning to become part of the mise-en-scène of the story that will unfold as they proceed through the permanent exhibit.[54]

The first gallery after the movie screen rises is called Barriers, a playground-sized village of a racially segregated townscape, where visitors can drink from segregated water fountains or sit on a segregated school bus. Upon leaving the village, visitors pass the Corner Café storefront, where a sign on an overturned crate reads, "*Please* Take One Copy and Spread the Word," a pile of handbills staked next to the place card. The handbill contains information about the arrest and jailing of Rosa Parks because she refused to give up her bus seat for a white person and encourages everyone to "stay off of all buses Monday" when her case goes to court. A visitor reading the handbill is addressed as a black subject. Handbills historically functioned as a means of organizing within the black community and to circulate information impossible to so do through the white-controlled mass media.[55] The Birmingham Civil Rights Institute offers sightseers faux participation as they walk through the space of the theater screen onto a preconceived racial townscape designed for their consumption. Even heritage attractions that appear static, such as monuments, are promoted as interactive and participatory. For example, the brochure for the Southern Poverty Law Center's Civil Rights Memorial in Montgomery, Alabama, asserts: "Visitors to the Memorial can touch the words and see themselves in the water."[56] Civil rights heritage attractions based on participant interaction offer visitors, regardless of their race, a temporary experience of a particular historical black subjectivity.

Upon leaving the Birmingham Civil Rights Institute, visitors can walk across the street and enter the site where civil rights incidents documented in the museum occurred, Kelly Ingram Park. In 1963, protesting black youth were attacked by police with water hoses and police dogs in the park; media coverage of these incidences held by many scholars as a significant contributor to the eventual passage of the Civil Rights Act of 1964.[57] Most sites where civil rights movement incidents occurred are anti-climatic, plain, and sometimes aesthetically ugly, and Kelly Ingram Park is no exception. Because of the topological everydayness of such sites and their lack of any noteworthy visual characteristics, accoutrements are necessary to supply tourists with knowledge that will allow them to endow the banal and commonplace with historical meaning; hence, historical markers and memorials acquaint them with information such as Rosa Parks being arrested on this site on 1 December 1955, providing the impetus for the year-long Montgomery bus boycott that ended racial segregation on the city's public transportation.[58] As Kirshenblatt-Gimblett observes, "heritage interpreters often locate truth in what cannot be seen, in the invisible heart and soul of the site. Their expressed desire to make sites real and vivid indicates that sites cannot do this for themselves. The inability of sites to tell their own story authorizes the interpretation project itself."[59]

The Freedom Walk located inside Kelly Ingram Park offers just such an interpretive project but one that offers visitors primarily not historical

James Drake sculpture *Police Attack Dog* on the Freedom Walk in Kelly Ingram Park. In order to continue along the walk, one must past through the sculpture, becoming part of the mise-en-scène of the historical event depicted. Photograph by author.

information but an interactive racialized experience of black subjectivity regardless of the visitor's race. The park originally was part of a black business district and community that was thriving until the area deteriorated during the 1970s; it eventually became part of a newly designated Civil Rights District in the 1990s. The Civil Rights District also includes the Fourth Avenue Business District, the Alabama Jazz Hall of Fame, Sixteenth Street Baptist Church, and the just-discussed Birmingham Civil Rights Institute. In confirmation of Kirshenblatt-Gimblett's argument that heritage is "an instrument of urban redevelopment," Kelly Ingram Park received a major renovation in 1992 that transformed it from just a park into a shrine in honor of the civil rights movement and the specific incidents that occurred there.[60] As part of the renovation, a circular pathway called the Freedom Walk was added to the park. The sidewalk passes through three sculptures created by James Drake that enshrine

James Drake sculpture *Fire Hosing of Demonstrators* on the Freedom Walk in Kelly Ingram Park. The sculpture is constructed so that a visitor walking along the pathway is guided to interact with the statue as a black subject, offering transient transracial subjectivity to white visitors. Photograph by author.

the three main media images associated with the local civil rights campaign that occurred there: children being bitten by dogs, sprayed by water hoses, and arrested by police. While the park is the actual site where these events occurred, the re-presentations installed in the park are not mimetic ones but rather playful abstract structures containing realistically shaped figures.

The three sculptures are designed so that pedestrians must literally pass through them in order to continue along the Freedom Walk pathway around the park, placing them literally within a mise-en-scène of these three historical events as one of the children to whom they occurred. In *Police Attack Dog* (1993), visitors walk between two walls from which the bodies of three dogs leap out, their mouths wide open, snarling and yapping. Just as a visitor casually swings left to avoid the first dog jumping out from the right, another dog strikes out from the left causing a shift back to the right again where a third dog awaits. Their menacing presence causes a reflexive action back and forth as one walks through the sculptural space. Circling on around the pathway, a visitor next walks between two water hoses and enters the sculpture *Fire Hosing of Demonstrators* (1992). A wall, crossing the walkway, contains a horizontal rectangle cutout that must be traversed in order to continue walking along the Freedom Walk. The opening functions as a doorway and a cutout next to it resembles a window. Upon reaching the doorway, the water hoses point directly at the visitor, now standing as a fellow schoolmate next to a kneeling boy and a standing girl contorting their bodies in an attempt to protect themselves from the sting of the invisible spraying water. Finally, visitors walk between two massive walls, each with a large window full of jail bars—this is a piece titled *Children's March* (1992). The 1963 Birmingham campaign with its jail-in was the first time high-school students were used as a tactic in a civil rights demonstration, and the strategy at the time received wide criticism from both blacks and whites. In the jail window located on the side of the walkway facing toward the center of the park stand a boy and a girl in front of the bars, with the words "I AIN'T AFRAID OF YOUR JAIL" inscribed underneath them. The inscription above the other jail window appears upside down and backwards, as though that half of the sculpture had been installed upside down. If turned right side up, the inscription reads, "IS A SIN." Although not technically a palindrome, if treated as a loop it relays the same thing regardless of which direction it is read and from which side.

All three of the sculptures work on a purely experiential and visceral basis as they position strollers on the Freedom Walk as participants in re-presentations of popular media images associated with the 1963 Birmingham campaign. Interaction with the sculptures provides sightseers, regardless of their race, the opportunity to vicariously and temporarily experience black suffering for citizenship at the hands of racists, without the risk of the bodily danger that historically accompanied that struggle. Just in case visitors are not aware that the violence depicted in the sculptures is directed toward blackness, two of the three sculptures include realist statues of black children, and for the third sculpture a traditional statue representing the same incident exists in another location of the park composed of a black child being attacked by a dog controlled by a white police officer. (And if a tourist is coming from the Birmingham Civil Rights Institute, he or she has just seen the historical media footage of the three incidents.) In contrast to this traditional statue, the agents of the racists' actions are only implied in the Freedom Walk statues rather than depicted directly. While snapping dogs and water hoses are represented, no white men are depicted holding the dogs' leashes or guiding the water hoses. As a result, the racists are de-racialized, allowing white visitors walking the Freedom Walk to experience black suffering without having their conscience bothered with the knowledge that their own race was responsible for inflicting that pain. Of course, a pedestrian on the Freedom Walk is not deterministically positioned as such, he or she may respond with indifference or even jump off the path and stand behind one of the water hoses and pretend to be spraying it like a racist. I am not arguing for a preordained Althusserian interpellation—although I do believe many institutional structures and discursive apparatuses exist that hail individuals as subjects (but no guarantee exists of their success).[61] In this case, the sculptures of the Freedom Walk are constructed in such a fashion that a visitor walking along the pathway is guided to interaction with the statues as a black subject struggling for citizenship. They not only are a material manifestation of black cultural citizenship in this particular locale but they offer non-blacks the opportunity to temporarily position themselves as such a racialized citizen. Although most civil rights heritage attractions impute a unified collective body politic to blacks as a racial group within the United States, those that privilege interactivity (such as the Freedom Walk) transform blackness into a mutable racial position, offering transient transracial subjectivity.

Southern Discourse, Bi-Civic Heritage, and Biraciality

Today, the memory of the civil rights movement has assumed a parallel civic heritage (for blacks and racially progressive whites) similar in structure to that held by the memory of the Civil War (for conservative whites). In 1999, the city of Selma, Alabama, released a television advertisement to encourage tourists to visit the city. A voice-over narrator declares, "You don't have to travel far for a trip back in time," as the words "Selma, Alabama" appear over a shot of the Edmund Pettus Bridge, the bridge crossed at the beginning of the now-famous 1965 March from Selma to Montgomery and the site of Bloody Sunday.[62] Footage of an older home with a white picket fence follows this shot. The narrator continues: "Witness the war between the states and the site of the last stand of General Forrest's Confederate troops." Accompanying these words is a scene of a white woman dressed in an antebellum dress walking to a window and peering out, succeeded by two shots of a Civil War battlefield re-enactment, with marching men firing guns in the first shot and men running up a small hill in the second, with an American flag prominently displayed in both. "Retrace the steps of voting rights heroes," the narrator recommends as a still photograph of the March from Selma to Montgomery appears, followed by a zoom onto a monument composed of, among other elements, a bust of Dr. Martin Luther King Jr. with the words "I Had a Dream" inscribed on it, while the steeple of Brown Chapel AME Church peers out from behind the monument in the corner of the film frame. The advertisement ends with the narrator requesting the viewer to "experience our past as part of your future" because "history lives in Selma." Shots of three local historical buildings appear in succession: first, the Old Depot Station; then, the St. James Hotel; and, finally, a white, two-story antebellum mansion with large columns.

The Selma advertisement combines verbal references to Civil War leader Nathan Bedford Forrest, who after the Civil War was the first national leader of the Ku Klux Klan, with visual references to civil rights movement leader Martin Luther King Jr. Images of lost military battles by whites for political secession and won civilian battles by blacks for political inclusion are positioned side by side as equivalent struggles. The structure of the ad highlights two popular spring tourist events in Selma—the Civil War re-enactment of the Battle of Selma and the civil rights re-enactment of the crossing of the Edmund Pettus Bridge, called the Bridge Crossing Jubilee. The byline "history lives in Selma" can be taken literally, as residents and visitors re-enact historical events from the Civil War and from the civil rights movement. The ad frames the March from Selma to Montgomery led by Martin Luther King Jr. in terms of "voting rights" rather than as part of a broader struggle by blacks for social and economic justice as well as political equality. By framing the civil rights movement in terms of voting rights, the passage of the Voting Rights Act of 1965 (closely associated in popular perceptions with the Selma civil rights campaign) can be viewed as providing closure to, and fulfilling the goals of, the movement. As a result, the movement becomes part of the past—"back in time," "our past," "history"—rather than a struggle still in process today. This is confirmed by the inscription on the Martin Luther King Jr. monument in the ad, which rewords the title of his famous "I Have a Dream" speech, given at the 1963 March on Washington, into "I Had a Dream," transposing the dream from the present to the past, implying that either the passage of the Voting Rights Act of 1965 fulfilled it or else it died with Martin Luther King Jr. in 1968. An appeal to history and tourism in the advertisement weaves the two seemingly incongruent elements of the Civil War and civil rights into a seamless whole, with both institutionalized as part of the city's civic heritage. While the ad never explicitly invokes the regional, only the local, it partakes of images that over the years have become coded as "southern." The southern discursive supplement in the ad linking the local to the regional operates primarily at the level of the audiovisual rather than the linguistic, in particular clothing and architectural structures.

Around the same time of the Selma tourist ad, Don Siegelman was elected governor of the state of Alabama. His inaugural speech on the steps of the state's capitol invoked the location as a place where President Jefferson Davis and Dr. Martin Luther King Jr. both stood prior to him, his speech honoring General Robert E. Lee and Dr. Martin Luther King Jr., each "for his courage, his sense of duty and his sacrifice."[63] The parallel linguistic structure of his speech positioned the Civil War and the civil rights movement as equivalencies; he invoked race without mentioning it directly, and these two historical events functioned as acknowledgment of his white and black constituents, respectively. Siegelman did not invent this parallelism; it was already encoded in the state's law for the third Monday of January, which was an official state holiday for Lee and King jointly. The states of Mississippi, Georgia, and Arkansas similarly celebrate the two men through a joint holiday, and Florida's Lee holiday periodically falls on the same date as its King holiday. Given the context of the state, the yoking of the Civil War and the civil rights movement results in racially coding them as white and black, contributing to the discursive framing of the region as biracial indirectly through a strategy of parallelism that maintains racial separation rather than integration.

Charles Reagan Wilson argues that a "Southern civil religion" emerged in the aftermath of the Civil War. Because of its origins in the defeat of the Confederate States of America (aka the Lost Cause), it "offered confused and suffering Southerners a sense of meaning, an identity in a precarious but distinct culture."[64] Although presumed but not specified, this is a *white* civil religion. According to Wilson, because it linked memory of "a profound historical experience based in [white] suffering" with "deeply felt Christian forms," this Lost Cause religion was existential in outlook yet "promoted the self-image of virtue and holiness and thus helped maintain the cohesiveness of [white] Southern society in a critical postwar period."[65] This institutionalization of the memory of suffering within a civil framework with religious overtones is reminiscent of how the historical memory of the civil rights movement functions today. The church and Christianity played an integral role in the civil rights movement, so its history is drenched with explicit religious overtones. Although Wilson's concept of civil religion could easily be applied to the civil rights movement, I prefer to approach it through civic heritage. But one place where the civil religion of the Civil War assumes material form is civic heritage attractions, and one could argue those manifestations provides the model for civil rights heritage.

As sites of cultural citizenship and civic disciplining, civil rights heritage attractions (similar to Civil War heritage attractions) offer explicit expressions of racialized citizenship. The popular writing of history through civil rights heritage attractions institutionalizes memories of black suffering in the name of citizenship. While Civil War heritage, with its Lost Cause perspective, celebrates the virtue exhibited in a horrific but failed attempt at white citizenship, civil rights heritage celebrates the virtue exhibited in a frightful but successful attempt at black citizenship (and the implementation of democracy for all citizens regardless of their race). The main focus of the civil rights movement was racial integration (and the abolition of white supremacy). It was not an anti-white movement (although it envisioned a different version of whiteness than that associated with Civil War heritage). As the movement moved into the terrain of memory (aka the past and history) and became civic heritage, it was racially coded as black and thereby associated with black cultural citizenship in the popular consciousness. Today, these two historical periods of the Civil War and the civil rights movement are the raw material for the formation of racial citizenry in the present. This means whites who desire to enunciate a progressive racial position through a *southern* framework must do so through aligning with civil rights and therefore indirectly with blackness.[66] This is an emotional and intellectual alignment, not the mimicry of black-articulated sociocultural practices. I am talking about an affinity by whites with blackness, not an imitation of it.

Just as Charles Reagan Wilson argues that the Lost Cause emerged as a civil religion (in my formulation, civic heritage) after the Civil War as a way for whites to socially deal with a military political defeat, one could similarly claim civil rights heritage has emerged to socially deal with an electoral political victory. In other words, Civil War and civil rights heritage emerged during periods of social change as the populace adapted to a new social era that resulted from a failed or successful event of historically transforming proportions. Heritage is concerned with history and thus the past. According to David Brett, "the preoccupation with the past is ... born of the stress experienced when one social 'habitus' is being replaced by another."[67] The change of "social habitus" which this new civic heritage signals is not the introduction of blacks onto the political arena but the more difficult task of blacks coming to terms with being a constitutional component of that political order (although in most cases the overall economic power base in these municipalities and states still resides predominately within their upper-class white communities).

Because southern discourse is not systematic or unitary, it contains emergent, dominant, and residual elements simultaneously. Raymond Williams notes that it is hard to distinguish between those emergent elements that will become a new phase of the dominant formation and those that will be an alternative or opposition to it. Emergent formations can become either, depending on the historically situated outcome of the struggles between them.[68] As demonstrated in my discussion of civil rights heritage attractions, a strong strain of black racial citizenry has now been introduced into southern discourse. Is this an emergent or dominant formation? If no longer emergent, is it an alternative to the dominant or an element of it? Or is it currently in a struggle for dominance with the white citizenry derived from mechanisms such as Civil War heritage? On a pragmatic level, the institutions associated with both types of civic heritage are obviously in a struggle for the same limited governmental and foundational funding. My concern is not with this economic institutional struggle, which is often tied to tourism polity at the municipal, state, and federal levels, but the broader issue of the discursive struggle they represent within southern discourse concerning the racialization of the region.

Because these two civic heritages are typically believed to be mutually exclusive, few incidents of synthesis or syncretism occur between their discursive racializations of the region.[69] Although blackness is no longer an emergent discursive component of southern discourse, it has not *replaced* the previous dominant of whiteness. But neither is it an *alternative* to the dominant because it is an integral, constitutional component of it. If the two are in a "war of position" in the Gramscian sense, then that struggle has dissipated into hegemony through the banner of biraciality.[70] (Of course, once it has been established, hegemony is not innately permanent but must be continually maintained.) The two currently coexist in hegemony although one may be more prevalent in a particular micro context. But at the macro level, neither is *the* dominant within southern discourse. Because of the racial coding of the region that accompanies these two civil heritages through a southern supplement, their simultaneous presence contributes to the formation of a bifurcated racial hegemony within southern discourse that is routinely labeled biraciality—the existence of two separate races, black and white. While this bi-civic heritage is not the cause of this hegemony, it is one manifestation of it. Ironically, although a key component of the civil rights movement was racial integration, it has been racially institutionalized as a "separate but equal" civic heritage. This "separate but equal" bi-civic heritage is an institutionalized manifestation of what Tara McPherson calls lenticular logic on the terrain of cultural citizenship. However, unlike its earlier manifestation through forced segregation—declared unconstitutional by *Brown v. Board of Education*—that reinforced the discursive association of the region with whiteness, this is voluntary segregation—which articulates race to cultural citizenship and on a certain level offers an expression of self-determination—that discursively associates the region with biraciality through a southern supplement.

Though not explicitly stated in racial terms, a site where the negotiation of this bi-civic heritage assumes material form is the Alabama vehicle tag. The slogan on the tag was "Heart of Dixie." To most black (and progressive white) residents, the phrase was an ode to segregation and invoked white supremacy, an association made all the more obvious if one considers that it was only added to the tag in the early 1950s, just as the civil rights movement was becoming more prominent. The tag was changed in January 2002 to "Stars Fell on Alabama." Although the phrase has a number of etymologies, its most common reference point is the title of a 1930s song recorded by artists such as Ella Fitzgerald, Billie Holiday, Frank Sinatra, and Johnny Mathis, as well as, more recently, Harry Connick Jr. and Alabama native Jimmy Buffett. Because black state politicians had unsuccessfully attempted to have the old tag line removed, some whites perceived the white Democratic governor's introduction of the new tag line as political payback to black Alabamians for their votes. Although the song had been recorded by white as well as black artists, the tag line was perceived by numerous whites to be racially tainted with blackness. If the state's vehicle tag is observed closely, however, the initial paradigm persists in the shape of a tiny heart with the words "Heart of Dixie" inside. Although, on the road, the star is hardly noticeable, state law requires that it appear on every vehicle tag.[71] It serves as a material signifier that one of the stars shinning over Alabama is the residue of white supremacy. The two civic heritages of the Civil War and the civil rights movement exist in an incongruent whole, typically not through direct representation but second-order racially coded representation, as in "Stars Fell on Alabama" and "Heart of Dixie." But hegemony is never finished; it is only maintained through constant struggle. This resolution of the struggle between the two civic heritages was renegotiated again before the end of the decade. In January 2009, while the "Heart of Dixie" miniature heart logo remained, the "Stars Fell on Alabama" tag line was replaced by the title to a Lynyrd Skynyrd song, "Sweet Home Alabama," to complement the adoption of the slogan the year before by the state's department of tourism. State representatives claim they chose the tag line to promote tourism because the song is third behind "New York, New York" and "I Left My Heart in San Francisco" for most popular destination songs. Though a rap version of the song exists, "Sweet Home Alabama" retains a closer association with whiteness than blackness, an association reinforced when one considers that the movie with the title presented a racialized landscape of the state in which blacks were almost nonexistent.[72] The institution of the state in places like Alabama is a site of contradictory impulses, sometimes swinging back and forth between progressive and regressive articulations of race while at other times articulating both simultaneously. The southern supplement accompanying the dual heritages that have emerged in many locales in the aftermath of the civil rights movement assists to reinforce the hegemony of biraciality within southern discourse.

Conclusion

Prior to the civil rights movement, civic heritage attractions typically racialized citizenship as white. One of the successes of the movement was the reestablishment of the ability of all blacks to act on the right to vote that was illegally denied most blacks after Reconstruction. This reinstatement of political citizenship eventually translated into cultural citizenship as the movement became institutionalized as a civic heritage. The southern discursive supplement accompanying such civic institutions assisted in the reconfiguration of the region from the equivalent of whiteness to also include blackness. Although civil rights heritage attractions typically construct blacks as a monolithic group, they also provide visitors the opportunity to vicariously experience blackness regardless of their race. The civic institutions of Civil War and civil rights heritage align citizenship along racial lines of white and black, respectively, thereby framing civic heritage as biracial. This bifurcated civic heritage uses past struggles for citizenship to create something discursively new in the present, a biracial region.

While southern discourse frames the region predominately as biracial, periodically multiracial formulations appear, but not frequently. Some significant examples in print include the Fall 1994 special issue of *Southern Exposure* on "Beyond Black and White," the 1998 anthology derived from the 1996 Southern Anthropological Society conference, *Cultural Diversity in the U.S. South*, and more recently *The New Encyclopedia of Southern Culture: Volume 6: Ethnicity*.[73] Such discursive framings of the region as multiracial, however, typically receive limited circulation and currently do not constitute a serious challenge to biraciality—although more academic research is appearing each year related to the matter. Care should be taken not to assume these recent acknowledgments of multiracialism are synonymous with the recent arrival of racial diversity to the areas. Some of the local manifestations of racial diversity are new while others are long-standing, such as those presented in the documentaries discussed in chapters five, six, and seven. In other words, many locales scattered across southeastern states have a history of multiraciality and polyculturalism despite the current dominance of a discourse that the region is biracial. While this chapter considers race through the framework of citizenship, the next chapter shifts the focus to performance. The documentary *bro•ken/ground* (Margaret Wrinkle and Chris Lawson, 1996), about race in Birmingham, Alabama, will serve as the focus for that exploration.

Chapter Two

"God-created difference": Racial Performance, Regional Exceptionalism, and *bro•ken/ground*

Introduction

While the permanent exhibit of the Birmingham Civil Rights Institute begins with a segregated townscape for visitors to roam, devoid of people but with spaces clearly designated as white or black, it ends with a human tableau of around a dozen pasty-white, life-sized figures through which visitors must walk, a representation of the 1965 March from Selma to Montgomery. Upon closer inspection of the George Segal-style statues, one can estimate the age, sex, and race of the figures using stereotypical phenotypes. A certain element of incongruence exists in coloring all figures white for a march about black civil rights. The gallery immediately preceding this one is on the 1963 March on Washington and its central display is an audiovisual presentation of Martin Luther King Jr. delivering his "I Have a Dream" speech. Contained within that speech is King's basic philosophy of race: "I have a dream my four little children will one day live in a nation where they will not be judged by the color of their skin but by the content of their character."[1] Having just heard this speech, the white sculptures can be read as representing this condition in which skin color no longer serves as a basis for judging people. In other words, they visualize the adage "we are all one race, the human race." While whiteness can theoretically be viewed as the absence of color, it is still perceived aesthetically as a color. This human race becomes one based on the normalcy of whiteness. If viewed as a homage to color-blindness, then the statues inadvertently expose the white advantage that underpins the implementation of the concept.[2] This uniform whiteness can be read symbolically as everyone obtaining the civic (and social) rights previously reserved only for whites as a result of the political changes wrought by the successful mass protests of the civil rights movement. (An alternative reading is that the participants needed to act white in order for the movement to succeed.) The decision to use one color, white, equates metaphorically the movement's goal

The 1965 March from Selma to Montgomery is represented in the Birmingham Civil Rights Institute by a group of pasty-white, life-size figures through which visitors must walk. The question arises: why use the color white to represent racial unity? Photograph courtesy of Birmingham Civil Rights Institute.

of equality with that of sameness and the goal of integration with the attainment of white stature. The sculptured figures ultimately elide racial difference, reducing it to crude approximations based on stereotypical facial phenotypes. While the preceding galleries as discussed in the last chapter write a history of black collective cohesion, this last gallery dissolves it into a general humanity. One of the clearly espoused goals of the civil rights movement was the elimination of race as a category for discriminating against people, whether legally or socially (a situation that unfortunately continues to this day). Is the accomplishment of this goal dependant upon the disintegration of race as a social category?

This chapter continues the focus begun in the last chapter on the particular locale of Birmingham, this time using the documentary bro•ken/ground (Margaret Wrinkle and Chris Lawson, 1996) as an artistic-inspired ethnographic expression of the residents' racial conception of the world during the mid-1990s. This conceptualization and its relationship to film form will be explored in terms of, first, common sense as informed by popular religion, and second, social praxis, which I will engage through the framework of racial performativity.

Race and "the exceptional situation in the South"

Today, most scientists maintain that race does not biologically exist; in other words, no genetic basis exists for dividing humans into groups based on physical characteristics such as skin color. Similarly, most social theorists view race as a social classificatory system that retroactively constitutes the groupings to which it refers. To put it another way, race does not describe a preexisting condition but rather, as an applied social label, actively forms any difference believed to exist. As a result, some scholars advocate the discontinuance of race as an analytical concept because it only contributes to further reification and naturalization of race as an essence.[3] Scholars such as Robert Miles and Rodolfo D. Torres advocate replacing the concept of race with that of racialization, redirecting attention from an end result (one that can easily slip linguistically into reified biological categories) to a process.[4] If race is a category constructed through social practice, then it only exists because the populace uses it as a frame of reference for perceiving the world. This means that racial categories can be constructed just as easily as being perceivable natural categories as societal ones. Although idealists may desire to eliminate race as a social category, many people do not want to abandon their race—although they do desire to eliminate the discriminatory value judgments that socially accompany the racial category with which they identify.

One of the key theoretical articulations of race as a social practice is Michael Omi and Howard Winant's now-canonical book *Racial Formation in the United States*. They expand Antonio Gramsci's concept of common sense, the philosophy of the masses, to include race. They hold that this common sense provides us with the "rules of racial classification" through which we are "inserted in a comprehensively racialized social structure,"[5] with racial formation being the result of both cultural representations and social structures. Omi and Winant hold that since the 1920s race "has not been afforded explicit theoretical primacy" in the United States because it has been subordinated to the paradigms of ethnicity, class, and nation, thereby "the manner in which race has been a *fundamental* axis of social organization in the U.S." has been missed.[6] They offer the concept of racial formation as a means to engage race theoretically in its own right, unsubordinated to these other approaches. According to Omi and Winant, the ethnicity paradigm emerged during the 1920s to contest the "then predominant biologistic and Social Darwinist conceptions of race" and maintained dominance until the mid-1960s when class- and nation-based racial paradigms arose to challenge it.[7] This competition lasted until the 1980s, when the ethnicity paradigm resumed preeminence.

While their concept of racial formation has become generally accepted standard practice among academics (often informing discussions even if they are not mentioned by name), their dubious axiomatic that explicit racial thinking has been subordinated to the concepts of ethnicity, class, and nation has fortunately been ignored.[8] This axiomatic, however, provides the foundation for their configuration of race through southern discourse. While they use the phrases "Jim Crow" and the "civil rights movement" in relationship to the region, they define it indirectly through a racial narrative, one already familiar from the work of historians such as Carl Degler (discussed in the introduction), only this time it is framed theoretically. Like Degler, they define this region as having two key characteristics: first, it differs from the rest of the country and, second, this distinction is the result of race—racial practices for Degler, and racial understanding for Omi and Winant. They hold that while the racists' biological-based approach was replaced in the 1920s with the ethnicity paradigm, it "lived on in the South" until the mid-1960s, when the civil rights movement destroyed this last holdout.[9] In Omi and Winant's framework, the civil rights movement began there because it was the only area in the country where an explicit formulation of race still existed and, therefore, the ethnic paradigm could function as a challenge to the racial status quo. As a result of the civil rights movement, the region finally accepted this "nationally dominant" racial paradigm of ethnicity, ending "the exceptional situation in the South."[10]

The region discursively constructed by Michael Omi and Howard Winant is a common one; many would claim it is *the* most common one. Although one would expect this region to disappear along with its exceptionalism, references to the region continue to appear in their book when discussing the post-civil-rights era. It is defined only indirectly though, primarily through reference to "the southern strategy," which was developed by Nixon Republicans in the wake of the 1968 presidential run by George Wallace. It assumes that because few blacks will vote for a particular candidate, the number of white votes he or she receives in southeastern states can be increased by using coded anti-black messages.[11] In other words, although the strategy will in all likelihood alienate black voters in those electoral districts or states, the significant increase in white voters that can be achieved outweighs this consequence and will lead to election.[12] While, on the one hand, Omi and Winant conceptualize the region as holding in the post-civil rights era the same racial paradigm as the rest of the country (that of ethnicity), on the other hand, they concur that its whites act differently on race (adoption of the ethnicity paradigm presumably had no effect on their racism). Two consequences emerge from the joint presence of these two axioms. First, taken together they decouple the commonly held association of belief with praxis, splintering them, thereby making the region a place where the national racial paradigm produces a different practice, an exceptional situation. If racial theory, as Omi and Winant hold, is "shaped by actually existing race relations" as well as "provides society with 'common sense' about race," then one would expect a correlation to exist between how people think and how they act, between knowledge and social practice.[13] Second, the co-presence of these two axioms results in the simultaneous claim that this region has lost its exceptional situation and continues to hold one. Omi and Winant seem unwilling to completely abandon their two basic characteristics of the region: that it is different from the rest of the United States and that this distinction is the result of race. Although the southern strategy implies a lack of national uniformity, Omi and Winant presuppose racial common sense and its accompanying racial formation as a national phenomenon, privileging the national—whether institutional or discursive—over the local; the latter is subordinated to the former. However, if common sense "is not a single unique conception, identical in time and space," as Gramsci holds, and racial formations are dependent upon historical context, then the conceptualization of race used by people in their everyday world could potentially vary in different sociocultural and geopolitical locales within the nation, differences that may not synthesize into a national racial formation (nor a regional one, although some trans-local expressions may be presumed by some to be the region).[14]

Antonio Gramsci developed his concepts—such as common sense and hegemony—to understand a particular concrete historical situation. This has not prevented scholars, however, from productively applying those concepts to other contexts. But while Gramsci's concept of common sense has been widely embraced, its complementary one, religion of the people, has not. Popular religion stands in relationship to the religion of the intellectuals much as common sense does to philosophy; both lack the intellectual order of their elite counterparts. Yet, per Gramsci, "The principal elements of common sense are provided by religion, and consequently the relationship between common sense and religion is much more intimate than that between common sense and the philosophical systems of the intellectuals."[15] While Omi and Winant extend Gramsci's concept of common sense to race, they ignore a similar move with popular religion because they assume secularity. Their trajectory that justifications for race changed in the eighteenth century from religious to scientific ("as a *biological* concept") and then in the twentieth century to political ("as a *social* concept") downplays the continued importance of religion today in some popular understandings of race.[16] Unlike traditional Marxists, Gramsci does not believe that religion is innately a "narcotic for the popular masses" and even holds that at certain times it has been a historical necessity, "a necessary form taken by the will of the popular masses and a specific way of rationalizing the world and real life, which provided the general framework for real practical activity."[17] Gramsci was interested in popular religion because of its function as "a unity of faith between a conception of the world and a corresponding norm of conduct."[18] In other words, for Gramsci religion entails not just beliefs but also social praxis (a community of the faithful) and this latter characteristic is what makes it for Gramsci the most serious threat to the socialist praxis that he advocates. If one accepts that race functions as a form of common sense, then it potentially has a corresponding popular religious expression.

Mise-en-scène, the Long Take, and bro•ken/ground

While the civil rights attractions discussed in the last chapter allowed visitors to position themselves within preconceived three-dimensional racialscapes derived from the mise-en-scène of historical photographs and audiovisual footage, bro•ken/ground enabled residents of Birmingham to construct and literally inhabit the mise-en-scène of the screen. This documentary, made by two visual artists in that city, Margaret Wrinkle and Chris Lawson, functions as a forum for city residents who did not otherwise have access to the media to talk about race. Given that their primary, though not only, raw footage was city inhabitants sharing their intimate thoughts on race, the filmmakers are amateur ethnographers as well as artists, and their documentary is an ethnographic one as well as performative. Proscriptions for ethnographic film over the years by scholars such as Margaret Mead, Alan Lomax, Karl Heider, and David MacDougall advocated the use of long takes with limited editing.[19] While interviewees in bro•ken/ground are typically shown in single shots, their conversations with the filmmakers have been sliced into numerous short units and dispersed throughout the documentary to enable the filmmakers to construct a collective voice. In contrast to this long-take proscription, ethnographic filmmaking as an applied practice has historically incorporated a diversity of filmmaking techniques, with few documentaries fulfilling this proscriptive demand and many of those that do seen by academics as unsatisfying as cinema. Such proscriptions insinuate a concern that aesthetics will overpower evidentiary documentation and the safest way to guard against such an occurrence is minimal filmic techniques. Although bro•ken/ground privileges editing over the long take, it does capture a community wrestling with how race is socially lived among its inhabitants during

The city divided

Filmmakers hope 'Broken Ground' builds racial unity

By **Bob Carlton**
News staff writer

The white woman says she fantasizes about walking into a black women's wig shop "and not being looked at like I'm insane."

The black woman says sometimes when she sees a white person, she cringes. "I don't like to feel that way," she says, "but I do."

The white man talks about how blacks and whites are afraid to ask each other questions about race "out of fear that something offensive will be said inadvertently."

The black man talks about how his friends in Tennessee are afraid to come to Alabama. "I've always wanted to know," he says, "where are people in Alabama scared to go?"

Black and white, male and female, young and old, they're all subjects in the new film *Broken Ground*, an "experimental documentary" about race relations in Birmingham. A joint labor of love by writers-producers-directors Chris Lawson and Margaret Wrinkle, the picture will premiere Friday at the Carver Theatre.

Nine months in the making, *Broken Ground* comes on the heels of a recent survey that indicates blacks and whites in Birmingham remain divided on many key racial issues. The project, though, has been swimming around in the filmmakers' heads for almost two years, ever since they finished shooting another documentary, *Set the Record Straight: How Life Is in Central City*, about life in Birmingham's Metropolitan Gardens.

Lawson, who grew up in Roebuck and graduated from Transylvania University in Kentucky, said he hopes *Broken Ground* will help blacks and whites come together by learning more about what separates them.

"It was conceived and produced not to be explosive (but) to deal with topics," Lawson says. "To me, when I think about it, it's like all the people, all the voices (in the film), are in communion with one another."

Ms. Wrinkle, who grew up in Mountain Brook, graduated from Yale University and taught in a refugee camp in the West Bank, said when she moved back to Birmingham in 1990, she discovered that, despite its reputation, it was not as racially divided as other cities where she had lived.

"There may be divisions, but everybody still feels that this is their community and we're all tied to each other because of our past and because all of us feel this is our home," she said. "I think everybody is motivated because of that sense of community."

For *Broken Ground*, Lawson and Ms. Wrinkle, both of whom are white, compiled hours of interviews with about 100 Birmingham and Alabama residents to get their views on how blacks and whites get along — and why they sometimes don't.

They attended a Million Man March assembly at the Alabama Theatre and went to a Ku Klux Klan rally in Pulaski, Tenn. They talked to students, schoolteachers, artists, administrators, ministers, social workers and civil rights leaders.

See **Film**, Page **6C**

Details

What: Premiere of *Broken Ground*, a film by Chris Lawson and Margaret Wrinkle.
When: 8 p.m. Friday.
Where: Carver Theatre, 1631 Fourth Ave. North.
Admission: Free.

Chris Lawson, left, and Margaret Wrinkle hope their film gets blacks and whites talking to each other.

An announcement in the 11 April 1996 edition of the *Birmingham News* about the premiere of Margaret Wrinkle and Chris Lawson's 1996 documentary bro•ken/ground. The documentary functioned as a forum for Birmingham residents who did not have access to the media to talk about race. Its screening around town resulted in the flow of words in the documentary being enacted by the audiences that viewed it.

a particular time. It originates out of the city on multiple levels. Besides its inhabitants' lives providing the basic raw material, it was funded through local grants and contributions of in-kind services. And once completed, the documentary was screened in local churches and classrooms, featuring discussion groups afterwards, resulting in the flow of words in the documentary by city residents being enacted by the Birmingham audiences that viewed it, thus blurring the line between the activities of production and consumption.

No narrator exists in the documentary, although in some sequences interviewees' words are edited into voice-over montages separate from their image track. In addition, none of the interviewees are identified, neither by name or an informative subtitle such as "minister," "artist," or "business executive." The lack of a narrator—combined with interviewees not being identified—places all of the voices within the documentary on an equal plane of authority with no division between experts and subjects. Although based on the aural sound of their voices and visual image of their bodies, their race, sex, and general age can be hypothesized (e.g., young black woman, middle-aged white man, etc.). While in general the interviewees disclose little autobiographical information, their words routinely position them racially. Hardly a talking head passes across the screen without the interviewee verbalizing on some level a reference to race. They speak of "white people," "black people," "blacks," "whites," "white Americans," "African Americans," "white community," "black professionals," "race," "different races," "racial divide," "color," "color thing," "racism," "racist," and so forth. According to Colette Guillaumin, "Just talking about race means that it will always be there in residue."[20] In other words, talking about race contributes to its continuance as a relevant social category. If the Birmingham interviewees captured in bro•ken/ground are indicative of the residents of that city, then race will play a significant role in it for a long time.

While race is performed by the interviewees within the mise-en-scène space of the screen, its conceptualization emerges through the combination of those individual shots. In other words, enunciation transpires not through narrative means (or even narration) but associative logic created through editing that must be connected by the listening viewer. These multiple juxtapositions amass to form a meaning greater than that spoken by any talking head in a shot. While traces of ethnic, class, and national understandings of race appear in bro•ken/ground, they are isolated voices in comparison to the main expression of race enunciated in the documentary. These approaches are isolated as anomalies, their meaning literally contained within the mise-en-scène of a few shots, segregated from the collective voice that forms through editing. Through editing, separate shots are integrated to form a meaning not contained within any individual shot. As a result of these techniques, ethnic, class, and national understandings of race are associated aesthetically with segregation, and the direct engagement with race aligned aesthetically with integration.

Dispersed throughout the rushing flow of talking heads that constitute a significant portion of the documentary are intertitles containing words, often accompanied by definitions. The words and definitions on the screen typically shake, with their definitions fragmented and/or blurred, thus literalizing the instability of words and the difficulty of discerning their meaning and literalizing the problem of anchoring language; the listening viewer must attempt to comprehend the polyphony of spoken words spewing from the screen. The intertitles function as guideposts for organizing and ascribing meaning to the barrage of voluminous words aurally encountered. An attentive listening viewer will glean that although people often find themselves "trafficking" in "race" "stereotypes," racial "difference" between "white" and "black" does exist as a result of different "perception[s]" of "truth" and experiences within society which have led whites to "fear" blacks and blacks in turn to feel anger toward whites. If people are to move beyond the "stereotypes" and to "heal" the racial wounds of history, in particular those of the 1960s, then people must have "faith" and be willing to "work for forgiveness" by entering into honest dialogue with each other, respecting racial differences while maintaining "hope" that racial reconciliation will ultimately be achieved. The title of the documentary, *bro•ken/ground*, when juxtaposed with the popular civil rights phrase "common ground" accentuates this reading. In other words, broken ground separates the races in Birmingham and, in order to find common ground, racial perceptions must be discussed so cross-racial understanding can be obtained and the chasm bridged. The documentary advocates a community activism based not on confrontation, exposure, or agitation but rather on reconciliation and healing through candid racial interaction.

Jennifer Fuller holds that "[m]edia and political discussions of race in the 1990s were dominated by a discourse that might be best characterized as fear of a 'racial divide,'" and *bro•ken/ground* definitely falls into that purview.[21] She holds that this discourse of racial divide shifted the measurement of racial progress from the elimination of "discrimination and economic inequality" to the attainment of "racial harmony," "from creating social *equality* through policy to fostering racial *harmony* between individuals."[22] Although this new approach, framed through racial reconciliation, dominated popular culture in the 1990s, Fuller also holds it was challenged by progressives and civil rights activists. Fuller focuses on nationally circulated media and assumes a national perspective. In contrast, *bro•ken/ground* deals with a concrete locale that, like many other locales across the nation, is not necessarily representative of the national. In this particular case, the discourse of racial divide functions differently than on the national level as she defines it; the separation of the socioeconomic from the interpersonal, easily maintained at that level, is practically impossible to sustain at the local level. A local call for racial reconciliation lacks the abstraction available at the national level because it is addressed to a particular lived situation with its own specific history. As a result, such a call simultaneously raises the issue of why there is a racial divide in our community that needs to be reconciled, thereby invoking such tangible matters as housing, education, and employment, linking interpersonal feelings—getting along—to broader social conditions of parity.[23] After briefly considering isolated expressions of ethnic, class, and national articulations of race in bro•ken/ground that occur within a few isolated shots, I will explore the collective understanding of race it enunciates through editing, followed by a consideration of racial performativity within the mise-en-scène.

Traces of Ethnic, Class, and National Articulations of Race in bro•ken/ground

Of the rushing flow of voices in bro•ken/ground, only three express ethnic, class, or national understandings of race. In one shot, a middle-aged white man proclaims, "For me the overwhelming divide is an economic divide," while in another a different middle-aged white man declares, "The number one problem affecting the survival of this nation is race mixing, and I am opposed to it because every civilization in the past that has practiced uncontrolled amalgamation of the races has gone down the tubes." The first interviewee espouses a primarily class-based understanding of race while the second a nation-based understanding. The former, a racial progressive, appeals to economic structures to explain racial inequality while the latter, a racial conservative, uses nationalism to justify white supremacy. The editing of this last comment pulls the remark about racial intercourse in two directions. In the shot immediately preceding it, a black youth ponders the one-drop rule for determining who is black. He explains to a filmmaker: "But if one of the brothers and you get together and mix blood, that next baby produced is going to be considered black. You see what I'm saying? So, therefore, I would be increasing my population and I would be decreasing your population." This comment frames race mixing as sexual intercourse. But in the shot immediately succeeding the white supremacist's pronouncement, a professional black man contends: "I think most people want to keep separate their history and their knowledge and their pride. But I think they do want to cross racial barriers. I don't think that—and then you always have the extremist here and extremist there who want an all-black state or an all-white country, which is stupid." This comment, in contrast, frames race mixing as social intercourse. It serves to ridicule and marginalize the sole articulation of nation-based thinking of race in the documentary but does so in a manner than includes its black form as well as its white form. The combinations of shots exemplify the elasticity of the phrase "race mixing" and its ability to simultaneously invoke intercourse as both social and bodily. Because the "different types of human bodies" associated with race "reproduce themselves," as Richard Dyer argues, "[a]ll concepts of race are always concepts of the body and also of heterosexuality."[24] The addition of the word "mixing" to "race" makes explicit the sublimated (hetero) sexual component of race.

The only interviewee in the documentary to explicitly mention ethnicity—a black woman—talks about it in terms of white people. She claims that whites fear interacting with blacks as equals because of "what it is that white people think they need to give up" in order to do so; she also asserts that "because whiteness has been constructed in such a way that means power, that means possessions, means things—not ethnicity—white people feel that if they give up all the things that come with whiteness then they won't exist." She advises that whites will have "to give up the artificiality of that construction . . . in order to claim a self." She does not use the word in its popular meaning of national decent, such as German American or Italian American, but rather as a synonym for race. But her use of the words "possessions" and "things" invokes both economic and social power, yoking whiteness to the visibility of class but invisibility of race. Her comment is informed by Richard Dyer's position that whiteness is simultaneously nothing (invisible) and everything (the norm). Per Dyer: "Whites must be seen to be white, yet whiteness as race resides in invisible properties and whiteness as power is maintained by being unseen. . . . The slippage between white as a colour and white as colourless forms part of a system of thought and affect whereby white people are both particular and nothing in particular, are both something and non-existent."[25] Per this interviewee, whites define whiteness through class privilege (thereby making it invisible). This comment shares affinity with Nell Irvin Painter's position that at the beginning of the twentieth century "the word *white*, unless modified, indicated a member of the upper class and *black*, unless modified, equaled impoverished worker. So deeply embedded in racial categories were assumptions about class that deviation from these assumptions required the use of the adjectives; *poor* white, *middle-class* black."[26] Rather than reposition race as a form of class, the comment highlights how the two social positions have at times been historically constructed as so intertwined that they are presumed to be synonymous. Even today this assumption periodically informs comments made by journalists and commentators in the news media. In other words, to acknowledge as this interviewee does that white privilege has economic benefits (as well as social benefits) does not collapse race into class but rather recognizes their intricate interconnectedness. Such a position defines whiteness not as an attitude of racial superiority but as access to certain socioeconomical privileges because of one's race, which indirectly frames racism as being about social structures rather than personal feelings. While interviewees in the documentary routinely talk in terms of personal experience and emotions, a sense of race as an "axis of social organization" also informs their conversations with the filmmakers. Unlike popular culture that primarily frames racism as a problem related to personal feelings, thus routinely ignoring the issue of instructional structures, the common-sense understanding of race enunciated in bro•ken/ground comingles the personal and the social, the emotional and the institutional, rather than treating them as separate, competing conceptualizations—although ultimately greater emphases is placed on the interpersonal. (One could presume this is because interviewees believe social praxis follows from personal feelings even if one's beliefs are shaped to justify ones actions.)

The Enunciation of Race in bro•ken/ground

If ethnic, class, and national expressions of race are rare in bro•ken/ground, then what articulation of race dominates? The associative editing of the many voices within the mise-en-scène enunciates a local common sense in which the principal elements are provided by popular religion, that of a constructed difference within essential sameness. On the one hand, the voices espouse that, fundamentally, "no differences between black people and white people" exist because "God created everybody the same," while on the other hand, they acknowledge that "in this society we treat people differently based on race . . . and that creates experiences that certainly have an impact that then lead to differences." So, although on a basic human level "we're all the same," the different societal experiences encountered by certain groups as a result of how others perceive their human body construct racial difference. While an appeal to a scientific-based biological essentialism may have been abandoned, most residents of Birmingham (as presented in bro•ken/ground) do not filter race through the lens of ethnicity nor have they disposed of essentialism per se. Instead, they embrace religion as an alternative essentialist model to provide a foundation for understanding race. Essentialism is used for very different purposes in these two approaches, science in the past for racism, religion now for anti-racism.[27] The created order of God, once claimed by whites to have preordained blacks first to slavery and later to inferiority and subordination, has been transformed into a justification for racial harmony between them. While religion is invoked to invalidate race through the claim that all humans are created in God's image (and are therefore equal), it simultaneously frames race as an essence because it implies God created race, although the problem of how this reconciles to an origins story of one couple, Adam and Eve, is ignored. The claim espoused that God "glories in difference" functions to justify racial difference as a manifestation of God's diverse creation, this difference, unlike past uses of religion, undifferentiated by varying degrees of value. Religion is used to justify the simultaneity of sameness and difference, depriving difference of hierarchical ranking in terms of social worth because of the presence of an essential sameness.

Essentialism, per Diana Fuss, "underwrites theories of constructionism and . . . constructionism operates as a more sophisticated form of essentialism."[28] The religiously influenced understanding of race espoused in bro•ken/ground is no different. While race is framed as just another form of bodily difference created by God, it is simultaneously perceived as constructed through social interaction. If every "body" is of the same worth in the eyes of God, then to treat people differently based on their bodies is an act of bad faith. While biological-based racism was based on classifying certain types of bodies as innately inferior, bro•ken/ground offers a foundation for racism based instead on a constructionist perspective. Race is a natural, God-given difference within a basic sameness that derives from all individuals being created in God's image, but racism is a socially learned disorder. In other words, racism occurs when this God-created difference is hierarchicalized through the assignment of different levels of worth, an action in the social sphere based on a theological misconception. Michael Omi and Howard Winant define a racial project "as *racist if and only if it creates or reproduces structures of domination based on essentialist categories of race.*"[29] I find their privileging of the operation of an essentialist position in their definition of racism rather surprising, for it seems domination should be the primary component of racism, not essentialism. As this discussion of bro•ken/ground demonstrates, essentialist understandings of race are not innately synonymous with racism but rather can offer anti-racist justifications as well, just as constructionist formulations of race can offer racist understandings of racial difference. The religiously inflected understanding of race enunciated in bro•ken/ground provides a predominantly, although not exclusively, essentialist understanding of race while offering a constructionist understanding of racism.

Most Birmingham residents appearing in bro•ken/ground reject the either/or mandate in which a choice must be made between perceiving race "as an *essence*, as something fixed, concrete, and objective" or else "as a mere *illusion*," a "construct which some ideal non-racist social order would eliminate."[30] They prefer theoretical "race mixing" in their religiously inflected common sense rather than the racial theoretical purity of either essentialism or constructionism. The persistence of Christian thought provides the foundation for an articulation of race grounded in a form of essentialism not dependent upon the racist biological paradigm. And the secular understanding of race as constructed through sociocultural difference slides incongruently into this God-created difference. The sameness touted in claims of color-blindness presumes the dissolution of difference. In contrast, this configuration of religious essentialism allows not only for the simultaneous acknowledgment of sameness and difference but results in a common-sense understanding of race that allows an individual to support racial integration without necessitating the disintegration of racial difference—in other words, to hold racial difference as an invalid category for assigning social worth while celebrating its existence and the richness it adds to culture and society. As one black interviewee calmly exclaimed, "Without color it would be boring."

As noted earlier, Antonio Gramsci holds that in some historical situations religion is an important means through which the populace makes sense of "the world and real life" in a way that provides a constructive avenue for "practical activity." bro•ken/ground provides documentation of one such expression. The question arises: what conditions in this particular spatial locale at this particular temporal conjuncture does a religious articulation of race negotiate? Manifestations of the populace not expressed through institutional structures and technological mediation are typically hard to find after the fact. This situation is one of the motivating factors behind endeavors, despite their problems, such as salvage anthropology and oral history. bro•ken/ground offers a populace expression of race in Birmingham during the mid-1990s, one obviously mediated through the filmmakers, a condition innate to all such audiovisual presentations seeking to document the social rather than the individual self of the filmmaker. The documentary was made in the aftermath of the solidification of the local civil rights movement as part of the city's heritage, as discussed in the last chapter. The 1963 civil rights event most closely associated with the city—in which children were attacked with police dogs and water hoses—resulted in a perceivable dismantling of certain (but certainly not all) elements of segregation in the city. In contrast, the process of establishing a new sociopolitical equilibrium transpired slowly over decades, a reminder that social change occurs gradually as well as swiftly.

While earlier political and social theories were often constructed around rapid change through revolution (such as those of Marx) or were fatalistic about the possibility of such change (such as those of some members of the Frankfurt School or Louis Althusser), in the aftermath of the 1960s disappointment on the left with the lack of timely change, some of the most popular theories have been those that theorize change as a slow process.[31] Some such theorists who immediately come to mind are Michel Foucault (discursive formation), Raymond Williams (structures of feeling), Deleuze and Guatterri (desiring machine and assemblage), and Pierre Bourdieu (field and habitus).[32] The social movements of the 1960s in the United States are commonly historicized as emerging from the impetus of the civil rights movement, including, not only the Black Power movement, but the student movement, the antiwar movement, the women's movement, the Chicano movement, the gay and lesbian movement, and the environmental movement. These social movements that followed in its wake were secular, and the positioning of the civil rights movement within this trajectory often obfuscates its defining characteristic as a religious movement. The civil rights movement stands as an American example par excellent of Gramsci's belief that "religion is always political."[33]

Because the civil rights movement was a religious-based movement (with a political aim), organized often through religious institutions (many actual churches), its historical presence contributes a religious component to race in many of those locales where such activities occurred. Gramsci notes: "Previous religions have also had an influence and remain components of common sense to this day."[34] Although Gramsci is discussing Italy and alluding to pre-Catholic primitive religions, a similar process transpires in the Birmingham context. As part of the city's religious (as well as racial) expression, the civil rights movement continues to reverberate today not only through civic (racial) heritage but by contributing a religious component to the city's common-sense understandings of race.[35] And popular religion, similar to common sense, "cannot be reduced to unity and coherence even within an individual consciousness, let alone collective consciousness."[36] The religious expressions of the social actors in bro•ken/ground exhibit this incoherence, with religion used to simultaneously justify the irrelevance of race and to celebrate it—to simultaneously repudiate racial difference and embrace it. Its emergence cannot be traced to any particular events (such as those of 1963) because it developed gradually over time as residents struggled to deal with the transition not only from a racially segregated city to an integrated city, but also from a white-majority city to a black-majority city. Charles Connerly links the city's white flight to how it implemented federal urban renewal and interstate highway programs during the 1950s and '60s, which disproportionately destroyed black neighborhoods and resulted in a housing shortage for black residents who then sought housing in white neighborhoods, thereby leading to white flight.[37] One of those urban renewal programs was the Southside Medical Center (now the University of Alabama at Birmingham campus), which enabled the city "whose economy was foundering in the 1950s and 1960s to convert from a dying iron- and steel-based economy to an economy focused on the dynamic health care field."[38] By the 1990s, the changes resulting from these disruptions had became the norm in Birmingham—the city predominately black (with black residents in control of city government), and the medical and health care industry budding from the medical school, now the largest segment of the city's economy—and residents struggled to negotiate the new racial dynamics that emerged along with them, dynamics very different from what previously existed.

Based on his ethnographic status as a participant-observer of the Alabama political system as both an academic and politician, Glen Browder argues that "the monolithic struggle of good-versus-evil [associated with the civil right movement] morphed into a relatively normalized political system by 2000" in which although "polarizing in national elections, Southern whites and blacks have accommodated themselves to functional co-existence in state and local affairs."[39] By the 1980s, Birmingham had transformed into a predominately black urban city surrounded by predominately white suburban towns, the fastest growing ones over-the-mountain, streaming south from the city through Jefferson and Shelby counties.[40] The United States congressional districts for Alabama were realigned in 1992 to replicate this division when a new gerrymandered peninsula snatched the city from the encircling suburbs and added it to the Black Belt, creating a majority-minority (that is, a black-majority) district.[41] This redistricting resulted in the 1992 election of the first black U.S. congressional representative from the state since Reconstruction. The redistricting of the city to a majority-minority U.S. congressional district, and its changing racial composition due to white flight, necessitated that white city residents learn to become a minority.[42] While black citizens were historically used to having to rely on white politicians to address their concerns (including the present, when they did not constitute a majority), this was a new situation for white residents of the city who now had to come to terms with this common minority quandary.[43] While whites held proportional representation on the Birmingham City Council, because council seats were elected citywide, the whites elected were those approved by the local black political organization, the Jefferson County Citizens Coalition (JCCC), which dominated the city's politics. This dependence was eliminated in 1989, when a single-member district (SMD) was imposed upon the city as a result of a lawsuit filed by a group of white residents. SMD is commonly used to rectify the underrepresentation of minorities that typically occurs in at-large elections. Birmingham was an unusual situation in that the minority was white. The change broke the JCCC's monopoly, relieving white residents of dependency on the goodwill of black residents for proportional representation on the city's council.[44] SMDs, however, depend on segregation to accomplish the goal of diversity, which means the city replicates internally the racial segregation of the city in relationship to the suburbs.[45] And many interviewees in bro•ken/ground mention frustration and dissatisfaction with the racial separation that is a prominent feature of the Birmingham cityscape. While initiatives such as these provide racial political security, they are based on racial separation rather than racial coalition and indicate the persistence of cross-racial mistrust even after the profound changes that had transpired within the city over the preceding decades. They also contributed to the solidification of a new interracial baseline. bro•ken/ground captures residents at the juncture of intellectually negotiating this new interracial baseline within their everyday lives. And fortuitously for the documentary filmmakers, during the period when they recorded interviews the issue of race was a hot topic of discussion in the city not only because of the recent O. J. Simpson trial that had captured national attention, but also the city's recent political election in which an ad on behalf of the black mayor referred to two black candidates as "handkerchief head, weak-kneed Uncle Toms" and linked the white candidate to Mark Fuhrman, the infamous ex-Los Angeles police detective of the Simpson case.[46] Although the radio ad—aired primarily on radio stations catering to a predominately black audience—never explicitly mentioned race, it was perceived by many as race-baiting, a use of color-blind racism by a black political candidate.

A survey on local racial perceptions sponsored by the Community Affairs Committee of Operation New Birmingham (ONB) was conducted in late 1995, with the results released six weeks prior to the premiere of the documentary.[47] At the time, Operation New Birmingham was an approximately thirty-five-year-old civic organization with the dual objectives since the late 1960s of promoting downtown economic development and racial harmony, with its Community Affairs Committee composed of local business and political leaders charged with addressing the latter concern. Although bro•ken/ground was independently made, ONB served as the fiscal agent for processing grants received by the filmmakers, a logical alliance given that the documentary and survey covered the same terrain. Similar to the documentary, the ONB survey showed a disparity existed between black and white perceptions regarding the degree of progress made in Birmingham toward racial equality and

ONB's executive director claimed the documentary was just "a different way of presenting these same differences in perceptions."[48] Because of the inherent limitations of surveys, however, it did not capture the religiously inflected common-sense understanding of race found in the documentary (or the racial performativity that will be discussed in the next section). Neither of these matters would emerge if the survey was the basis for one's knowledge of this time period because if the question is not asked, then the information is not gathered. In contrast, the filmmakers allowed interviewees to say whatever they wanted on the issue of race; consequently, the documentary offers, to borrow Clifford Geertz's term, a "thick description" (instead of the "thin description" of the survey).[49] Although, in general, religious institutions in the city are segregated, religion is a popular endeavor across races, thereby providing a common discursive terrain (even if not an institutional one) for interracial negotiation. In the aftermath of this sociopolitical realignment, popular religion offered a "way of rationalizing the world" that provided a "general framework for real practical activity": that of cross-racial interaction, which, while acknowledging racial differences in perceptions, assisted in the everyday negotiation of this new interracial baseline (even if not the elimination of interracial contentions).

Racial Performativity and bro•ken/ground

When theorizing society and culture, tension exists between whether to privilege social structures or personal agency, with the outer theoretical edges sharing similar terrain as the religious debate between predestination and free will. In other words, do structures deterministically shape people or do individuals have the ability to determine their own destinies? While the former position denies the ability to act, the latter denies the limits placed on that ability. This tension shapes the trajectory of Michel Foucault's research, which began with a consideration of how structures discipline individuals and ended with how individuals form themselves. He called the former technologies of power and the latter technologies of the self. Technologies of power "determine the conduct of individuals and submit them to certain ends or domination, an objectivizing of the subject," while technologies of the self "permit individuals to effect by their own means or with the help of others a certain number of operations on their own bodies and souls, thoughts, conduct, and way of being, so as to transform themselves in order to attain a certain state of happiness, purity, wisdom, perfection, or immortality."[50] Most social spheres entail some permutation of both, although for many scholars those of power tend to prevail. As Judith Butler notes, "self-determination becomes a plausible concept only in the context of a social world that supports and enables that exercise of agency," only "to the extent that social norms exist that support and enable that act."[51] The difficult task is figuring out how to integrate the two technologies in a single analysis.

As numerous scholars, including F. James Davis, have noted, during the segregation era a dual system of laws and social rules of etiquette existed in many areas of the United States, in which "racial etiquette was the chief means of maintaining white dominance in personal contacts that were unavoidable."[52] The violation of this etiquette could have brutal consequences. While today such incidents as the 1955 murder of Emmett Till in the Mississippi Delta for allegedly whistling at a white woman are well known, whites were also the target of punishment in some locales, although of a less severe nature. For example, during the 1920s the Birmingham Ku Klux Klan flogged a white store owner and his teenage daughter because she waited on black customers in the store.[53] Grace Elizabeth Hale observes that "the troubles to which especially southern blacks must go to appease whites . . . revealed the very performative nature of segregation."[54] She notes that although white retail outlets served blacks, white customers still held performative expectations of deferment by blacks in those integrated commercial spaces. Racial difference was regulated and maintained just as much through the daily performances of racial roles within the social sphere as by the law. In other words, race was not only imposed on individuals from outside through the law but performed by them from within through the internalization of social norms.[55] While racial etiquette was just as much a technology of power as Jim Crow laws for the production of race, it contained the potential to also serve as a technology of the self, a potential realized in the aftermath of the civil rights movement as the blatant regulation of racial behavior through the law deteriorated. Because the particular system of racial etiquette associated with segregation (whether de jure or de facto) disappeared along with the era, new forms of racial performativity have subsequently emerged.

Erving Goffman claims that "the expressiveness of the individual (and therefore his [or her] capacity to give impressions) appears to involve two radically different kinds of sign activity: the expression that he [or she] *gives*, and the expression that he [or she] *gives off*."[56] The former is verbal and explicit, the latter nonverbal and theatrical and must be gleaned through a symptomatic reading of the individual's body. Individuals seek to control the conduct of others in social interaction by influencing "the definition of the situation" by expressing a self that leads others to act in accordance with their own plan.[57] Performers, Goffman holds, may not necessarily be aware of this projection or their intention may derive more from social group norms than conscious goals. While it is easy for an individual to manipulate the verbal expressions he or she gives, according to Goffman what an individual "gives off" contains "ungovernable aspects."[58] He uses a dramaturgical model in which social actors are performers who evoke characters. According to Goffman, one's self is the product of social interaction and changes as the situation changes. This means the self is not stable but constantly shifting depending on the social situation. For members of racial and sexual minorities, this presentation of the self contains a strong aural and visual component manifested through vocal inflections and bodily posture. Such minorities are all too aware of the need to express a particular self in certain situations in order to survive, whether to keep from being "nigger knocked" or "fag bashed." But whites today are also aware of the fluid nature of the self. While rarely spoken about publicly by white people, they typically know which of their white acquaintances are racist and which are not. While explicit expressions of racism are, in general, frowned upon today in the public sphere, the private realm is another matter. As a result, a person can be courteous toward racial and sexual minorities but express hostility and antagonism toward them in interpersonal exchanges that exclude such minorities. Who we are depends on whom we are interacting with socially, and different people know a different us. Individuals determine what is appropriate etiquette based on the situation and that includes not just matters such as whether the event is formal or casual but also the racial and sexual composition of the participants.

While Erving Goffman highlights that an individual's racial attitude and behavior can be fluid, his approach does not assist in understanding the social formation of race through performativity. A differentiation is typically drawn between performance, which is a presentation or exhibition (hence theatrical), and performative, which is an "utterance that executes, enacts, or performs the action that is uttered, for example, *I apologize* . . . , or the *I do* of the marriage ceremony."[59] Of course, as most queer scholars are quick to note, performativity retains connotative associations of theatricality despite this distinction. The most widespread theory of performativity is Judith Butler's related to gender.[60] While rules of racial etiquette may no longer guide its performance, race continues to be performative because as a social category it is formed as much through how people act as what they believe. In other words, race functions similarly to Butler's formulation of gender, constituted through "the stylized repetition of acts through time," emerging "within a highly rigid regulatory frame that congeal over time to produce the appearance of substance."[61] This repetitive performance within the social sphere assists to form the racial categories through which we view the world.

Although within Goffman's conceptualization performance produces the self, and the self is fluid, his metaphorical use of theatrical performance to describe human social interaction leaves a residual trace of an essence under the façade. In contrast, Butler's theorizing of performativity leaves no such residue.

One of Bill Nichols's six modes of documentary film is the performative; the other modes are poetic, expository, observational, participatory, and reflexive.[62] According to Nichols, the performative mode is not concerned with realism or the mimetic qualities of cinema but the evocation of a personal perspective that provides viewers with insight into the subjective experience of an underrepresented social group. This knowledge is conveyed not through rhetoric or detached observation but artful presentation. Rather than present facts in one of the documentary styles that the public associates with objectivity (such as the detached observation of direct cinema or expository voice-of-God narration of cable television networks like the History Channel), performative documentaries use experimental film styles to relay a group's subjective perspective, including performance art, poetry, and dramatic sequences (as opposed to re-enactments of events that transpired). Such documentaries acknowledge that objectivity (as well as documentary realism) is ultimately a style that changes from one historical period to another. Nichols's definition of the performative documentary mode prioritizes performance over performativity, as attested by such documentaries typically identified by their inclusion of theatrical performances that are not re-enactments. As a result, they blur the line between documentary and experimental film as well as between documentary and fictional.

One of the most celebrated performative documentaries and one that seems to embody its ideals is Marlon Riggs's *Tongues Untied* (1989), a documentary that influenced the makers of *bro•ken/ground*. Performative documentaries are not only typically about social groups that are underrepresented in the mainstream media but also are typically made by individuals from them. In other words, they are embodiments of self-representation. *bro•ken/ground*, however, is a hybrid documentary, combining elements of the performative and participatory modes, theatrical sequences from the former and talking heads from the latter. But unlike *Tongues Untied*, which foregrounds the filmmaker's voice (both as a textual enunciation and a physical presence within the text), *bro•ken/ground* privileges a collective voice arising from its social actors (the filmmakers, though referenced by participants, never physically appear within the text). While the dramatic sequences in the documentary offer artistic performances of race, racial performativity emerges from its social actors—that is, the talking heads. While certain racial patterns occur

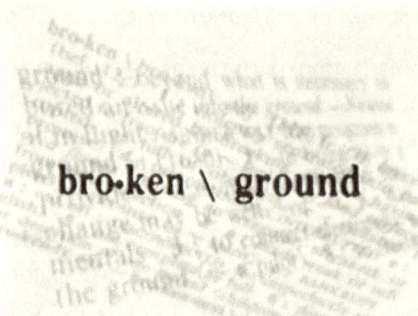

bro·ken \ ground

The order of the three dramatic sequences in Margaret Wrinkle and Chris Lawson's 1996 documentary *bro•ken/ground* forms a racial narrative.

The first theatrical sequence presents black fear of white terrorism, which is exorcised through confrontation and exposure of racism.

The second theatrical sequence presents white fear of black interaction, which is exorcised through negotiation of lingering racist impulses.

The third theatrical sequence presents black and white unity that emerges when these fears are overcome as the three actors from the other two sequences recite a poem about productive ways a discarded Klan robe can be recycled; the Klan outfit is a signifier par excellence of white supremacy.

across these two different modes, the talking heads offer a much greater critique of the way whiteness is enacted in the post-civil rights era.

Most of the dramatic sequences in *bro•ken/ground* are grouped together in one section that contains two sketches and a poetry reading. While the segments are separate performances, their ordering conforms to the dominant configuration of race within southern discourse as biracial, the first sequence from a black perspective, the second a white one, and the third a joint one. In the first one, a black woman walks across a field and lifts the veil of a Ku Klux Klan hood to confront her fear of the unknown underneath and leaves having exposed it, while in the second one, the white man just seen under the KKK hood sits across a table from a black man who encourages him to confront his lingering racist urge to say the word "nigger," which he does, excising the word's power by shouting it into the air in front of the black man. These two dramatizations are followed by the three performers reciting a poem listing productive ways to discard a KKK robe, such as use it for compost or as a scarecrow. The two dramatized sequences deal with fears that hinder blacks and whites from interacting, while the poem celebrates the result of overcoming those fears—the disposal of racism.[63] In addition, the sequences move from antagonistic confrontation to negotiated interaction to joint cooperation. The first theatrical sequence centers on black fear, aligning with the argument made by bell hooks that whiteness signifies terror for many blacks because of white supremacy.[64] The KKK outfit—the signifier par excellence along with the noose of white supremacy—signifies this form of whiteness. In contrast, the second theatrical sequence deals with white fears, but rather than physical harm this fear is of personal embarrassment. In other words, whites fear interacting with blacks because they are afraid they might say or do something that will be perceived as racially offensive.

Some scholars have argued that in the post-civil rights era, whiteness has lost its previous invisibility and become racialized, resulting in "a crisis of white identity."[65] Yet historian Grace Elizabeth Hale has documented that during the segregatation era, though whiteness may have functioned as the societal norm, it was not invisible.[66] The classic signifier used today to visually represent the segregation era—separate water fountains labeled "white" and "colored"—highlight the everyday visibility of whiteness. Regardless of whether whiteness was invisible in the past or continues to be so in the present, in the post-segregation era it has encountered not a representational crisis but a performative one as a result of the need to socially articulate new forms of whiteness to replace the now-socially unacceptable incarnations based on white supremacy and privilege. While the first dramatic sequence presents this older version of whiteness grounded in superiority, the second one offers an alternative based on ineptitude. Because the white man is played by the same actor in both sequences, their juxtaposition implies a conversion from white supremacy to racial negotiation. This change in the performance of whiteness from hatred to incompetence elicits a corresponding change in the performance of blackness from fear to compassion, placing the burden for the achievement of racial reconciliation on blacks. Whether the performance of whiteness generates black fear or black compassion, the performance of blackness remains tied to an appeasement of whites, although now the goal of such action is racial reconciliation rather than racial subordination (enacted for physical safety). It still requires blacks to serve whites—except now, rather than black manual labor benefiting whites physically, it requires black emotional labor benefiting whites psychically. In other words, it is a passive-aggressive means of "maintaining white dominance in personal contacts." The performance of whiteness through interracial ineptitude distributes unequally the responsibility for racial interaction. These scripted dramatizations offer a white liberal fantasy of white conversion and black compassion.

In contrast to the racial performance by the theatrical actors, the racial performativity of the social actors offers very different configurations of not only white fear but the black response to interracial incompetency as an enactment of whiteness. Because the social actors are encountered only as talking heads, racial performativity emerges primarily through the interviewees' attitudes and verbal utterances rather than their physical actions. While the dramatic sequence offers a version of white fear as a consequence of insecurity about interacting with blacks in a non-racist way, some black interviewees articulate an additional form of white fear that they often encounter, one resulting from panic that blacks will inflict harm. A black man professes, "If I'm walking and some [white] woman is in a car and she stops and I'm walking cross the street, I can—you can hear, you can hear that lock, lock." Two other black men in the documentary describe similar experiences of whites locking their car doors when they are seen. This enactment of whiteness elicits a response of anger from the black interviewees who mention it. Along a similar line, a young black woman shares: "I was on the elevator and this old white lady came on the elevator and she grabbed her purse. And I'm like, 'Lady, look, I don't want anything from you.'" These acts appear to be the contemporary corollary to the little white child pointing at Frantz Fanon in the early 1950s and exclaiming: "Mama, see the Negro! I'm frightened!"[67] But key differences exist. First, today the verbal component has been eliminated because it violates the contemporary social etiquette of not identifying others explicitly through race. Second, the physical expression has become indirect through the performance of an action that expresses the fear but only implies the source instead of pointing directly at it. Finally, while the expression of fear continues to racialize both parties, as a result of the above two changes the construction of whiteness now receives greater visibility than before. While on the surface this version of white fear may seem the inverse of the black fear defined in the dramatic sequence, it is not because it lacks justification in a historical pattern of violence; it elicits a defensive bodily action rather than a conciliatory one. A shift appears to have transpired with the cultural burden for the performance of race residing predominately on whites rather than blacks. In other words, while during the segregation era racial difference was often enacted on a societal level through black performance of servitude or appeasement, today public spaces are more often racialized through white performativity, as in displays of fearful panic and interracial ineptitude, although the latter tends to occur more often in semi-public and private spaces.

While the black response in the theatrical sequences to the enactment of whiteness through interracial incompetence is one of compassion, many of the black social actors in the documentary exhibit a different reaction. While they *are* sympathetic toward whites who desire to learn how to interact with blacks as equals, they also express frustration at whites for not taking responsibility for their own racial education. Throughout the documentary, whites and blacks alike concur that whites do not understand blacks while the inverse is not so. As one black interviewee shares, "blacks in particular have to pay a lot of attention to every nuance of white attitudes, psychology, feelings," while a white interviewee discloses, "I don't think I know how black people feel." While the enactment of whiteness through a fearful display of harm from blacks is obviously racist and a continuation of white supremacy, its rehabilitation through the enactment of interracial ineptitude does not resolve the problem of cross-racial interaction because it still perpetuates white dominance, only now through a passive maneuver rather than a hostile maneuver. Because the documentary includes a diversity of social actors, *a* common racial performativity does not exist as it does with the dramatized sequences, and I have only highlighted the ones that contrast with those sequences. But one thing remains clear, white performativity continues to be problematic for some racial progressives in certain locales of the United States.

Conclusion

Although the word "biracial" is never spoken in *bro•ken/ground*, the documentary frames race as such, with the social actors constantly referencing race in terms of black and white.[68] One lone young white woman mentions another race when she confesses: "I feel at my age I should know a lot of things about black people or Asian people or all these different cultures but I don't." In the few incidences where the racial imagery moves beyond the binary colors of black and white, it occurs in an unrealistic, phantasmic form, one individual referring to "black or white, red or green or blue" and another to "red, black, green or blue." Such references imply that racial difference is an artificial construct that should be moved beyond. The design of the March from Selma to Montgomery gallery in the Birmingham Civil Rights Institute similarly attempts to move beyond racial classification but does so through making everyone white. Unlike the racial pallet spoken about in *bro•ken/ground* that extends racial categories into the whimsical realm of the rainbow, the sculptures in the Selma gallery visually reduce race to a monochromatic scheme of whiteness.[69] Both are attempts to destroy the usefulness of race as a social category, the former through a strategy of expansion, the latter contraction. The few occurrences in the documentary that conceptualize race beyond the black and white binary are quickly submerged and forgotten in the overwhelming bombardment of references that define racial difference as synonymous with black and white. The overall effect creates an image of Birmingham as biracial.

bro•ken/ground documents one particular locale's understanding and enactment of race. While Michael Omi and Howard Winant discursively construct the region as holding the same understanding of race as the nation (ethnicity) but acting upon it differently (the southern strategy), *bro•ken/ground* depicts the inverse: a city, Birmingham, that holds a different understanding of race than the nation (religious essentialism) but performs it similarly (white fear, white ineptitude, black compassion, black frustration, black anger). Enacting whiteness through the display of fearful panic or interracial incompetence is not unique to any area of the country. In other words, while the documentary is about one specific locale, it does not present nor argue for a local exceptionalism, much less a regional one. The issue arises as to whether other locales also base race on religious essentialism. It may be a trans-local phenomenon, if not a national one. Even if the documentary presented an example of a local exceptionalism, that would not be proof of a regional exceptionalism. The documentary is a discursive manifestation of a particular locale, and the local has a tenuous relationship to the regional, sometimes incorporated into the regional through a discursive supplement, other times ignored. While local references such as "Birmingham" and "Alabama" periodically occur in the documentary (and these labels accompanied its circulation), regional references such as "southern" rarely occur. Yet at the end of the documentary the local manifestations represented in it are discursively connected to the regional explicitly. This connection transpires through an intertitle with a quotation from Martin Luther King Jr.: "I like to believe that Birmingham will one day become a model in southern race relations . . . that the negative extremes of Birmingham's past will resolve into the positive and utopian extreme of her future."[70] If listening viewers accept that Birmingham is representative of "southern race relations," then the region becomes discursively similarly shaped as biracial, with other possible Souths—such as multiracial—forsaken.

Part II

Biracial Denial One—Miscegenation

Chapter Three

"In slave time you know everything happened": The Racial Closet, Southeastern Expatriate Road Film, and *Family Name*

Introduction

While documentaries that deal with one or more southeastern states or locales within them are typically defined based on that focus rather than on common textual structures (be it narrative patterns or audiovisual stylistics), in the 1990s content and form were fused for one particular group of documentaries that I call the southeastern expatriate road film (and which I will refer to by the acronym SERF for convenience).[1] Taking a cue from the trail plowed in the prior decade by Ross McElwee in his 1986 documentary *Sherman's March*, a number of filmmakers located at the time in New York City made similar first-person documentaries about their road trips back to the region of their birth. These documentaries include *Greetings from Out Here* (Ellen Spiro, 1993), *Dear Jesse* (Tim Kirkman, 1997), and *Family Name* (Macky Alston, 1997). Lest we forget, the subtitle of McElwee's documentary is "a meditation on the possibility of romantic love in the South during an era of nuclear weapons proliferation," and he spends much of the screen time tracking down former girlfriends and chasing potential new girlfriends. Just as McElwee's sexuality plays a key role in *Sherman's March*, so too with these filmmakers who followed in his wake, except they were all gay and lesbian rather than straight. In addition, their sexual orientation enters the narrative structure of the documentary cycle not through the blatant means of sexual pursuits, a la McElwee, but rather in the form of the closet and, its related corollary, coming out.[2] While they approach the closet as related to gays and lesbians, they move beyond this traditional definition to encompass the primary focus of their documentaries as well. This chapter, after tracing the generic contours of the southeastern expatriate road film and exploring its element of the closet, focuses at the conclusion on the particular southeastern expatriate road film *Family Name*. Because this documentary chronicles the white filmmaker's search through his family's history for descendants of slaves owned by his ancestors and potential black relatives among them from miscegenation, it frames the closet as racial.

The 1990s saw a renewed interest in the issue of miscegenation, the concern often funneled through a focus on its occurrence in a southeastern state. Manifestations of this concern appeared across many media, from print forms (such as newspaper columns and nonfiction books) to audiovisual forms (such as television movies and documentary films). The 1990s saw nonfiction books such as Edward Ball's *Slaves in the Family* and Carrie Allen McCary's *Freedom's Child: The Life of a Confederate General's Black Daughter*, theatrical films such as *A Family Thing* (Richard Pearce, 1996) and *Cookie's Fortune* (Robert Altman, 1999), documentaries such as *Family Name*, and TV movies such as *A House Divided* (John Kent Harrison, 2000).[3] Of course, earlier films dealt with miscegenation in a southeastern state, including *Pinky* (Elia Kazan, 1949) and *Band of Angels* (Raoul Walsh, 1957). But while these older films tended to focus on a mixed-race person who narratively is presumed to be a black person who is passing as white, these contemporary films center around defining family *across* races.[4] A number of media events during the decade brought the issue of miscegenation to the national forefront, capturing the fascination of journalists and audiences alike and leading to widespread discussion in newspapers, network and cable news programs, and radio and television talk shows. Besides Ball's 1998 book, two other important media events were the 1998 publication of DNA tests results demonstrating a match between the white descendants of Thomas Jefferson and the youngest son of his slave Sally Hemings and the 2003 public announcement by seventy-eight-year-old Essie Mae Washington-Williams revealing that she was the illegitimate daughter of recently deceased white United States Senator Strom Thurmond of South Carolina, her mother a black maid in his parent's house.[5] (Thurmond was a segregationist and long-time opponent of the civil rights movement.) Despite this increased public acknowledgment of the matter, familial and social tensions continue to exist around whether it should remain in the racial closet or come out. Although a national phenomenon, it was framed as a regional one when accompanied by a southern supplement.

Although at particular historical moments certain configurations of race within southern discourse dominate, southern discourse is a site of continual re/negotiation. Biraciality has not eliminated earlier articulations of race within southern discourse, such as the region being white; it has only achieved temporary preeminence. And even the meaning attached to this dominant is not fixed but is instead open to redefinition. The word "biracial" has typically circulated within southern discourse to indicate that the region is composed of two separate races—black and white—similar to its application to a couple composed of two individuals from different races. But the 1990s media coverage and interpersonal conversations surrounding these cultural products and historical events that dealt with miscegenation expanded the available interpretations of biraciality, layering another interpretation that aligns with the word's usage when applied to an individual: that of mixed race. This alternative definition of biraciality shifts the emphasis from a region in which blacks and whites share the same space to the same genes. The familialization of the region across races, of course, is not new. The Christian-inspired language of "brothers and sisters" was routinely used during the civil rights movement and thereafter. But a key difference exists between these two configurations; the theologically based familial reference of the civil rights movement ultimately functioned metaphorically rather than literally, being concerned with the body politic rather than the physical body. This newer familialization of race within southern discourse reframes racial difference as existing not just between colleagues and neighbors but relatives. Unlike the dominant definition, this emergent definition does not foreground separation and thereby does not necessitate the addition of another concept such as religion to promote integration (if that is one's desired goal). While *Family Name* operates out of the axiomatic that the region is biracial, it utilizes this emergent definition of biraciality rather than the earlier definition.

Southeastern Expatriate Road Film

Although first-person autobiographical documentaries appeared in the 1970s, after the 1980s successes of *Sherman's March* and *Roger and Me* (Michael Moore, 1989) an explosion of such documentaries occurred the following decade, in the 1990s. For Michael Renov, the autobiographical documentary combines the "documentary impulse" with representation of the filmmaker's "own subjectivity."[6] He holds: "The new autobiography, far from offering an unself-conscious transcription of the artist's life, posits a subject never exclusive of its other-in-history. In so doing, it challenges certain of our staunchest aesthetic and epistemological preconceptions."[7] Alisa Lebow makes explicit this "other-in-history" component by positioning relationality alongside subjectivity as defining characteristics of the autobiographical documentary because it "implicates others in its quest to represent a self, implicitly constructing a subject always already in-relation—that is, in the first person plural."[8] Renov specifically associates the new autobiography with the "construction of subjectivity as a site of instability—flux, drift, perpetual revision—rather than coherence."[9] As Lebow acknowledges in her consideration of Jewish autobiographical documentaries, the "most common" ones are "artless, sincere, direct-address video[s] that make no attempt to deconstruct the subject or allow the subjectivity of the film its full range of complexity."[10] She chooses, instead, to focus on those that meet Renov's definition of the *new* autobiography, ones in which both aesthetics and the self are engaged innovatively and creatively. From the perspective of such concerns, the southeastern expatriate road film is rather perfunctory, falling within a "most common" category. While audiences encounter a conflicted and/or embattled self in the southeastern expatiate road film, a partial or fragmented one rarely appears. Although full of personal information and connections (splattered all over the audiovisual screen for all to encounter), due to its structure as a road trip to re/search a particular matter, that larger social issue takes precedence in the southeastern expatriate road film over the personal in the overall perception of the documentary. The autobiographical, although palpable, ultimately functions to channel the broader social concern, thereby making the social rather than the individual self the ultimate focus, although within the documentaries the former would not have occurred without the latter. In other words, the autobiographical southeastern expatriate road film is ethnographic as defined by Catherine Russell, who holds: "Autobiography becomes ethnographic at the point where the film- or videomaker understands his or her personal history to be implicated in larger social formations and historical processes."[11] She borrows Mary Louise Pratt's term "autoethnography" to describe the result.[12] While the SERF does not fit easily into the theoretical framework through which film scholars have typically engaged both the autobiographical and autoethnographical documentary (which privileges the experimental, both in terms of aesthetics and constructions of the self), it does, however, fit comfortably into a particular popular cultural form invoked by the documentary cycle's initiator *Sherman's March*.

At various points in *Sherman's March*, Ross McElwee searches for Burt Reynolds, the lead actor in *Smoky and the Bandit* (Hal Needham, 1977) and prototype star of the 1970s good ol' boy hick flick. The appropriation, appropriately enough, parallels the overall structure of his film as a road trip, albeit one in a documentary rather than fictional form. The association of the region with the rural in certain strains of southern discourse (which today is more likely to be framed as non-metropolitan) was the mainstay of the hick flick, a film genre that blossomed in the 1970s with the mainstreaming of its previously independent, low-budget moonshine version that centered around a road trip that entailed evading the law because of transporting illegal liquor through one or more southeastern states.[13] *Thunder Road* (Arthur Ripley, 1958) is considered by many film critics and scholars to have initiated the genre with *Smoky and the Bandit* the most popular and widely known. McElwee's pursuit of Burt Reynolds—which always ends in failure—can be viewed as a cinematic tribute to the hick flick popularly associated with him during the 1970s and which shares structural parallels with his own film.

While the documentary southeastern expatriate road film is narratively similar to the fictional moonshine version of the hick flick, it differs in two significant ways. These differences relate to (1) the characteristics of the protagonists, and (2) the nature of the chase. First, while continuing to be racially white, unlike the hick flick where the protagonist resides in a southeastern state, the protagonist of the SERF is an expatriate who lives in the northeast and has only returned to the area for the road trip. Because the filmmaker is only visiting the region, a narrative time frame emerges in which the mission needs to be accomplished before the trip ends. While Ross McElwee does not explicitly express why he left North Carolina, it is obvious in the film that he prefers living in the northeast. For the gay and lesbian filmmakers who followed in his wake, a sense of urgency and peril informs their descriptions of why they left.[14] So whether the filmmaker "ran away" from North Carolina, like Tim Kirkman, or "took off" for New York City, like Ellen Spiro, that flight did not cancel a continuing emotional tie to the homeland of their childhood. Though that place may be posited as a dangerous space that should be left, as a site of homophobic or racist bigotry, a desire for knowledge (whether about one's own family or about why people similar to one's self decided to stay rather than leave) draws the expatriate back to that supposedly perilous place. This sudden emotional willingness to encounter this once-believed-to-be danger zone through a physical return is, as might be expected, framed as the result of a family matter, a disruption in family arrangements, whether physically because of a break-up with a lover (McElwee, Spiro, and Kirkman) or psychically because of learning a disturbing family secret (Alston).

The second way the southeastern expatriate road film differs from the moonshine version of the hick flick relates to the motivation for the chase. While the protagonist's motivation in the hick flick is external, to allude police, for the SERF the motivation is internal, resulting from the filmmakers' desire for insight. Although the southeastern expatriate road film contains plenty of time in the car and on the road, rather than involving a physical chase, it entails an ethereal chase for knowledge. Ross McElwee, in *Sherman's March*, searches for personal love as he follows Sherman's March through the Carolinas and Georgia; Ellen Spiro, in *Greetings from Out Here*, searches for cultural expressions of gays and lesbians in various southeastern states; Tim Kirkman, in *Dear Jesse*, searches for responses and (re)actions to politician Jesse Helms and his legacy in North Carolina; and Macky Alston, in *Family*

Name, searches for the descendants of slaves owned by his family in North Carolina prior to the American Civil War. The purpose of the road trip is to investigate some element associated with one or more southeastern states or locales within them that has acute personal meaning for the filmmaker. Although the filmmaker's motivation may be inward rather than outward, it still involves a chase. But rather than outrunning the law, the SERF filmmaker is attempting to beat time, to acquire the insight and knowledge they are pursuing before time and financial resources expire. Midway through *Sherman's March*, McElwee declares, "I was broke, and I had to return to Boston to take a film editing job," and at the end of *Dear Jesse*, Kirkman confesses, "By the time summer arrived I was running out of film and money, and I felt it was time to get back to my life in New York." The southeastern expatriate road film is also a chase with time in another sense. Because a viewer knows that the documentary will last approximately ninety minutes, an expectation emerges that the filmmaker will fulfill his or her search before that time has elapsed.

The Closet, Coming Out, and the Familial Norm

While these filmmakers acknowledge the closet as a metaphorical trope of a sociopolitical phenomenon historically related to gays and lesbians, they move beyond this traditional definition to encompass the primary focus of their documentary as well. As Eve Sedgwick reminds us, approaching the closet as an "all-purpose phrase for the potent crossing and recrossing of almost any politically charged lines of representation" does not evacuate the trope of its historical gay and lesbian specificity.[15] And such is the case with these southeastern expatriate road films in which the closet functions simultaneously in its gay and lesbian sense but also in the broader sense of the specific topic of the documentary itself. Thus, the closet becomes in Spiro's documentary related to health (being HIV-positive), in Kirkman's to politics (supporting Jesse Helms), and in Alston's to race (denying miscegenation). While the closet can provide physical safety and psychic comfort (and can even be a means of agency through the withholding of acknowledgment), it can also entail willful denial and/or dreadful fear (of disclosure). The closet is conceptualized in popular usage as a means of silencing, whether bodily or discursively, audiovisually or scripturally, mediated-technologically or interpersonally. This negation results in not only invisibility but illegibility and illegitimacy, as coming out is routinely touted as the means to eliminate this positioning and its resulting consequences. And accompanying the archetype of the closet in these documentaries is its presumed corollary, coming out.

Coming out of the closet is a confessional act in the Foucauldian sense because it is a procedure "by which the subject is incited to produce a discourse of truth" about him or herself.[16] Michel Foucault argues in *The History of Sexuality, Volume One* that "Western societies have established the confession as one of the main rituals we rely on for the production of truth," which includes not only "justice, medicine, education, family relationships, and love relations" that are specially mentioned by Foucault but also the cultural industry associated with the mass media.[17] He defines four characteristics of the confession:

> [First] a ritual of discourse in which the speaking subject is also the subject of the statement; [second] it is also a ritual that unfolds within a power relationship, for one does not confess without the presence (or virtual presence) of a partner who is not simply the interlocutor but the authority who requires the confession, prescribes and appreciates it, and intervenes in order to judge, punish, forgive, console, and reconcile; [third] a ritual in which the truth is corroborated by the obstacles and resistances it has had to surmount in order to be formulated; and finally [fourth], a ritual in which the expression alone, independently of its external consequences, produces intrinsic modifications in the person who articulates it.[18]

Power in the confessional resides not with the confessant who speaks but the interlocutor who listens (traditionally thought in terms of a priest, a judge, or a psychiatrist but, in the context here, a filmmaker) who compels the speech. In his later works, such as "About the Beginning of the Hermeneutics of the Self" and "Pastoral Power and Political Reason," however, Foucault expanded his formulation of the confessional as he realized that it can function not only as a technology of power but also of the self, in which "the self is like a text or like a book that we have to decipher" through "an art of interpretation," verbalization "a way of sorting out thoughts which present themselves."[19] This type of confessional that facilitates self-formation results from the enactment of "pastoral power," a type of power in which the purpose is "to ensure, sustain and improve the lives of each and every one," both as individuals and as a "flock."[20] The confessional can operate in diverse ways; the key difference, as Judith Butler notes, the interlocutor in the latter "is no longer understood primarily as governed by the desire to enhance his [*sic*] own power but to facilitate a transition or conversion through the process of verbalization, one that opens the self to interpretation and, in effect, to a different kind of self-making in the wake of sacrifice."[21] (Although Foucault secularizes the concept, lest we forget—as is evidenced by such terms as "pastoral" and "flock"—that the confessional in this latter sense entails not just self-making through verbalized introspection but engagement with the divine as part of that process and also transpires within a communal context rather than in isolation, issues that will be engaged with further in the next chapter.)

Certain forms of documentary film have been associated with the confessional. One of the most famous is Jean Rouch's Cinéma Vérité, a connection acknowledged when he remarked: "I discovered the camera was something else: it was not a brake but let's say, to use an automobile term, an accelerator. You push these people to confess themselves and it seemed to us without any limit. . . . It's not exactly exhibitionism: it's a very strange kind of confession in front of the camera, where the camera is, let's say, a mirror, and also a window open to the outside."[22] The southeastern expatriate road film contains interviews with social actors and diary entries by filmmakers, both of which often assume the form of confessional utterances. Michael Renov differentiates between first-person video confessions in which the "speaking subject" is "simultaneously the enunciating subject" (because the confessant conceives, shoots, and edits the text and therefore is the author of the audiovisual enunciation) and the traditional talking head in "documentaries of the interactive mode in which the interview format prevails" where confessants, he argues, "are more spoken than speaking."[23] This differentiation is based not only on the confessant in the former having an "editorial agency" in the textual presentation that the latter lacks but also the confession being addressed to an "absent, imaginary other" rather than an interlocutor (which tends to be the filmmaker in the participatory mode).[24] Renov holds that "taped self-interrogation can achieve a depth and a nakedness of expression that is difficult to duplicate with a crew or even camera operator present."[25] But is self-interrogation the same as confession? And can confession be severed from the social and still be a confession? Finally, does the absence of other people during the taping equate to the absence of an interlocutor, especially if we approach the confessional within the context of the audiovisual arrangement (which includes the listening viewer during reception as well as the pro-filmic event during production)?[26] While I agree that the confessional is a form of self-interrogation, because I hold it is also a social act, then not all self-interrogation is simultaneously a confession. In other words, while the two overlap, they are not synonymous. Plus, the act of taping one's confession introduces the possibility of an audience that would not exist otherwise (be that an audience of one, 100, or 1,000); this potential audience is not an "imaginary other" but an actual audience that can be realized. This audience becomes possible through the act of taping, which introduces an interlocutor into the process. If all documentary confessionals have an interlocutor, then the salient question becomes not whether they are first-person (by a solo filmmaker) or talking heads (in the participatory mode), but rather: who is the interlocutor and does the interlocutor use that position for self-power or to assist in the production of new selves in confessants? This question speaks to the heart of the political efficacy of documentary as a venue for progressive political and social change.

The logic of the confessional is integral to the southeastern expatriate road film due to its particular generic construction of a search by the filmmaker for knowledge about a particular topic, which the filmmaker desires to disclose through his or her filmed journey. As a result, the filmmaker (either on-screen or through voice-over) and the social actors the filmmaker encounters on that trip are expected to produce a truth on the matter, even if that truth is partial, inscrutable, or absent. The interlocutor function is fluid within the southeastern expatriate road film with the filmmaker, a social actor, or the potential audience fulfilling it at different points. While the filmmaker is most often the interlocutor for the interviewees, at times the relationship reverses. Because the interviewees are typically shot in their own environment, with the interview often performed conversationally with the filmmaker, the interviewee periodically assumes the role of interlocutor, questioning the filmmaker, who is therefore compelled to speak. While the viewing audience listening to the confession during the reception process is not an interlocutor, its potentiality does at times function as an interlocutor during the production process, especially when the filmmaker directly addresses the camera or the interviewee verbally references the future audience.[27] A singular or consistent interlocutor does not exist within the documentary audiovisual arrangement of the southeastern expatriate road film; the confessant and interlocutor positions are unstable, fluctuating among the various participants (filmmaker, social actors, and possible audience).

While the potential audience can function as an interlocutor during the production process, the actual audience that hears the confession during the screening does not, except in the psychoanalytical sense of misrecognition associated with Jacques Lacan's mirror phase. While Jean Rouch associates the mirror with the social actor who appears in the documentary, film scholars have traditionally aligned the mirror with the spectator engaging the audiovisual text within the cinematic apparatus. During the mirror phase, while being held by the mother, the infant sees his—the pronoun is intentional—image reflected in the mirror. Although the infant lacks "co-ordination of his own motility," he perceives himself through the visual as coherent, "an ideal unity," hence misrecognition.[28] For Lacan, the mirror phase is part of the imaginary order and a means through which the child begins to access the symbolic order associated with language and the Oedipus complex. Although this is a simplification of Lacan's complex formulation in which the child also sees himself as an other and forms a split subject, for the association I want to make between the audiovisual arrangement and the confessional, this is the salient piece. Christian Metz applied Lacan's mirror phase to the cinematic apparatus, acknowledging upfront that it is just an analogy, not a scientific explanation of spectatorship. According to Metz, unlike the mirror phase, the spectator is absent from the screen but this absence is not a problem because the spectator is not a child and cinema transpires within the symbolic, rather than the imaginary, order. This situation enables it to function as an imaginary signifier "which induces by means of visual images the same sorts of identifications which occur early in the subject's life."[29] Because the spectator is absent from the screen within the cinematic apparatus, Metz argues he or she identifies with the omniscient look of the camera, thereby aligning misrecognition with the spectator perceiving him/herself as the origin of the projected audiovisual world represented on the screen.[30] Although I assume predominately Foucauldian and/or Deleuzian approaches, here the Lacanian-inspired concept of audiovisual misrecognition is appropriate. In other words, in order for the audience listening to and watching a documentary to enter into the confessional arrangement, not only must a textual confession by filmmaker(s) and/or social actor(s) exist on the screen but audiovisual misrecognition by the spectator must transpire off the screen, thereby inscribing the listening viewer as an interlocutor.[31] While the audiovisually documented confession may enact a change in the confessant (be it the cultural worker or social actor), most filmmakers and documentary proponents desire the confessional utterance that occurs every time the documentary is screened to produce a change in the audience as well (be it in thinking or acting). Like Jane Gaines with her concept of "political mimesis," discussed in the introduction, I too am interested in the sociopolitical efficacy of documentaries. Because the possibility of change resides with the confessant and the only position available to the audience is that of the interlocutor, the confessional style appears to be an ineffective strategy for producing change. But the interlocutor is an influential position because it impacts the lives of others. Thus, if one's concern is not with changing the audience but empowering it, then the confessional becomes a training simulator for developing psychic confidence in one's ability to affect others. Of course, no guarantee exists that that audience will then enact such ability in the world beyond the documentary textual encounter.

However, my interest in the confessional arises here not because I think it is necessarily a productive way for engaging with documentary as a means for producing social change but rather because coming out, which is typically considered the solution to eliminating the closet, is a type of confession. The concepts of the closet and coming out are intricately linked through the normal. Coming out, whether through a bodily or linguistic confession, is an act of border crossing, a traversal of the societal boundaries established by the normal, disclosing what the closet silences.[32] As Michael Warner reminds us, the normal is not a statistical average but rather an evaluative concept that has "came to mean right, proper, [and] healthy."[33] The norm, per Judith Butler, "governs intelligibility, allows for certain kinds of practices and action to become recognizable as such, imposing a grid of legibility on the social and defining the parameters of what will and will not appear within the domain of the social."[34] The normal is a means of social regulation, an element of what Michel Foucault calls disciplinary power that produces subjectification, a technology of power.[35]

While the normal establishes the boundaries constituting the closet, Mary Douglas's concept of pollution engages the closet from the perspective of crossing the threshold of the normal.[36] She holds that societies with strictly defined social structures require the creation of pollutants to symbolize what must be kept outside of that system's boundaries if cultural purity is to be maintained; she calls these pollutants "dirt," which she defines as "matter out of place."[37] An individual can become a polluting person if he or she "crossed some line which should not have been crossed and this displacement unleashes danger for someone."[38] To cross the doorsill of the closet and come *out* is a societal manifestation of dirt; such individuals become "matter *out of place*" because they have left their proper place of the closet through a confessional utterance that brings "hidden content out into the open."[39] The association of the region in southern discourse with a "sense of *place*" disseminated through the writings of both academicians and popular writers is the *place* of the closet for those considered "matter out of *place*" if they were to come out. The southeastern expatriate road film deals with subject matters—both in terms of people and topics—that have discursively been consigned to the closet within southern discourse but which the documentaries disclose, breaking the silence that enables their closeting. As a result, the film texts themselves become material manifestations of matter out of place, that is, dirt. Although Douglas frames her discussion in terms of "pollution," the title of her book also includes the word "taboo." And within the United States the public acknowledgment of miscegenation has historically been taboo (an association that is gradually changing with the rise of a mixed-race movement of people refusing to declare a singular race). Although a national phenomenon, mixed-race individuals (as well as interracial heterosexual couples which can potentially create such individuals) still routinely function within southern discourse as pollutants consigned to the racial closet to inhibit them from redefining the meaning of biraciality, which currently within southern discourse is conceived as the coexistence of two separate races, not their blending.

As highlighted by a number of writers, the family is a key social site for the formation and preservation of racial divisions in the United States; the two social formations are intricately connected through their association with ancestry and descent. Hierarchies of race, gender, and class become, as Patricia Hill Collins argues, "normalized" because they are "associated with [the] seemingly natural family processes of family households."[40] This process results from the family being simultaneously a social formation and a discursive formation. Pierre Bourdieu holds that the latter impacts our perception of what is considered natural in the former. In other words, while the family exists within the social sphere, its structure is not innate. Rather, the discursive component naturalizes "this arbitrary social construct" which is a "product of a labour of *institutionalization*" that is based on "social conditions that are in no way universal."[41] This discursive element frames certain configurations of the family as normal while disqualifying other as legitimate. The history of matters such as miscegenation, polygamy, adoption, and gay marriage highlight how the perceived naturalness of the family is socially constructed. While no innate social norm of the family exists, its discursive manifestation routinely frames certain social configurations as a universal norm, one of those being that families are composed of only one race. Kimberly McClain DaCosta holds that anti-miscegenation laws and the one-drop rule simultaneously racialized the family and familialized race. As a result of such mechanisms, the family has been constructed as mono-racial and a race not having kinship in other races.[42] According to DaCosta, the interconnectedness of these two social categories—how "people construct racial identity through notions of family, and family identity through notions of race"—becomes most noticeable in the practice of disowning.[43] As DaCosta notes: "Under the logic of disowning, 'mixed' relations and their parents are exiled outside the family, because they have gone outside 'the race.' In other words, relatedness to a person of another racial group disqualifies one from membership in the family because it disqualifies one from full membership within the 'race.'"[44]

Historically, various components of the collective social formation identified as the family have been discursively positioned as outside of the societal norm and consigned to the closet. Two key sites for the struggle over how to define the family currently are race and sexuality. Today, public debate typically centers on whether gay marriage (and sometimes gay adoption) should be legally recognized as a normal family arrangement. Although miscegenation laws have been declared unconstitutional, the matter of race and the family also continue to be socially contentious despite this legality, in particular biracial marriage and cross-racial adoption. The dominant definition of biraciality—two separate and distinct races—associated with the region in southern discourse allows miscegenation to be denied because it presumes racial purity; it consigns miscegenation to the racial closet. In contrast, the emergent trend in the 1990s within southern discourse of recoding biracial as mixed race reconfigures the region in relationship to race, making the familial a literal descriptor similar to neighbor and citizen rather than a primarily metaphorical descriptor, as discussed in the last chapter. While shades of ambiguity do exist within the theological framework regarding whether such claims as "we are all God's children" are metaphorical or literal, this new, emergent definition of biracial removes all such ambiguities regarding the familial. To date, this alternative definition of biracial has remained marginal within southern discourse, where it resides quietly as a possible South.

The 1990s Culture War and the Southeastern Expatriate Road Film

These gay-and-lesbian-made post-McElwee southeastern expatriate road films emerged during the 1990s, a period often referred to as playing host to the "culture war," in which political and religious conservatives initiated a public battle against homosexuality and abortion.[45] The attack as it relates to gays and lesbians busted onto the public consciousness with the 1989 controversies surrounding the planned (but eventually canceled) exhibition of Robert Mapplethorpe's photographs at the Corcoran Gallery of Art in Washington, D.C., and the broadcast of Marlon Riggs's documentary *Tongues Untied* on many PBS stations across the country as part of the independent documentary series *P.O.V.*[46] Unlike the first decade of the twenty-first century, when the controversy surrounding gays and lesbians centered primarily on the right to marry (even though gays, lesbians, and transgender people continued to lack basic civil rights protection in employment, housing, etc. in most areas of the United States), during the 1990s the clash centered around not just whether basic civil rights should be extended to gays and lesbians but the validity of any social approval of homosexuality as exemplified by the fundamentalist Christian-produced documentary *The Gay Agenda* (1992). Although called a "culture war," the attacks were not just against governmental support of gay and lesbian artistic expressions but political access, leading to the nationally visible 1992 anti-gay initiatives in Oregon (Ballot Measure 9, which failed) and Colorado (Amendment 2, which passed) to specifically strip gays and lesbians of any civil protection, overturning any such laws at the municipal level within the state and invalidating legal enforcement of any such corporate policies within the state.[47] A part of this campaign included an explicit attack on the comparison of the struggle for black civil rights in the 1950s and 1960s with that of gays, lesbians, and transgendered people, arguing that the latter are special rights, not civil rights, in such documentaries as *Civil Rights/Special Rights: Inside the Homosexual Agenda* (1993). The documentary uses, as Allan Bérubé observes, "racialized class to undermine alliances between a gay rights movement portrayed as white and movements of people of color portrayed as heterosexual."[48] The insidiousness of the campaign led Coretta Scott King, the widow of Martin Luther King Jr., to speak out on behalf of gay and lesbian civil rights, believing it was the logical extension of her husband's concern with peace and social justice, a move that resulted in her being attacked by numerous black pastors.

While none of the southeastern expatriate road films were caught in the snares of the culture war as an object of derision, because they were made during its siege, they address the proposition circulating at the time by the Christian radical right that gays and lesbians were not a legitimate social minority similar to racial minorities (and, by extension, their request for civil rights was a demand for special rights). While this issue is challenged through more than one means in the documentaries, the most dramatic means in *Greetings* and *Dear Jesse* use a black gay or lesbian interviewee, thereby also challenging the popular presumption within mainstream American culture at the time that equated gayness with whiteness. The connection arises organically throughout *Dear Jesse* because of its topics. Jesse Helms, after all, used blacks as a social scapegoat for political gain before he turned his sights on gays and lesbians for the same purpose. The comparison, however, is made explicitly by Mandy Carter, a civil rights activist working at the time for a gay and lesbian group organized to support the Democratic candidate running against Helms in the 1996 election. As she and the filmmaker walk through a town park, she emphasizes that the goal is not to legislate people to like gays and blacks but rather to ensure that "no one can take away your fundamental rights." Carter opines, "A lot of us can't be out for whatever reason but we're already here," as she offers the examples of losing a job or child custody only because you are (known to be) gay or lesbian. The comment is immediately followed by another remark about being rejected only because of your skin color. Her conclusion directly connects the two: "What the heck is the difference? A prejudice is a prejudice—and it's an amazingly emotional feeling of you're less than, you're not worthy. It's just, I mean I've been on the receiving end of both of those and I'm telling you it feels exactly the same." As a political activist, Carter frames the similarity between racial and sexual minorities through the issue of discrimination—in other words, civil rights. But this intellectual argument grounded in civil rights becomes psychological through an appeal to personal experience. Therefore, while race and sexuality may be different, from the perspective of what it feels like to be rejected because of some component that constitutes one's self, they are indeed similar. While Carter begins from a position out of the closet ("already [out] here"), the other two documentaries explicitly use the closet and the confessional to establish a connection between racial and sexual minorities.

Although *Greetings* also uses a civil rights correlation, the matter is framed through a more controversial rhetorical move. In this case, James Cox, a preacher whose father was a civil rights activist in Jasper, Alabama, confesses: "I've been in some issues not only dealing with civil rights issues, with racism, but even my identity ... I'm a gay man and I'm happy with that today, because I can be free enough to speak about it." Later, he notes: "I always had to hide it here in Alabama. It wasn't anything I could just come out and express." The struggle with race, whether through internal self-loathing or external racism, is paralleled with that of homosexuality. And just as racism needs to be overcome so too does homophobia. When discussing the embrace of his sexuality, Cox takes the analogy a step further: "It has taken me to this point to where I can begin to be free with it [homosexuality], just as free as when some of my ancestors were released from slavery. That same freedom I feel inside of me being able to speak my mind and go where I want to go and do what I want to do." He not only compares homophobia to racism but coming out to freedom from slavery. In other words, the closet is a form of slavery, and just as the abolition of slavery provided blacks with freedom, the abolition of the closet performs the same release for gays and lesbians. Cox frames the freedom of coming out as not just an inner psychic freedom but also an outer physical freedom—an ability to steer public space. As implied through the stories he relays, the social consequence of being a member of a racial minority and a sexual minority are the same from the perspective of having societal limitations imposed upon the physical mobility of one's body and the threat of bodily danger that accompanies entering certain public spaces. But his comparison of coming out (the abolition of the closet) to the abolition of slavery makes me uncomfortable, and I must confess I find it rather scandalous. To be freed from slavery is to no longer be the property of another person—that is, of finally owning one's own body. The freeing of the self seems to be the similarity that Cox holds between the two. Cox associates the closet with internal homophobia and thereby a mechanism that constrains the self, hence a technology of power, while the coming out confessional provided him with a technique of the self.

In contrast to the other documentaries, in *Family Name* the connection is not made by a black gay or lesbian interviewee but the filmmaker himself, using a story about his father. Rather than approach the matter from the inside out, the experience of the minority, *Family Name* does so from the outside in—through the experience of the non-minority (who, after an internal struggle, comes out in support of the minority). Macky Alston recounts how in North Carolina his dad "fought for [black] civil rights," even enrolling him in a black public school as a child. He continues: "I did see him struggle with the gay issue. It took me walking in and telling him I'm gay for him to look at his prejudice. Now he's started speaking out for gay rights." Although this is a form of coming out, the process is framed as a conversion narrative similar to the "white southern racial conversion narrative" outlined by Fred Hobson. According to Hobson, this literary genre shares similarities with the earlier Puritan conversion narratives because it consists of "a recognition and confession of the writer's own sins and the announced need for redemption, as well as a description of the writer's radical transformation—a sort of secular salvation."[49] While the association of sexual minorities with racial minorities through an appeal to civil rights finds explicit expression, the application of the racial conversion narrative to gays and lesbians occurs through an implied analogy. The equivalence is based on the perspective of how a non-minority individual comes to support the social acceptance and legal equality of a subjugated social group. Because the conversion narrative is a public acknowledgment of support for a stigmatized group, it is a confession; in this case, however, the closet is silencing not the subaltern group but rather others who advocate for the elimination of the social injustice perpetrated upon that group. Regardless of the specific topic of the documentary, the post-McElwee southeastern expatriate road film presumes the struggle by racial and sexual minorities for social inclusion and legal equality share common ground, an affinity that does not, however, evacuate the differences that exist between these two sociopolitical movements nor deny their interlacing constituencies. These documentaries also differ from *Sherman's March* in that the closet is an integral component of their construction; the closet is used not only in its traditional sense as related to gays and lesbians but also in terms of the specific topic of the documentary.

The Closet and the Southeastern Expatriate Road Film

When these filmmakers reference the closet in its traditional sense related to sexual orientation, they heed Michael Brown's warning to regard the closet as "not *just* a metaphor for the concealment, erasure, or ignorance of gays' sexualities," but also as having "spatiality, an existence in space that has location and situation, which signifies placement, interaction, movement and accessibility."[50] In other words, "the closet materialises in social space."[51] In *Greetings from Out Here*, when discussing her move to New York City and becoming a gay activist, Ellen Spiro confesses: "But there was something funny about this picture. Here I was being an out dyke and back home I was still in the closet." Similarly, in *Dear Jesse*, Tim Kirkman muses: "Sometimes I feel as if I live in two worlds, one in New York where I'm totally out of the closet and one here [back home] where I find myself going back in." In *Family Name*, Macky Alston confesses: "I've always felt like a bit of an outsider in my family. Probably the main reason is because I am gay. For a long time it was something I felt I couldn't talk about." For these filmmakers, the closet is not only a discursive operation but a territorial space, one that the filmmakers assign to the physical location of "back home," where they grew up and their families still reside. From the position of living in New York City, "back home" becomes the place of one's biological family—for Kirkman and Spiro, North Carolina and Virginia, respectively—and one's ancestral family—for Alston, North Carolina, where he lived as a child and where his grandmother continues to reside. During their journey, the filmmakers are "out of place," both in the sense that they no longer live in the place of "back home" and that their sexual orientation is out. While references to specific locales (both municipalities and states) dominate, the filmmakers and social actors do occasionally mention "the South." Several of these instances are meant to be simply a convenient shorthand reference to the geographical area of the southeastern continental United States, devoid of any evaluative associations (similar to the way I use the word "southeastern" in this book). Other instances, however, are imbued with signification and affect, enacting southern discourse. Although the documentaries deal with very specific manifestations of the local, such discursive operations link the closet of "back home" to the regional as well as the local. The road trips that are captured in the documentaries explore the contours of this "back home" closet, outing it.

These two ways of conceiving the closet—the traditional way related to gays and lesbians, and this new way related to the region—are fused in *Greetings from Out Here* because its primary topic is "southern gay subcultures." The president of a gay rodeo association shares that the organization has never allowed such an interview "on camera before," and Spiro's voice-over narration highlights that a gay Mardi Gras Ball has not been "videotaped [before] for outsiders to see," expounding further, "All across the South it seems gay folks are beginning to come out on camera." None of the faces in the documentary are blurred or in shadows, and although voice-overs occur we never hear disembodied voices for which we are unable to assign a visual face. In the documentary, images of gays and lesbians from local organizations in several southeastern states that had never been "on camera before" function metonymically to represent the invisibility of the closet being forsaken, this legibility claiming a place of legitimacy within their respective local communities. And through the operations of a southern supplement—such as "all across the South"—the local becomes regional.

In *Greetings from Out Here*, the closet is associated not only with its main topic of gays and lesbians in southeastern states but another topic closely linked to homosexuality in the early 1990s: AIDS. Prior to making *Greetings*, Spiro was part of the bustling New York City AIDS activist scene, and the footage she includes to illustrate her gay activism is typical of documentary work in AIDS activism at the time. Prior to *Greetings*, she made *DiAna's Hair Ego* (1991) about the South Carolina AIDS Education Network run out of DiAna's beauty parlor and *Party Safe! With DiAna and Bambi* (1992), about safer sex parties. During the opening sequence of *Greetings*, Spiro's AIDS activism is closeted through careful camera framing and muffled chanting of demonstrators, with all indicators as to the specificity of the type of demonstration she is participating in having been removed. This closeting of AIDS activism at the beginning of the documentary foreshadows the explicit association of AIDS with the closet that occurs later on. This association emerges in the section on John Blansett from Okolona, Mississippi, who informs the viewer, "I decided not to call AIDS cancer when I got it," lamenting, "My little brothers shouldn't have to get it simply because someone didn't want to talk about it." The prohibition against talking about AIDS as AIDS (rather than as one of its symptoms) positions the disease in the closet. According to Blansett, this act of silence contributes to the continual spread of the disease; therefore, those with AIDS must confess their medical condition and come out of the closet about it. During the decade preceding Spiro's documentary, HIV-positive status (HIV being the virus that causes AIDS) was routinely configured within local gay communities as a closet. Discussions abound about whether HIV-positive men were obligated to disclose their status to their sexual partners. In other words, a second closet existed within the gay community, one regarding HIV status. Just as one can live in mainstream society and be in the closet about his or her sexual orientation, so too one can be active in the gay community and be in the closet about his or her HIV-positive status. Safer sex was presented by some as a means to circumvent the social paradigm of the closet that was becoming attached to HIV status. If everyone practiced safer sex, then disclosure would be unnecessary, thereby making coming out an irrelevant confessional utterance.

Dear Jesse and *Family Name* differ from *Greetings from Out Here*, in which the main topic of the documentary is explicitly related to gays and lesbians. Even so, the closet still functions metaphorically in these documentaries to describe their main focuses. *Dear Jesse* explores United States Senator Jesse Helms's conservative politics of hatemongering and fear that uses anti-homosexual rhetoric to win elections. While earlier in his political career Helms routinely used blatant anti-black rhetoric to appeal to white voters, after the civil rights movement changed the tone of public discourse on the matter, he turned to coded racial messages; his blatant expressions of disdain and hatred were now reserved for gays and lesbians. Even though Helms had numerous supporters (otherwise he would not continually be re-elected to Congress), Kirkman found on his road trip few people "would go on camera in support of Jesse Helms." As he muses, "It was as if they were in the closet about it." While Helms supporters in North Carolina are a majority, they are not willing to come out on camera the way the gay rodeo president and gay Mardi Gras Ball participants did in *Greetings*. The documentary frames the closet as being political, one occupied by Helms supporters unwilling to publicly confess their support for him on camera. The closet in this particular case is adopted to prevent being publicly associated with an individual who espouses positions that, while popular at the local level of a state, are no longer as popular at the national level of the country as they once were. The closet in this case functions as an invisibility cloak for the local in relationship to national media in an age before Fox News as well as a means to avoid accountability within the broader society for the regressive social consequences of supporting warmongering.

Subsequent to Ross McElwee's *Sherman March*, the closet has become a defining characteristic of the southeastern expatriate road film that emerged in its wake. Besides being used in its traditional sense as a sexual closet for gays and lesbians, the closet simultaneously functions as a paradigm for the very subject matter that each documentary makes visible, both in the literal sense of being shown and the cerebral sense of making known. Because the purpose of each road trip is different, the closet is reconfigured in each documentary uniquely. The closet becomes a medical closet in *Greetings*, with AIDS patients publicly denying their health status; a political closet in *Dear*

Jesse, with Jesse Helms voters publicly denying their support for him; and, as will be discussed in the next section, a racial closet in *Family Name*, with white descendants of slaveholders publicly denying their black relatives.

Family Name and the Racial Closet

While the post-McElwee southeastern expatriate road films do not avoid the issue of race, it is not typically their main focus, except for *Family Name*, where it takes center stage. At the beginning of the documentary, Macky Alston, who is white, reminisces about elementary school in North Carolina, where he first met blacks with the same last name as his own, which caused him to wonder, "How could this be?"[52] After learning the reason (that his ancestors had been one of the largest slaveholders in the state of North Carolina), Macky decides to return to the state to search for descendants of the slaves previously owned by his family. He equates this family secret that his father kept from his children with his own "keeping secrets" from his parents and siblings—that of being gay. He pushes the similarity further, noting that, like his father, he knows "what it feels like to not speak the truth" and "how it contorts your sense of self." Just as Macky struggled with his gayness and coming out, so did his father with this knowledge about the family's history as slaveholders in North Carolina. Macky's father acknowledges his own struggle when, after Macky tells the family about his initial search for descendants of the family's slaves, his father responds: "You don't know the kind of . . . destructiveness that came out of that provincial familial southern life. I have been trying to break away from that all my life . . . I don't want any part of it." For his dad, some secrets are better kept in the closet. Unlike his father, Macky immediately and enthusiastically confessed the family secret. He attributes his personal experience of the sexual closet as the reason why he alone among his siblings feels a need to open this racial closet, which he does through documenting his road trip to learn the story behind the family's name.

Macky's search for descendants of former slaves owned by his family quickly transforms on the trip into a search for blood relatives among them.[53] His desire to find a black cousin permeates the tone of the documentary, manifesting itself both implicitly in his attitude and explicitly in his words. Throughout, the documentary is punctuated with declarations such as, "I want to know the truth" and "I have to find out." Yet he never adequately addresses why he is so compelled to prove he has a black cousin other than with his equation of the legacy of miscegenation with that of homosexuality through the trope of the closet. As presented in the documentary, a sense of desperation

The Racial Closet, Southeastern Expatriate Road Film, and *Family Name*

Macky Alston interviewing a participant at a black Alston family reunion for his 1997 documentary *Family Name*. A black Alston family reunion and a white one are held just miles apart during the same week yet each is unaware of the other. Photograph by Brooke Williams. Courtesy of Macky Alston.

Filming an interviewee at a black Alston family reunion for *Family Name*. When asked by Macky Alston if they could potentially be kin, she replied, "We could be some related. In slave time you know everything happened." Photograph by Brooke Williams. Courtesy of Macky Alston.

permeates his search, as he makes two major attempts to find a black relative, first with the living classical musician Fred Oliver Alston Jr. and then with the deceased painter Charles Henry Alston, who died in 1977. Eventually, Macky is able to prove, based on legal documents, that his ancestors owned Fred's. He is actually disappointed that he could prove only a slavery connection and not a blood connection; nonetheless, he continues his search for the latter with Charles. Macky is able to make a slavery connection with Charles, and when he informs the listening viewer about discovering Charles, he displays a picture of him on the screen, exclaiming, "His skin is almost as white as mine," fueling Macky's hope that he might be a cousin because he visually appears mixed race. Because Charles is dead and cannot be interviewed, Macky interviews his sister, Rousmaniere, instead. During their conversation, the issue of passing for white arises, and she confesses that she had sometimes done so. Charles and Rousmaniere's father, Primus, was born a slave. Because his owners, Nathanial and Patsy Alston, had no children and his mother, Primelia, was a house servant, Macky makes the leap that Nathanial is Primus's father. He admits, "I will probably never be able to prove it but I believe it's true."

Early in the documentary, Macky asks a woman at a black Alston family reunion, "If I'm an Alston from around here you think there's a chance we're kin?" She replies: "We could be some related. In slave time you know everything happened." The woman nervously laughs and then continues: "You knew that. Don't you?" The interviewee seems unwilling or unable to openly say what happened, as though it is not something to mention in polite company. Despite her use of vague and evasive language, her meaning still comes across. She assumes the answer to the question is already known so it does not have to be explicitly stated—she assumes that it is an open secret, something everyone knows but no one openly acknowledges knowing. Macky admits that the underbelly of his search for a black cousin is the historical fact of sexual liaison between masters and slaves. But he never grasps that his search for a black cousin is not just about "the legacy of slavery," an idea that emerges as rather quaint in the documentary. What he seeks is not about just masters and slaves but rather white *male* masters and black *female* slaves. It is about the legacy of rape. Rape is the "everything happened" that no individual in the documentary will openly express. Macky never acknowledges that any black descendents he finds will in all likelihood be the result of rape between a white male master and black female slave. He prefers to talk about miscegenation during slavery as one of sex rather than violence and power, basing his argument that Charles is a cousin on the fact that Primus's mother, Primelia, "was a house servant and therefore easily accessible to Nathaniel." He is so intent on proving he has a black cousin that he ignores what would have transpired for that to be the case. Rather than acknowledge the violence that this implies, he sutures it with "easily accessible." While the documentary chronicles in detail his investigation of two potential black male cousins, its construction displaces the historical violence enacted on the black female body that would enable such a relative to exist.

As discussed in chapter two in relationship to *bro•ken/ground*, a common discursive configuration of cross-racial interaction is white fear/black anger. Because Macky assumed this particular understanding of cross-racial interaction (even acknowledging that he asked questions to invoke such responses), he is disappointed when he does not find black anger and only few expressions of white fear from the Alstons he encountered. The expectation of black anger seems to have inhibited Macky's sensitivity to more common responses, and its absence seems to have lulled him into a forgetfulness of the violent terrain he was excavating. As a result, he is surprised and puzzled when everyone he interviews does not know anything about their family history. When searching Charles's family history, interviewees continually respond in frustration to his questions with comments like, "I don't know . . . [My father] didn't tell me anything about that" or "Our parents never told us anything about those days." Families are routinely presented within popular cultural expressions of southern discourse as passing along detailed family histories from generation to generation, a part of the routine association of the region with the past. The interviewees in *Family Name* exhibit just the opposite characteristic. One of the commonalities between the blacks and whites that Macky interviews is their lack of knowledge about their family's history in relationship to slavery, a legacy that was typically not talked about in personal terms from generation to generation. Black Alstons in the documentary acknowledge that their parents kept them in the dark about such painful events in an attempt to protect them from the harsh realities of the past as they sought a better life for their children in the future. And even Macky's white father did the same thing in terms of his children in order to protect them from what he saw as the "bigotry and prejudice and narrowness and meanness and destructiveness that came out of that provincial familial southern life."

As mentioned earlier, Macky aligns the closet with his family's secret of having been one of the largest slaveholders in North Carolina, this closet being a racial one not only because it concerns whites owning blacks but also because of the miscegenation that accompanied this violence-maintained asymmetrical relationship. Macky hints at a way to move beyond this simple analogy when he asks: "Is something a secret if everybody knows it but nobody talks about it?" The question reframes the issue, moving it away from the framework of a secret (and its corollary, the closet) to that of an open secret. Michael Taussig defines the open secret as a "secret which is in fact 'known' but for reasons of power cannot be articulated and creates, in its stead, dissimulation and fabulation."[54] The open secret, then, is not about the lack of knowledge—"the relations of the known and the unknown"—associated with the closet.[55] According to D. A. Miller, the social function of the open secret "is not to conceal knowledge, so much as to conceal the knowledge of the knowledge."[56] While many people who consider themselves to be a southerner may have, to parrot Fred Hobson's famous book title, a rage to "tell about the South," here is a situation in which they clearly do not want to talk.[57] The filmmaker's search is *the* narrative driving force in the southeastern expatriate road film and Macky's incessant need to find a black relative blinds him to the fact that his search is actually a challenge to the open secret. While a secret is a component of the closet, an open secret is not. It is a different paradigm and functions differently. Although Macky rhetorically asks whether the legacy of slavery (and the related issue of miscegenation) is an open secret, he acts as though it is closeted and that all he needs to do is open the door (by asking the right questions) for it to be revealed. In contrast, the social actors he encounters operate from the open-secret paradigm and, as a result, their answers to his questions are continually evasive as they attempt to politely answer his questions without openly enunciating the issue. The documentary does not open the racial closet door about white and black miscegenation during slavery because no racial secret exists to be so revealed. Yet, despite Macky's naïve (but earnest) liberal racial politics that saturate the narrative thrust of the film, the documentary does demonstrate that the construction of race in many areas of North Carolina has an open-secret component, that of miscegenation, whether from rape during slavery or voluntary union now. Although Macky operates from the paradigm of the closet, his documentary ends up demonstrating the workings of the open secret as a result of the social actors' reactions to him.

Toward the end of *Family Name*, Macky introspectively reflects on what is he trying to accomplish by the search through his family's past. He muses: "Does getting to the truth about history really change anything?" As presented in the documentary, Macky's father is part of that rare Christian tradition of social justice that fueled such events as the civil rights movement, a segment of the Christian faith overshadowed during the 1990s—as well as today—by the politics of hate espoused by the Christian radical right. His father tells him: "Stop looking at history. Do you see now, right around you and are you making your stand now?" In response to his father's question, Macky admits that nothing has really changed as a result of his journey. Following his father's advice about focusing on the now rather than the past,

Macky organizes a concert for Fred at Cherry Hill, an old Alston plantation that had been converted into a classical music foundation. The concert was an attempt to move from researching the past to acting in the present, with the concert serving as a site of reconciliation for white and black Alstons. Although civil rights heritage attractions and documentaries privilege spectacular images of white violence against blacks, they also emphasize racial reconciliation. Macky's documentary, too, follows this latter classic civil rights tradition. When confronting the issue of social change, he admits, "I tend to look for drama, for revolution," but he has learned through his search "that change can happen in subtle ways." In other words, Macky would like the profilmic that he captures to be sensuous images of struggle, which Jane Gaines argues political documentaries rely on for their power (the sort one routinely finds in civil rights documentaries). Instead, he has polite conversations with the various people he encounters who speak from the paradigm of the public secret. His documentary is, after all, a road trip, which means it centers around personal visiting, not mass protest. The concern with documentaries creating social change is grounded in a one-to-one, cause-and-effect understanding of historical change. While social change does result from dramatic singular events (such as the end of a war, the fall of a government, or a natural disaster), it is more likely to occur slowly over time, unnoticed as social change per se until after it has solidified, as discussed, in relation to Birmingham, in the last chapter. This type of social change is not comparable to coming out of the closet with its dramatic change from "in" to "out."[58] While *Family Name* may not create dramatic change, nonetheless it does contribute to gradual change by being one more manifestation of a shifting discursive terrain that conceives the familial relationship routinely used within southern discourse to describe the relationship between blacks and whites as not only metaphorical but literal, connected not only through spatial proximity but bodily familiarity.

Conclusion

While emergent configurations of race within southern discourse that equate the region with multiracialism and residual configurations that equate it with whiteness contest in varying degrees the current dominant of biraciality, challenges can arise not only through a maneuver of substitution but also recoding. As the limitations of biraciality, in its current conceptualization to engender racial integration, materialized during the 1990s, an alternative definition emerged: biracial as mixed race. The familial metaphor of "brothers and sisters in Christ," used by the civil rights movement (and which continues to hold sway in some locales), is literalized in this competing meaning of biracial. Unlike nineteenth-century concepts such as muleology, which used a husbandry analogy to frame mixed-race individuals as "an unnatural act of mating" and thereby a societal pollutant consigned to the place of the racial closet, this recoding of biracial within southern discourse functions as a discursive mechanism for racial unity.[59] The acknowledgment of miscegenation brings home that "[b]iologically speaking, we are all mixed," that "there never have been any pure races," and that racial categories are not exclusive although many people may like to think they are.[60] Because this competing definition of biraciality concedes the mutability of the color line, it challenges the common-sense racialization of the family as mono-racial.

White supremacy racializes the family as mono-racial, familializes races as having no kinships across races, and frames any violations of these two postulates as degenerate. While biraciality appears progressive when compared to the previous dominant of white supremacy, its definition as two separate races legitimizes the continuance of these two postulates. The metaphorical layering of the familial onto race functions within southern discourse to suture the fissure that the persistence of these two postulates generates. (This layering also functions as a maneuver to make race an integral component of the regional as opposed to a competing one.) The recoding of biracial as mixed race literalizes the familial characteristic routinely attached to biraciality through appeals to religion and challenges these postulates that persist with its metaphorical usage. Given the region's prior dominant association with whiteness, the dominant definition of biracial as two races allows blackness to be poached on within southern discourse to signify the region so that it can maintain relevance in an age in which racial difference signifies differently than in the past. In contrast, the emergent definition of mixed race necessitates a serious negotiation of the porous nature of the boundaries between blackness and whiteness. While this chapter explored biraciality through the funnel of race as bodily, the next chapter does so through race as cultural.

Chapter Four

Praying Pigs and Wooden Peg Legs: Racial Poaching, Redemptive Ethnography, and 1970s Southeastern Documentaries

Introduction

While academics typically approach race through the anti-essentialist lens of the social, residents in locales such as Birmingham, Alabama—as captured in *bro•ken/ground* (Margaret Wrinkle and Chris Lawson, 1996), discussed in chapter two—continue to avail themselves of predominantly essentialist understandings of race which are anchored through religion rather than science. While it would be easy to fame these two approaches as aligning, respectively, along a cultural and biological divide, neither approach is so easily separated from these two elements. The social formation approach is, after all, based on perceptions of the body. Whether cultural difference preceded the bodily classification or resulted from it is not my concern; instead, my concern is only that race is articulated as both a cultural and bodily category in each of these approaches. The biracial component of southern discourse configures race similarly—not only are there black and white bodies but also black and white cultures. Although the dominant discursive racial framing of the region continues to be biracial, with its assumption of two (separate) races, the instability of the line dividing those two races is beginning to be acknowledged, both at the level of the body, as discussed in the last chapter, and the level of culture, as will be engaged here.

This chapter explores southern discourse from the perspective of race as culture, using 1970s southeastern documentaries as a site where it assumes material form and thereby is accessible for analysis. After a general consideration of intercultural exchange as formulated through cultural assimilation (often referred to as acculturation), cultural appropriation, and cultural appreciation, I approach the matter through the avenue of cultural poaching (which, in light of the topic under examination, can also be called "racial poaching").[1] This discussion then informs the remainder of the chapter, which explores 1970s southeastern documentaries in light of the crisis of legitimacy that engulfed southern discourse during that decade. Although the crisis was framed at the time as being about whether the region would continue to exist, because the regional is a discursive practice, to bemoan its demise paradoxically contributes to its continuance. Instead, the crisis was ultimately about the need for new presentations of the region to replace the older ones that were under assault as a result of the historical changes that were occurring in many locales in the aftermath of the civil rights movement. Because the older presentations had been now transcoded as negative, if the region was to continue in a positive light, new presentations were needed.[2] I label these 1970s southeastern documentaries "redemptive ethnography" because they sought to redeem the region through the exploration of local cultural expressions. They introduced new signifiers for the region untainted by the "massive resistance" to the "second reconstruction" and, through a southern supplement, were circulated as evidence that the region was distinct but also that this distinctiveness was good.[3] Many of these documentaries focused on either previously underrepresented white cultures that were not associated with the legacy of slavery and the Civil War, such as the Appalachian and Cajun areas, or on black cultural practices. The former group of documentaries redeemed the region through the reconstruction of whiteness; the latter group did so through the use of black subjects to present the region. As with civil rights tourist attractions developed in the decades following their production, this latter group of documentaries, when accompanied by a southern supplement, contributed to the discursive reconfiguration of the region as biracial through the incorporation of black culture practices into what constitutes southernness. Because these filmmakers were often white, the issue arises regarding whether they were racial poachers, a consideration that concludes the chapter.

Racial Poaching and an Ethics of Love

Just as the various cultures brought by African slaves to the area eventually known as the United States intertwined over generations to became known as black rather than African, such was also the case in some areas of the country with European immigrants in relationship to whiteness. This similarity, of course, did not disrupt the power differential existing between the racial formations and accompanying articulations of culture, which continue to privilege the latter formation. But while cultures exist that are articulated to certain races, like all cultures, these too are not static, bounded, or coherent. Despite periodic claims of cultural absolutism on both the left and the right, by both racial minorities and whites, cultures are dynamic, thereby changing over time; they are fluid, thereby affected by other cultures, and contested, thereby sites of struggle.[4] (Isolation has become almost impossible in today's environment.) I would also add that racially articulated cultures are not homogenous but rather heterogeneous; thus, cultural difference transpires not just between social formations but within them. The identifying of cultures as black or white, rather than African or European, creates a hurdle for races and ethnicities not considered black or white. As will be discussed in chapter five, this meant Italian and Spaniard immigrants were considered European ethnicities in some areas of the United States (rather than white Americans) because their cultures did not conform to this New World formation. And as will be discussed in chapter seven, this framework ignores the influence of the cultures of native peoples on these African and European derived cultures. While many cultures exist in the United States, intra-racially as well as interracially, culture is routinely referred to rhetorically as black and white (within an implied national framework), sometimes with the adjective "southern" before the terms, with this linguistic supplement discursively articulating those particular cultural manifestations with the regional.

The articulation of race to culture raises expectations of certain correlations between practitioners and cultural expressions. Some people insist that only those individuals who had the particular social experience of a race can understand the culture articulated to it (a minoritizing view), while others hold that anyone can potentially learn such cultures if they have the aptitude to intellectually and emotionally grasp the social conditions that contributed to its formation (a universalizing view).[5] Holders of the former position often treat non-alignments between the race of the cultural practitioner and the racial coding of the cultural practice suspiciously, be it a white artist performing rap music or a black one playing classical music. In *Family Name*, discussed in the last chapter, Jeff Alston complains that other blacks often give his father a hard time for being a classical musician, constantly telling him: "You shouldn't be playing the white man's music." Of course, as Joan Scott warns: "It is not individuals who have experience, but subjects who are constituted through experience."[6] Therefore, experience does not offer an explanation but rather is that which needs to be explained. While the minoritizing position can easily lapse into absolutism, the universalizing position risks minimizing power differentials between the social groups involved.

Given that cultures are by definition fluid, when a minority group adopts the cultural practices of the dominant group in order to assimilate into the mainstream, the process is referred to as acculturation, while when the dominant group adopts subcultural practices of a minority group in order to invigorate the mainstream, the process is referred to as cultural appropriation. Because unequal power exists between the two groups, damage is presumed to occur to the subculture in both cases—potential annihilation through the process of cultural assimilation, most likely distortion through the process of cultural appropriation. Paul Gilroy holds that the "assimilation of blacks is not a process of acculturation but of cultural syncretism."[7] While the dominant culture within the United States is typically described as white, certain black cultural expressions are also part of it. (Rap, for example, moved from being a subcultural practice to an integral component of the mainstream music industry.) And certain forms of white culture are also the result of syncretism. Although constrained by an allegiance to a discourse of biraciality that erases Native American cultures, Charles Joyner provocatively argues that not only does "every black southerner" have "a European heritage as well as an African one," but that "every white southerner has an African heritage as well as a European one."[8] Although the former is routinely acknowledged, with jazz commonly invoked as an example, the latter is not. John Edward Philips makes a similar claim, holding that the study of the African heritage of white America has been ignored.[9] One of his examples is the banjo, the most common musical instrument associated with white Appalachian music like bluegrass.[10] If asked to racialize the banjo, the overwhelming response by most Americans would be white. But researchers have long agreed that the banjo is of African origin, some going so far as to claim that traditional mountain banjo music is closer in style to African music than blues. Joyner and Philips shake up the presuppositions that white cultures are uninfluenced by the African cultures brought to the United States by slaves and therefore purely European derived—the under-acknowledged cultural complement of white bodily purity. Although racialized cultures exists within the United States, black cultures can no longer be conceived as separate from the mainstream or white cultures as non-syncretistic. Within the American context, syncretism is not the cultural exception but the norm, although the degree of its presence varies from one sociocultural formation to another.[11]

Given the prominence of syncretism in American cultures, in combination with the increasing segmentation of the mainstream and the routine production and/or consumption of minority cultural expressions within mainstream spaces (as well as the expected subcultural spaces), a complicated interplay between minorities and the mainstream now exists, blurring the traditional distinction between cultural assimilation (acculturation) and cultural appropriation, as well as the presumption of intrinsic damage to the subculture.[12] Today, while some minority cultural expressions are produced within subcultural spaces, others transpire within mainstream spaces; in other words, some minorities have been incorporated into popular culture, with this incorporation often actively sought by such minorities. While the former are typically referred to as independent and the latter popular culture, the boundary between them can at times be opaque.[13] Given this situation, Stuart Hall warns of perceiving such negotiations with popular culture through a binaristic "either/or" model of "either total victory or total incorporation."[14] Instead, he proposes approaching the matter in terms of cultural hegemony which "is never a zero-sum cultural game" but "about shifting the balance of power in the relations of culture," "changing the dispositions and the configurations of cultural power, not getting out of it."[15] In other words, whenever minority culture transpires within mainstream apparatuses, it is the result of a negotiation (often including a reconstruction), not an imposition by one side or the other. Of course, given that power disparity exists between racial formations and their articulated cultures, cross-cultural interaction may affect them differently. Despite their theoretical problems, concepts such as cultural assimilation (acculturation) and cultural appropriation are attempts to recognize when such situations are not beneficial to the weaker formation. Of course, because minority groups are not homogenous, which cultural interactions are perceived as such is an ethics question.

Although concerned only with the narrow issue of consumption, bell hooks frames this ethics question in terms of "eating the other" or "loving blackness," the former being cultural appropriation, the latter cultural appreciation.[16] Eating the other—or, more specifically in her case, eating blackness—is using black culture as "spice, seasoning that can liven up the dull dish that is mainstream white culture."[17] Although she is pessimistic regarding the mass commodification of black culture for white consumption, she admits: "Luckily, there are individual non-black people who have divested of their racism in ways that enable them to establish bonds of intimacy based on their ability to love blackness without assuming the role of cultural tourists."[18] For hooks, the differentiation between appreciation and appropriation resides in not just whether one loves that cultural expression but whether one loves the social group that produces it.[19] The concept of love is thought of rather skeptically within academia today but it has a long history within philosophy; most major philosophers address the matter at some point in their oeuvre.[20] In a subsequent book on love, hooks defines love as "an action, a participatory emotion. Whether we are engaged in a process of self-love or of loving others we must move beyond the realm of feeling to actualize love. That is why it is useful to see love as a practice."[21] This position can be traced back to Søren Kierkegaard, who interpreted the "thou shall" of "the biblical commandments to love God and to love one's neighbor as categorical imperatives," thereby making love "dependent on appropriate action rather than feeling or inclination."²² To think of love as an action shifts the focus from the psychological to the sociological. In other words, love manifests itself in the outward behavior of the lover toward the beloved. If one desires to retain a sense of interiority, then the lover's inner condition can be read from his or her outer actions. Of course, the main critique of this position is that some people are good actors. But if love is a practice actualized in behavior, whether interiority exists becomes irrelevant because within such a definition when one stops acting in a loving manner one stops loving. Of course, just because a person loves a particular cultural form does not mean that they also love the people who create it, as attested by racist whites enjoying over the years black-created music like soul, funk, and rap. Defining love as an action rather than emotion shapes the ethics question as one of social consequences rather than intentions. Hooks broadens the ethics of cultural appropriation to encompass not just the act of cultural borrowing but also the larger context of how that borrower acts toward the social group that produces the cultural expression. As a result, the ethical question becomes not "what are the consequences of one's borrowing a particular cultural expression on the social group that originally produced it," but rather "what are the consequences of one's actions *in general* on that social group?"

Because the concept of cultural appropriation implies the existence of a rightful owner of cultural expressions, it also presumes illegitimate borrowing can transpire. As noted earlier, all sociocultural groups borrow from one another (some of it even occurring because of individuals being simultaneously members of more than one cultural formation). What makes cultural interactions an ethical issue is not some imputed socially illegal act of borrowing that violates ownership rights but the asymmetrical power differentials that exist between the social groups articulated with those cultural expressions, a process that can be intra-racial as well as interracial. Henry Jenkins, building on Michel de Certeau's association of popular readers with poachers, offers the term "textual poachers" to describe fans borrowing mainstream texts as "the raw materials for their own cultural productions and the basis for their social interactions."²³ Many of the textual poaching practices Jenkins describes entail copyright infringement problems, and cultural appropriation is conceptually entwined with illegitimacy, albeit socially or ethically rather than legally. Because cultures are unbound, dynamic, and contested, cultural poaching as a form of cultural borrowing is a multilateral affair. For Jenkins, poaching is not consumption per se but the reshaping of the borrowed cultural expression into a new expression. While I do not want to adopt Jenkins's framework of textual poaching because of this presumption, I do want to borrow the concept of poaching itself and apply it to the borrowing of racially articulated culture in order to make explicit the issue of legitimacy that discussions of cultural appropriation typically imply—in other words, racial poaching. The members of many social formations have a strong sense of ownership toward the cultural expressions articulated to them. My aim is not to diminish the validity of this attachment (for, though unfortunately at times expressed in absolutist terms, it often derives from the important role such cultural expressions play in forming a sense of belonging among such social groups in negotiating sociopolitical—and routinely economic—marginalization); instead, my aim is to highlight that determining when an act of borrowing constitutes poaching is not amenable to an easily solvable mathematical equation of legitimacy. Given the fluid nature of culture in general, the entwining of mainstream and minority cultures in an era of conglomerate media segmentation, and the prevalence of syncretism within American cultures, ownership is not the determining factor of cross-cultural interaction as an ethical issue but rather the asymmetrical power relations that exists among the various sociocultural formations involved. In other words, how is this power differential enacted? Does the group with the social advantage act lovingly toward the other party whose culture it poaches—with love not as sentimental feelings but consequential actions, love not as patronizing charity but respectful support? As will be discussed in the last section, documentary film production, when it emerged in most southeastern states during the 1970s, traversed this terrain of racially articulated culture and racial poaching.

1970s Crisis of Legitimacy and Documentary Film

Cultural studies sociologists such as Paul Gilroy and Kobena Mercer hold that during the 1970s England underwent a representational crisis of nationalism as the country confronted colonial decline and increased immigration from former colonies. Rather than recourse to "genetic or essentialist notions of racial difference" the New Right used "the *cultural* construction of Little England as a domain of ethnic homogeneity," a claim of monoculturalism.[24] This emphasis on culture, per Gilroy, "allows nation and race to fuse. Nationalism and racism become so closely identified that to speak of the nation is to speak automatically in racially exclusive terms. Blackness and Englishness are constructed as incompatible, mutually exclusive identities. To speak of the British and English people is to speak of the *white* people."[25] During the 1960s, a crisis of legitimization also arose within southern discourse, one which peaked in the 1970s.[26] Although race played a significant role in both crises, and one could argue they both contributed to the emergence of what is now referred to as the New Racism in their respective countries (one that functions through coded language), significant differences existed between them, including the fact that within the United States blacks were not recent immigrants and the crisis was precipitated by the emergence of a thriving black social movement for equality. While recourse to culture in the English context enabled the solidification of a white supremacy solution to the crisis, because of the prevalence of cultural syncretism within the American context, recourse to culture functioned differently, contributing to the emergence of the discursive framing of the region within southern discourse as biracial. Rather than its exclusion, blackness (and articulated cultural expressions) was discursively incorporated as regional as well as racial.

During the 1960s and '70s, the existence of the region was typically legitimized within southern discourse on the basis of it being distinct from mainstream America. Debate arose during this period over whether the region was losing its uniqueness as a result of a broad range of changes occurring at the time, the primary culprits being the dismantling of legalized segregation as a result of the civil rights movement, the homogenizing effects of an expanding national-based mass media, and the industrialization of the economy in many locales of southeastern states. Arguments in support of an "enduring South" and a "disappearing South" were advanced in books and articles; the latter position typically presented the region as being in the process of disappearing (thereby losing its exceptionalism)—although sometimes it was framed as suggesting that any difference between the region and the nation has always been minimal (therefore, the region never was exceptional).[27] As one might expect, given that the regional as an object is one of knowledge, not corporeality, the debate began within academia before spilling over into the print media consumed by the educated populace. The alarm was rung as early as 1957 by academic and New Critic Louis D. Rubin Jr., who warned: "What has been distinctive and Southern about the South threatens to disappear, and the South threatens to become a thriving but undistinguished replica of the North and West, dependent upon the national industrial economy as never before."[28] One of the earliest challenges to the common-sense proposition within southern discourse at the time that the region was unique (i.e., exceptional) was Howard Zinn's 1964 book *The Southern Mystique*. Zinn, a white northerner who had taught from 1956 to 1963 at the historically black women's college Spelman in Atlanta, wrote periodically for magazines such as the *Nation*. While he agreed with the common assessment within mainstream American society that "[t]he South is . . . racist, violent, hypocritically pious, xenophobic, false in its elevation of women, nationalistic, conservative, and it harbors extreme poverty in the midst of ostentatious wealth," he countered that "the United States, as a civilization, embodies all of those same qualities." Because "the South possesses them with more intensity simply makes it easier for the nation to pass off its characteristics to the South, leaving itself innocent and righteous."[29] In other words, rather than an exception, "the South is but a distorted mirror image of the North."[30] Zinn's book was not only reviewed unfavorably but relegated to page fifty-four of the *New York Times Book Review*, while page three of the same issue was devoted to James McBride Dobbs's *Who Speaks for the South?*, Dobbs being a writer included in the 1957 anthology by Rubin, who espoused the orthodox position of southern distinctiveness.[31] Zinn's book captured enough attention, however, that the dean of southern history at the time, Yale professor C. Vann Woodward, felt a need to publicly challenge its thesis.[32] A decade later, when the debate was no longer quite so marginal, John Egerton's book *The Americanization of Dixie: The Southernization of America* was released in 1974. It was not only reviewed favorably but placed on page three of the *New York Times Book Review*.[33] Based on the title of Egerton's book, the region appeared to be disappearing because of two intersecting processes: its distinction from the nation declining because of the former's acculturation to the latter, and the latter's appropriation of the former. These were processes of reduction and expansion, respectively. (In other words, difference can be eliminated by making it the norm as well as through outright annihilation.) But Egerton frames the interaction not in terms of acculturation and appropriation but rather syncretism, as when he asserts: "The South and the nation are not exchanging strengths as much as they are exchanging sins; more often than not, they are sharing and spreading the worst in each other."[34] Although the debate over whether the region's distinctiveness was disappearing peaked in the 1970s, it continued into subsequent decades.[35]

Although the 1970s crisis of legitimacy assumed the form of a debate over whether the region was disappearing, it was ultimately not about the region's continuance but its presentation. As cross-race interaction and blackness were reconfigured within national discourse through the civil rights and Black Power movements and the Cold War debate (all transpiring in the shadow of a recent war against anti-Semitic racism), the white supremacy underpinnings of most mass cultural presentations of the region was finally being publically acknowledged as problematic. One of the most popular presentations of the region during the first half of the twentieth century was the plantation genre, which includes films such as *The Birth of a Nation* (D. W. Griffith, 1915), *Gone with the Wind* (Victor Fleming, 1939), and *Band of Angels* (Raoul Walsh, 1957). Given this social context, as one might expect, it gradually disappeared after 1957, although *Gone with the Wind* continued to hold sway with numerous re-releases in the 1960s.[36] Within such a sociopolitical context the genre's romanticism of white supremacy became unsustainable. Its demise accompanied the decline of Hollywood and the rise of television as the premier national audiovisual medium. Of course, contradictory presentations of the region exist simultaneously in a Gramscian war of position for hegemony. In the early 1960s, entertainment television programs, in general, ignored blacks but included a few all-white rural shows aligned with the region through a southern supplement (although the specific location of the setting was typically unspecified). This situation contrasted sharply both in terms of quantity as well as quality with the televisual presentation seen on nightly network news telecasts. During this time period, when it came only to news stories related to the state of Alabama, stories included the 1961 burning of a Freedom Riders bus in Anniston, the 1961 beating of Freedom Riders at the Birmingham bus station (also covered in a CBS News documentary, *Who Speaks for Birmingham?*), the 1963 attack of children with fire hoses and police dogs in Birmingham's Kelly Ingram Park, the 1963 symbolic blocking of Vivian Malone and James Hood from entering the University of Alabama at Tuscaloosa (also covered in a NBC News documentary, *Crisis: Behind a Presidential Commitment*), the 1963 bombing of the Sixteenth Street Baptist Church in Birmingham that killed four little girls, the 1965 murder of Jimmie Lee Jackson by state troopers in Marion, and the 1965 tear-gassing and clubbing of protesters on the Edmund Pettus Bridge in Selma.[37] Despite a variety of presentations, the association of the region with white hostility and violence against blacks prevailed. The news media typically framed the struggle in sharp terms of good versus evil, with the civil rights movement generally covered sympathetically with reporters ignoring, per Sasha Torres, "the journalistic imperative to neutrality" because of, on the one hand, "the moral authority commanded by movement participants, who acted with remarkable courage in the face of the violent reprisals and economic deprivations that accompanied their activism," and, on the other hand, "the self-evident bankruptcy of the segregationist position."[38] While these news events were also covered by the print media, they became visceral and kinetic spectacles because of television. Torres holds that coverage of the civil rights movement provided television "precisely the cultural capital the new medium needed," allowing "network news not only to report, but also intervene in national culture and political discourse."[39] In other words, coverage of the civil rights movement served as a mechanism for the new medium of television news to claim an important role in shaping public opinion and thereby a national force to be taken seriously. During the 1960s, the news supplanted entertainment as the most widely circulated presentations of the region. Although the shift did not disrupt the continued association within southern discourse of the region with white supremacy, the previously unacknowledged brutalizing and dehumanizing consequences for blacks was now being shown. While the region is closely associated with the Civil War and the civil rights movement, it is also closely associated with the civil as "proper social decorum." For those desiring the presentation of the region to be socially acceptable, new regionally specific forms were needed that were not based (or at least not so obviously) on white supremacy.[40]

It was during this 1970s crisis of legitimization within southern discourse and its underlying dilemma of presentation that independent documentary filmmaking emerged in most southeastern states. Its emergence resulted from a ripple effect of a broader national trend that began in the 1960s because of such diverse factors as the introduction of lightweight 16mm cameras with synchronized sound, the increase in television documentary production, the emergence of a youth counterculture, the developing interest in American folk cultures, and a shift in acquiring production skills from Hollywood apprenticeships to college education and media centers. Documentaries were, of course, made in those states prior to the 1970s. The now-classic 1930s U.S. government-sponsored documentary *The River* (Pare Lorentz, 1937) focused on the creation of the Tennessee Valley Authority, and *People of the Cumberland* (Elia Kazan, 1938), made by the New York City-based leftist Frontier Film Group, centered on the Tennessee mountains. But such documentaries were rare. And when the three major television networks began to make documentaries in the early 1960s to counter their image problem as a "vast wasteland," documentaries on locales within southeastern states appeared among them, such as *Sit-In* (NBC White Paper, 1960), on the Nashville, Tennessee, civil rights sit-in campaign by Fisk College students, and *Harvest of Shame* (CBS Reports, 1960), on the conditions of migrant agricultural workers in Florida. These TV documentaries were typically made not only by visiting film crews from outside the area but more importantly framed the region as a problem, partaking of the common presentation of the region within the various news media during the 1960s. Regardless of these precursors, the emergence of independent documentary film production during the 1970s provided a new source for the presentation of the regional. And unlike Hollywood films, New York City publishing, and network television documentaries, they were not burdened by preexisting medium-specific generic forms of presentation of the region, a fortuitous coincidence during a time of crisis over presentation. As a result, the elements these filmmakers focused on—if accompanied by a southern supplement—became an intervention, however unconscious, however minor, into that crisis through contributing to the discursive reconfiguring of the elements associated with the region.

Since 1970, hundreds of documentaries have been made not only about various locales within southeastern states but oftentimes by individuals who resided or grew up in them. And rather than present the area as deficient, in need of fixing, these documentaries celebrated the various cultural expressions found there, which stood in sharp contrast to the afterimage of 1960s television news presentations whose residue still strongly lingered within national memory during the 1970s.[41] The documentaries are typically short in length—often from fifteen minutes to one hour—with feature-length documentaries being the exception. The restraints of available exhibition outlets (such as airing on public television and screening in classrooms) dictated this length. I would not use the phrase "regional movement" to describe the filmmakers who created this body of work because the term would ascribe an unwarranted intentionality and unity to them. Yet these dispersed documentaries have been routinely woven together, through production context, distribution circuits, and critical reception. They have been intertwined thanks to screenings at film festivals, holdings in college library media collections, airings on state educational television stations, presentations at media arts centers, reviews in newsletters and journals, and touring on the Southern Circuit.[42]

While observational documentaries of contemporary events ruled the 1960s and early 1970s, during the 1970s participatory documentaries on previously neglected histories also became popular, such as *With Babies and Banners: The Story of the Women's Emergency Brigade* (Lorraine Gray, Anne Bohlen, and Lynn Goldfarb, 1977), on women's roles in a 1930s factory strike, and *The Life and Times of Rosie the Riveter* (Connie Field, 1980), on women welders during World War II. Ironically, given the close association of the region in southern discourse with history and the past, 1970s southeastern documentaries did not follow this trend. Although a few such documentaries appeared, in general they focused on contemporary rural cultural practices, partaking of ethnographic filmmaking. Examples of documentaries made during the 1970s include: Yasha Aginsky's *Sonny Terry: Shoutin' the Blues* (1979); Les Blank's Cajun life films, such as *Spend It All* (1971); Tom Davenport's films for the Curriculum in Folklore at the University of North Carolina, such as *It Ain't City Music* (1973); Blaine Dunlap and Sol Korine's films for Georgia Public Television, such as *Mouth Music* (1980); *Red, White and Bluegrass* (Elliot Erwitt, 1973); William Ferris and Judy Peiser's films for the Center for Southern Folklore, such as *Mississippi Delta Blues* (1974); Alexis

Krasilovsky's *Beale Street* (1978); Ross McElwee's *Charleen: or How Long Has This Been Going On?* (1978); Gretchen Robinson's *The People Who Take up Serpents* (1974); Marjie Short's *Kudzu* (1976); Ross Spears's *Agee* (1978); and Stanley Woodward's *It's Grits* (1978).[43] In addition, the Appalshop Media Center in Whitesburg, Kentucky, made over two dozen films during the decade about Appalachian Mountain life. This focus on rural cultural practices continued well into the 1980s; the epitome of the trend was the 1990 five-part PBS series by Alan Lomax, *American Patchwork: Songs and Stories of America*, which, despite its title, focused on a few local cultural formations in several southeastern states, with the material constituting the series recorded over the preceding two decades.[44] Unlike *Mai's America*, discussed in the introduction, in *American Patchwork* these locales were allowed to represent America, but in this case as arcane remnants of folk cultures from the past rather than in the shape of its present condition.

Redemptive Ethnography and Racial Mutability

Within the 1970s crisis of legitimacy, these ethnographic-inspired documentaries—when accompanied by a southern supplement—served a dual function, one related to the present, the other to the future. For the present of the 1970s, they provided evidence confirming regional distinctiveness. In contrast, for the future they provided documentation preserving the "disappearing South." These two concerns—persuading the current generation that the region is unique, and salvaging for future generations a vanishing world—are governed by a larger concern: to show that this disappearing distinctiveness is good. I call this larger concern "redemptiveness," which reframes the other two, persuading and salvaging, into acts of witnessing. Although they are manifestations of salvage ethnography, rather than saving through preservation, redemptive ethnographies rescue through revaluation.[45] The concern is ultimately not physical disappearance from the material world but reputable disappearance from the social world; consequently, it preserves not through corporeal mummification but social recoding. Socially belittled and/or disparaged cultural expressions are redeemed through re-signification; the profilmic is endowed with positive connotations. These documentaries perform a double redemption: first, that of the specific cultural expression recorded that is the function of all redemptive ethnographies, and, second, that of the region articulated with these particular cultural expressions through a southern supplement, a connection often only appearing during the circulation and reception processes of the texts rather than within the texts themselves. Unlike salvage ethnography, in which the recording of a cultural expression accomplishes the act of preservation, with redemptive ethnography, achievement is dependent upon the reception of the text, not its production.

Although these redemptive ethnographies are not concerned with the issue of civil rights, neither in terms of capturing contemporary events nor historicizing prior ones, its legacy saturates the milieu from which they emerge. Although, as will be discussed in the next section, three primary presentational forms appeared in these documentaries, the most prominent was blackness, whose discursive reverberation with redemptive suffering from the civil rights era provided the underpinnings of redemptive ethnography.[46] The idea that suffering has redemptive powers is an old religious belief but, with the civil rights movement, it became widely associated with blackness. Throughout his speeches and publications, Martin Luther King Jr. espoused a deep belief that "unearned suffering is redemptive," the concept even appearing in his famous "I Have a Dream" speech.[47] If the quotation by King about Birmingham at the end of *bro•ken/ground* that was discussed in chapter two had not been cut short, it would have concluded: "that the sins of a dark yesterday will be redeemed in the achievements of a bright tomorrow."[48] Within Christian theology, redemption results from an act of love; Christ freely accepted the suffering of the cross in order to be the sacrifice that reconciles humankind with God, with his death being the payment for that restoration.[49] For King, blacks perform an analogous role in American society; their unwarranted brutalization and murder being the price of redeeming the United States wandering from the democratic ideals of freedom and equality for all people.[50] Like many scholars, he conceives of love not as sentiment or emotion but action, an act specifically of "redeeming good will for all men."[51] Therefore, love is socially perceivable through its "seeking to preserve and create community" and anyone "who works against community is working against the whole of creation."[52] In a secular society, this position appears both naïve and romantic—but it is meant to be concrete and practical. Although black nationalistic strains appear in King's rhetoric, through his recourse to black pride and blacks holding a special role within society, he was at heart an integrationist.[53] And, for King, this "beloved community" is based not on racial affiliation but a commitment to peace and (social and economic) justice that emerges from a "thoroughgoing integrated community in which persons are intentional about living in accordance with the meaning of agapé love."[54]

The concept of the beloved community shares an affinity with Jacque Ellul's earlier conceptualization of the role of the Christian in the world. For Ellul, the Christian must plunge into social and political problems in order to have an influence on the world, not in the hope of making it a paradise, but simply in order to make it tolerable—not in order to diminish the opposition between this world and the Kingdom of God, but simply in order to modify the opposition between the disorder of this world and the order of preservation that God wills for it—not in order to "bring in" the Kingdom of God, but in order that the Gospel may be proclaimed.[55]

Christians are called not to establish a utopia on the earth nor to simply wait for the realization of one in an afterlife. Instead, they are called to preserve the world from disintegration into disorder, corruption, and injustice by signifying the coming kingdom of God through one's life. The Christian

has to carry into the actual world of the present day elements which belong to the *eschaton*. In so doing he [sic] fulfills a prophetic function . . . for the prophet is not one who confines himself [sic] to foretelling with more or less precision an event more or less distinct; he [sic] is one who already "lives" it, and already makes it actual and present in his own environment.[56]

Although Ellul writes here in terms of *the* Christian, he holds that such a life is only possible collectively within a beloved community (although he never used that particular phrase). In other words, the "carry[ing] into the actual world of the present day elements which belong to the *eschaton*," which he describes as the presence of the kingdom, is similar to King's beloved community. This "persons-in-community" entails not only the spiritual but also the material, as the beloved community lives the future in the present through an ethics of love that materializes (even if only partially) a possible world of peace and justice in concrete form.[57] While politicians in the United States routinely invoke Christianity, as a political force it is closely associated with the evangelical and fundamentalist religious right, which, since the 1980s, has "plunge[d] into social and political problems in order to have an influence on the world." But is this religious activism the actualization in the present of the presence of the kingdom of God, as envisioned by such Christian scholars as Jacques Ellul and Martin Luther King Jr.? The social, economical, and political consequences of the laws they seek enacted indicates a commitment to religious dogma rather than an ethics of love. Words such as "justice" and "freedom" can be interpreted very differently. For the religious right, these two particular words are typically aligned with, respectively, "law and order" and "free markets." Such definitions stand in stark contrast with the meaning attributed to them within an ethics of love and a beloved community.

For example, access to medical care based on financial resources rather than physical need would be unjust within an ethics of love, as would be laws that contribute to the concentration of wealth and power in the hands of a few or that destroy human lives through imprisonment for drug abuse rather than offering rehabilitation and counseling. James Robinson holds that, when considering Jesus's message from the perspective of the "sayings Gospels," its core concern is "God reigning" (a phrase commonly translated "kingdom of God"). He defines this situation as "God acting [that is, reigning] through those who trusted him [sic]," "trusting God for today's ration of life, and on hearing God's call to give now a better life to neighbors, indeed to enemies."[58] In other words, God reigns through us, and like the concept of love, the concern is not with sentiment and spirituality but action and materiality. For example, the references to "bread" and "debts" in the Lord's Prayer are to food and money. Robinson summarizes the message thus: "The human dilemma is, in large part, that we are each other's fate. We become the tool of evil that ruins another person as we look out for ourselves. . . . But if we each would cease and desist from pushing the other down to keep ourselves up, then the vicious cycle would be broken. Society would become mutually supportive rather than self-destructive."[59] Whether or not one uses the phrase "beloved community," "the presence of the kingdom," or "God reigning," this is a form of Christianity almost nonexistent in the public sphere, unlike that of the religious radical right, which too often dominates politics and the media.[60]

While redemptive ethnography is not part of a beloved community or the presence of the kingdom per se, it is the materialization in the present of a possible South that redeems the region from its association with white supremacy. By the 1970s, the afterimage of blackness as redemptive of America, made popular during the civil rights era, shifted as applicable to the region as well, a slippage made possible by the tendency to interpret the civil rights movement (unlike the Black Power movement) as addressing a racial problem in southeastern states rather than the nation.[61] I realize the concept of redemptive ethnography may appear rather illusive and seem quite mystic. Because redemption occurs through social recoding, its achievement is dependent upon reception, not production. But in this particular case, the concern is not with recoding the meaning of a preexisting media text but with reconfiguring a discursive terrain through the presentation of new signifiers. The form of the texts, therefore, is important in the process. To function as redemptive, however, did not necessitate the depiction of black suffering as displayed in documentaries and heritage museums on the history of the civil rights movement. To do so as a contemporary phenomenon would only continue to indict the region. While blackness provides the basic underpinnings of redemptive

Peg Leg Sam Jackson who dances in Tom Davenport's 1976 documentary *Born for Hard Luck*. Photograph by Tom Davenport.

ethnographies through the discursive reverberations of blackness as redemptive from the civil rights movement (and, as will be discussed shortly, blackness as a Third World in the First World from the black liberation movement), such documentaries are not limited to presenting black social actors. Because the crisis of legitimacy within southern discourse arose from the primary presentations of the region being expressed through white supremacy, any marginalized subculture not explicitly associated with white supremacy was able to function similarly. These other subcultures do not become honorary blacks nor do they use a black style. Rather, these discursive features of blackness enabled the formation of a filmic space, that of redemptive ethnography, which was racially mutable with an elasticity that enabled functionality with any similar positioned subaltern sociocultures, even those that may be white (or those not previously discursively articulated with the region through a southern supplement). For example, Les Blank, renowned for his Louisiana Cajun documentaries in the 1970s, began filming black blues musicians in east Texas in the late 1960s. More often, this mutability is not so obvious.

Instead of suffering, these 1970s (and 1980s) southeastern redemptive ethnographies capture playfulness and innocence, a key textual element being the material manifestation on screen of the pro-filmic interaction between filmmaker and social actors, although editing periodically contributes as well. If one compares them to Errol Morris's 1981 documentary *Vernon, Florida*, this textual feature quickly becomes apparent. Morris presents a portrait of the residents of Vernon, Florida, an outrageous collection of bizarre characters as enunciated in the documentary. The impression conveyed is one of weirdness, of people who deserve to be laughed at, if not ridiculed, for their odd stories. Although the camera does move periodically, the overall effect is one of a motionless camera that creates a distancing effect from the film subjects to whom listening viewers are invited to feel superior. Although these redemptive ethnographies also capture what is eccentric behavior from an outsider's perspective, a sense of humor as well as respect for the social actors being recorded permeates the screen. And the typically handheld camerawork signifies intimate interaction with the social actors. The fictional French film *Amélie* (Jean-Pierre Jeunet, 2001), known for its whimsical stylistics, could incorporate an excerpt of Peg Leg Sam Jackson dancing around on his wooden stump leg from Tom Davenport's 1976 documentary *Born for Hard Luck* on the basis of its purely visual oddity alone, and because it also displayed a playfulness similar to the rest of the film. Spectators are prone to laugh *with* the social actors of redemptive ethnographies rather than *at* them.

If approached from the perspective of whether the social actors show or tell, physically demonstrate or verbally describe, respectively, *Vernon, Florida* falls into the category of telling, while redemptive ethnographies privilege showing. Rather than typically immobile social actors who verbally drone on as in *Vernon, Florida*, the performance of the participants in these documentaries privilege the non-linguistic, although they routinely speak as well. This performance ranges from producing cultural objects with their labor to executing physical actions with their bodies to generating nonverbal or musical sounds with their vocal cords. The listening viewer is offered an audiovisual experience *of* the matter under discussion rather than a linguistic-based experience *about* it. When the few social actors in *Vernon, Florida* do show us something, it is a stagnate object related to the story being told, such as a possum held by the tail, a bullet hole in the seat of a police car, or varnished plaque of turkey feet. They function as mere illustrations to the story rather than constituting the story itself, as with these redemptive ethnographies. Although these documentaries may not be in the performative documentary mode discussed in chapter two, the pro-filmic material captured by the camera and sound recorder are theatrical performances. While many famous observational documentaries of the 1960s and 1970s also capture artists performing, these ethnographic filmmakers and their equipment do not assume a fly-on-the-wall, noninterventionist posture. While the documentaries have an observational feel, because they use handheld cameras in the field, the social actors routinely acknowledge through their attitude and actions the presence of the filmmaker. While sometimes an anonymous audience may be present, in general they tend more often to perform either directly for the camera or an intimate group of family and friends, of which the filmmaker is one. The interaction between the filmmakers recording and social actors performing is a fluid dance that flows between observational, participatory, and reflexive modes of documentary practice.

The civil rights movement in the United States occurred concurrently with national liberation movements in colonial countries around the word, with Africa as a key site. As a segment of the freedom struggle morphed into Black Power during the mid-1960s, writers associated with this decolonization movement, such as Frantz Fanon, provided an alternative black intellectual framework to that of Martin Luther King Jr., one that was secular rather than religious, framed in terms of black liberation rather than civil rights, nationalism rather than integration, violent force rather than civil disobedience.[62] The production of these ethnographic documentaries occurred not only in the afterimage of blackness as redemptive, reverberating from the civil rights movement, but also blackness as a Third World within the First World, reverberating from the black liberation movement. This discursive alignment with Third Worldism occurs primarily through recourse to exoticism via the presence of colorful, eccentric social actors (who connote strange) in combination with rural, semi-tropical locations (which connote nature), odd cultural practices (which connote primitivism), and impoverished settings (which connote underdevelopment).[63] As mentioned in the introduction, eccentricity is a common component of southern discourse. Rather than the traditional conceptualization of eccentricity as a mental illness (a personality disorder), in "On Eccentricity" George Marcus approaches it through social positioning (a judgmental social label). He associates it with dynastic families, arguing that their ancestral authority rests on claims of distinctive personhood and, for mature dynasties in decline, that distinction becomes not virtuous character but eccentricity.[64] Given this definition, its inclusion as an element of southern discourse appears misplaced. Besides the class component, his definition contains two primary elements that are familiar from earlier discussions—that of distinctiveness and decline. These two factors define the 1970s crisis of legitimacy within southern discourse over whether or not the region was disappearing due to the decline of its distinctiveness (often framed as a result of Americanization). Marcus's underlying argument—that social groups defined by distinctiveness turn to eccentricity for the basis of that distinction when in decline—applies to a prevailing trend within southern discourse during this period. Marcus restricts his definition to situations of affluence because "the bearing of great wealth or the exercise of great power," first, produces "distortion effect or excess" and, second, is "exotic in the imaginations of most people."[65] But these same two claims can be made about poverty. Distorting effects result from bearing great poverty and powerlessness, and this condition is considered exotic to most people. Poor people have to take what is readily available, often considered refuse by others, and use it in creative ways, whether for everyday existence or artistic expression, hence their behavior is viewed as eccentric and often considered primitive. Such is the case of the rural working-class cultural practices captured in these redemptive ethnographies, whether it is a snake-handling congregation, tongue-popping musician, or hog-roasting party. A good example of this occurs in *Fannie Bell Chapman: Gospel Singer* (William Ferris and Judy Peiser, 1975), when Chapman makes a decorative table covering from the plastic holders that fasten a six-pack of can drinks. I hold that inhabiting the extreme borders of the financial continuum—with either too much money or not enough exists—facilitates the emergence of eccentricity.

The visual evocation of Third Worldism in these redemptive ethnographies—in conjunction with a southern supplement that connects them to a crisis of legitimacy linked to Americanization—aligned them with the paradigm popular at the time of cultural imperialism. Although critiqued today for its determinism and presumption that consumers are passive, in the 1970s cultural imperialism was framed as the exportation around the world of American culture, thereby spreading American values and habits, dominating local cultures and homogenizing them. Cultural imperialism conceives of cultural practices and economic power as intricately intertwined, reinforcing each other.[66] This feared Americanization of world cultures, however, was of a particular kind of Americana, one seldom aligned at the time through southern discourse with the region. Kirby nicely sums up the prevalent tenor of the decade: "the South has always been a media colony, an elsewhere for the

American majority's amusement or negative example."⁶⁷ This is not to deny that some cultures articulated with the region through a discursive supplement were exported, but those cultural expressions—such as Delta blues and bluegrass music—tended to be associated with folk rather than popular culture, with traditionalism rather than commercialism. The 1970s debate over whether the region was in danger of disappearing due to Americanization aligned with this other cotemporaneous concern of various cultures around the world being adversely affected by the worldwide spread of American culture. The 1970s saw the beginning of the well-known ethnographic film series on subaltern cultures around the globe, "Disappearing World." These redemptive ethnographies, enabled by the crisis of legitimacy, partook of this ethos.

Through recourse to blackness and connotations of Third Worldism, these redemptive ethnographies offered a discursive realignment of the region with the subaltern rather than white supremacy. Given the limited distribution and circulation of these documentaries, their ability to actualize this possibility was severely constrained. Also, since these local cultural practices were only articulated as southern through a discursive supplement, that supplement could easily not coalesce, with the redemption graced only to blackness or Cajunness or Appalachianness. When fusion did occur, however, it was not because the region was of the Third World (whether economical, social, cultural, or ethical) but rather as a result of the fusion the two shared presentational space within the United States. The southern supplement accompanying these ethnographic films contributed—albeit in a minor way—to the gradual realignment of the region with blackness as well as whiteness, thereby reconfiguring the presentation of the region to one socially acceptable within public opinion at the time, by framing it as biracial rather than white.

1970s Southeastern Documentaries and Blackness as Presentation of the Region

While a few documentaries about locales within southeastern states appeared during the 1970s that dealt with history or biography, they primarily focused on cultural practices. These cultural expressions fell into three basic categories: (1) humorous depictions of cultural elements previously associated with the region in popular perception, such as grits and kudzu, (2) cultural depictions, especially musical ones, of previously undervalued white subcultures, in particular southwest Louisiana Cajuns and Appalachian Mountain hillbillies, and (3) depictions of black cultural expressions.⁶⁸ While a few documentaries on the history of the civil rights movement were made, the most famous one at the time being *King: A Filmed Record, Montgomery to Memphis* (Ely Landau, 1970), such historically focused documentaries did not begin to proliferate until the late 1980s and early 1990s, when the popularity of these culturally focused documentaries waned. While the documentaries on black cultural expressions and undervalued white subcultural expressions differ in terms of race and locale, they both share a common focus on rural and working-class cultures. The white subcultures of the Appalachian Mountains and Louisiana Cajuns were not discursively tainted with white supremacy at the time. Therefore, they were safe terrain for negotiating an alternative to the association of the region with white supremacy as perpetuated by the media coverage of the civil rights movement the two preceding decades.[69] The presentations of these two types of documentaries complement one another, the former rehabilitating whiteness and the latter incorporating blackness into southern discourse as a defining feature. The stylistic similarities between them in terms of form and performance were unifying, despite the racial difference of the social actors. This correspondence, on the one hand, naturalized the incorporation of blackness as a constitutional component of southern discourse to accompany whiteness; on the other hand, it transmuted the white subcultures as redemptive similarly to blackness. My concern here is with the third category listed, the poaching on blackness by primarily white filmmakers and, whether intentional or not, their contributing to the discursive reconfiguration of the region, cleansing its blemished presentation that resulted from 1950s and 1960s media coverage.

The strategy of using black cultural practices to present the region conflates presentational with representational, blackness presented as representative of the region. Of course, the use of blackness by white people is nothing new. The mass media in the twentieth century is full of such cultural appropriations, of what Susan Douglas calls "racial ventriloquism."[70] The first major feature-length film made in the United States, the blatantly racist *The Birth of Nation*, is full of white actors in blackface, and the most popular show during the network radio era, *Amos 'n' Andy*, featured two white actors mimicking stereotypical black voices. And the film considered the first feature-length talking picture, *The Jazz Singer* (Alan Crosland, 1927), combines blackface and blackvoice in Al Jolson's performance. A long history exists of the appropriation of blackness by whites for their own ends. Yet the use of blackness in these 1970s southeastern documentaries is not as straightforward as in these fictional texts. Although their poaching on rural working-class cultures articulated as black may indirectly re-signify what constitutes as being southern, they also exhibit a respect (and admiration) for those cultures without being, to borrow hooks's expression, cultural tourists.

Racial Poaching, Redemptive Ethnography, and Southeastern Documentaries   147

Tom Johnston and his pigs who pray in Judy Peiser and Bill Ferris's 1978 documentary *Hush Hoggies Hush*. Photograph by William Ferris (William Ferris Collection, Southern Folklife Collection, Wilson Library, University of North Carolina at Chapel Hill).

Bill Ferris with his camera during the 1970s. Photograph by Hester Magnuson (William Ferris Collection, Southern Folklife Collection, Wilson Library, University of North Carolina at Chapel Hill).

The documentaries of Judy Peiser and Bill Ferris, made for the Center for Southern Folklore in Memphis, Tennessee, during this decade, are exemplary in terms of using blackness to present the region as worthy. While nothing in the documentaries per se indicates that they are to be perceived as regional, rather than local, expressions, the organization through which they were produced provides the discursive supplement that articulates these local expressions as regional. Their documentaries, such as *Hush Hoggies Hush: Tom Johnston's Praying Pigs* (1978) and *Bottle Up and Go* (1980), focus primarily, although not exclusively, on black cultural practices in rural Mississippi. *Hush Hoggies Hush* combines two of the categories I mentioned earlier, humor and blackness. In the four-minute documentary, Tom Johnston demonstrates how he has taught his pigs to pray before they eat. Their action appears more the result, however, of conditioned reflexes rather than spiritual piety. The pigs stand frozen in place as Johnston prays holding a stick prominently displayed in his hand, knowing punishment awaits them if they move. But as soon as Johnston says "Amen," they rush to the troth and devour the slop. Although the pro-filmic action is bizarre, even absurd, the filmic presentation contains no element of ridicule. Rather, just as Johnston tells the off-camera filmmaker that it's just "a play thing," so too does the documentary treat his actions as such. The documentary screams for an Althusserian reading using interpellation, in which the religious practice hails the pigs as subjects, or a Foucauldian one using disciplinary power, in which religious practice polices the pigs' behavior, leading to subjectification. But can pigs practice religion? Can pigs be subjects? In his later work, Michel Foucault differentiated between technologies of power and technologies of the self. While the Christian practice of confession informed his formulation of the former, his exploration of early Christian practices of pastoral care contributed to the formulation of the latter. In the documentary, however, the religious practice of prayer is reduced to an instrument of power leading to an external action that connotes piety. *Hush Hoggies Hush* problematizes the issues of interiority and knowledge formation; the behavior of the pigs indicates praying, but listening viewers know a pig cannot understand the human concept of God. Can humans similarly perform practices that they do not comprehend? Does comprehension matter?

While much could be made about the irony of an animal considered in some religions to be unclean performing one of their major ritual acts, the documentary offers little in terms of the articulation of race to religious cultural practices. This matter is made clear if John Thompson's commutation test for analyzing screen acting is applied to it. The test involves the theoretical substitution of one actor for another, followed by observing whether the switch produces a change in meaning, and if so, what kind.[71] Jane Gaines has already applied Thompson's test to race, holding that American race movies of the segregation era that used white Hollywood formulas but with black actors resulted in

> an ensemble effect in which every character alters the meaning not only of the narrative but produces a slight shift in the system of meaning itself so that race movies are always the same but different, and different because they are white-not.... So black casting was not a grammatical change in the individual film text, and neither was it a complete translation into another language as from English to French. And yet it was a semiotic modification that never left the text the same.[72]

Although developed for fictional film, application of the tool can assist in deciphering the racial articulation of culture and thereby racial poaching. Blues, zydeco, Cajun music, and bluegrass (as well as traditional mountain music in general) are all heavily coded racially, the former two with blackness, the latter two with whiteness. As a result, changing the race of the social actors in the documentaries on these musical styles would result in textual incongruence for many audience members.[73] In contrast, in the documentaries focusing on other rural and working-class cultural practices, this is not the case. A switch in the race of the social actors would in many cases not modify the text, which would remain primarily the same. Though most of Peiser and Ferris's short documentaries focus on black subjects, the cultural practices captured therein are often practiced by whites too. For example, *Black Delta Religion* (1973) captures a black religious service and river baptism, but other filmmakers have recorded whites performing in the same style, as in *The High Lonesome Sound: Kentucky Mountain Music* (John Cohen, 1962), made a decade earlier, and *Chase the Devil: Religious Music of the Appalachian Mountains* (Jeremy Marre, 1982), made a decade later. Similarly, in Ferris's solo project, *Made in Mississippi: Black Folk Arts and Crafts* (1975), the quilting and basket-weaving practices displayed in the documentary are also performed by whites. And some cultural practices, such as those captured in *Gravel Springs Fife and Drum* (Judy Peiser and Bill Ferris, 1971), are so unknown that unless the listening viewer is an academic specialist or amateur enthusiast, he or she is unlikely to be familiar with a racial articulation of the particular cultural practice demonstrated. Nothing in *Hush Hoggies Hush* necessitates that the practitioner must be black. No racial incongruence would have occurred if the practice had been performed by a white social actor rather than a black social actor. The cultural practice was racially mutable, indicative of rural and working-class conditions rather than race.

Rather than exploring the African elements that are a part of cultures articulated as white, these predominately white filmmakers routinely poached on cultural practices articulated with blackness as their documentary material. While, on the one hand, they usurp the cultural capital that blackness had acquired in certain circles of the United States during the 1970s (as a result of the civil rights and Black Power movements), on the other hand, they contributed to the discursive incorporate of blackness into the definition of the region. In other words, blackness functioned as a redemptive agent to rearticulate the discursive configuration of the region from synonymous with whiteness to that of biracial by including blackness as southern. Although these white filmmakers poach on blackness, the documentaries are not necessarily examples of racial ventriloquism nor of cultural appropriation (as the term is typically used). Because redemptive ethnographies were not dependent upon black social actors, they also contributed to the fracturing of whiteness through the presentation of various white subaltern cultural expressions that were not articulated with white supremacy.

Conclusion

While some of the cultural expressions captured in these 1970s redemptive ethnographies have strong racial articulations, others were weak due to the prevalence of cultural syncretism. But regardless of whether that racial articulation was strong, weak, or nonexistent, in general the documentaries are mono-racially focused, their filmic separation of racialized bodies naturalizing the racial articulation of the documented cultural expressions. Even the closely related (white) Cajun and (black) zydeco music of southern Louisiana typically appears in separate documentaries. This occurrence is a material manifestation of what Tara McPherson calls lenticular logic. The objective of these documentaries is typically to document specific subcultural practices (and sometimes offer historical contextualization). While their narrow focus resulted in capturing a rich and detailed account of these various subaltern cultures which would not have audiovisually existed otherwise today, they often inadvertently perpetuate cultural non-syncretism. Because of their concern with documenting subcultures in threat of disappearing, acknowledging syncretism would detract from their claims to traditionalism and uniqueness, two features expected at the time to legitimize concern with the disparaged subculture. In addition, through a southern supplement they perpetuate framing the region as composed of two separate races, each with its separate culture, even if a variety of subcultures exists within each one.

While the past two chapters considered the first denial of biraciality, that of bodily and cultural miscegenation, the remaining three chapters ponder the second denial of biraciality, that of other races and ethnicities. These chapters will look specifically at other races and ethnicities beyond the black and white binary of biraciality that currently dominates southern discourse, considering how biraciality functions as a hurdle they must overcome in their pursuit of recognition.

Part III

Biracial Denial Two—Existence of Other Races and Ethnicities

Chapter Five

"Wonder if our culture will survive": Racial In-Betweenness, Cultural Preservation, and the Sound of Ethnicity in *Mosquitoes and High Water*, *Living in America*, and *Nuestra Communidad*

Introduction

Given the dominance of biraciality within southern discourse and the saturation of so many locales with a southern supplement, other races and ethnicities must negotiate this presumption if they desire to establish social recognition outside of its binary structure. The remainder of this book explores the second denial that results from this dominance, the existence of other races and ethnicities in the region. These chapters focus on local sociocultural manifestations of race or ethnicity (which in turn have geopolitical ramifications for those locales) as presented in documentary film. These documentaries contribute to the discursive formation of the region through not a metadiscourse about the region but a southern supplement to the local. Similar to the 1970s redemptive ethnographies that came before them, discussed in the last chapter, these documentaries contain thin southern supplements so are dependant upon extra-textual material for the enunciation of this association. And their limited circulation impeded the emergence of such extratextual material. As a result, their impact on the reconfiguration of southern discourse has been minimal and their ability to actualize a possible South severely curtailed.

Southern discourse tends to frame the region as a site of racial, not ethnic, difference. But expressions of ethnic difference can be found, both in the past and the present, at the level of the local in many southeastern states. This chapter focuses on the issue of white ethnicity through the framework of racial in-betweenness using the documentaries *Mosquitoes and High Water* (Louis Alvarez and Andrew Kolker, 1983), *Living in America: One Hundred Years of Ybor City* (Gayla K. Jamison, 1987), and *Nuestra Communidad: Latinos in North Carolina* (Joanne Hershfield and Penny Simpson, 2001). The documentaries explore three Spanish-speaking communities, respectively: Los Isleños [pronounced ees-lane-yos] of St. Bernard Parish, Louisiana, who entered the United States in the eighteenth century from the Canary Islands of Spain; Ybor City [pronounced EE-bore] of Tampa, Florida, who (except for the Afro-Cubans) entered the United States in the nineteenth century from Spain and Italy; and Latin American immigrants in North Carolina, who recently entered the United States primarily from Mexico (as well as other countries). Their status as Spanish-speaking communities paradoxically raises an issue routinely associated with the region, that of accents. Michel Chion claims that the cinema is vococentric, that "it almost always privileges the voice, highlighting and setting the latter off from other sounds."[1] Although he is referring specifically to fiction film, his assertion is even more relevant for nonfiction film, where talking heads and/or voice-over narration typically dominate. The visual track is often relegated to an illustrative role of the vocal soundtrack. The voice is composed of not only a linguistic element but also nonverbal ones, what researchers call "paralanguage," the non-linguistic qualities of the voice such as rate, pitch, volume, tone, and rhythm. This chapter considers the interplay between race and ethnicity in these three documentaries, along with the issue of cultural preservation (with its slightly different accentuation than the more common frameworks of cultural retention and cultural assimilation). This latter matter will be explored through a discussion of how the aural sound of language functions within the documentaries. In other words, the spoken words in the documentaries relay information not just through the means of oral sounds but aural ones too. These paralanguage elements structure meaning in these documentaries and provide clues as to where each community stands in the process of ethnic cultural preservation as they negotiate the challenge of maintaining ethnic distinction while participating in mainstream society.

Racial In-Betweenness and Cultural Preservation

A common misconception holds that, after the initial wave of immigration that formed the United States, subsequent waves of immigration did not include southeastern states. Yet, at the local level, numerous cases of immigration exist, even if southern discourse marginalizes them. Two well-documented cases are found in Birmingham, Alabama, and Tampa, Florida. In the late 1970s, a local history project, Birmingfind, began in Birmingham to research the histories and cultures of six city neighborhoods and five of the city's oldest ethnic groups "in order to make local residents more aware of

Mosquitoes and High Water, Living in America, and Nuestra Communidad

1981 Birmingfind calendar. Birmingfind was an early-1980s project directed by Jeff Norrell that researched the histories and cultures of various neighborhoods and ethnic groups in Birmingham to make residents more aware of the city's diversity (Tutwiler Collection of Southern History and Literature, Birmingham Public Library).

the cultural diversity and the varieties of historical experience" in the city.[2] The project, directed by Jeff Norrell, resulted in the production of photography exhibits, booklets, and calendars in the early 1980s that documented the Greek, Lebanese, Jewish, black, and Italian communities in the city.[3] Around the same time, two Florida university professors, Gary Mormino and George Pozzetta, studied the Ybor City community in Tampa composed of Spaniards, Italians, and Afro-Cubans, resulting in their 1987 book, *The Immigrant World of Ybor City: Italians and their Latin Neighbors in Tampa, 1885–1985*. Oral histories were integral to both of these projects.

Beginning in the 1880s, both cities needed laborers for the recently opened coal mines in Birmingham and the recently transplanted cigar industry in Tampa. In Tampa, the immigrants followed the settlement pattern of the North and West Coast, establishing a separate community from the Anglo residents that was called Ybor City. In Birmingham, Italian immigrants were spread throughout the surrounding towns, although one particular town, Ensley, developed an area that became known as Little Italy due to its concentration of Italian immigrants. By the 1910s, foreign-born workers accounted for 20 percent of the miner workforce, with half coming from Italy. The community was so large that the Catholic Church assigned an Italian priest to the city.[4] Practicing Catholicism, along with being considered "a little too dark," differentiated the Italian immigrants from other whites in the city.

David Roediger claims that during the first half of the twentieth-century new immigrants from eastern and southern Europe occupied a space of racial in-betweenness in the United States, in-between "hard racism and full inclusion—neither securely white nor nonwhite."[5] In other words, they "often existed between nonwhiteness and full inclusion as whites, not just between black and white."[6] According to Roediger, European immigrants viewed the racial structure of the United States "as a line (or a ladder) with African Americans at the far back (or very bottom)."[7] Whether this racial in-between space was perceived at the time to be biological or cultural is unclear, but after World War II they were fully assimilated into whiteness by building a racial alliance with whites through naturalized citizenship.

Chinese and Italian immigrants entered states such as Mississippi and Alabama in the latter half of the nineteenth century because of the need by plantations for labor. Although one group is a racial minority and the other a white ethnicity, the experiences of the two groups (while not identical) were similar—that of racial in-betweenness. Both groups found plantation work unpleasant and (after a detour through the coal mines for the Italians) they sought better paying, less physically grueling work and stumbled across the same entrepreneurial solution. As will be discussed further in chapter six,

Chinese immigrants in the Mississippi Delta opened grocery stores to service black residents. Italians did the same thing in Birmingham, with both groups becoming "trading minorities."[8] Chinese and Italian immigrants shared two common characteristics. First, they were not accepted into the white community, although they were not black, and second, because they were unfamiliar with local racial customs, they did not harbor prejudice against serving blacks commercially. Chinese in the Mississippi Delta and Italians in Birmingham prospered as small retail grocers catering to the local black clientele. Although one social group is considered a racial category and the other an ethnic category, in these two particular segregated locales they both initially occupied the same in-between social space that allowed them to exploit an economic vacuum caused by lack of black capital, white violence toward black economic success, and distaste by whites for serving blacks, regardless of the financial reward. This issue raises the question: How does one differentiate between race and ethnicity?

Michael Banton, in his overview book *Racial Theories*, succinctly recaps how researchers often distinguished between the concepts of race and ethnicity. His summary contains three key components: (1) race is used to refer to physical difference while ethnicity to a shared culture; (2) race is derived from an objective assessment by an outside observer while ethnicity is a subjective response by voluntary self-identification; and (3) race is used to exclude people within society while ethnicity is used to create an inclusive group.[9] Although white ethnicities, such as Italian Americans, Irish Americans, etc., are those most often discussed in the United States, all races have ethnic differences. Although whites and blacks in Mobile County, Alabama, view the Southeast Asians in Bayou La Batre as one social group (Asian American), they actually consist of three different ethnic groups (Laotians, Vietnamese, and Cambodians) that affect their internal politics as a racial group.[10] Of course, the inverse is also true—an ethnic group can have racial differences within it. The most common example of the latter is Latinos, treated by the United States census as an ethnicity and breaks the category down along racial lines of black, white, etc. As discussed in chapter four, race is articulated through culture as well as the body so it cannot be so easily separated from ethnicity by invoking a body/culture split. Similarly, ethnic groups also have been identified based on physiology for exclusion from the mainstream, as Italians upon arrival to Birmingham discovered. And some Latinos claim a brown race that is neither black nor white, as well as an ethnic Hispanic culture.

Because biraciality is configured within southern discourse as black and white, the cultural expressions articulated racially to them are also framed as black and white rather than African American and European American, respectively. During the first half of the twentieth century, Chinese and Italian immigrants were positioned similarly because both groups were viewed as practicing different cultures from those articulated with blackness and whiteness, with their cultural difference including a linguistic component too. As the twentieth century progressed, subsequent generations of Italian Americans in Birmingham eventually integrated into the life of the local white community. Because of their higher income status, the Chinese Americans in the Mississippi Delta sent their children away to college, which often led to them entering other professions and therefore migrating out of the region. David Roediger's concept of in-betweenness applies to both Asian Americans and Italian Americans in these two particular locales prior to World War II because race was conceived through the narrow lens of black and white, not European and African decent. Yet, despite their numerous similarities, the experiences of these two groups after that war differed significantly. Unlike Italian Americans (who became white), assimilation for Asian Americans (as well as Native Americans) could only progress to white social acceptance, not whiteness itself. Because whiteness was not an option for eliminating their position of in-betweenness, it persists today. Chapter six focuses on the negotiation of this conundrum by Chinese Americans, while chapter seven does so for Native Americans.

Because the three communities captured in *Mosquitoes and High Water*, *Living in America*, and *Nuestra Communidad* speak predominately Spanish and perform cultural practices that lack a southern supplement, they are perceived as ethnic rather than regional. As with the redemptive ethnographic films discussed in the last chapter, the practices captured in these documentaries fall within the purview of folk, rather than popular, culture, although that does not prevent those associated with the two older communities from being commercialized for tourism, typically as an intentional strategy for survival through recourse to preservational discourses and structures. The three groups chronicled in these documentaries are threatened with cultural loss not through the mainstreaming of their practices (as is routinely confronted by blacks and gays and lesbians today), but through insufficient cultural reproduction to the next generation, which these three documentaries show to be a concern common to the new group as well as to the two older groups.[11] For example, in *Mosquitoes and High Water*, about a long-standing Spanish-speaking community, the narrator confesses: "With the changes coming to St. Bernard, we're trying to recall our Spanish heritage before it's too late." Similarly, in *Nuestra Communidad*, about a new Spanish-speaking group, Lidia Johnson comments: "We don't want to forget our cultural traditions. So as our children grow up here they learn about our culture and traditions, we ensure that these traditions are not lost over time by continuing to celebrate them." While the new Spanish-speaking group is in all likelihood unaware of the long-standing one, its members are mindful that their fate may be the same regarding the cultural reproduction of their ethnic distinctiveness.

Such concerns about cultural loss are typically framed through the concepts of acculturation and assimilation; the latter has traditionally been defined as a process where "ethnic minorities shed themselves of all that makes them distinctive and become carbon copies of the ethnic majority." Recognizing that "American society is far from homogenous" and that "immigrant ethnicity has affected American society as much as American society has affected it," Richard Alba shifts the emphasis of this definition from the "endpoint, the disappearance," to the process itself, "the decline ... of an ethnic distinction and its allied differences."[12] While not explicitly stated, his definition conceives of assimilation as an *ongoing negotiation*, which could potentially result in cultural annihilation but that "does not require the absolute extinction of ethnic difference."[13] Alba conceives of assimilation "as changes in two (or more) groups ... [that] shrink the differences and social distance between them."[14] Maintaining ethnic distinction and participation in the mainstream does not have to be an either/or proposition, even if it operates on a sliding scale, but rather, because it is a negotiation, the resolution can assume numerous forms, although one typically held in perpetual tension of reformulation. In other words, while the interaction between the two contains the risk of obliterating ethnic distinction or turning it into what Herbert Gans calls "symbolic ethnicity," the two can also be compartmentalized as well as integrated.[15] In addition, the difference between two groups can be reduced not just by a subculture shedding portions of its difference from the mainstream but the mainstream incorporating portions of that subculture's difference as a part of itself. In other words, "the expansion of the mainstream culture to include elements of the minority culture ... reduces the apparent differences between the two sides."[16] (The question arises, however, of whether such a framework has moved so far beyond the terrain of cultural assimilation, as it is typically theorized, as to become another concept.) In terms of the three communities chronicled in these three documentaries, such a perspective means that while the elimination of Spanish is not required for participation in mainstream American culture, a proficiency in English is. While the acquisition of English does not necessitate the eradication of Spanish, this situation does place it in a subordinate position. While the concept of assimilation emphasizes the deterioration (and eventual loss) of ethnic distinction, the concept of ethnic retention (referred to as pluralism in sociology literature) emphasizes the continuation of that distinction, even if only at the level of social ties. To accentuate the ongoing struggle to maintain cultural difference within a context of social incorporation, I approach the matter from the more narrow perspective of cultural preservation. For a new group, such as the Latin American immigrants in North Carolina who are just beginning that process, the struggle is with determining the cultural practices worthy of preservation; for an older group, such as Los Isleños and Ybor City, the struggle is with preventing the cultural vestiges remaining of annihilation. Although not necessarily the intended subject of these documentaries, their depiction of the interaction between the dominance of English and the marginalization of Spanish within the United States speaks to this issue. I examine the documentaries in relationship to the aural though a consideration of the broader issue of cultural preservation of ethnic distinction along with that of the blurriness of the distinction between race and ethnicity that they inadvertently raise at times.

Mosquitoes and High Water

The documentaries made by Louis Alvarez and Andrew Kolker during the 1980s for their Center for New American Media focused on cultures not typically associated with the region because of the hegemony of biraciality within southern discourse that contributes to the racial articulation of culture as black and white. A decade before the popularity of multiculturalism, the documentaries of Alvarez and Kolker captured such cultural complexities, primarily in southern Louisiana. Their 1980s films include *The Ends of the Earth* (1982), *Mosquitoes and High Water* (1983), *Yeah You Rite! The Way They Talk in New Orleans* (1985), and *American Tongues* (1987). The last two center on the issue of language as an expression of culture. While *American Tongues* explores the diversity of language usage and dialects in the United States, *Yeah You Rite!* does the same thing for the city of New Orleans. The documentary portrays a linguistically rich city as a result of the diverse racial and ethnic groups residing there. After viewing it one quickly realizes that to speak of *a* New Orleans accent is reductive because no single way of speaking exists. *Yeah You Rite!* stands as a reminder that while cities are sociopolitical entities, they are also discursive ones that homogenize certain elements of the neighborhoods that constitute them. Many of the ethnic dialects presented in the documentary are not associated with New Orleans in the popular perception constructed through tourism and the national news media. Although the documentary centers on racial and ethnic diversity as manifested linguistically at the neighborhood level, it firmly situates that diversity in relationship to class.

Irvan Perez, an onscreen interviewee and the voice-over narrator in Louis Alvarez and Andrew Kolker's 1983 documentary *Mosquitoes and High Water*. Perez championed the preservation of Los Isleños culture, performing décimas at numerous folk festivals during his lifetime. Photograph courtesy of the Center for New American Media.

Louis Alvarez and Andrew Kolker filming for *Mosquitoes and High Water*. The Isleños had been fishers, hunters, and fur trappers, remaining relatively isolated in St. Bernard Parish, Louisiana, until the 1920s. Photograph courtesy of the Center for New American Media.

In terms of white ethnicities, *Mosquitoes and High Water* focuses on one of the least known groups in the United States: Los Isleños—the Islanders—who reside in St. Bernard Parish outside of New Orleans.[17] As a voice sings in Spanish, script in English scrolls up the screen: "They are descendants of Spaniards and Canary Islanders who came to the New World 200 years ago." What we are not told is that after France ceded Louisiana to Spain and Britain in 1766, Spain was fearful of an attack by the British against this new territory in an attempt to acquire a base for eventually attacking Mexico. In response, between 1778 and 1783 Spain sent thousands of immigrants to the area from its Canary Islands colony to develop it, thereby creating a buffer zone between the British territory and Mexico. The Isleños began as farmers on land granted by the Spanish government. They initially provided produce to the city of New Orleans but then turned to fishing, fur trapping, and hunting, and remained relatively isolated until the 1920s. Although for centuries they spoke an archaic dialect of Spanish and therefore are Hispanic, they do not define themselves as Latino as the term is commonly used in the United States. They fit the older definition for Creole, before the term became popularly associated with being mixed raced. The term formerly meant Spanish or French people who were born in the Americas rather than their homeland. The last words of the documentary, appearing before the credits and sung in Spanish by Irvan Perez (both an on-screen interviewee and voice-over narrator), convey just such a perspective: "With pain and torment and the help of God, in the towns on the coast in the parish of St. Bernard, long live Spain and her flag. With all our hearts we're Americans; but we have Spanish blood."[18] Rather than viewing American and Spanish as mutually exclusive categories, which one much be chosen over the other, they embrace both.

Although *Mosquitoes and High Water* provides a little bit of historical background, its primary focus is on the situation of Los Isleños when the documentary was made, 1983, considering their current way of life and cultural expressions. The interviewees are primarily elderly because a key argument is that the local culture of the Los Isleños is under threat due to factors such as young people not learning the language, locals moving away to find work, weekenders from the city—called "chivos" by Los Isleños—encroaching on the area as a resort, and commercial development of the area. While interviews are in Spanish, toward the end of the documentary, when it switches to the question of the continuance of Los Isleños as an ethnic group because of the disappearance of signifiers of their ethnic distinction, some interviewees speak English to aurally emphasize the replacement of Spanish with English. Although the documentary considers such elements of their social life as fishing and fur trapping, its main focus is on the cultural practice of the decima, a ten-stanza song they brought with them from the Canary Islands. The Spanish-speaking narrator informs us: "When something usually happened in St. Bernard or if someone needed to be taken down a few notches, they'd make a decima about it." Decimas are a form of oral tradition because earlier generations were illiterate. Performances of decimas are included throughout the documentary. Like the salvage impulse of redemptive ethnographies, the narrator informs us: "Few people remember decimas any more or the people who wrote them." It is an oral cultural practice that is dying out, which the aural structure of the documentary emphasizes. The film's form and content work in harmony. Just as its primary focus is on an aural cultural practice, sound is similarly structured to relay meaning beyond the linguistic component. The first decima sung in the documentary is one about Los Isleños coming to America. Subtitles provide its English translation: "In 1777 some families left the Canary Islands bound for Cuba and southern Louisiana. In south Louisiana on land given to them, they became farmers to support their families." At the end of the documentary, words from the decima lyrics reappear in the spoken narration, its English translation provided again by subtitles: "In 1777 our ancestors came from the Canary Islands. They brought with them many customs and traditions. For 200 years these customs flourished with us. Today, as our children leave to make new lives in the city, we who stay behind wonder if our culture will survive." After the first sentence, barely audible under the words, a song is heard, a reminder that what would have been a sung decima in the past has today become spoken words due to the fact that young people are not learning this musical tradition. The audio track is constructed to emphasize lost aural culture, which is the focus of the documentary as indicated by its concern with, first, sung songs—the decima—and, second, spoken language—Spanish. As noted earlier, ethnicity is often differentiated from race by it being a voluntarily shared culture. Although Los Isleños appear to confirm this definition, the decima lyrics quoted earlier frames their affiliation as one of "Spanish blood" as well as culture. But unlike nonwhite racial groups, as the twentieth century progressed they were accepted as white.

Arising from concern that their heritage was disappearing, in 1980 a Museo de los Isleños was established to preserve it. Subsequently, as the museum grew into a complex, its name was changed to the Los Isleños Heritage and Multi-Cultural Park in an attempt to recognize the diverse cultural groups in the area with whom they historically interacted, including French (Cajuns), Germans, Filipinos, and Native Americans (Houma).[19] Although heritage tourism is about economic development, it is also about preserving history. But unlike the civil rights heritage tourism discussed in chapter one, with its dedication to memorializing history and remembering the past, here heritage tourism is being used as a mechanism for maintaining (not remembering) ethnic distinction amidst an accelerating acculturation that is perceived to threaten it with annihilation. Prior to the landmark 1954 *Brown v. Board of Education* case that outlawed segregated education, some Native American communities that were not recognized by the federal government obtained the right from some states—such as the Poarch Creeks in Alabama and the Lumbees in North Carolina—to operate their own separate elementary schools. Such schools functioned as material signifiers for the surrounding neighbors that the group was not black or white but Indian. Such signifiers of Indianness were important because, as will be discussed further in chapter seven, these groups were typically indistinguishable from their black and white neighbors in terms of language and culture. The Los Isleños Heritage and Multi-Cultural Park can also be viewed as a similar material signifier. But, in this particular case, the institution functions as a means to maintain group awareness through institutionalizing the formation of collective memory and the propagation of cultural expressions as those differences diminish in the everyday. Los Isleños in St. Bernard Parish, Louisiana, are not the only Spanish-speaking community with a long history in a southeastern state. Ybor City in Tampa, Florida, which I consider in the next section, is another such community—although they have not fared as well.

Living In America: One Hundred Years of Ybor City

Like Italians in Birmingham, the ethnic residents of Ybor City also dissipated in the decades after World War II, although for different reasons. Union organizing and mechanization led to the decline of the cigar industry in Tampa, which, combined with the dispersal effects of World War II, suburbanization, and urban renewal, resulted in the deterioration of Ybor City.[20] *Living in America: One Hundred Years of Ybor City* recounts the neighborhood's history of Spaniards, Italians, and Afro-Cubans. The filmmaker's grandparents lived in Ybor City, and Gayla Jamison uses her childhood memories of the neighborhood as a starting point to explore its history, from thriving ethnic community to urban blight (although, subsequent to her documentary, this situation changed). Stylistically the documentary is typical of the period in which it was made. It combines contemporary footage with old photographs. History documentaries typically also include archival audiovisual material but *Living in America* contains no such footage, an indicator of the general indifference toward the community by the rest of society as of the date of her film. In addition to old buildings and elderly people, the other physical remainder of Ybor City's past is the cigar boxes from the various brands made in Tampa. Instead of archival audiovisual material, the audience is proffered images of three-dimensional commercial products with insignias of the businesses that made them, a fitting tribute given Ybor City's past history as "the fine cigar capital of the world." The documentary briefly touches on numerous issues related to the neighborhood, including racism against black Cubans, the practice of socialized medicine through mutual aid societies, promotion of ethnic affiliation and culture through clubs, Anglo-Tampa prejudice against Ybor residents, labor organizing and strikes, and the harmful effects of urban renewal. The issues are so complex and the material so rich that in such a short time period—less than an hour—they can only be skimmed. Nonetheless, Jamison presents a concise overview.

The documentary differentiates between race and ethnicity in that black Cubans experienced explicit racism in comparison to the Spaniards and Italians. As a result, many left Tampa for New York City and the North, although at the time Jamison was making the documentary in the mid-1980s, some were beginning to return because the racial situation that initially led to their flight was finally changing. Although such "hard racism" was not experienced by the Spanish Americans and Italian Americans, the film highlights two of the issues mentioned earlier related to white ethnicity—first, the in-between position of white ethnicities and, second, that ethnicity contains a bodily component as well as a cultural one. Both of these issues emerge in the comments made by Judith Villavisanis, an artist who at the time had recently returned to Tampa. She informs us that she never really thought much about her heritage until she went to a public junior high school. She muses: "That's when I started feeling a little bit strange about my heritage and was ashamed of it—the fact that my mom had an accent and the fact that people would come up to me and say things like 'Oh yeah, you're Spanish because you have a darker olive skin complexion.'" She shares a story from the early 1960s about visiting a friend who told her that she had to leave before her parents came home because she was not allowed to have any "Spanish friends in the house." As the comment highlights, Spanish Americans were not treated as completely white. Although it was acceptable to have a Spanish American friend, it was not acceptable to have such a friend in the house. The hard racism of total rejection that blacks experienced does not occur, but neither does the full acceptance that someone considered white would experience, hence an in-between social status. Villavisanis's comment indicates how ethnicity was perceived to have a bodily component too. She was singled out as different not just because of cultural elements, but because of her skin complexion—in

Gayla Jamison and crew filming cigar workers in a factory for her 1987 documentary *Living in America*. At the beginning of the twentieth century, handmade cigars were an economic mainstay of Tampa, Florida, with most workers residing in the Ybor City neighborhood. Photograph courtesy of Gayla K. Jamison, Lightfoot Films, Inc.

other words, the physical appearance of the body, a domain typically associated with race. Ethnicity cannot be easily separated from race by a culture versus body split. Culture and the body are both articulated with race and ethnicity. But the one way they do differ is that while ethnicity in America is socially mutable, race typically is not (although historically some individuals have changed their race by moving to a new location where their family is not known).

I am focusing on the last part of *Living in America* because, although the documentary is a history, it charts that history up to the mid-1980s, when Jamison made the film. Like 1970s redemptive ethnographies, when the documentary moves to the present, it focuses on cultural practices—in this particular case dancing, baking bread, and brewing coffee. The final section focuses on two issues: first, the continuance in the neighborhood of cultural remnants from the past that are unique to Ybor City and, second, the new trend of artists moving into the neighborhood. The opening sequence of the documentary includes brief shots of dancers in a studio performing a Spanish dance, workers in a bakery kneading bread dough, and coffee and milk being simultaneously poured into a diner coffee cup. The shots of the last two

Filming interviewees Juan and Evelia Mallea for *Living in America*. Because of the discrimination that existed against Afro-Cubans, Juan and Evelia left Tampa in the 1930s for New York City but had recently moved back. Photograph courtesy of Gayla K. Jamison, Lightfoot Films, Inc.

cultural practices are references to the "Cuban sandwich" and "Cuban coffee" of Ybor City, which the final section of the documentary considers in detail, arguing that the names are a misnomer because they are a product of the unique history of Ybor City. When the owner of the Silver Ring Sandwich Shop is interviewed about his Cuban sandwich, he notes that it does not taste like one from Cuba because of the bread, a difference he attributes to either water quality or cooking technique. We are then shown workers making bread at Segunda Central Bakery, implying they supply Silver Ring. Similarly, when the owner of Naviera Coffee Mill is interviewed about his Cuban coffee, he relays a history explaining why it is not really Cuban coffee—even though the locals call it such. He informs us that because the Spaniard and Italian immigrants were from Europe, they preferred their coffee dark, more like espresso, than the lighter roasted coffee of Latin American countries. In addition, because the residents of Ybor City were working class they had to be frugal, and darker roasted and more finely ground coffee allowed them to stretch a pot of coffee further. Although Ybor City is today touted in local boosterism literature as the "Tampa Latin Quarter," the documentary specifically positions the community as developing its own cultural expressions as a result of the unique combination of immigrants that settled in the neighborhood. The sandwich and coffee produced in the neighborhood may be called "Cuban" but they are really "Yborian." The opening voice-over informs us: "Most of Ybor City exists now only in the memories of the people who lived here and in their stories." One might also add that Ybor City also continues to exist in the commercial cultural products of bread and coffee, which are lingering traces in the present of a once-vibrant community life.

While on the surface the section of the documentary on the present (the 1980s) appears to be salvage ethnography, it presents a local community that does not conform to what is typically associated with the region within southern discourse at the time. But *Living in America* never enunciates an explicit connection to the region itself, a feature common to all three of the documentaries discussed in this chapter. When mention of "here" occurs in the documentary, the reference is to the local, Ybor City, not the regional. Yet, ironically, while linguistic references to "the South" are absent, remarks about "the North" are not. Twice Ybor City is positioned in relationship to the North, a reference not to upstate Florida (or the panhandle) but "the North" as the complement to "the South." Besides its appearance as the unspoken inverse of "the North," only one other reference discursively connects Ybor City to the regional. That connection is also indirect, a mention of Jim Crow laws in relationship to Afro-Cuban residents who moved to New York City to escape them. As the discussion of Michael Omi and Howard Winant in chapter two highlighted, the phrase "Jim Crow" connotes "the South." Because the documentary contains a thin southern supplement, it does not transform the ethnic community it captures into an expression of the region—and neither did the extra-textual material accompanying its distribution and exhibition.

Nuestra Communidad: Latinos in North Carolina

Both of the documentaries discussed above focus on Spanish-speaking communities with a long history in a particular locale of a southeastern state. In comparison, *Nuestra Communidad: Latinos in North Carolina* considers a recently arrived Spanish-language group within a much broader area than a local community, that of a particular state. This group is not culturally unified but rather includes a variety of national cultures (although Mexican tends to dominate), a position most succinctly asserted in the documentary by Maria Ines Robayo who comments: "As Latinos, many of us are not familiar with the traditions of the Costa Ricans, or the Mexicans don't always know about the customs from Ecuador or what Chileans or Colombians do, or vise versa." As with the other two documentaries, however, *Nuestra Communidad* does construct them as a coherent group in terms of their social positioning within North Carolina through an appeal to a pan-ethnicity grounded in speaking Spanish.[21] Although Spanish-language communities may be a relatively recent phenomenon in North Carolina, as the other two documentaries demonstrate, it is not to states along the Gulf Coast.

Nuestra Communidad explicitly frames Latinos in North Carolina as an ethnicity. For example, after images of an INS citizenship ceremony, Ivan Parra, the director of El Centro Hispano, shares in Spanish: "There's a great myth that people have come here only for a short time and then they will leave.... It's like any community, or any ethnic group. There are always people who will come and go but I think the majority of us are here to stay." As mentioned previously, ethnicity is not de facto a subset of race but rather can traverse numerous races. If these new Spanish-language immigrants are an ethnicity, then the question arises: what is their race? When addressing this question the documentary relies not on the perceptions of the group's neighbors but rather its leaders and supporters. It adopts an active role in constructing the race of these new Spanish-language immigrants before others have a chance to do it for them and, in that undertaking, assumes biraciality. In other words, brown is not an option so therefore they must align as either black or white. The activists captured in the documentary position the Latino ethnicity as a white one. Joel Najar, of the National Council of La Raza, asserts:

> When we last saw a giant wave of immigration at the turn of the century, we had Poles, Russians, Italians, Jews from southern Europe and Irish coming-in in great numbers. And there was the same kind of responses. In fact, Benjamin Franklin had called the German Americans stupid, that they would never be able to adjust to life in the United States and he said they would never learn English. These are the same arguments we're hearing today. And yet Irish Americans, Polish Americans, German Americans are all considered part of mainstream white America.

Najar is one of the few Latino interviewees to respond in English. His rebuttal to the criticism regarding language as a barrier to full citizenship is performed both aurally and linguistically. Not only does he speak in English, thereby being an aural repudiation of the cultural and linguistic arguments against immigrants, but he speaks without a trace of an accent, neither one aurally associated with Latin American countries nor one aurally associated with areas of the southeastern states. Toward the end of the documentary, Father John Heffernan raises the issue of European immigrants again, but as a member of a white ethnicity. He declares in English: "From time to time, I try to point out to people my own ancestral experience of coming to this country, of Irish who came during the potato famine and their experience in New York and then the Italians who came at the turn of this century. There was always a similarity and there's always a transformation." Rather than allow language to separate Latin American immigrants as different from other Americans, the documentary uses it to construct a shared history with earlier European immigrants. In other words, these new immigrants are the same as the whites who now inhabit the country and whose ancestors spoke a language other than English, such as German or Italian.

This position is reinforced with coverage of an anti-immigration rally at Silver City held by David Duke and the Ku Klux Klan, which is framed as being about immigration, not race, as indicated by one of the few anti-immigration signs shown in the documentary from the rally, which states: "The Melting Pot Is Boiling Over." The sign references terminology that became popular at the beginning of the twentieth century, when a significant increase in European immigrants occurred. In contrast, among the counter-protestors, a small group of University of North Carolina students are briefly seen carrying signs with slogans such as "UNC Students & Silver City United against Racism." The student activists perceive the rally as using the cover of anti-immigration to advocate an anti-Latino position, an action that they label as racist. Of course, their position assumes that Latinos are a nonwhite race and not a white ethnicity as the documentary enunciates. To raise the issue of racism (as opposed to that of race) would invite comparison to African Americans and their long struggle for equality within the United States, a comparison that occurs only once in the documentary when a Latino storeowner is interviewed about the rally. He states: "What I see is that the demonstrators don't care for Hispanics or for Jews or African Americans. They are in the minority because in Silver City the people don't want to harm the Hispanics. I think they are happy to see them working here and they admire their work ethic." Ignoring the allusion to discrimination as a personal prejudice rather than part of societal structures, the comparison leaves open the question of whether Latinos are similar to Jews, and therefore are a white ethnicity, or similar to African Americans, and therefore are a nonwhite race. Other than these few fleeting moments, the possibility that Latinos may be racially perceived as other than white is avoided in the documentary. Dispersed throughout are scenes of diverse cultural events from Latin America ranging from religious processionals to community festivals, displaying food, music, dance, and clothing different from those typically associated with blacks and whites in the state. Although these cultural events are from an array of Hispanic cultures, within the rhetoric of the documentary they become unified as Latino. The documentary assumes a cultural logic beyond black and white while simultaneously operating from a racial logic that does not.

Unlike *Mosquitoes and High Water* and *Living in America*, which dedicate a significant portion of their screen time to a social history of the particular local community and an exploration of its cultural practices that continue into the present, *Nuestra Communidad* focuses primarily on economic, political, and social issues confronted by Latin American immigrants in the state of North Carolina at the time of its production, cultural manifestations typically thrown in as visual wallpaper to break up the monotony of the talking heads (although they also serve to reinforce the contention that Latinos are a different ethnicity based on culture rather than race). While all three documentaries display an attitude of support for the community they capture and rely heavily on community leaders as their informants, *Nuestra Communidad* lacks the overall ethnographic impulse that informs the other two. As a result, the viewer walks away with not so much an audiovisual sense of the life of the community as with its professional management. The inclusion of professional civil rights activists and representatives of social service organization providers, instead of enriching the presentation of the social group, results in the categorization of them as a social problem that needs solving rather than a dynamic group negotiating a new lived environment. Consequently, the documentary captures the political strategy used by those professionals to advance the acceptance of Latin American immigrants into the life of the state rather than the group's self-understanding in this particular historical situation. This strategy is a continuance of the one that emerged with the appearance of Mexican American civil rights organizations in the 1930s. Neil Foley, in his history of such organizing, argues that for many Mexican Americans it was "not the color line per se that was the problem in American life and culture" but rather "the way in which they were consigned to the nonwhite side of the line." As a result, "Mexican American civil rights organizations sought to expand the civil rights of Mexicans by expanding the boundaries of whiteness to include, to use their own phrasing, 'the Spanish speaking people.'"[22] The documentary continues this tradition, with its alignment of immigrants from Latin America as being similar to earlier immigrants from Europe, with the implied corollary that both are white. The documentary enunciates this racialization both linguistically and visually. For example, the non-Latin community organizers, social workers, governmental representatives, and other parties interviewed in the documentary are white, except for the brief appearance of a school teacher and an artist, both of whom are black. The latter two are not presented in an official talking-head fashion similar to the stream of Latinos and whites who are interviewed nor are they identified with a subtitle that identifies them by name and profession. As a result, the visual presentation structurally aligns Latinos and whites not only through numerical quantity but visual presentation, neither characteristic which is shared in the documentary with blacks. The issue of the color line is not even raised in the documentary, much less challenged; rather, it rhetorically operates out of a biracial logic of black and white that assumes Latinos in North Carolina are a white ethnicity. If this is the case, then they bypassed the stage between white and nonwhite that David Roediger argues other white ethnicities experienced before achieving "full inclusion as white" in the United States.

While the documentary acknowledges that Latin American immigrants are culturally diverse, it never admits what is visually present on the screen: that they are also physically diverse, some indistinguishable from the local whites, others with very different skin tones and facial phenotypes. The racial ambiguity that surrounds many Latin American immigrants in the state of North Carolina is vanquished from consideration. And the documentary's enunciation of Latinos as white stands in sharp contrast to the social science research that is emerging on how Latinos perceive themselves racially within North Carolina. For example, when Helen Marrow looked at two counties in eastern North Carolina, she found that while the black/white racial binary continues to dominate, Latinos have not been incorporated as white but rather "operate within a 'nonblack' zone that exhibits greater overall distance from blackness than from whiteness."[23] In other words, they perceive themselves as a racialized ethnicity beyond the black/white binary that the biracial southern supplement to local structures necessitates that they discursively navigate. Numerous scholars have argued that as we enter the twenty-first century, the traditional black/white color line is being reconfigured as a result of changed immigration patterns and increased interracial marriages. Whether they conceive of the result as a biracial dual system with a provisional group awaiting allotment or a tri-racial hierarchical system with a permanent intermediary racial group, the consensus is that the distinction between black and nonblack, rather than between black and white, will become the determining factor within race. Because the documentary constructs Latinos as a white ethnicity instead of a racially ambiguous intermediary group, no need exists to differentiate them as nonblack. To acknowledge that Latinos in the state may be brown rather than black or white would necessitate a negotiation of this emergent differentiation between black and nonblack. In spite of how race is enunciated in the documentary, only time will tell whether Latinos in North Carolina are racially incorporated into the state's citizenry as a white ethnicity or as a brown race beyond black and white.

Conclusion

While an explicit concern about the issue of cultural preservation is expressed linguistically in all three of these documentaries, the concern also finds non-linguistic textual enunciation through the display of particular types of bodies or spaces in conjunction with environmental sounds and/or subtitles. In *Mosquitoes and High Water*, the narrator and nearly all of the interviewees speak in Spanish, with their words translated into English through subtitles printed at the bottom of the screen. As the narrator speaks toward the beginning of the documentary, the subtitles translate "our way of life is changing; our kids don't speak Spanish," and then, later on, "[t]he younger Isleños don't speak Spanish; in one more generation no Spanish will be spoken here." The audiovisual presentation reinforces these words; the space of the screen is occupied primarily by elderly subjects whose aging bodies signify the culture dying—no young people are visibly seen to signal that it will continue. And the presence of English subtitles at the bottom of the screen signifies that the linguistic performance that we aurally hear is not the norm and therefore must be translated in order for most viewers to comprehend it. As a result, the spoken Spanish functions for these members of the audience not linguistically but aurally, with the quality and texture of the sound signifying cultural difference instead of relaying knowledge verbally. The Spanish spoken by Los Isleños is an arcane dialect unique to this particular community due to its physical isolation and thus can only be perpetuated by members from this single community.[24] In *Mosquitoes*, preservation is presented as dependent on the presence of young people; their absence from the screen signals the dire situation of Los Isleños.

Just as *Mosquitoes and High Water* presents Los Isleños as concerned about preservation, *Living in America* presents residents of Ybor City (past and present as well as descendants) sharing the same concerns. But while the former documentary uses aging bodies to visually signify a community in decline, the latter uses aging buildings (and the presence of their absence, vacant lots) for that purpose. These visuals mesh with how the problem of decline is framed in each documentary, through language attrition in the former, geographical dispersal in the latter. In other words, cultural reproduction is failing because bodily skills involving the larynx are not being transmitted in the former case and corporal spaces involving land in the latter case. As a result of the dispersal of the residents of Ybor City, the syncretistic cultural expressions that emerged from that particular combination of ethnic groups—Spaniards, Italians, and Afro-Cubans—sharing the same neighborhood are at risk of disappearing. Especially at risk of disappearing are cultural expressions related to food, like the coffee and the sandwich. Unlike *Mosquitoes and High Water*, all of the spoken narration and interviews in *Living in America* are in English. But a constant stream of Spanish saturates the environmental sound of the social clubs, bodegas, and restaurants captured in the documentary where elderly people in the background are casually heard speaking to one another in Spanish. While the loss of cultural expressions is associated with the death of the older generation in both documentaries, *Living in America* aligns such loss with spatiality—that is, the loss of the physical locale of the neighborhood itself. Both of these communities are the result of a reterritorialization that occurred after an earlier deterritorialization as a result of migration, with that reterritorialization re-linking the now-altered culture to the new place, over time naturalizing it as simultaneously foreign and indigenous.[25] Ybor City is a reminder that territory *does* still matter, that sometimes cultural expressions are embedded in particular social relations facilitated through particular geographical configurations of space and that their detachment (i.e., deterritorialization) is an act of destruction that, instead of leading to the production of something new through reterritorialization, just leads to demise. In *Living in America*, preservation is presented as hinging on the persistence of a particular space, not a particular form of language; the absence of livable housing on the screen signals the dire situation of Ybor City.

These two documentaries capture communities confronting the possibility of extinction due to a failure of reproduction, their futures unclear at the time the documentaries were made in the 1980s. Subsequent to the filming of *Mosquitoes and High Water*, the threat of language loss for Los Isleños escalated in the wake of Hurricane Katrina in 2005 as the community was physically scattered as a result of the extensive damage wreaked to St. Bernard Parish. As a result, today Los Isleños also confronts the key problem facing Ybor City in the 1980s: spatial dispersal impeding cultural reproduction. In contrast, subsequent to the filming of *Living in America*, Ybor City became a trendy entertainment district, fulfilling the prophecy of artist Richard Sorrentino, interviewed in the documentary, who noted that, after artists rehabilitate old spaces and make them chic, the real estate investors descend, resulting in the area becoming too expensive for them.[26] The 2004 song "Killer Parties" by the Hold Steady references Ybor City as one of the sites where the singer attends a killer party. Gayla Jamison's timing was fortuitous for she caught a neighborhood in decline just before gentrification. Urban planning was one of the factors contributing to the neighborhood's destruction, as well as the shape its revitalization assumed—that of economic development via heritage tourism.

This rejuvenation of the buildings physically saved the neighborhood but not the existence of the community intricately tied to that space.

As noted above, *Nuestra Communidad* differs from the other two documentaries in that it focuses on a newly arrived Spanish-speaking group, in this particular case within certain locales of North Carolina. (Of course, the arrival of Spanish-speaking immigrants is not a region- or statewide phenomenon but a trans-local one, restricted to specific municipalities and counties, although at times state legislations have intervened with statewide policies meant to impact the immigrants in such locales within their state.) The documentary audiovisually signifies their status as a new group by, in contrast to the other two documentaries, including written subtitles on the screen to translate the spoken English into Spanish as well as the expected spoken Spanish into English. This visual presence indicates a potential audience that is not uniformly fluent in English, the reason why, of course, being because some of them are new to the country. Being new, the group aspires to learn English so that they can function in their new environment in a way that is economically advantageous; the matter is stressed numerous times throughout the documentary as interviewees mention wanting their children to learn English. The documentary even includes a section devoted to English-language classes. Cultural preservation emerges within the documentary, as indicated by Lidia Johnson's comment quoted earlier, as a problem of not the loss of language but the loss of cultural practices. As enunciated in the documentary, the group conceives of cultural assimilation as not an either/or proposition but a both/and proposition, a negotiation between how much of the new culture to embrace and how much of the old culture to retain. The simultaneous presence of the two is not incongruent. In other words, cultural assimilation is framed not as the operation of impersonal social forces but as a process of collusion. While some viewers may perceive this position as wishful thinking, it demonstrates a self-awareness of the social dynamics at work and an attempt at agency within the terrain of the cultural even if such agency may be lacking within the realm of the social.

These three documentaries are a reminder that a diverse array of local ethnic and racial manifestations can be found scattered across the landmass of southeastern states and that the local does not always conform to the prevailing discursive construction of the regional—in this case, as biracial, black and white. Because the region is not an aggregate of the locales within some physical geographical area but a discursive practice that forms an object of knowledge, the local can easily be ignored. But the local offers a reservoir of possible Souths for the discursive reconfiguration of the region. While books dealing with the region may include examples of local diversity, they typically frame them as anomalies, eliding them as articulations of the regional. This occurs as a result of the cultural presentations of such locales containing a thin southern supplement. While these three documentaries do not contain within them as texts a sufficient southern supplement to make that connection, extra-textual materials such as the discussion of the documentaries in this book potentially can. When the cigar industry arrived in the 1880s, according to Gary Mormino and George Pozzetta, Tampa was "populated by people identifying with the values and attitudes associated with traditional southern society," but because of the influx of immigrants to work in the cigar industry the city "faced no simple black-and-white equation in its race relations."[27] As I will flesh out in the next two chapters, the situation of "no simple black-and-white [racial] equation" was (and is) a more common experience than is typically acknowledged within southern discourse as a result of the dominance of biraciality.

Chapter Six

"So that we have our own color": Racial Negotiation, Textual Posturing, and *Mississippi Triangle*

Introduction

Documentaries accompanied by a southern supplement typically presume biraciality, even if the focus is only on one race. Of course, while biraciality may be the dominant articulation of race within southern discourse, it is not the only one. The rare documentaries that do not assume such an approach typically embrace a multiracial perspective, such as *Displaced in the New South* (David Zeiger and Eric Mofford, 1995), which focuses on recent Latin American and Asian immigrants in the suburbs surrounding Atlanta, Georgia. Unlike *Nuestra Communidad: Latinos in North Carolina* (Joanne Hershfield and Penny Simpson, 2001), discussed in the last chapter, which enunciates Latinos as white, because *Displaced in the New South* does not operate from a presumption of biraciality, it explicitly engages with the issue of Latin American immigrants upon arrival to Georgia having to deal with being racialized, something they did not encounter in their country of origin. After three decades, the replacement of biraciality with tri-raciality in *Mississippi Triangle* (Christine Choy, Worth Long, and Allan Siegel, 1984) remains unique even among the exceptions. Its representation of race as tri-racial accentuates, in a way that multiracialism cannot, the problems associated with attempting to negotiate a racial position that is neither white nor black when a discourse of biraciality dominates.

Mississippi Triangle explores the tri-racial configuration of black, white, and Chinese in the Mississippi Delta.[1] The documentary's structure progresses topically, beginning with a consideration of the entrance of the Chinese into the Mississippi Delta during the nineteenth century, followed by an examination of the cotton industry, the Chinese grocery store, the Mississippi River, Chinese segregated education in the past, Chinese interracial marriage with blacks in the past, the black civil rights movement, integrated education in the present, interracial relationships in the present, Chinese acculturation to white norms (in particular, Christianity), black work/white leisure, and the future. The documentary has been praised for its open-ended style, which critics claim does not privilege any particular viewpoint and thereby allows the listening viewer to determine what conclusions to draw, and for its complex, ethnographic portrait of the Chinese in the Mississippi Delta.[2]

The first half of this chapter reconsiders the validity of these two commonly repeated truisms about the documentary that only recently have begun to be questioned. I argue against both, countering that the documentary only creates a spectatorial position that *feels* open-ended and only *poses* as an ethnographic study.[3] Through its film form (in particular its editing style and mise-en-scène), the documentary enunciates a position on the tri-racial situation in the Mississippi Delta that reproves the Chinese for their alliance with whites because it excludes blacks. In other words, it is an exposé. The film form, albeit in a manner similar to the dissonant music that opens the documentary, frames this racial coalition in de facto negative terms rather than advance an ethnographic understanding of the complex quandary confronted by the Mississippi Chinese as they attempted to negotiate a racial position outside of the dominant biracial paradigm. This failure results from the documentary privileging race over class as the basis for the coalition. Because *Mississippi Triangle* focuses on tri-raciality, it serves as an ideal venue for exploring the problems a multiracial locale confronts when a discourse of biraciality dominates. The latter part of this chapter examines the documentary in light of the representational problems confronted by groups who view themselves as neither black nor white and strive, in the words of one Chinese interviewee, to "have our own color."

Open-ended Text or Enunciated Position?

Both the filmmakers in interviews and film reviewers and scholars in articles and books typically claim that *Mississippi Triangle* is open-ended. For example, Christine Choy stresses: "The film doesn't tell you anything; it doesn't say go this way or that. If you look at individual issues or areas you might not digest the recurring themes."[4] Jun Xing argues: "In stressing both intra-ethnic and intra-Asian American community concerns, *Mississippi Triangle* comes to grips with the complexity of the Chinese American experience in the South. No one person monopolizes the voice, so there is no 'official' story or point made in the film."[5] Similarly, Gina Marchetti claims that "[n]o single, unified point of view dominates; rather a number of perspectives vie for the viewer's attention and support" and that "no point made by the film is brought to a conclusion."[6] I believe the documentary is not as open-ended as claimed by either its makers or reviewers. A closer look reveals that, while the movement from shot to shot provides a space for multiple voices, as a text it does enunciate a particular position.

The presentation of conflicting information spoken by interviewees, left unreconciled, functions in the documentary to signify narrative openness and multiple viewpoints. The editing, however, causes these shots to comment upon one another and enunciates a meaning not contained in any particular one. For example, in the sequence on the present state of education after the integration of public schools, a shot of students in front of the public Greenville High School dissolves by multiple diamond irises into one of children in front of another school as a female voice (whom we latter see is Chinese) asserts, "Washington School is a private school with an open door policy. We say that anyone—any race, creed, color—can come to our school." The voice-over words contrast sharply with the racial characteristic of the student population seen in the film frame, who are all white, and these white private school students contrast sharply with the diverse racial configuration of black, white, and Chinese just seen at a public high-school prep rally. In succession, three different interviewees comment on the public school versus private school issue. A white middle-class woman, Ellen Douglas, explains: "There's a split now between the white people who have gone with the private school system and those who have stayed with the public school system. . . . It's called by the name of quality education, but in fact they don't want their children to go to school with black people." Immediately following Douglas's comment, Luck Wing, the Chinese mayor of Sledge, Mississippi, asserts: "The reason I send my kids to private school is because I thought they could get a better education." In turn, following Wing's declaration, "Spunky" Woods, a white working-class man, ponders: "There may be a few more opportunities in a private school because of the simple fact that you have a high social class of people maybe involved in the whole function of the school. In other words, this group of people may be able to do a lot more things, you know, out of their pocket that, say, people in a public school couldn't do." While the middle-class justification of flight to private schools (whether by whites or Chinese) is based on "better education," the middle-class critique is based on racism, that adults are sending their children to private schools primarily because they do not want their children educated with blacks (the unspoken presumption being that the presence of blacks lowers the quality of education their children will receive because blacks are intellectually inferior to whites). Ironically, while the white middle-class interviewee sees the racial justification, she does not see the class justification. The editing melds the comments

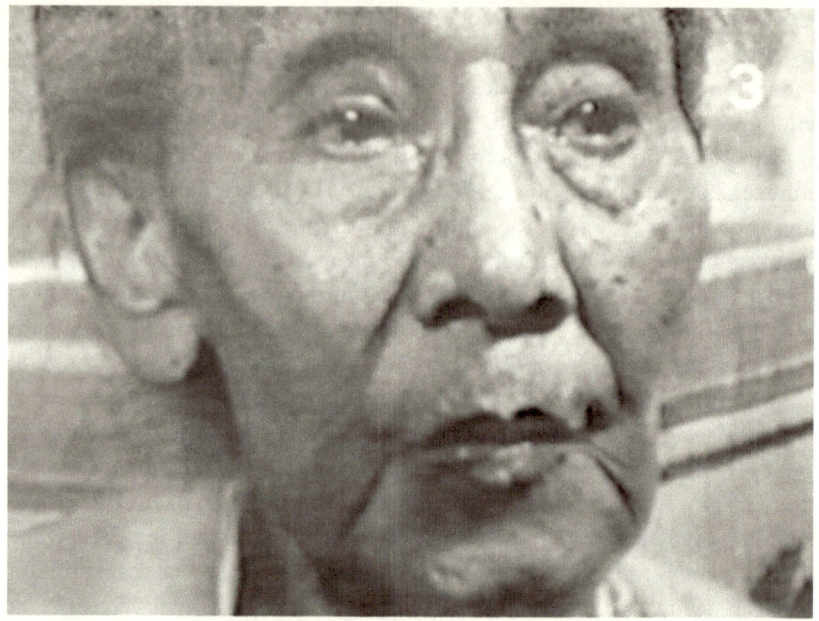

Arlee Hen, the elderly black-Chinese woman who is framed through editing in Christine Choy, Worth Long, and Allan Siegel's 1984 documentary *Mississippi Triangle* to function as a critique of the Mississippi Chinese. Photograph courtesy of Third World Newsreel.

by Douglas and Wing into an enunciation that (middle-class) Chinese are identical to (middle-class) whites in their prejudice against blacks. Through such editing, the documentary uses the very words of the Chinese to pass judgment on them.

While no one interviewee monopolizes the documentary in terms of time allotment, the narrative framing privileges the perspective of Arlee Hen, an elderly black-Chinese woman who, subsequent to the prologue, speaks the first and last words in the documentary. At the end, as a casket lowers into a grave, she discloses: "I couldn't be buried in a Chinese cemetery. I'm mixed with Negro, you know." Hen signifies the past social relations that the Mississippi Chinese want to not only move beyond but to forget. The section of the documentary on acculturation of the Chinese to white norms shows a Chinese church service in which the members, led by a white minister, take Communion, followed by Hen, sitting alone in her backyard, receiving Communion from a black minister. The interweaving of the two Communions indicts the Chinese for excluding Hen because she is racially mixed with black. Communion is a ritual of personal introspection, and, in his preparatory speech, the white preacher comments: "God is saying to us that we need to examine ourselves and see if we are worthy to undertake, and partake, of the Lord's Supper." Hen is then shown receiving Communion alone, her isolation presented as that for which the Chinese congregation needs to examine itself. Her recitation of the Lord's Prayer while taking Communion functions as a retort to the Chinese community for excluding her: "Forgive us our trespasses as we forgive those who trespass against us." Meaning in this sequence derives not from the content of the individual shots themselves but rather from the relationships between the shots formed by the editing. These relationships enunciate amidst the patchwork of voices a textual viewpoint—that is, a critique of the Chinese for their alliance with whites based on an exclusion of blacks.

The absence of a voice-over narrator, whether in the style of a voice of God or of a personal diary entry by the filmmakers, contributes to the feel that the text is open-ended. Yet the appearance of many voices that have to be negotiated by the listening viewer does not negate the textual system of the documentary from enunciating a position that rises above them. As Pascal Bonitzer notes: "To 'let the event speak' is to let it be spoken by the spectators, according to the paths traced in silence by the film and guided by the signposts of montage. It is thus important to analyze the structure, the montage, which conveys the 'event' and what historical capacity is distributed to it."[7] Meaning in *Mississippi Triangle* arises not from individual shots or necessarily from two juxtaposed shots. After all, juxtaposed shots that contradict simulate irresolution and uncertainty as well. Instead, meaning builds from the multiple relationships of shots upon shots.

Racial Narration

The three filmmakers of *Mississippi Triangle*—Christine Choy, Worth Long, and Allan Siegel—self-identify as, respectively, Asian American, African American, and European American. Articles about the documentary and interviews with the three filmmakers typically stress the shooting strategy they employed, that of three separate crews—one Asian American, one African American, and one European American—each shooting interviews with individuals of their own racial affiliation. "The whole point of the film," Choy has said, "was to show different points of view on race relations. If we did not allow different points of view we would have been perpetrating racism—racial tension. That's why we decided to present a different point of view from each different racial background."[8] The filmmakers believed that individuals would be more open with a film crew of their own race than one containing

A Chinese grocer waiting on a black customer, one of three patterns of cross-racial interaction captured within the mise-en-scène of *Mississippi Triangle*. These three patterns form a logic equation that makes the documentary's primary argument about the triangular relationship between the Chinese, blacks, and whites in the Mississippi Delta. Photograph courtesy of Third World Newsreel.

members of a different race. In other words, they thought this particular shooting strategy would allow them to obtain an insider's perspective from each of the three racial groups.

This strategy typically results in each racial group in the Delta being recorded separately; consequently, they rarely interact within the documentary. The few scenes in which the races interact within the mise-en-scène fall into three general categories. First are sanctioned commercial situations of Chinese or whites interacting with blacks, such as a Chinese grocer waiting on a black customer in the sequence on the Chinese grocery store or a black worker assisting a white boss with cotton in the sequence on the cotton industry. Second are sites of cultural assimilation of whites instructing Chinese, such as a white minister conducting Communion at a Chinese church or a white wedding coordinator providing instructions at a Chinese couple's wedding rehearsal. Both of these sequences occur in the section on the acculturation of the Delta Chinese to white norms. Third are social interactions of Chinese with blacks or whites. Only three such sequences occur in the documentary, two involving Chinese and blacks and one involving Chinese and whites; all occur in the section on interracial relationships in the present.⁹ The differences between these two types of cross-racial social interactions are significant. In the two sequences between Chinese and blacks, the participants openly discuss the issue of race, while in the sequence involving Chinese and whites they do not. Although comments about race fill the documentary within intra-racial contexts, only in these two scenes between Chinese and blacks is the topic discussed within an interracial context.

Both incidents of social interaction between Chinese and blacks center around a Chinese girl stating that most Chinese hold blacks in disdain but she does not. In the first case, an unidentified Chinese girl plays Monopoly and swims with two black girls. As her friends listen in the background, she relays a story about a Chinese girl at church who did not like black kids because "they don't go with her color." She concludes: "But I don't think like that. I just think like any color people's my friend just as long as they get along with me." In the other case, Linda Wing, whose name we learn from her voice-over narration, dances and plays pool with an unidentified black man. When he asks her why "[y]our people don't want you to be seen with me," she replies, "they think that black shouldn't belong with Chinese people. My people want me to marry somebody my own color so that we have our own color because of the blood. Shouldn't mix the blood up. . . . I ain't going to turn against black people because my people tell me not to." In both situations, the young Chinese girls feel compelled to justify for the camera their social association with blacks who are seen on the screen interacting with them. This defensiveness contrasts sharply with the only sequence in the documentary to show social interaction between Chinese and whites. As an unidentified white man deejays at country music radio station WSVM in Greenville, Mississippi, a close-up of his left hand reveals a wedding ring. Then, outside the radio station, he opens a car door for a Chinese woman; this is followed by shots of them working in a Chinese grocery store. The couple offers no justification for their behavior.¹⁰ Because on-screen conversations between the various races are so rare, these three occurrences acquire the status of a microcosm of the Mississippi Delta. This presentation of Chinese socialization with whites as not requiring comment, but such interaction with blacks as needing justification, contributes to the documentary's enunciated critique of the Chinese alliance with whites because it necessitates social separation from blacks.

Adria Bernardi documented the objections raised by the Delta Chinese community against *Mississippi Triangle* when it premiered at the Clarksdale, Mississippi, public library in 1984. The audience at the premiere, according to Bernardi, thought that the documentary did not adequately portray the advances that had been made by the Mississippi Chinese and did portray the

Chinese as more closely aligned with blacks than whites, a depiction with which they disagreed.[11] Implicit in this second criticism is an assumption that association with blacks is an undesirable connection. In addition to the two sequences of Chinese girls socializing with blacks previously mentioned, Henry Goon, a Chinese man who married a black woman, confesses: "Now what I do, what I done, is something different, you see, but I'm still Chinese." Unlike the Chinese woman married to a white man, he has to declare his Chineseness because of the attempts to exclude him from its definition on the basis of his wife's race. When an interviewer asks Ray Joe why the Chinese stopped associating with Chinese who married blacks, he explains that in Mississippi "everything separate from the white to the black" and "if you want to be on white people side you must behave yourself." That behavior includes not socializing with, dating, or marrying blacks. Although the dialogue captured in the documentary indicates that the Chinese community does not endorse interaction with blacks except in the narrow arena of commerce, the mere representation of a few exceptions seems to have disturbed the Delta Chinese community. The reason, of course, can be found in Joe's comment.

The three patterns of cross-racial interaction shown in the documentary form a racial narrative logic. They enunciate the following racial postulates: first, Chinese and whites hold similar relationships to blacks, that of economic domination, with one a buyer of labor and the other a supplier of goods; second, Chinese are willing to learn white culture, but not black culture; and third, Chinese have to defend social interaction with blacks, but not with whites. These postulates fuse into the documentary's primary argument: whites and Chinese in the Mississippi Delta participate in a social pact that excludes blacks. Of course, as in most social situations, exceptions to the basic rules exist. Rather than ignoring those exceptions, *Mississippi Triangle* uses their status as unacceptable to define the dominant racial patterns.

Ethnographic Film or Political Exposé?

As just noted, discussions about race among individuals of different races are the exception in *Mississippi Triangle*, the examples above being the only ones. In general, dialogue between social groups (whether race- or class-based) is created through editing, not the recording of pro-filmic interaction. Do people act differently in a same-race group than they would if other races were present? Obviously, the filmmakers believed so or they would not have gone to the trouble of ensuring that the race of the shooting crews matched that of the interviewees. Given the twentieth-century history of highly coded rules governing social interaction among the races, the assumption of behavioral differences between same-race and mixed-race groups seems reasonable. If this difference does exist, then the editing style of the documentary presents intra-racial conversations as interracial conversations, except for the two scenes described above. Its editing strategy stitches these individual private pieces into a public whole. In other words, the documentary creates a public dialogue among the three racial groups out of each group's internal conversations about racial interaction.

The three filmmakers openly acknowledge that each racial group in the Delta was not aware during the three years of shooting that members of the other racial groups were also being interviewed and recorded. To maintain their "autonomy," they chose not to be in the Delta at the same time except for one short period. That the filmmakers perceived their mission as clandestine manifests itself in a remark Allan Siegel makes when asked in an interview about the production strategy. He discloses: "Once Chris [Choy] and I met in a Pizza Hut, in the middle of the night, to exchange equipment, and that was it. People didn't know we were operating together."[12] Similarly, Christine Choy describes the undertaking to film Hen in covert terms. She comments:

> No one wanted us to talk to the elderly black-Chinese woman who became a major character in the film. So we made an announcement in Greenville that we were leaving town. Word traveled quickly from Jackson, Mississippi, to Memphis, Tennessee. All the gossips spread the word. We went down to Jackson, spent the night, and then sneaked back into Greenville. We parked the car in an alley behind the woman's house, and stayed in her home for two days of filming. The Chinese community didn't know we had any relationship with this woman. When they saw the final film they were very upset.[13]

Although the filmmakers claim the documentary is an ethnographic study, such extra-textual discourse that frames the production process as secret rendezvous, undercover missions, and back alleyway meetings in the middle of the night positions the documentary as an exposé instead. This practice means that the interviewees were, in effect, deceived into believing that they were participating in a documentary about their own racial group in order to illicit unguarded responses from them. Yet the editing style positions these intra-group private conversations as inter-group public dialogue meant for all to hear. Social etiquette in many locales necessitates that certain topics not be discussed in the public arena although they may dominate private conversations. The forthrightness and vulnerability of the comments made by Chinese in the documentary far exceed any of those made by whites and blacks. They reveal a deep trust in Choy and her film crew, as well as a willingness to accept them as members of their community and thereby allow them access to their private conversation. The violation of their hospitality might assist in explaining why the Mississippi Chinese were so upset with the documentary. Though the filmmakers describe the documentary as "a study of race relations," it is ultimately about how three racial groups each conceive of their relations with the other two groups rather than about how these three racial groups actually behave (i.e., relate) in the presence of each other.[14] The production process prohibited the latter and, as a result, footage capturing the internal dynamics of the three separate groups is presented through the editing as though it is cross-racial interaction. In-group communication is presented as inter-group communication although, as discussed in chapter two, our performance of the self typically differs depending on who is the other party.

Although Choy maintains that the documentary itself "doesn't say go this way or that," she clearly expresses the same perspective that I argue the documentary itself makes, despite the appearance of multiple viewpoints. She proclaims: "And these Chinese who are in between the blacks and whites have inherited, as neocolonizers within the system [business owners in black neighborhoods], the values of the capitalist system. They have become racists; they think they are socially white. They have become the dividers."[15] Although in general I agree with Choy's extra-textual critique of the Mississippi Chinese during the early 1980s, I find dubious her claim that this critique is not made in the documentary itself. In addition, although in general I agree with the documentary's critique of the Mississippi Chinese at that time, I am skeptical of the production strategy used to capture the footage that is used to construct that critique. Claims that the documentary is open-ended functions as a disavowal of its critique, which is often textually made through the way the words of members of the Chinese community are edited with other shots. This disavowal allows the filmmakers to distance themselves from the critique should it be noticed by others and thereby deflects attention from the ethical issues raised by the use of deceptive production practices to obtain the filmic representations that make the critique. The suspicion is that Choy parlayed her own racial status in order to obtain acceptance and, thereby, access to what otherwise would have been denied to a non-Asian-American filmmaker. Given the demands by identity politics at the time for group solidarity, the claim of textual open-endedness allows this violation to be dodged. Of course, deception is a cornerstone of undercover reporting, but such deception is typically justified by an appeal to a higher cause. What is the higher cause here? Why the urgent need for exposure? To claim that the documentary is an exposé rather than an ethnographic study would draw attention to the critique that it makes (and that the filmmakers and most film reviewers and scholars deny exists) because an exposé is expected to disclose something unsavory, not to provide nonjudgmental insight into the social position and culture of a group.

In addition to being praised for its open-ended narrative, *Mississippi Triangle* is also routinely touted as presenting an intricate portrait of the Delta Chinese community. Yet the documentary excludes numerous matters that would complicate the representation of the Chinese's interaction with other races and assist in explaining why the Mississippi Chinese made the choices that they did. In particular, it neglects the protests targeted at Chinese grocery stores by black activists during the civil rights movement, the displacement Chinese confronted when they decided to stop living in the back of their stores located in black neighborhoods and to move into residential homes (they wanted, and could afford, better housing than that found in the black neighborhoods but were initially prohibited, despite their financial capability, from purchasing homes in the white middle-class neighborhoods), and the disparity between their economic status and their social status (in the 1960s the average income among Chinese in the Mississippi Delta was twice that of the average income among whites in the area).[16] Although *Mississippi Triangle* focuses on economic structures such as the business operations of the cotton industry and the retail grocery store, it withholds information that would complicate the socioeconomic position negotiated by the Chinese. The absence of such information in the documentary contributes to its textual transvestitism, allowing it to pose as an ethnographic study and thereby disguise its investigative social critique.

As mentioned earlier, one of the two criticisms made against the documentary by the Mississippi Chinese was that it did not show the progress that they had achieved. The basis for this complaint resides in its focus on rural Chinese grocery stores, which many Mississippi Chinese regarded as "the history" and "down side of things."[17] The desire for the documentary to focus on present successes rather than past hardships is a desire (common to many minority groups, as Choy acknowledges) for films to show positive images. Ella Shohat and Robert Stam note: "Rather than deal with the contradictions of a community, 'positive image' cinema prefers a mask of perfection."[18] While part of the reaction against the documentary can be attributed to this preference for a positive portrait, I believe the desire for "a mask of perfection" does not completely explain the negative reaction toward the documentary upon its release in the 1980s. The editing style that positions private conversations as public interaction most likely contributed significantly to the negative reaction as well because it violated social etiquette. As the filmmakers' comments on the production process and the Chinese community's reactions to the final documentary suggest, the practices used to capture the footage that composes the documentary ironically partakes of the same neocolonialist impulse toward its subjects as Choy criticizes the Mississippi Chinese for adopting toward Delta blacks. Marchetti maintains that the documentary "create[s] a different sort of viewing experience and a very different relationship to the ethnic community it examines" than Hollywood mainstream films.[19] I am not sure the Mississippi Chinese, who felt betrayed by their representation in the documentary, would agree that it treated them any better than a Hollywood film would have. Marchetti's claim does not hold up unless one excludes the Mississippi Chinese from the "ethnic community" of Chinese in the United States. Being a rural Chinese community rather than an urban one, as was more common in the United States at the time, necessitated that the group pursue different social and political strategies.

Unlike documentaries in general, those claimed to be ethnographic—whether that claim is made within the text itself or extra-textually—deserve to be evaluated on how well they fulfill the general objective of ethnography—that is, to understand the cultural and social values that a particular group finds meaningful, to ascertain and represent a group's self-understanding.[20] While the documentary often achieves this goal at the level of the individual racial groups within the Mississippi Delta, it does not for the Mississippi Delta as a whole, the society within which these three racial groups interact and the espoused focus of the documentary. Besides the production strategy itself, this failure also results from the presumptions within the documentary that (1) race, not class, is the overarching characteristic of the coalition built among these groups, and (2) for a coalition to be progressive it must be built with blacks, not whites. These presumptions, when a discourse of biraciality dominates, create problems for racial groups who try to negotiate a social space separate from both blacks and whites, and such presumptions also ignore race's entwined articulation with class.

Anti-Black or Not-Black?

Christine Choy charges: "A lot of filmmakers are conditioned by what they want to see because it's in the South. They want direct conflict. There are surface conflicts, and conflicts below the surface."[21] "Direct conflict" seems to imply the mass demonstrations and marches associated with the civil rights movement (still fresh in the national consciousness at the time), while "surface conflicts" suggests public confrontations easily captured audiovisually.

Southeastern Indians and Mississippi Chinese, in general, did not choose the strategy of mass protest in their quest for political and social acceptance. In some locales of southeastern states, blacks constitute a majority or near-majority that enables mass collective action to be a highly effective means to accomplish societal change. These civil rights protests eventually translated into local political power for blacks (although not necessarily economic power) and a change in how whites dealt with them. This approach for improving a group's societal position was unavailable to the Mississippi Chinese because of their relatively small numbers. Therefore, coalition-building was necessary. The issue became: a coalition with whom? Because they engaged in "conflicts below the surface," their actions typically—although not always—went unnoticed by the media.

Historians claim that originally the Mississippi Chinese were sojourners who came to the United States in order to make money for their families in China and expected to return home one day. As a result, they were unencumbered by, and willing to ignore, the racial etiquette of the area and lived in the back of their grocery stores, which were typically located in black neighborhoods. It was only when they switched from being sojourners to immigrants, and therefore saw themselves as permanent residents in the United States, that they acquired an active interest in their social standing in the Delta. According to Choy, the 1971 book *The Mississippi Chinese: Between Black and White* by James Loewen was one impetus for the documentary. As part of the preproduction process for the film, Loewen performed additional field research, which he then used to update his book in 1988. Loewen argues that "the Chinese majority profited from the image of fellowship with blacks established by the minority of merchants who did have close ties, including marriage, with members of the Negro community. These ties were therefore not discouraged until they hindered the advancement of the group into white institutions."[22]

A focus on what the Chinese and white coalition in the Delta excludes results in an understanding of it as race-based, formed through an exclusion of blacks, while a focus on what the coalition includes results in an understanding of it as class-based, formed through an exclusion of the working class, this exclusion including whites and Chinese as well as blacks. While the financial status of many Mississippi Chinese within the context of the Delta was middle class, their social status was initially low because of their race. But they were able to parlay the common middle-class financial status that they shared with certain whites in the area, thereby raising their overall social status. Of course, as Loewen notes, it was not money alone that enabled the Chinese to cross the black/white "color bar" and move from being "classed with blacks" to being "viewed as essentially 'white,'" but rather the use of their money "to establish a life style and image different from that of the black majority."[23] The section of the documentary on Chinese acculturation to white norms implies it was their performativity of whiteness that sealed the deal. In other words, the improvement of the Chinese social standing within Delta society required an intricate negotiation of the cultural accoutrements of whiteness. Missing from this analysis is that it was not the adoption of white culture per se but a particular kind of white culture, one associated with a particular class formation. Given the rural context, the elements of being "country" that crossed class formations was not a disqualifier for such coalition-building but adoption of the accoutrements particular to white working-class culture would have been. As I will discuss in more depth in the next section, because of the way the intersection of race and class is enunciated in *Mississippi Triangle*, the documentary ultimately prioritizes race over class as the dominant component determining the coalition between the Chinese and white middle classes in the Mississippi Delta.

As mentioned in the last chapter, David Roediger claims that during the first half of the twentieth century European immigrants occupied a space of racial in-betweenness, "between nonwhiteness and full inclusion as whites."[24] After World War II, however, they were able to eliminate this in-between position and become accepted as fully white. Although the situation of Asian Americans (as well as Native Americans) in the second half of the twentieth century may also be one of in-betweenness, it differs in a number of significant ways from those of European immigrants in the first half of the twentieth century. First, the intermediary position that Asian Americans (and Native Americans) strive for is not a temporary stepping stone before absorption into one of the binary racial categories—a strategy that reinforces the binary—but the establishment of a permanent third (and fourth) racial category that is no longer a liminal space of in-between. Their task is much more difficult to achieve because it appears to challenge biraciality, thereby necessitating discursive suturing—typically performed through claims of anomalism—and/or socially disavowing it in order to maintain at least the appearance of the binary. Second, Irish Americans, Italians Americans, and Jewish Americans became white, but Mississippi Chinese (and Southeastern Indians) only obtained social acceptance from whites. Obtaining white social acceptance is not the same as acquiring white racial status. Physiological difference continues to be associated with these groups, that bodily difference accompanied by a lingering suspension of cultural difference, regardless of how culturally white they look, sound, or act. In other words, their situation is not one of acquisition of honorary whiteness but rather of white approval.

Difference from whiteness does not cease to exist and, unlike the case of European Americans, is not eradicated through cultural assimilation. One could argue that for the Mississippi Chinese, that approval was conditional upon their adopting a racist attitude and behavior toward blacks similar to that predominate among older whites at the time.[25]

Finally, the in-between racial space that Asian Americans (and Native Americans) negotiate in the second half of the twentieth century is not between the same end points as those of European immigrants in the first half of the twentieth century—that of nonwhite and white. But neither is it a racial space in-between nonwhite and black. Because of the discursive dominance of biraciality and the persistence of white privilege—as well as continued strains of white supremacy—the enactment of a nonwhite position by Asian Americans (and Native Americans) runs the risk of being folded into blackness.[26] As a result, these groups need to negotiate a position between nonblack and black in order to secure a third (and fourth) position that is neither black nor white. Such a nonblack stance requires an active separation from blackness, making the more appropriate descriptor "not-black." The adoption of a not-black stance by a non-black-or-white racial group is not the same as an anti-black stance because it purports to call attention to a racial category outside of the dominant paradigm of biraciality.[27] But significant dangers accompany the social maneuver of a not-black stance. It can easily be received by others as anti-black—regardless of the intent of the non-black-or-white group not to be so—or slip unnoticed into an anti-black stance within that particular group. And this latter is what appears to have happened to the Mississippi Chinese as captured in *Mississippi Triangle* and documented by Loewen in his book.

Many scholars have written about the recurring history of disenfranchised racial and ethnic groups within the United States achieving broader social inclusion on the back of blacks, with Toni Morrison's expression of the phenomenon probably among the more frequently cited ones.[28] I find this argument hard to refute. While from an ethical perspective one might expect disenfranchised social groups to form affinities with one another, from a pragmatic perspective such alliances may not necessarily be strategically productive. The dominance of a binaristic understanding of race as black and white, in combination with the persistence of unequal value judgments attached to those two elements, has historically limited the ability of this strategy to be a successful means of social advancement for non-black-or-white groups. While the incorporation of a third term into the binaristic system of biraciality might fracture the system, making it now three components instead of two, such incorporation will not necessarily disrupt the basis of the system as long as unequal value judgments continue to be associated with the various components. In other words, as long as white supremacy continues to exist, even if in a muted form, the hierarchical system persists, only now with more layers, whether that is one more layer, two, or three. And many scholars hold that even within multiracial frameworks, in practice racial hierarchicalization persists with blacks positioned at the bottom.[29] This situation raises the ethical issue of whether a particular disenfranchised group should prioritize its own advancement over the broader issue of equality for all subaltern groups. A dreary downside of post-1960s identity politics (and a reason why many scholars and activists have moved away from it) was the isolation of the concerns of particular groups from a larger overarching framework of interconnectedness and interstitiality. It appears the pursuit (and achievement) of a particular subaltern group's advancement at the expense of the broader goal of creating a just society for all is the underlying philosophical basis that informs Christine Choy's critique of the Mississippi Chinese, a philosophical position that I share. But from a pragmatic perspective, given the social and discursive context that they navigated in the Delta, a coalition with blacks at the time would not have enabled the Mississippi Chinese to achieve a non-black-or-white position—in other words, to have their "own color"—because it would have led to their being folded into blackness. But I question the now-standard mantra that the Mississippi Chinese raised their social position within the Delta through a coalition with whites because the thesis erases a key factor that seems to have been integral to their success—namely, the class basis of the coalition.

Mississippi Chinese or *Mississippi Triangle*?

Most writers focus on the representation of the Mississippi Chinese in the documentary. However, its title is *Mississippi Triangle*, not *Mississippi Chinese*. As Choy emphasizes in interviews, unlike "most films about race relations" in which "it is always two groups, black versus white," the documentary is about "race relations in a tri-racial situation."[30] Because the documentary centers on a triangular relationship, the question needs to be asked: How does it present the three racial groups in the Mississippi Delta? And, in particular, how does this presentation intersect with class? In the section on the future, Henry Goon, who owns a rural grocery store, notes: "You, in this society you going to have class. The poor class and the rich class. You know the poor are not going to mix with the rich. Just can't. One with million and one with nothing. You know he not going to be rub shoulder with each other." Numerous manifestations of class differences occur in the documentary among whites and among

Chinese, resulting in the two races being presented as economically stratified. In contrast, the documentary fails to acknowledge that class differences exist among blacks; instead, it represents them as one unified racial underclass.[31]

The documentary's enunciated critique of the racial alliance between whites and Chinese, because it is based on the exclusion of blacks, is naturalized through the class presentations of these three groups. Also, the inclusion of only archival film footage for blacks, from a stylistic perspective, separates blacks audiovisually from whites and Chinese, while simultaneously reinforcing the latter two as being similar. But fissures exist within the documentary that challenge its enunciation of blacks as one mass undifferentiated working-class body. The archival footage falls into two basic categories: blacks as laborers and blacks as civil rights workers.[32] Two of the three black interviewees serve similar functions; one, John Dorsey, describes the hardship of picking cotton, and the other, Hartman Turnbow, relates the struggle of the civil rights movement. The third black interviewee, Unita Blackwell, however, is a town mayor. The mayor's presence signals not only the presence of black political power, but also a black professional class capable of performing such tasks. Yet neither matter is explored in the documentary. Although interviewees discuss the issue of class, in particular Spunky Woods and Henry Goon, their comments ultimately function to cordon off class difference to only whites and Chinese. The documentary naturalizes the alliance between whites and Chinese by presenting them as structurally similar (economically variegated with diverse opinions) as opposed to blacks (a uniformed oppressed underclass). Paradoxically, despite this presentation of class differences within these two races, the coalition between middle-class Chinese and middle-class whites is ultimately framed as one between Chinese and whites, erasing its class component. One sequence in the documentary, which I call "black work/white leisure," makes an overly simplistic and reductionistic argument associating whites with leisure and blacks with labor. The segment ignores both the emerging black professional class and the white working class. The documentary frames the coalition in racial terms, forgoing a serious engagement with its class component. The coalition was neither simply race-based nor class-based but rather a complex intersection of both.

Conclusion

Several elements contribute to *Mississippi Triangle*'s enunciation of a critique of the Mississippi Chinese's negotiation of their social and racial positions in the Mississippi Delta. The extra-textual discourse surrounding the documentary directs attention to this reading through a variety of means, from direct comments by the filmmakers (such as Choy's explicit condemnation of the Mississippi Chinese) to the framing of the documentary as revealing the underbelly that the Chinese community did not want exposed (especially the past and present associations of Chinese with blacks). Besides these extra-textual sources, the text itself also frames this reading through its mise-en-scène and editing. Textual manifestations, such as Chinese having to justify their interaction with blacks when shown socializing with them, as well as the way in which shots are combined to comment upon one another, enunciate this critique.

The preeminence of biraciality affects not only what documentaries are made about the region—hence the dearth of documentaries about Southeastern Indians, such as Malinda Maynor's *Real Indian* (1996), and those about Asian Americans, such as *Mississippi Triangle*—but also creates a discursive barrier that non-black-or-white groups have to negotiate in order to have their "own color." The next chapter will explore this situation in relationship to Native Americans by using the short documentary *Real Indian*. For Native Americans, however, the problem emerges as one of racial legitimacy rather than racial negotiation.

Chapter Seven

"Too much bad blood": Racial Legitimacy, Representational Strategies, and *Real Indian*

Introduction

A popular belief exists that removal to Oklahoma eliminated American Indians from southeastern states. The framing of the region within southern discourse as biracial, composed of blacks and whites, not only functions to justify this belief but indirectly encourages its unconscious acceptance. The presumption of biraciality led Joel Williamson, discussed in chapter one, to erase the biological influences of native peoples in his book *New People*. Similarly, it led Charles Joyner, discussed in chapter four, to erase their cultural influences in his book *Shared Traditions*. Both miscegenation and cultural syncretism have a long history in many areas of southeastern states, but that history begins before the introduction of slavery. It includes not only black and white (sexual, cultural, and social) intercourse during the antebellum period but native and non-native (sexual, cultural, and social) intercourse during the earlier contact period as well as afterwards.

As discussed in prior chapters, race as a social formation is typically articulated to culture as well as the body. This chapter explores these two articulations in relationship to the indigenous inhabitants of the southeastern United States. The adaptive strategies many of these groups implemented to survive the onslaught of European invaders and their African slaves makes both ways of defining race problematic; consequently, their racial legitimacy as Indian is often questioned. Because Native Americans are expected to practice an ancient culture and exhibit certain bodily phenotypes, these groups confront the problem of how to represent their Indianness given that they often lost their culture and intermarried yet retained over generations the memory that they are native peoples. Although native tribes are political affiliations, not racial ones, the latter has become so intertwined with the former in public discussions and popular representations that the validity of federally non-recognized tribes has been called into question at times because of apprehensions about their racial legitimacy. After exploring the historical situation that led to this contemporary problem, using Malinda Maynor's 1996 short documentary *Real Indian* on the Lumbee Tribe of North Carolina located predominately in Robeson County, I explore the articulation of race with the body and culture for Native Americans when a discourse of biraciality dominates.[1] The chapter concludes with a consideration of the representational strategies used to counter challenges to their native legitimacy as enunciated in the documentaries *Snowbird Cherokees* (Rich Panter, 1995) and *The Chief: Calvin McGhee and the Forgotten Creeks* (Max Shores, 1995), with the focus primarily on the counterintuitive strategy of appropriating the Hollywood Indian stereotype.

Indigenous Strategies of Survival and Non-Native Criteria of Racial Legitimacy

Gerald Sider holds that "in the pre-contact southeast," "clearly demarcated and separated 'tribes'" did not exist but rather the "social landscape ... was constituted by networks of native villages and towns with multiple and diverse kinds of connections between them."[2] The arrival of Europeans and their African slaves onto this territory disrupted this arrangement through physical dislocation and organizational change (for example, switching from communal farming and hunting to commercial deer hunting for European traders). According to Robbie Ethridge and Charles Hudson, "[i]n the seventeenth and eighteenth centuries, the southeastern Indians had to put themselves together into new societies in which they could cope with the terrible new world in which they found themselves," what Ethridge and Hudson call "coalescent societies—the Creeks, the Cherokees, the Chickasaws, the Choctaws, the Catawbas."[3] As a result of the migratory flux created by European encroachment, native groups considered separate by Europeans, merged, split, and recombined; they also moved geographically as they adapted to the dangerous situations they confronted as a result of that invasion. In other words, native groups have not been stagnant but rather have changed over time, both societally and geographically. In such a disruptive environment, native peoples tried different strategies for survival, one being social isolation. Sider argues that the

> Europeanization of native peoples [who moved into relatively isolated regions, especially swamps in the borderlands between different colonies] was *not* simply acculturation but the framework for *social* isolation—for being left alone, for being seen as neither Black nor Indian nor, in some profoundly ambiguous ways,

White—an isolation revealed by the long-lasting, continuing separateness of many of these peoples, who have endured as distinct groups until the present.[4]

These isolated groups, according to Frank W. Porter III, "adopted many of the outward accoutrements of White society" and, thereby, became in many ways "indistinguishable from the lower stratum of eighteenth century rural White society."[5] In other words, some native peoples outside of the large coalescent societies sought to isolate themselves from whites by living in remote areas and adopting cultural codes that would not mark them as different. Both of these strategies were attempts to exist undetected by whites. Because they were culturally indistinguishable from most of their white and black neighbors, observers mistook them as mixed race rather than Indian. Cultural assimilation verged on racial annihilation, not integration, for such native communities.

In the post-World War II period, a minor field of inquiry emerged in the disciplines of anthropology and sociology concerned with pockets of people in the eastern United States that were considered neither white nor black. Researchers proffered various names to describe these communities, such as "racial islands," "little races," "marginal people," and "racial orphans," with the most popular term being "tri-racial isolates," which came to commonly describe the field of inquiry.[6] Although associated with the eastern United States, most researchers pointed out their predominance in southeastern states.[7] One would expect a group that is a mixture of three races to constitute the fourth racial group in that society. But such is not the case according to the tri-racial isolate researchers. While the tri-racials were considered to be a mixture of white, black, and Native American, the society in which they lived was viewed as biracial, composed of whites and blacks, with tri-racials an anomalous intermediary group in some locales. Although writers in the tri-racial isolate school of thought alluded in passing to a native connection for many of these communities, they quickly asserted on their behalf a mixed-race identity. Many researchers claimed that these groups preferred to be considered white but, failing that achievement, settled instead for being considered Indian because, given the social hierarchy of race that existed at the time, that would be better than being classified as black in terms of social benefits. As this argument goes, since they are rejected by whites and they refused to be identified as black, they came to occupy an intermediary racial position between black and white. Tri-racial isolate researchers typically ignored the self-understanding held by these various communities, privileging the public opinion of their surrounding neighbors, which was typically steeped in prejudice. Although most of these writers openly acknowledged the socially constructed nature of race, they ignored their active role as social scientists in writing a particular racialized version of ethnohistory for these groups.[8]

Many of these previously isolated communities eventually organized as official native tribes and sought federal recognition of government-to-government relationships. This phenomenon is so closely associated with the southeastern United States that one former employee of the Bureau of Indian Affairs' Branch of Acknowledgment and Research calls it "The Southeast Syndrome," although similar federally unrecognized native groups exist in the northeastern and Midwestern states.[9] While federal guidelines technically focus on ancestry—tracing a petitioning group's history back to a native tribe in the past—and not blood quantum, some researchers hold that the issue of blood (that is, interracial marriage) is indirectly playing a role in federal denials of recognition. Most scholars now hold that native peoples prior to European contact did not hold a conceptualization of race so therefore did not perceive intermarriage as an issue but over the years, as a result of federal policy, eventually internalized this European derived way of thinking.[10] Ward Churchill maintains that

> by 1830 at the latest, the notion of defining "Indianness" in terms of race had been rendered patently absurd. It has been reliably estimated that something approaching half of all Native people still residing east of the Mississippi River were at that point genetically intermixed not only with one another, but with "Negroid and Caucasoid racial stock," a demographic pattern which would spread rapidly westward during the next half-century. There is little if any indication, moreover, that most indigenous societies viewed this increasing admixture as untoward or peculiar, much less threatening, in and of itself (that is as opposed to their often bitter resistance to the cultural, political, and material encroachments of Euro-American "civilization").[11]

Similarly, Jack Forbes argues that "the idea of an absolute cleavage between African, white, and Native American is false, as is the notion of a 'two-caste' society."[12] Despite the limited circulation of the tri-racial isolate theory, the construction of race through the prism of biraciality enacted by these academicians on behalf of these communities in the past—that they are mixed race and therefore cannot be native—has become a presumed historical reality today, forming an administrative obstacle—the belief in "The Southeast Syndrome"—that they have to overcome in order to prove they are legitimate native peoples.

While an argument can be made that the experiences of native peoples in the eastern United States are on a basic level similar, I believe today that two elements influence mainstream representational perceptions of southeastern Indians that are not confronted on the popular front by their counterparts in other areas of the United States—removal (aka the Trail of Tears) and black slavery.[13] The forced relocation of the "five-civilized tribes" (Cherokees, Creeks, Choctaws, Chickasaw, and Seminole in the Carolinas, Tennessee, Georgia, Alabama, and Mississippi) to present-day Oklahoma in the late 1830s is often perceived as having eliminated native peoples from the southeastern states, and the discursive framing of the region as biracial—from a legacy of white planters owning black slaves—in turn functions as a confirmation of that elimination.[14] A consequence of the simultaneous acceptance of these two postulates is that many native peoples in southeastern states had their legitimacy called into question through much of the twentieth century, a situation that continues to exist for some in the twenty-first century.

The reframing of the region within southern discourse as biracial in the wake of the civil rights movement occurred at a time politically sensitive for these previously isolated native communities who were just beginning to seek federal acknowledgment of being Indian tribes. Because "Indians did not want integration into mainstream American society . . . [but rather] sought recognition of their sovereign rights as Indian nations," their goals did not mesh with those of the civil rights movements, so therefore they typically kept their distance from that movement.[15] In other words, while the primary focus of blacks in Alabama during the civil rights era was racial citizenship, as discussed in chapter one, for native peoples it was racial legitimacy because of the routine reduction of their political aspiration to a racial one by nonnatives. Racial legitimacy was not a problem for blacks because of the dominance of the one-drop rule for defining who is black. In addition, while blacks in Alabama constituted a majority in a sufficient number of locales as to form an electoral political force for citizenship, native peoples did not, even if that had been their goal. But, more importantly, because of the colonial relationship that legally structures native nations as wards of the United States, in order for federally non-recognized native tribes to obtain legal sovereignty they must be unilaterally recognized as such by the United States, with the recognition of that political legitimacy often dependent upon an unacknowledged racial legitimacy. In other words, a strategy that may be advantageous for one minority group may not be for another because their goals may not necessarily be identical.

When the national media focused on Alabama during the 1960s, it centered on the civil rights movement in Birmingham and the Black Belt where

Montgomery and Selma are located (a part of the state that formerly was Indian country until the loss of the Creek War of 1813–14 resulted in the forced removal of the native peoples residing there during the 1830s).[16] Two of the federally non-recognized native communities in the state at the time (today known as the MOWA Band of Choctaw Indians and the Poarch Band of Creek Indians) are located between the Black Belt and the Gulf Coast where the 300-year-old city of Mobile stands.[17] These two groups resided in an area that, for a century, was a borderland between the French and Spanish settlements on the Gulf Coast and the native peoples within the interior of present-day Alabama. In other words, it was literally an in-between space, its geography paralleling their social experience as such. Although the Poarch Creek in the area of Atmore, Alabama, obtained federal recognition in 1984, their southwestern neighbors, the MOWA Choctaw in the vicinity of McIntosh, Alabama, were denied federal recognition in 1997. At the beginning of the twentieth century, this latter group was called "Cajan" by local whites and visiting writers, a term they never used to describe themselves. As a result of others using this term in documents, they now face a de facto presumption that they must overcome, that they are Cajan, a mixed-race community, instead of Native American. Although documentation exists that verifies native peoples remained in the area after removal, and the group's oral history can be traced back to that time, the group could produce no written document by outsiders prior to the late nineteenth century. This gap contributed to the success of their strategy of social isolation, but it hurts them today from an administrative perspective since it left a gap in terms of written documentation by outsiders. Like the United Houma Nation in Louisiana, they were declared by the federal government to not be legitimate Indians.[18] Are such groups wannabe Indians, as the tri-racial isolate researchers and "The Southeast Syndrome" proponents claim—a position ratified by the federal government in rejecting their petitions for official recognition—or are they reconstituted native groups that "lost all vestiges of their native culture, except for their identity as American Indians" as a result of successfully implementing a survival strategy of social isolation?[19] That survival strategy had bodily ramifications (from intermarriage) as well as cultural ones (from acculturation). But if racial legitimacy cannot be validated by a bodily or cultural appeal, then what basis should be used for determining Indianness? Malinda Maynor's short documentary *Real Indian*, about the Lumbee Indians, who have had their legitimacy as Indians called into question for just these reasons, confronts this quandary head-on.

Real Indian and the Issue of Racial Legitimacy

At the beginning of *Real Indian*, over old family photos, Maynor's voice-over informs us: "When I was a kid, I didn't question my identity much. My parents were Lumbee Indians and they taught us to be a good Lumbee. When I left home, I discovered there were real Indians and fake Indians. Lumbees are definitely fake—at least according to some people."[20] The documentary examines why "some people" consider the Lumbee "fake Indians." While the Lumbee were officially recognized as a native tribe by the state of North Carolina in 1885, the federal government did not do so until the 1950s and only then with the caveat that such recognition made no concession of federal wardship toward them. In other words, they were not considered a sovereign nation by the United States government, a situation that puts them in a similar position as federally non-recognized tribes. In her history of the tribe published subsequent to the documentary, Maynor argues that the lack of federal recognition never negated the tribe's understanding of itself as a sovereign nation.[21]

Like many documentaries, *Real Indian* mixes modes, in this particular case primarily the talking heads of the participatory mode and the artistic creations of the performative mode. These various modes are interwoven throughout the documentary. As a result, the construction of the text parallels that of the Lumbee themselves, who for "some people" have "too much bad blood" to be legitimate Indians, a common criticism levied toward many federally non-recognized tribes. This particular combination of modes results in a documentary that interweaves an aesthetic of realism (talking heads) with that of the fantastic (performative shots); these two aesthetic forms function metonymically with the narrative concerns of real and fake. Given this combination, as one might expect, rather than a historical chronicle or ethnographic study the documentary is Maynor's first-person exploration of what it means to be a Lumbee Indian, interspersed with two interviewees from federally recognized native tribes who comment on why other native peoples question the Lumbees' legitimacy as Indians. As a result, the personal is intermixed with the social, but that social context is not that of mainstream American society but rather that of native peoples. In other words, the issue of the Lumbees' racial legitimacy is focalized not through the interracial conflict between natives and non-natives, but rather the intra-racial conflict between native peoples themselves, although the historical results of the former conflict informs the latter conflict, especially in terms of popular Indian stereotypes.

The two interviewees discuss why the Lumbee are considered "fake Indians" by many native tribes; the objections enunciated in the documentary

In her 1996 documentary *Real Indian*, Malinda Maynor smears war paint across her face as she recollects being asked: "How can you be Indian if you have curly hair?" Photograph courtesy of Women Make Movies.

align along two axes, one bodily, the other cultural. Of the two interviewees, both of whom are unidentified, one visually resembles an Indian based on the stereotypical phenotypes, while the other, who has pale skin and light-colored hair, does not, although she verbally identifies herself as Apache. This contrast in the physical appearance of the two women serves to highlight the problem of using visual signifiers, whether bodily or culturally, to define Indianness. And this issue is one both women specifically address in their comments. The Indian-looking interviewee notes that "Lumbees, along with a lot of eastern tribes, . . . don't look Indian" in terms of the physical characteristics popularly associated with Indians in the mainstream media nor do they "have any Indian culture or language or tradition." Keeping with the aesthetic, structural, and narrative motif of mixing and multiple layers, these two ways of defining Indianness—the body and culture—are interwoven throughout the documentary rather than presented linearly.

As the Indian-looking interviewee notes, one reason why the Lumbee are often not considered legitimate Indians is because they are thought to be too mixed with other races. While posing in a traditional frayed Indian dress, Maynor raises her hand to sign "how" and smears streaks of make-up across her cheeks in the fashion of Indian war paint. Her voice-over recollects how she has been asked: "How can you be Indian if you have curly hair?" In other words, she does not physically look like what people think an Indian should look like. She positions this visual perception as being specifically derived from popular culture as she continues, "I'm not a John Wayne, Pocahontas, cigar store Indian. War paint just doesn't become me." The question raised by Maynor's inquisitor regarding hair derives from an understanding of race as defined by certain physical characteristics of the body, whether facial structure, skin color, or hair texture. In this particular case, Indians are supposed to have black straight hair, not curly hair. But native peoples in the southeast routinely do not fit the phenotypes associated with the popular stereotype. Why? Because, in the words of the Indian-looking interviewee: "They're mixed with black." But as Maynor's voice informs us earlier in the documentary over old family photos: "My grandfather used to say that some Lumbee families have good blood, meaning white, and bad blood, meaning black. My grandfather's family, the Sandersons, were proud of their good blood. They tried to fit into white society, to be acceptable Indians." In other words, the Lumbee intermarried with whites as well as blacks. But it is their intermarrying with blacks that causes both whites and other native peoples to have a problem with their Indianness.

Academic liberals will be quick to read the comment by Maynor's grandfather as exhibiting racism toward blacks and internalized self-hatred of being Indian, although these same critics would be quick to concede that this was a result of the prejudice he experienced at the hands of whites. I think such a response does not fully recognize the historical conditions faced by native peoples such as the Lumbees and the limited options available to them if they wanted to survive. Rather than assume the easy position of moral superiority by disdaining the "white is good" and "black is bad" alignment presented here and pronouncing it offensive, I prefer to follow the path of attempting to understand it from the perspective of how race operates in the United States in relationship to Indianness. The distinction Maynor's grandfather makes between good and bad blood needs to be read through the bias of (1) the one-drop rule, in which any black ancestry is considered to racially trump any other racial ancestry, and (2) white supremacy, in which any nonwhite ancestry is considered to racially trump white ancestry. In the case of Indianness, this means intermarriage with blacks result in erasure; therefore, from the perspective of preservation, it is bad. In contrast, intermarriage with whites does not result in erasure of Indianness; therefore, it can be viewed as good. From such a perspective, the distinction is not about moral goodness and badness but rather about the effects on Indianness resulting from the social construction of blackness through the one-drop rule and whiteness through supremacy. Under such conditions, the acknowledgment of any blackness functions as a form of Indian extermination.

The resistance by native peoples to being classified as black was often misunderstood as a racist reaction by most whites (and some blacks) instead of an attempt at self-determination in the midst of a society dominated by a discourse of biraciality. Although Native Americans differ from Asian Americans in numerous ways—chief among them their status as First Peoples and resulting concern with the issue of sovereignty—the existence of white supremacy (even if one believes it is only residual in the post-civil rights movement era) necessitates assuming a not-black stance in order to be recognized as non-black-or-white. As discussed in the last chapter, such a maneuver carries the risk of slipping into an anti-black stance, which it does at times. Some activists, however, hold that a not-black stance is inherently anti-black because it leaves white supremacy intact, only now with an intermediary group while blacks still are socially, economically, and politically on the bottom. Recently some scholars have gone so far as to argue that during the segregation era—which informs our present situation—some native peoples appropriated the rhetoric of segregation to their own advantage for the purpose of native sovereignty. According to Theda Perdue, because of the dominance of a "racial binary," "Indians made choices that sometimes were at odds with other people of color ... for example, [they] supported segregation—as long as it made room for them as Indians—and used it to legally establish their identity as Indian."[22] In other words, native peoples adopted separatism as a mechanism to achieve some modicum of self-determination, this action often supported by whites because it was perceived as an affirmation of their own practice of segregation. This same dynamic can be seen with the Mississippi Chinese discussed in the last chapter. Although biraciality does not prevent coalition-building among racial subalterns, because separation continues to be a key component of its discursive framing (often yoked to a strain of racial essentialism), it does create an impediment because too often alliance formation becomes framed for non-black-or-white groups as an either/or choice between either blacks or whites.[23] In terms of Native Americans, this means, per Melanie Benson Taylor, "Gradually, the Native South became inextricably bound in not just a racial society but a biracial one that increasingly demanded alliance with either a white power structure or a black, laboring underclass."[24]

The second reason the Indian-looking interviewee offers to explain why the Lumbee are often not considered legitimate Indians is because they have no indigenous culture. As she underscores, "[t]he biggest opponents to Lumbee inclusion was those people whose culture is a pan-Indian culture, a powwow tradition, which is not their own tribal tradition or culture but that which has been borrowed from other tribes." When discussing her curly hair mentioned earlier, Maynor displays a number of cultural signifiers associated with

Indianness—a nonverbal communication sign ("hello" hand sign), a style of clothing (a fringed leather dress), and facial make-up (war paint). In addition, she verbally references figures that immediately conjure visual images—John Wayne, Pocahontas, and a cigar store Indian. Maynor holds that none of these representations of American Indians within mainstream popular culture align with how she looks or how she perceives herself. Based on such stereotypes from popular culture the Lumbee *are* "fake Indians." Over an image of a teepee, the Indian-looking interviewee remarks: "Native people have begun to use those same stereotypes in terms of their own identity." Native peoples in the southeast never lived in teepees, nor were they nomadic. They resided in stable farming communities, even living in log cabins constructed of vertical logs rather than horizontal ones. The cultural stereotype based on plains Indians does not apply to native peoples in the eastern United States, and historically they adopted a number of very different strategies for coping with European invasion than their western counterparts. The interviewee regards the adoption of stereotypes by native peoples as symbolic because they tend to focus on "the outward manifestation of one's identity," such as beads, buckskins, feathers, and hairstyles, stereotypes ultimately based upon the "European perspective from the Enlightenment period." She confesses that many native peoples "probably aren't even aware that they are stereotypes."

The non-Indian-looking interviewee notes that Indianness has become associated in the popular consciousness with the Western stereotype perpetuated by the mass media in which "all Indians look like Anthony Quinn in those old movies, kind of the bronze guy in the buckskin pants on a horse." As numerous writers have noted, Hollywood has created a "homogenized Native American, devoid of tribal characteristics or regional differences."[25] Although homogenized, this Hollywood Indian does borrow heavily from one particular region, enough so that Ward Churchill claims "the Plains stereotype ... has assumed proportions of a valid archetype in the public consciousness" as representative of all native peoples.[26] But, as the interviewee reminds the listening viewer, more than one type of Native American exists; the "five hundred different tribes from coast to coast, [were] religiously, culturally, linguistically, as different as European nations are from one another." Although popular culture presents native peoples as a single cultural group, a diversity of cultures exists among them. Along similar lines, in popular culture American Indians are associated with the past. Those "old movies" referenced by the interviewee are Westerns, a genre set at the end of the nineteenth century. But even when Native Americans are allowed to make a filmic appearance in the present, they are expected to at least exhibit cultural signs of the past in their clothes, hairstyles, etc. This expectation is a filmic expression of a broader societal one.

In other words, that Native American as a "*cultural* category . . . must remain unchanged in order to be considered 'Indian.'"[27] While a cultural expectation may accompany race in general, for Native Americans it rises to the level of a requirement for legitimacy. As a result, non-natives are more likely to conceive of sovereignty in cultural, not political, terms. From such a perspective, whether on film or in-person, racial legitimacy derives from the exhibition of cultural traits from the past that are thought of as uniquely Indian.

Malinda Maynor draws attention to the role of aural and visual culture to signify Indianness when she shows a Barbie doll slowing turning on the screen wearing an Indian outfit and professes: "Other Indians even argue that Lumbees can't be real Indians because we're not traditional enough. No reservation, no ancient language, and too much bad blood." The juxtaposition of an Indian outfit on Barbie highlights the hollowness of visual signifiers to represent Indianness in popular culture; the right outfit does not make Barbie, the embodiment of whiteness, into a Native American. The dress is to being native what Barbie's body is to being female. Although not explicitly stated, the theatrical performances in the documentary, in conjunction with the talking heads, raises the question: Why does the performance of white-derived Indian stereotypes not call into question a native tribe's legitimacy (a matter that will be discussed further in the last section), while the loss of one's original culture does? The loss of native cultures by many southeastern Indians is the result of their adopting a survival strategy of isolationism.

If bodily and cultural signifiers are problematic for determining Indian legitimacy, then what criteria should be used? Both interviewees in *Real Indian* advocate that, rather than outward stereotypical manifestations or federal guideline compliance, the basis for determining who is a legitimate Indian should be based on "one's outlook, one's behavior." They agree that there *is* "something" that "is recognizable as Indian," although that "something" is "hard to put into words" and cannot be measured through visual signifiers, such as dark hair or powwow dancing, or auditory ones, such as war yelps or spoken dialect. Indianness, they concluded, is constituted by "a connection to home" and a "sense of place," a connectedness "with the generations that went before." This definition is one shared by Maynor. The documentary ends the way it began, with old family photographs passing along the screen. Over the photos, Maynor affirms that her Indian tradition is her family and community, "and that's what's real." In other words, "real Indians" are defined not by signs that can be registered on their body (whether physical or cultural) or outward manifestations, such as facial features or hair, clothes or dances, many of which are white stereotypes, but rather by a philosophical perspective toward family and relationships that sustains them through constantly changing times. A number of writers also conclude that kinship is the foundation of being native. For example, Jack Forbes claims that for many Native Americans "identity begins with a family identity," "a kinship unit," and that "the family is the key element in all native social, economic, and political life."[28] Similarly, when Frank Porter III lists the main elements that contributed to the social cohesion and eventual survival of eastern native peoples, key among them is "the maintenance of family unity," in other words, kinship.[29] So, Indianness is collective, not individualistic, and is determined by social relations, not outward manifestations. The idea of family closeness as characteristic of a particular social group is not unique to Native Americans, however, and the trait is a common stereotype applied to minorities. Similar references are routinely made about Latinos, blacks, and gay men (they take such good care of their mothers, bless the dears). So it cannot be read as a characteristic unique to a particular group. But it is this history of family relationships—kinship, not tribal name—that makes the group native.[30] Cultural expressions can be adopted and dropped without affecting that core relationship. Similarly, the group can absorb outside members of other races without affecting the core. As a result, Indianness moves beyond the bodily and cultural and into the relational, a terrain for which currently shorthand audiovisual signifiers have yet to be adequately developed similarly to the other two. Although the family is not separable from race, as discussed in chapter three, defining Indianness relationally aids in reinstating its political dimension.

Representational Strategies of Legitimacy and Mimicry of the Hollywood Indian

After World War II, some federally recognized tribes—in particular, the Cherokees of North Carolina and the Seminoles of Florida—used tourism as a mechanism of economic development. Although gambling is now more important than heritage tourism, a museum and/or gift shop on a reservation is still a common sight. And as one might expect, for sale in those gift shops are documentaries about the groups, some sponsored by the group itself, others produced with the group's cooperation. Two such documentaries are *Snowbird Cherokees* (Rich Panter, 1995), and *The Chief: Calvin McGhee and the Forgotten Creeks* (Max Shores, 1995), which I will consider in terms of aural and visual signifiers of Indianness. Both were produced for educational television with the native group's participation—*The Chief*, by the University of Alabama Center for Public Television and sold by the Alabama-based Poarch Band of Creek Indians, and *Snowbird Cherokees*, by the South Carolina

ETV and sold by the Eastern Band of Cherokee Indians in North Carolina.[31] Although these types of documentaries tend to be either promotional pieces or general histories, they often indirectly wrestle with the issue of signifying Indianness when a discourse of biraciality dominates. Such a discourse typically necessitates the demonstration of difference (as well as differentiation) from blacks and whites in order to be recognized as legitimate and one way of accomplishing that is through cultural expressions. Three such representational strategies appear in these documentaries: (1) adopt the culture associated with one of the Indian confederacies removed to Oklahoma, (2) adopt powwow pan-Indianism, or (3) adopt the Hollywood stereotype.[32] While the first two are considered legitimate native cultures, the last one is not. It is, of course, a fantasy concocted by whites. Yet, this latter means has been invoked by some native peoples to signify Indianness because it is what many non-natives associate with Indianness.

Given that the Indian confederacies removed to Oklahoma are perceived to be authentic Indians, the safest way to obtain legitimacy is to borrow the culture of one of those tribes. Hence, one routinely finds references in tribal names to one of the five confederacies with the prefix "band" attached to it. Both documentaries represent ties between the southeastern tribe and an Oklahoma tribe, with the narrator explicitly making the connection verbally for the listening viewer and audiovisual shots showing the two tribes participating in a joint cultural activity. *The Chief* references both an Oklahoma tribe and powwow culture simultaneously when, over images of people dancing in a circle, the narrator interjects, "Poarch Creeks join members of the Muskogee Creeks of Oklahoma in a stomp dance. It is a symbolic reunion of people separated for over 150 years." Ironically, the joint activity does not have to be Indian. In *Snowbird Cherokees*, an annual gospel singing festival functions as the mechanism for a reunion between the Eastern and Oklahoma Cherokees. Over images of audience members seen through a chain-link fence and accompanied by gospel music on the soundtrack, a voice recounts: "The Trail of Tears separated the tribe and isolated the eastern band from the larger Cherokee nation in Oklahoma." The images switch to people serving themselves buffet-style from a picnic table as the narrator continues: "But reconnections have been made over the years at events like the Trail of Tears Sing." In other words, once fenced off from each other by distance and unawareness, now the two groups commune as one family. As musicians play and sing gospel music, a voice asserts that the event is "an annual Cherokee tradition . . . which strengthens the bonds between the eastern and western Cherokees." Gospel music is an Indian tradition? With its barbershop quartet-style harmonies, the gospel music sung is of the white variety, not that of black gospel's free-flowing call-and-response routine. One way Indian groups in the eastern states maintained social cohesion was by adopting such Euro-America institutions as the church and its accompanying Christianity. Because the Eastern Band of Cherokee Indians has a long history of continuous interaction with the United States government, receiving formal federal recognition in 1868 and a reservation in 1889, their legitimacy as Indians has not been called into question. Sharlotte Neely maintains:

> Because the Cherokees, unlike many other southeastern groups, have reservation land, an Indian language still spoken by a few Cherokees, unique crafts, an undisputed relationship to prehistoric and historic Indians, and other characteristics that non-Indians associate with "real" Indians, the Cherokees have not had to "prove" their Indian identity despite intense intermarriage with whites and the loss of many traditional traits.[33]

As a result, they are free to use non-Indian elements as a basis for reunion and reconnection with the Oklahoma Cherokees. The 1838 Trail of Tears removed "most of the acculturated 'mixed-blood' population [in the hill country] . . . while most of those Cherokees who remained [in the mountains] were 'full-bloods' and conservatives," cultural traditionalists.[34] The Snowbird community, where the Trail of Tears Sing takes place when held in the southeast, is one of the more traditionalist communities of the Eastern Cherokee, so they are secure in their use of Christianity and gospel music without having their Indianness doubted. And though the number of Cherokee speakers in the tribe was steadily decreasing because it was not being passed along to the younger generation, the documentary's audiovisuals highlight its continued presence with images of elderly residents of Snowbird speaking Cherokee and its resurgence with images of young children in a classroom learning the language. The situation for the Poarch Creeks is just the opposite. They at one time lost their language and culture, although they are now reacquiring it through contact with the Oklahoma Creeks. Because their interaction with other Indian groups began before they received federal recognition, signs of Indianness were of utmost importance to them, hence the adoption of the culture of an Oklahoma tribe or the practice of powwow culture in order to be perceived as legitimate Indians.

While the strategies of practicing powwow culture and adopting the culture of an Oklahoma tribe assist in obtaining legitimacy as an Indian group, the strategy of appropriating and performing the Hollywood Indian can ironically do so too. This is not to deny that the strategy is fraught with problems and potential liabilities. This third strategy appears in both documentaries.

However, given the different histories of the two groups in terms of economic development and federal recognition, the matter of performing the Hollywood stereotype is also situated very differently in the documentaries, framed through tourism for the Eastern Band of Cherokee Indians and governmental recognition for the Poarch Band of Creek Indians.

In the 1930s, the United States established the Great Smoky Mountains National Park on the border of the Eastern Cherokee reservation. After World War II, the park brought people to the reservation area in numbers previously not seen. As a result, the Eastern Cherokee adopted tourism as a key component of their economy. In *Snowbird Cherokees*, as a voice informs us the town of Cherokee "expanded enormously to accommodate the tourism," shots appear of signs stating "Red Skin Hotel" and "Honest Injun Trading Post," of streets crowded with stores such as "Pow Wow Gift Shop" and "Golden Arrow," and of a Hollywood-looking Indian on the side of the road. Following these shots of tacky tourist attractions in the town of Cherokee, interviewee Dr. Michael Abrams of the Cherokee Heritage Museum and Gallery remarks that tourists are typically "disillusioned that the Cherokee don't live in teepees." Because of the expectations that tourists bring with them about what "the Indian looks like," Cherokee men, Abrams explains, dress up "in regalia that looks like the war bonnets and the like [that] you see in the John Wayne Hollywood movies of cowboys and Indians." The headdresses are in the Plains Indian style, a style not historically worn by native peoples such as the Cherokee. The adorned Indians allow tourists to have their picture taken with them in exchange for money. Some people, Abrams acknowledges, charge the men with selling out their own people. He counters: "They don't realize that . . . it's nothing more than street theatrics." On a basic level, these performances are parodic from the perspective of the Native Americans but not from that of the tourists; after all, parody is based on an insider's knowledge of text and context. Although tourists may recognize the representations being quoted as those of old Hollywood movies, because the tourists typically do not have a basic understanding of the Cherokee, they are incapable of seeing the historical inappropriateness and thereby the parodic self-display inherent in the spectacle paraded by the street Indians for their consumption. The re-enactment of the Hollywood Indian in *Snowbird Cherokees* is for tourist purposes, offering a white-derived image of the Indian to non-native tourists for an economic return.

In contrast to the Eastern Band of Cherokee Indians, the Poarch Band of Creek Indians only received federal recognition in 1984 and their performance of the Hollywood version of Indianness was for a very different purpose— that of racial and political legitimacy rather than economic gain. *The Chief*

Racial Legitimacy, Representational Strategies, and *Real Indian*

Portrait of Chief Calvin McGhee wearing his war bonnet. Photograph courtesy of Office of Archives and Records Management, Poarch Band of Creek Indians.

explores the life of Calvin McGhee, who in the late 1940s began campaigning for high-school admission of the local native youth. As a now-classic picture of McGhee—standing on a large rock in the woods, dressed in Plains Indian regalia with his arms crossed over his chest—appears on the screen, the voice-over narrator discloses that he began wearing the outfit around 1960 "for most of his public appearances and meetings with government officials." This scene is followed by a talking-head interview with Jack Edwards, a former U.S. congressman from Alabama, who confides: "I believe that he [McGhee] understood what he was about so well that he used that headdress in meetings such as mine and with other congressmen over the years to impress upon them the seriousness of what he was about. It was done in a very formal way. Not in jest at all. He got our attention almost single-handedly and I think wearing that headdress was an integral part of his effort." Toward the end of Edwards's speech, his talking head is replaced with old photos of McGhee crowned with his Plains Indian headdress. Throughout the documentary, pictures are shown of McGhee in his headdress with both state and national politicians, including John F. Kennedy and Lyndon B. Johnson. In contrast to the use of the Hollywood Indian by some Eastern Cherokee men to satisfy tourist demands, here the Hollywood Indian is used to transform the popular leader of a community mistaken in the past as being racially mixed into a legitimate Indian chief of a federally non-recognized native tribe. Because the Poarch Creeks had lost their Indian language and culture, they were without any of the popular signs typically associated with Indianness. McGhee chose to manipulate the symbols that non-natives associated with Indianness, using them as a badge of authenticity despite their obvious historical irrelevance to his own community. Anthony Paredes, in his anthropological writings on the Poarch Creeks, notes that the group has "imported much of the local color that bolsters their public image as Indian."[35] He discloses that some members of the group initially resisted the introduction of "wearing feathers and beads and putting on Indian dances," while others saw "appealing to the stereotyped public tastes for 'Indian culture' . . . as critical for gaining outside support for the Indian cause."[36] The Poarch Creeks began holding an annual Thanksgiving powwow in 1970, easily incorporating its pan-Indian element into the Hollywood stereotype used by Calvin McGhee a decade earlier with his headdress.

To compensate for the tendency of stereotype analysis to overly rely on character studies, Charles Ramírez Berg offers an approach that also takes into consideration film form (such as camera angles, lighting, etc.) as well as the reception process.[37] My concern with the Hollywood stereotype is not with its occurrence on the movie screen or its relationship to the listening viewer but rather with the Hollywood stereotype's migration off the film screen into social reality—in other words, its circulation within society. There is a certain irony in McGhee's borrowing of the "fake Indian" image produced by Hollywood in order to obtain sociopolitical legitimacy as an Indian. His performance of Indianness is a form of mimicry but one different than that theorized by Homi Bhabha. For Bhabha, mimicry entails the colonized subject adopting the external form and internal values of the colonizer, a process he defines as "almost the same but not quite." In other words, mimicry entails the copying of the colonizer's culture by the colonized. Bhabha makes explicit the cross-racial component of his version of mimicry when he rephrases "almost the same but not quite" as "almost the same but not white."[38] But McGhee mimics not whiteness but Indianness. He replicates not the colonizer's culture but rather the colonizer's fictitious image of the colonized culture. One could argue that although the focus is on the colonized culture and not the colonizer's, it still emerges out of the colonizer's frame of reference and perspective, and indeed it does. But this difference in focus has significant ramifications for the conception of mimicry and its relationship to mimesis.

The idea of mimesis—how close the replicated image is to reality—also underlies theories of stereotypes. To dispel the inaccuracies of negative images in film, characters are compared against social reality. But, as Stephen Neale highlights: "Although it claims the stereotypes it identifies . . . are measured against 'the real,' the actual object of comparison is other discourses *about* the real."[39] The reality replicated in McGhee's situation is a particular audiovisual discourse about Indianness—that of Hollywood films. Mimesis in his case is not grounded in non-media-based social reality but rather the mediated reality of the mass media.[40] Simplistic approaches to stereotypes just decry them. Such an approach could be applied here, McGhee's behavior condemned for its perpetuation of the false images created by Hollywood. Such an approach, however, misses the rich terrain present regarding how stereotypes can be used by the stereotyped to their own advantage. Stuart Hall notes that stereotypes can be countered by recoding them through such strategies as reversal and contestation.[41] Reversal entails reversing the popular evaluation of a stereotype by taking a negatively valued characteristic and perceiving it as positive. Of course, such a strategy does not undermine the stereotype because it still operates within its binary logic. Contestation, in contrast, entails contesting the representation from within by making the stereotype work against itself. Because meanings are never entirely fixed, this strategy focuses on the instability inherent in representation. McGhee's performance of the Hollywood Indian stereotype is neither a reversal nor a contestation.

As the interviewees in *The Chief* emphasize, he wore the costume with utmost seriousness. For Bhabha, mimicry is ironic. But no irony exists in McGhee's performance, which was in earnest, nor in its reception at the time, although from a purely conceptual perspective one could argue that it is ironic for those aware of the historical inappropriateness of the costume. For McGhee, the Hollywood Indian outfit was not an ironic statement. Instead, his mimicry resembles that of Harlem voguers, such as those captured in the documentary *Paris Is Burning* (Jennie Livingston, 1991), who also used media images as the basis for their mimesis rather than non-media-based social reality. The aim is not irony or parody but realness. Yet realness in both of these cases is based not on the mimicry of an image from non-media-based social reality but rather from media-based social reality, fashion magazines for voguers, Hollywood films for McGhee. Stereotype analysis compares the media image to non-media-based images in social reality to determine whether they are false (which they always seem to be). An inversion of stereotype analysis occurs here because a media image enacted in non-media-based social reality is compared to the media image to determine whether it is "real." McGhee, like Harlem voguers, seeks to replicate the media image in such a fashion that his performance is mistaken for it. The goal, to borrow Judith Butler's description of Harlem voguers, was "to compel belief, to produce the naturalized effect" through the "embodiment of norms."[42] Media images are the basis for judging the realness of his social performance. He sought to naturalize the performance of this "fake Indian" image appropriated from the mass media. For McGhee it becomes a representational strategy for legitimacy because the conceptualization of race for Native Americans includes a cultural component. In order to be considered a legitimate Indian, one must have a native culture. But, as discussed above, many southeastern Indians lost their native culture and have been mistaken as mixed race because they sometimes intermarried with non-natives. So what is one to do in such a situation if you want to be perceived as Indian? One solution is to turn to the most accessible and well-known Indian culture familiar to non-natives, that produced by the white media, the Hollywood Indian. And that is exactly what McGhee did, a strategy of performing the Hollywood Indian in order to obtain legitimacy as an Indian because one needed a recognizable Indian-specific form of signification in order to be accepted as such. The replication of "fake Indian" media images enabled McGhee to be perceived as a "real Indian." In his case, the underpinning of "the real" is "the fake." Ironically, this claim parallels Scott Romine's that "the fake South . . . becomes the real South through the intervention of narrative."[43] Except here, rather than narrative accomplishing that conversion, it is social performance, one that becomes performative as well, thus solidifying native legitimacy for this community that was federally non-recognized at the time.

Conclusion

Although native tribes are political entities, race is intricately linked to them through not only popular perceptions but tribal requirements such as blood quantum. The issue of race is especially acute for federally non-recognized native tribes because while race is a social position that must be negotiated, self-proclamations can easily go unnoticed or be discounted. Such is the position of many federally non-recognized native groups such as the Lumbee captured in *Real Indian*.

Conclusion

In this book I am not arguing that the discursive framing of the region as biracial is somehow false because it ignores the diversity of racial formations that exist at the local level across southeastern states, which range from monoracial to multiracial. Nor am I making a teleological argument that the region has progressed from being associated with whiteness to biraciality and now needs to be associated with multiraciality in order to more accurately depict the region. If any such associations exist, they are accidental or coincidental, because I hold that the regional is not an accumulation of locales but rather a discursive practice that circulates as a supplement to local, national, and global structures and formations, because regional structures are too weak to sustain the region as a viable arrangement. This means any element(s) presented as a defining characteristic of the region—as its distinctiveness—is always a mediated one(s) because no necessary correlation exists between the local and the regional; any element(s) that emerges as a dominate(s) is the result of the current régime of truth that determines the limits of the permissible and what can function as the truth(s) of the region. Also, a move to framing the region through multiracialism rather than biracialism is not inherently transgressive or transformative. In other words, diversity can easily be recouped and therefore is not inherently a challenger to systems of power, as demonstrated by the discussion of Asian Americans and Native Americans in the last two chapters.

Encapsulating many of the issues discussed in this book are the Melungeons as a mixed-race group and their enunciation in the documentary *Melungeon Voices* (Julie Williams Dixon, 2007). In the 1970s, Appalachians, similar to Cajuns, were perceived as a safe avenue for approaching the regional without the baggage of white supremacy, and numerous documentaries were made on them. But just as the emergence of zydeco music in the 1980s threw light on the problems confronted by black Cajuns (i.e., Creoles), the increased visibility of Melungeons in the 1990s functioned similarly in relation to Appalachia; this occurrence was attributed by many people to the 1994 publication of Brent Kennedy's book *The Melungeons: The Resurrection of a Proud People*, and the controversy that surrounded it both in academia and the recently popularized Internet. And Kennedy plays an important role as an on-screen

Julie Dixon interviewing Seven Gibson for her 2007 documentary *Melungeon Voices*.

interviewee in *Melungeon Voices*. Both the voice-over narrator and a couple of interviewees reference that Melungeons "hide things like their past," invoking the discourse of the closet in relationship to their race and ethnicity similar to the use of the closet in the southeastern expatriate road film that was discussed in chapter three. Darlene Wilson makes explicit the relationship of this closet to race when she asserts: "Brent has been controversial in that he has opened a much denied, well hidden closet door of racism in Appalachia. He opened that door. A lot of Appalachian people don't want to contemplate their mixed ancestry." And the documentary tropes on the voices of Melungeons now heard in the public sphere as the opening of that closet door. The documentary, however, offers no corollary aural or visualization to accompany this linguistic trope. Instead, the image track is full of old photographs similar to *Real Indian*, discussed in the last chapter, and invokes both close family ties and widespread discrimination, both legal and social, as factors contributing to their continuance as a social group. One visual motif, however, that recurs throughout the documentary is that of movement through traveling shots of landscapes rushing across the frame and of moving down roads. This motif is even created in some static shots through the use of time-lapse photography in which mists or clouds stream across the screen. Based on how the documentary enunciates the Melungeons, this movement alludes to both the historical movement of their forbearers from the eastern coastline to the Appalachian Mountains as well as their contemporary movement out of the closet and into the public arena.

Although there is general agreement that the Melungeons are of mixed ancestry, exactly what constitutes that ancestry is hotly debated. (Interestingly, just as no certainty exists regarding their origin, no one knows the origin of the word, "Melungeon," that is used to describe them.) Some scholars claim a Native American origin for them; others claim a black/native, black/white, or black/white/native origin (and in the past they have been classified as a tri-racial isolate, a theory discussed in chapter seven). Brent Kennedy's book was controversial because of its assertion that "most Melungeons had always disclaimed any appreciable Native American heritage," insisting they were "Portuguese, or occasionally Spanish or Turkish."[1] In the book, he argues that the first British explorers found the Melungeons already living in the hinterlands when they arrived. In *The Melungeons*, he uses his own family history to offer an intricate ethnohistory in support of "a mixed Iberian-Moorish-Turkish-Native American heritage for the Melungeons."[2] Although an academician, his book privileges the group's oral history over the written records of historians, anthropologists, and census takers, which he perceives as prejudicial. Although he does not reference Hayden White, who was discussed in the introduction, Kennedy's position shares certain affinities with his claims about writing history and our access to the past. Subsequent to the publication of Kennedy's book, two additional disciplines have been added to the arsenal of approaches being used to solve the mystery of the Melungeons' origin, archeology and genetics, and sections on each appear in the documentary.

Although not the concern of *Melungeon Voices*, the documentary indirectly highlights the two specific problems addressed in this book regarding the way biraciality currently circulates within southern discourse: first, it conceives of race as two separate and distinct categories, black and white, and, second, it ignores the existence of other races and ethnicities. These problems are compounded further because the former is accompanied by the assignment of unequal social values to the two supposedly separate categories, with whiteness privileged over blackness, and the latter operates as a barrier that non-black-or-white groups must negotiate in order to obtain recognition beyond the binary. The documentary narrator acknowledges: "From way back the Melungeons have claimed to be Portuguese, or port-o-gee, and from way back this claim was questioned by many who thought it was just a way of explaining away dark skin that might have been African in origin." And one interviewee, when discussing the potential results of DNA studies of the Melungeons, shares: "They're going to find that we are Portuguese. And that we are Indian. And that we are German. And that we have all of these different European genes in us as well as Mediterranean genes as well as Native American genes." Conspicuously absent from this litany of races and geographical associations is Africa. And the narrator reports that the preliminary conclusions of the most recent DNA study reveals "that some, but not all, of the Melungeon families that have identified as white for several generations in fact have African haplotypes." No one in the documentary denies an African element, but accusations that such denials occur are scattered throughout the documentary, sometimes made by an interviewee but more often by the narrator. Brent Kennedy explicitly acknowledges Africa as part of the mix and points to not only the Melungeon Heritage Association's official logo, "one people, all colors," but that at a Melungeon festival you see people of all colors. The only expression of such denial occurs through its absence from the list of potential origins by the interviewee mentioned above. Given Africa is a potential origin, its omission from the list of potential DNA findings is an act of denial in the modern covert form rather than that of overt expression; this occurrence is an indication that it is perceived as less desirable than those other races and ethnicities that are listed as potential sources of origin. Even in this celebration of multiracialism and multi-ethnicity, residual traces remain that seek to not only marginalize but exclude blackness from the mixture.

During the section of the documentary on DNA studies, Brent Kennedy allows the filmmaker to disclose his family's DNA test results, which reveal a combination of northern European, southeastern European (including Turkey), Middle Eastern, and South Asian. Such genetic studies added another group to the potential list of origins: Roma gypsies from northern India. Toward the end of the documentary, over a map of the world, words flow by describing some of the various Melungeon origin theories, with numerous intersections of locations, peoples, and times flowing across the globe and across history as potential forbearers prior to their emergence as a social group in the Appalachian Mountains. The documentary does not argue on behalf of any particular theory. Rather, it concludes by contemplating the meaning of their very existence and, in keeping with the trope of its title, the narrator declares: "The history books did not give voice to the Melungeons or other mixed-ethnic groups that pioneered and persevered in America's infancy. But now their voices are growing louder and stronger."

A number of lessons can be taken from the existence of the Melungeons. First, the diversity of potential origins for the Melungeons raises questions about our simplification of the past in American history. In the case of Appalachia, which is often associated with Scotch Irish whiteness, the traditional account of an encounter between the English and an indigenous population is expanded to include not only potentially African, Portuguese, and Spanish explorers and/or settlers but potentially individuals of Middle Eastern and South Asian descent. A discourse of biraciality functions to cloak local diversity, not only in the present but also the past. Second, the diversity of potential origins for the Melungeons raises questions about whether single origins exist to explain some groups. In other words, race and ethnicity are not fixed categories; indeed, new categories can emerge, such as the Melungeons (and Latinos), just as older ones can disappear. Change is not a singular, linear process but a multivalent one. In other words, the Melungeons as a social category in the Appalachian Mountains most likely emerged not as the result of one particular type of interracial and interethnic sexual interaction, but from many different kinds. As a result, although socially grouped together at the macro level, at the micro level they can have different family histories, some with African heritage and others not, some with Middle Eastern or Roma Gypsy heritage and others not.[3] In other words, their cohesion emerges not from internal uniformity but external separation. This means that at the level of the individual, a Melungeon might perceive him or herself as white, Native American, or African American, while simultaneously embracing a mixed heritage as Melungeon. So some categories that we perceive as either/or can be lived as both/and.

While the first half of this book discusses some transracial positionalities emerging from blackness within American culture—especially civil rights heritage attractions and redemptive ethnographic documentaries—the latter half of the book, by contrast, presents a bleak situation for blackness. The obfuscation of the existence of other races and ethnicities that arises as a consequence of the dominance of biraciality places a burden upon blackness in a way that it does not for whiteness, making it—as seen in chapters six and seven—that which must be repudiated in order to obtain a racial position beyond the black and white binary assumed by discourses of biraciality. Although biraciality emerged within southern discourse as a means to redeem the region as being still relevant (similar to the function of redemptive ethnographic documentaries discussed in chapter four), from a political perspective it functions as a divider of intergroup affinity and collective action and ultimately has negative consequences for blackness. Many possible Souths exist, each with different political and social ramifications. Let us work to actualize one that also contributes to the actualization of racial equality and justice.

Notes

Introduction

1. I do not believe the nation is an outmoded framework for analysis, for it continues to hold strong sway in practice even in an age of globalization. Rather, my concern is with claims of exclusivity.
2. Chatterjee, "Beyond the Nation? Or Within?" 57.
3. See Bradshaw, *Regions and Regionalism*, and Richard Maxwell Brown, "New Regionalism in America." Richard Maxwell Brown provides an excellent overview of the literature on American regionalism in the twentieth century up to the point of his writing in the early 1980s.
4. Haraway, *Simians, Cyborgs, and Women*, 201.
5. The classic apology for the study of the region through myth is Tindall, "Mythology." The approach continues to be used today as represented by the Lassiter and Crespino anthology, *The Myth of Southern Exceptionalism*.
    On the region as an idea, see Vandiver, "Introduction"; Smiley, "Quest for the Central Theme"; O'Brien, *Idea of the American South*; Richard Gray, *Writing the South*; and Humphries, "Discourse of Southernness." Jefferson Humphries uses the word "discourse" in its popular sense as language usage rather than in the Foucauldian sense (as it will be used throughout this study). As a result, he views the region as "an idea in narrative form" (120). The implementation of the region as an idea varies from viewing it as a belief similar to religion to considering it an intellectual framework for organizing and comprehending social reality. While this introduction proposes approaching the region as a discursive practice, such an approach is not a complete theoretical rupture with that of the region as an idea. Despite very different philosophical underpinnings, the two approaches share one major commonality—as long as the region continues to be discussed, it will continue to exist.
    The classic study on the southerner as ethnicity is Reed, *The Enduring South*. Reed claims that southerners are the only American regional group in the United States that function as an ethnic group as defined by Milton Gordon (10–12).
6. The approaches of "invented South" and "imagined South" are derived, respectively, from Hobsbawm, "Introduction: Inventing Traditions," and Anderson, *Imagined Communities*. These two books were published in the same year, 1983.
    Some examples of these two approaches, often used together, include Ladd, *Nationalism and the Color Line*; Kreyling, *Inventing Southern Literature*; Cobb, *Redefining Southern Culture*, 150–86; and Richard Gray, "Forward: Inventing Communities, Imagining Places."

Contemporary scholars are more likely to approach the southerner as a consumer lifestyle than as an ethnic identity, as proposed by earlier scholars such as John Shelton Reed. One version of this approach views product labels and advertisements as packaging southernness as a commodity that can be acquired through consumption habits; others view consumption habits as regional custom. Some examples of this approach include Hale, *Making Whiteness*, 121–97, and Elias, "Postmodern Southern Vacation."

7. Although my discussion focuses on one particular region of the United States, it is ultimately a general theory of regionalism.

8. See McPherson, *Reconstructing Dixie*; Duck, *The Nation's Region*; Jon Smith, *Finding Purple America*; Romine, *The Real South*; and Greeson, *Our South*. Some of these writers are concerned with both ideology and discourse.

9. Anderson, *Imagined Communities*, 6.

10. Although the term "sectionalism" signifies an area of the country, as does the term "regionalism," by the 1930s the term had come to imply a section of the country where concerns diverged to such a significant degree from those of the rest of the United States that its residents began to believe that continuance in the Union could prove detrimental to their future. Hence, sectionalism has an overt political component absent from regionalism, in particular that of a competing nationalism calling for legal seccession. The introduction of the term "regionalism" in the 1930s was an attempt to remove this element from discussions of the various areas of the United States. Although sectionalism is typically associated with the eleven southeastern states of the former Confederate States of America because of the Civil War, other cases of sectionalism have occurred in the history of the United States. For example, New England almost seceded from the United States when the country initiated the War of 1812. More recently, during the 2008 presidential campaign the sectionalist tendencies in Alaska received mention in the mainstream media as a result of the Republican Party's choice of then-Alaskan governor Sarah Palin as the party's vice presidential candidate. Along similar lines, during the 2010 Texas Republican primary for governor, that state's sectional tendencies arose once again. Texas, of course, after secession from Mexico was a separate country for a decade before it became part of the United States.

11. Bhabha, "Introduction: Narrating the Nation," 1–2.

12. Anderson, *Imagined Communities*, 6.

13. Parker, Russo, Sommer, and Yaeger, "Introduction," 5.

14. Anderson, *Imagined Communities*, 6, 7.

15. Ibid., 46.

16. Brennan, "National Longing for Form," 52.

17. Anderson, *Imagined Communities*, 12.

18. Immanuel Wallerstein ponders in "What Can One Mean by Southern Culture?" whether the proposition that "a cultural entity we may call the South" (1) exists is a meaningful claim. He concludes that it is not because "culture is so fluid and so flexible . . . [w]e do better to make projections about the world-economy and the world political system" (12–13). Wallerstein holds that the concept of culture is routinely used rhetorically for "a political program . . . in the South" (7). Although never explicitly stated, he implies southern culture does not exist, that it is only a rhetorical concept. While concurring, Wallerstein and I differ

in that he uses this conclusion in conjunction with the claim that the United States is in "geopolitical decline in the world-system" (12) to justify recourse to the global. In contrast, I perceive the matter as an opportunity for a serious engagement with the local.

19. Romine, *The Real South*, 14; Appadurai, *Modernity at Large*, 12.

20. Raymond Williams, in his now canonical definition of culture in *Keywords*, 87–93, explicates three primary ways the word is used: (1) "a general process of intellectual, spiritual and aesthetic development," (2) "a particular way of life, whether of a people, a period, a group, or humanity in general," and (3) "the works and practices of intellectual and especially artistic activity" (90).

21. Critiques of the concept of culture range from weak to strong. Some include Abu-Lughod, "Writing against Culture"; Mitchell, "There's No Such Thing as Culture"; Gupta and Ferguson, "Beyond 'Culture'"; and Wright, "Politicization of 'Culture.'"

22. Michel Foucault, known for his archival-based historical analyses, confessed in an interview compiled in *Foucault Live*: "I am quite aware that I have never written anything but fictions.... It seems to me the possibility exists to make fiction work in truth, to induce effects of truth with a discourse of fiction, and to make it so that the discourses of truth creates, 'fabricates' something that does not yet exist, therefore 'fictionalizes.' One 'fictionalizes' history starting from a political reality that makes it true, one 'fictionalizes' a political outlook that does not yet exist starting from an historical truth" (213). Although a number of core Foucauldian concepts about discourse are present in this quotation, as will become clear as the chapter progresses, I believe use of the word "fiction" has the potential to obfuscate the framework trying to be explained. Foucault had a propensity for quotation marks. The placing of this particular word within quotation marks is an attempt to indicate that this fiction is not *really* fictional as the word is commonly used. In *Michel Foucault: Genealogy as Critique*, Rudi Visker argues that Foucault offers "a critique which literally puts the scientificity of particular disciplines between quotation marks[,] . . . a model of critique which runs throughout his entire *oeuvre*" (2), though "the later works turn away from the problematic of the quotation marks without consciously breaking with them" (98). I have intentionally taken a position to use quotation marks only for actual quotations or around words to indicate a grammatical reference to the word or phrase. Despite Foucault's use of the word "fictionalize," if its use necessitates quotation marks in order to convey one's meaning, I prefer not to use it at all (nor any other such dependent words). As a habitual abuser of sarcasm and irony (which the use of such quotation marks typically imply), I have taken a vow of chastity from them for this project, along with words such as "invented," "imagined," and "fictive."

23. The word "civil" comes from the close association of the region in the popular consciousness with the Civil War and the civil rights movement. Although "civil" in these two phrases means "civic," I use the term in a dual sense to also include "civilized." In other words, the term "civil" as employed here incorporates both the political and the polite. It encompasses not only public polity but also public manners.

24. Sara Mills, *Discourse*, 48.

25. I approach the region through the theoretical framework of a discursive practice. An alternative theoretical approach, taking a lead from the "post" in postmodernism and

poststructuralism, is the postsouthern. The concept has been used over the last three decades by Simpson, "The Closure of History in a Postsouthern America" in *Brazen Face of History*, 255–76; Kreyling, "*The Fathers*: A Postsouthern Narrative Reading"; Romine, "Where Is Southern Literature? The Practice of Place in a Postsouthern Age"; and Bone, *Postsouthern Sense of Place*. Phrases used by these authors, such as "this postsouthern age," "our postsouthern moment," and "late capitalist post-South," imply the term means a chronological shift to a new epoch or condition, a time after "southern." Such a definition makes the term little more than a lament or celebration, depending on the user's perspective, of a vanished South, an old intellectual position now displayed in trendy jargon, as a new stage is entered after the region's demise. Recent usages of the term designate not a period after disintegration but rather the heralding of a new South in which the traditional signifiers of the region are muted as a result of the intrusion of global capitalism. If the term "postsouthern" is meant to signify a transformation of the region from agrarian to industrial, then why attach the prefix "post" to the word "South"? Why not "post-agrarian," because people still refer to "the South"? Sometimes the term appears to be a substitute for "postmodern," in which case "postsouthern" is the equivalent of "postmodern South." Application of the term in such situations is a misnomer because they describe reconfigurations of the region, not a period after it. To date, circulation of the term has been limited, its usage restricted primarily to academic literary analysis. The approach innately inscribes the South as exceptional unless other regions are also post. I do not, however, foresee calls for a post-western, post-Midwestern, post-northern, or post-New England. If one desires a term to indicate a change in the configuration of the region, Scott Romine's phrase "the late South," introduced in his *The Real South*, appears a more productive approach (although, as Romine notes, it does invoke a deceased as well as a later temporal period).

26. Given my conceptualization of the region as discursive, just as a temptation exists to appropriate Benedict Anderson's framework of "imagined community" and apply it wholesale to the region, it also exists in relationship to Edward Said's concept of "orientalism," overlaying his East/West distinction at the global level onto the South/North division within the United States and calling the result something like Dixieism. According to Said, orientalism is knowledge produced by the West about the East that transforms it into the Orient, a position of inferiority to the superiority of the West. In other words, orientalism is the West speaking for the East. In contrast, southern discourse is multiperspectival, its power dynamics neither hierarchical (with its dominant/subordinate model) nor binary. So southern discourse is not comparable to orientalism, nor is "the South" to "the Orient." On orientalism, see Said, *Orientalism*.

27. Foucault, *Archaeology of Knowledge*, 49.

28. Tomlinson, *Cultural Imperialism*, 61.

29. Foucault, *Power/Knowledge*, 131.

30. Scott Romine uses the words "simulacrum" and "simulation" in *The Real South* to make this same point that no original South exists. Although he uses Gilles Deleuze's concept of deterritorialization throughout the book, his use of the word "simulacrum" appears to be meant in the Baudrillardian sense. As Claire Colebrook distinguishes in *Gilles Deleuze*, for Jean Baudrillard the simulacrum—a copy with no original—entails "the lost or

abandonment of the real" while for Deleuze the simulacrum "*is* the real" (101). Toward the end of his career, Deleuze reassessed the usefulness of the concept, reflecting: "I have totally abandoned the notion of simulacrum, which is all but worthless" (Deleuze, *Two Regimes of Madness*, 366).

From a Deleuzian perspective, simulacrum could be included in my conceptualization of southern discourse, but not Baudrillard's version. I prefer, however, not to use the concept because, as typically conceptualized, it tends to be devoid of the power dynamics associated with struggle and contestation that I hold are integral components of southern discourse as a discursive practice. As a concept it also tends to foreclose the issue of multiplicity, which appears to be Deleuze's reason for forsaking the concept.

As opposed to considering the region as a simulacrum, another approach that also begins with the premise that no original exists is that of the "concept" as defined by Gilles Deleuze and Félix Guattari in *What is Philosophy?* 19–22. Being incorporeal, the concept lacks a referent. For them a concept is neither an idea nor a discursive formation, which thereby differentiates it from previous popular approaches to the region such as an idea and emerging ones such as a discursive practice.

31. Because I hold that the region is presented, not represented, I have tailored the common cinema studies phrase "self-representation" to align with this position. Although the phrase "self-re/presentation" would have indicated another presentation of the self, because the slash in such situations is often used to indicate the simultaneous presence of two concepts (in this case, repeat presentation and representation), and my intention is not to invoke the concept of representation, I have not used it. An alternative phrase is offered by Richard Gray in "Inventing Communities, Imagining Places": "southern self-fashioning." The concept of "self-fashioning" had previously been used in relationship to ethnography—"ethnographic self-fashioning"—by James Clifford, who borrowed it from Stephen Greenblatt's book *Renaissance Self-Fashioning*. See Clifford, "On Ethnographic Self-Fashioning" in *Predicament of Culture*, 92–113.

32. Foucault, *Power/Knowledge*, 98.

33. Ibid., 133.

34. For a discussion of the concept of bricolage, see Hebdige, *Subculture*, 102–106.

35. Degler, *Place over Time*, 1, 127.

36. Claval, "Region as a Geographical, Economic and Cultural Concept," 167.

37. I use the term "local" in the rather unorthodox way to include not just the municipal level but also the state, which one could argue is too large to be local. The state is not the region, so one is left with the local to describe it within the terminological framework of the local, regional, national, and global. Of course, the local is rarely synonymous with legal jurisdictions (although the names of municipalities provide easily accessible linguistic labels for referring to particular locales). A particular locale is, first, simultaneously part of numerous types of configurations (such as environmental, legal, economical, social, psychological, and cultural), and second, participates in multiple manifestations within each of these types of configurations, each with different flows that connect with other configurations. For example, the different industries within a locale form different manifestations within its economic configuration, which means that the connecting flows to other locales

vary in terms of quality and quantity. Unlike more easily definable political configurations, social and cultural configurations tend to be amorphous. The question arises: how large can such configurations develop in the absence of specific institutional structures dedicated to sustaining them? Although I do not believe the region is a sociocultural configuration, I do believe larger ones exist beyond those typically referenced through the shorthand use of municipal and jurisdictional labels—for example, the Mississippi Delta. Of course, the Mississippi Delta is simultaneously a discursive formation as well. At the local level, not only do multiple configurations exist simultaneously, with multiple manifestations within each of these configurations, but their connecting flows with configurations in other locales are often spatially noncontiguous—in other words, trans-local, which is something very different than regional.

Given this situation of overlapping multivalent configurations with various connections to other configurations, which often tend to be trans-local, I believe an argument could be advanced for shifting the discussion away from that of regions to that of assemblages, as proposed by Gilles Deleuze and Félix Guattari. If the world was approached from such a perspective, while most of the conceptual ways lived life is currently approached would continue to be important, I believe the region, however, would prove inconsequential.

On the assemblage, see Deleuze and Guattari, *A Thousand Plateaus*, 88–91 and 503–505. Manuel DeLand and Lawrence Grossberg have proposed conceptual frameworks that share affinities to varying degrees with Deleuze and Guattari's concept of assemblage. See DeLanda, *A New Philosophy of Society*, and Grossberg, *Cultural Studies in the Future Tense*.

38. Reed, *One South*, 28, 30.

39. While local structures may also contain a national discursive supplement, unlike the regional, the national is not dependent upon it for existence because it has sufficient and numerous types of institutional structures to sustain its formation—socially, politically, culturally, economically, psychologically, jurisdictionally, and discursively.

40. At first I read Scott Romine's creative term "microSouths" in *The Real South* as referring to multiple configurations of the region that exist simultaneously in contestation, although some may be more popular or prevalent than others, at least within certain social formations and institutional structures. But later I realized I had misunderstood his concept. As he attests: "Mapping the South is always a situated venture and always implicitly narrative: a way of mobilizing space in efforts of immense variety and scope, ranging from (at the macro level) the red state mythology of contemporary American politics to more localized efforts to generate more intimate and compelling microSouths" (9). In other words, microSouths are boutique subsets of the South, even if some are deterritorialized. I hold that the local and everyday are not the regional and exist in their own right but can sometimes become framed as expressions of the region through a discursive supplement. That supplement to the local is the regional, not the local itself.

41. See Duck, *The Nation's Region*, 33. Unlike Leigh Anne Duck, who equates the local with the regional, I hold this supplement occurs with the local as well as the national because the local and regional do not exist in a hierarchical relationship with the former innately a manifestation of the latter. As a discursive practice with insufficient regional institutional structures to sustain it, the regional must poach as a discursive supplement on other structures through which knowledge circulates, be they local, national, or global.

42. Culler, *On Deconstruction*, 103.

43. Derrida, *Of Grammatology*, 154–55.

44. I do not wish to frame the region as lack, although based on Jacques Derrida's definition of the supplement, such an approach appears justifiable. The most common intellectual framework founded on the concept of lack is the Lacanian definition of desire as lack in relationship to an object, the *objet petit a*. If the lack is within that which is supplemented (the local, national, and global), then the regional becomes the *objet petit a*, that which is desired. Therefore, the region must remain allusive of them in order to continue its existence because, once satisfied, desire dissipates and along with it the *objet petit a*. But, within the Lacanian framework, desire is perpetually deferred, which means the lack can never be fulfilled. This quandary would need to be reconciled in order to define the regional as lack through the framework of Lacanian desire because the supplement fulfills a lack, is a trace of its prior presence.

In Saussurian semiotics, a sign stands for something other than itself and is composed of two parts: the signified, which refers to the mental concept that the sign represents, and the signifier, the physical form the sign takes for perception by our senses. While written words are signs, photographs are too. The referent is the thing to which the sign refers. While the *objet petit a* is defined as a signifier without a signified and therefore without a fixed definition, it *does* have a referent. If one uses such Saussurian semiotic language to describe the region as I have postulated it, then the region is a signifier with a signified but no referent. Thereby, the region as a discursive practice proposed here is incompatible with the region as lack framed through the approach of Lacanian desire.

45. Duck, "Southern Nonidentity," 322, 329.

46. See Foucault, "Governmentality."

47. Bourdieu, "On the Family," 21.

48. Munslow, *Deconstructing History*, 2.

49. Ibid., 5.

50. White, *Tropics of Discourse*, 129.

51. Ibid., 95.

52. Ibid., 125.

53. See Metz, *Film Language*. After an exploration of film through linguistics, Christian Metz concludes that "the cinema is certainly not a language system (*langue*)" but "[i]t can, however, be considered as a *language*, to the extent that it orders signifying elements within ordered arrangements different from those of spoken idioms" (105).

54. Shohat and Stam, *Unthinking Eurocentrism*, 215.

55. Katherine Henninger laments in *Ordering the Façade: Photography and Contemporary Southern Women's Writing* the over-reliance on "southern orality and oral tradition" (16) and argues for a turn to the visual, a sentiment with which I agree. But her book, except for one chapter, is concerned with writing, which is after all from a Derridian perspective a supplement to speech, i.e., the oral. She justifies this focus because "without the words surrounding the pictures—as captions, newspaper items, diary entries, cultural criticism, or fictional narratives—the cultural meanings of these images remain largely obscure" (9). People learn how to read visual images just as they do printed words, acquiring sociocultural codes allowing them to be understood. This skill is typically mastered before learning

to read print. The former is not dependent upon the latter, as Henninger implies, although both *are* dependent on the acquisition of cognition, even if only at a crude level. While the meaning of visuals may be denser and more ambiguous than words, this does not translate into their meaning being obscure. While written material—which is historical documentation—is necessary for writing a history of how visual (and audiovisual) material was received by viewers when issued and how they circulated within society (that is, when no original viewers exist to interview about such), the determination of their meaning is not dependent upon such written words, neither today or at the time they were made, nor any period in-between. Because access to the past is only available through traces that remain in the present, written documentation (as well as visual, auditory, audiovisual, and three-dimensional documentation) is needed to gain access to it. This need emerges from the task of *writing history*, not in order to be able to understand visual (and audiovisual) material. (Her dismissal of oral tradition simultaneously dismisses ethnographic-based oral history as an alternative means to access, however tenuously, the meaning attached to these visuals by users.) Although Henninger's goal is to bring to the forefront the neglect of the visual in southern studies, her framework inadvertently continues to subordinate it to the written, the supplement of speech. Although she lists film and television among the visual media routinely used to present the region, she ignores the fact that, unlike photography, these media are *audio*visual ones, not visual ones. In her flight from the oral, she also banishes the aural.

56. Michel Foucault offers just as strong a critique of literary analysis as he does writing history. Unlike his contemporaries, French philosophers Jacques Derrida and Gilles Deleuze, he rarely used literary analysis for philosophical investigations. In "On Literature," one of the interviews compiled in *Foucault Live*, 150–53, Foucault observes: "There has never really been an analysis of how, given the mass of things that are spoken, given the set of discourses actually held, a certain number of these discourses (literary discourse, philosophical discourse) are sacralized and given a particular function. It seems that traditionally literary and philosophical discourse has been made to function as a substitute or as a general envelope for all other discourses. Literature had to assume the value for all the rest" (150). He proposes: "In order to know what is literature, I would not want to study internal structures. I would rather grasp the movement, the small process through which a non-literary type of discourse, neglected, forgotten as soon as it is spoken, enters the literary domain" (152).

57. Jon Smith, Review of *Reconstructing Dixie*, 669–70. Jon Smith subsequently explored aspirational Souths in his book *Finding Purple America*.

58. Romine, *The Real South*, 105.

59. As numerous scholars have reiterated, the real is not the same as social reality, but as Alisa Lebow observes in "Faking What? Making a Mockery of Documentary," "the Real nonetheless structures our semblance of reality" (233) and "[r]eality is itself implicated as a poor rendering, an unconvincing rendition of the unattainable ideal (of the Real)" (232). In other words, a connection exists between the two terms other than just through linguistic slippages. In addition to Lebow's article, for an engaging discussion of the Lacanian real in relationship to documentary film, see Cowie, *Recording Reality, Desiring the Real*.

60. Foucault, *Archaeology of Knowledge*, 117.

61. Foucault, "Politics and the Study of Discourse," 59.

62. Visker, *Michel Foucault: Genealogy as Critique*, 119.

63. Agamben, *Potentialities*, 179.

64. Ibid., 180.

65. While the possible exists in the present, it invokes the future. One academic site where the issue of the field of the possible is explicitly framed in terms of the future rather than the present is the antisocial thesis debate within Queer Theory, a debate best exemplified by the work of Lee Edelman and José Esteban Muñoz. A key part of the debate centers around the question of whether queerness produces no future (i.e., death) or, instead, new forms of sociability. In contrast to the singularity and negativity offered by Edelman with his Lacanian psychoanalytic inspired approach, Muñoz offers collectivity and futurity through use of Ernst Block's critical philosophy. See Edelman, *No Future*; Muñoz, *Cruising Utopia*; and Caserio, Edelman, Halberstam, Muñoz, and Dean, "Forum: The Antisocial Thesis."

66. Foucault, *Foucault Live*, 76. Just as Gilles Deleuze in this conversation with Michel Foucault refers to theory as "like a box of tools," a few years later Foucault refers to his books as being like "little tool boxes. If people want to open them, use a particular sentence, idea, or analysis like a screwdriver or wrench in order to short-circuit, disqualify or break up the systems of power, including eventually the very ones from which my books have issued . . . well, all the better!" (Foucault, *Foucault Live*, 149).

67. Within a Deleuzian framework, an alternative to the possible South is the virtual South. Gilles Deleuze uses the concept of "the virtual" in a specific philosophical sense, and joining it to "the South" risks conflation with the word's now-popular meaning of cyberspace. While the virtual is real, it has not yet been actualized. Therefore, its couplet is with the actual, not the real. This means one could avoid the risk within the humanities of a linguistic slippage into the Lacanian real when using the word. Of the two approaches, I prefer the possible, not only because of the linguistic confusion with virtual reality that will most likely accompany use of the phrase "the virtual South" but also because of, as will be discussed below, the way Gilles Deleuze and Félix Guattari eventually connect the virtual to the possible. David Lapoujade, the editor of *Two Regimes of Madness*, a collection of writings by and interviews with Deleuze, maintains that the last published article by Deleuze derived from his wanting "to flesh out the concept of the virtual which he felt he had left relatively unexplored" (Deleuze, *Two Regimes of Madness*, 416). For me the Deleuzian concept of the virtual continues to be a difficult one to grasp.

68. Rodowick, *Gilles Deleuze's Time Machine*, 86.

69. Deleuze, *Bergsonism*, 98.

70. Ibid., 97.

71. For a detailed discussion of the possible/real and virtual/actual in *Bergsonism*, see Hardt, *Gilles Deleuze: An Apprenticeship in Philosophy*, 13–19.

72. Deleuze and Guattari, *What is Philosophy?* 118.

73. Ibid., 177–78.

74. See Bogue, *Deleuze on Music, Painting, and the Arts*, 176–85, for a detailed discussion of the possible in *What is Philosophy?* Unlike the English edition of *What is Philosophy?* that uses the word "survey," Ronald Bogue holds that the phrase "fly over" [*survolent*] is more appropriate to describe how Gilles Deleuze connects the relationship of the event to the possible.

75. Bogue, *Deleuze on Music, Painting, and the Arts*, 185.

76. A second configuration of the possible exists in *What is Philosophy?* which I have not explored here. This version emerges through the "concept of the Other Person as expression of a possible world" (18).

77. Gilles Deleuze concludes his last published article thus: "There is a big difference between the virtuals which define the immanence of the transcendental field, and the possible forms which actualize them and transform them into something transcendent" (Deleuze, *Two Regimes of Madness*, 393). And Félix Guattari, in his final solo-authored work, *Chaosmosis: An Ethico-Aesthetic Paradigm*, interlaces the two couplets of possible/real and virtual/actual, theoretically synthesizing them into an assemblage of ontological functions with the virtual and actual each having a possible and real, and vice versa.

78. Deleuze, *Two Regimes of Madness*, 233.

79. Ibid., 234.

80. While I claim that today the region is formed through discursive practices, one could construct an argument based on the temporary geopolitical formation of eleven states as the Confederate States of America (CSA). From such a perspective, the emergence and demise of the CSA becomes an event in the Deluezian sense of the term (similar to how Gilles Deleuze and Félix Guattari apply the term to May 1968 in France, which after all was also a failed revolt). This event created the possibility of the South existing as a region, producing "a new subjectivity" which society needed to match with "collective agencies of enunciation" (Deleuze, *Two Regimes of Madness*, 234) in order to sustain the possibility. Deleuze and Guattari hold that France failed to do so in relation to May 1968. The question becomes whether such "collective agencies of enunciation" exist for the South. I hold that while a few do, they are too insignificant to sustain the region as a cultural, social, psychological, emotional, economical, or geographical formation (or some combination thereof). Therefore, in order to exist the region must poach on local, national, and global structures and formations as a discursive supplement. Any argument about the South based on the CSA is innately an argument of regional exceptionalism.

81. Foucault, *Foucault Live*, 130.

82. Although, as discussed in footnote 67, I think the concept of "virtual South" will result in too much linguistic confusion for it to be useful, ultimately I am arguing that the possible South actualizes a virtual South.

83. Agamben, *Coming Community*, 85.6.

84. I am not arguing that the region and documentary film are analogous. While both are discursive practices, an outside exists in relationship to the documentary discourse that is not present with the regional as I have defined it.

85. Cowie, *Recording Reality, Desiring the Real*, 42.

86. Elizabeth Cowie also maintains in *Recording Reality, Desiring the Real* that the truth of documentary film "arises not through being recorded reality" but "through the argument it makes in presenting the statements of others" (26)—in other words, emplotment.

87. For Gilles Deleuze "art" means *high* art. His cultural elitism is on full display in "The Brain Is the Screen," one of the pieces collected in *Two Regimes of Madness*, 287–96. Although he acknowledges the existence of an "art market," he differentiates between "commercial

works" and "creative works," maintaining "there is no such thing as commercial art," which is "a contradiction in terms" (293). Today, his position reads as a cliché. Channeling Theodor Adorno, he not only claims commercial works are tailored to "the lowest common denominator" (293) but offer "prefabricated models of emotions" as opposed to the "multiplication of emotion" and "the invention of new emotions" (294) associated with works of art. He disdains the type of position I am advancing here, espousing: "People today think they're being clever when they erase the distinction between the creative and the commercial" (293). Too bad Deleuze did not read Pierre Bourdieu's articles on art markets and cultural capital written during the 1980s, when he composed this essay. See Bourdieu, *Field of Cultural Production*.

88. Gaines, "Political Mimesis," 91.

89. Ibid., 93, 99–100. While mimicry may sometimes be a mechanical copying, such reproductions are not necessarily always mindless. Within certain contexts, mimicry can also have political valiance, as I discuss in chapter seven regarding mimicry of the Hollywood Indian by the leader of the Poarch Band of Creek Indians in Alabama as a strategy for political legitimacy. The main purpose of her comparison of the two terms, however, is to differentiate her use of mimesis from deterministic behavioral models of media effects.

90. Winston, *Claiming the Real II*, 152.

91. Ibid., 233.

92. Ibid., 232. In *Representing Reality*, Bill Nichols considers three ways to define documentary film, "from the point of view of the filmmaker, the text, and the viewer" (12), as respectively (1) a community of practitioners with specific institutional practices, (2) a corpus of texts, and (3) "a function of the assumptions and expectations brought to the process of viewing the text" (24).

93. Ibid., 233.

94. While the field typically perceives these two approaches for distinguishing between documentary film and fictional film—the relationship of the image to social reality and the audience's perception—as an either/or proposition, the association by Gilles Deleuze and Félix Guattari of science with the actual and art with sensations offers a potential means to integrate them using their philosophy, science, and art framework. I have not thought through this line of investigation so it may prove unfruitful. While Brian Winston rejects appeals to science to explain the real of documentary film, Elizabeth Cowie repositions the issue of science by framing it within desire. She perceives documentary film as inheriting discourses of science and of desire, addressing simultaneously the desire for scientific knowledge and for sensational spectacle, engaging both the "pleasure of the visual" and our "desire for the real" (Cowie, *Recording Reality, Desiring the Real*, 9).

95. One could go further and claim that this is a triple dose of the possible if I incorporate Gilles Deleuze and Félix Guattari's other conceptualization of the possible in *What is Philosophy?*—that "of the Other Person as expression of a possible world" (18). So the possible arises not only from being an art form and capturing a pro-filmic event but also capturing a pro-filmic "Other Person."

96. I use the word "transmission" in order to incorporate both the solid picture from an old-fashioned film projector as well as the continual streaming line of data on a screen, be it

analog or digital, be it a television set, game console, computer, or handheld device, such as a cell phone.

97. The word "enunciation" will be used as it commonly is in cinema studies. According to Francesco Casetti, "enunciation is what, starting from cinema's inherent potentialities, allows a film to take form and to manifest itself: to present itself as a *text*, as *this* specific text, and as this specific text in this specific *situation*" (Casetti, *Theories of Cinema*, 155).

98. Fairclough, *Discourse and Social Change*, 62, 63.

99. From the perspective of their effective engagement with the local, academic disciplines differ widely. In general, anthropologists tend to emphasize the local over the regional, literary scholars the regional over the local, and historians somewhere between these two poles. While the national is an important category within cinema studies, the regional has received only limited attention.

100. *Mai's America* was shot on video, not film. I will use throughout this book the word "film" to refer to the documentaries I discuss regardless of whether they were shot on film, video, or digital.

101. See Geertz, "Thick Description: Toward an Interpretive Theory of Culture" in *Interpretation of Cultures*, 3–30.

102. Steven Rosen, "Asian Film Fest Puts Spotlight on Vietnam," *Denver Post*, 30 May 2002.

103. "Philadelphia Festival of World Cinema: Another Week in the Hot Seat," *Philadelphia Weekly*, 10 April 2002.

104. R. A. Bell, "*Mai's America*," *Orlando Weekly*, 11 June 2002; Felicia Feaster, "American Nightmare: *Mai's America* Chronicles a Contemporary Culture Clash," *Creative Loafing*, 28 August 2002.

105. Degler, *Place over Time*, 7. Although Carl Degler mentions a number of ways in which he holds that the region is distinct (from hotter weather to greater ruralness to narrower range of religions) his primary historical argument rests on issues that tie into race.

106. Ibid., 17.

107. The word "articulation" is commonly used to refer to the linguistic expression of an idea. Just as I use the word "discourse" in a specific way (the Foucauldian sense), so too do I use the word "articulation." "Articulation" will be used as it commonly is in black British cultural studies: to refer to the linking (i.e., articulation) of race to other categories. For a detailed discussion of articulation, see Hall, "Race, Articulation, and Societies Structured in Dominance."

108. Since I began this project, a significant body of academic work has emerged that challenges this second denial, ranging from ethnographic studies to historical investigations to textual examinations. For examples of the latter, see Bow, *Partly Colored*, Milian, *Latining America*, and Taylor, *Reconstructing the Native South*, which consider Asian Americans, Latinos, and Native Americans, respectively, in relationship to the region. A split appears to be forming within southern discourse between its dominant configuration of race within the academy and within the popular.

109. Ayers, "What We Talk About," 82.

110. Dollimore, *Sexual Dissidence*, 33.

Chapter 1

1. "Central Alabama's Black Heritage Trail."
2. The civil rights movement is periodized in popular culture as lasting from the 1955 Montgomery bus boycott to the 1965 March from Selma to Montgomery. The movement, of course, preceded and succeeded these particular events.
3. Williams, *Marxism and Literature*, 122, 123.
4. Phillips, "Central Theme of Southern History," 31.
5. Immediately following the 2008 election of President Obama, the association of the region with whiteness frequently appeared on the twenty-four-hour cable news channels because John McCain captured a super majority of the white votes in most southeastern states. Of course, the same pattern occurred in the plains and mountainous states, too, so this was not unique or exceptional but the media often made it sound as though it was.
6. Tindall, "Central Theme Revisited," 126.
7. Reed, *One South*, 117. The article, coauthored with Merle Black, originally appeared in *Journal of Politics* 44, no. 1 (February 1982): 165–71.

Because of my predilection for theory and cultural and social analysis, one might assume that I am anti-empirical research. I find much of it not only fascinating but also helpful. Just like writing history, however, statistical-based studies have methodological weaknesses often disavowed through claims of scientific truthfulness. Our grasp of social reality is always tenuous and partial regardless of the method we use. None have a greater claim on truth and all are mediated constructions of social reality.

8. Reed, *One South*, 118.
9. Although Joel Williamson's *Crucible of Race: Black-White Relations in the American South since Emancipation* and David Goldfield's *Black, White, and Southern: Race Relations and Southern Culture, 1940 to the Present* rarely use the word "biracial" in their racial overviews of the region, as their titles indicate they frame the "crucible of race" and "race relations" as black and white—in other words, biracial.
10. Joel Williamson, *New People*, 109.
11. Ibid., 22. The most famous of these free mulatto communities was Cane River in lower Louisiana. For more on it, see Gary Mills, *The Forgotten People*. The documentaries *Women of Cane River* (Mark Cottrell, 1980) and *The Creoles of Cane River* (Bill Rodman, 2005) focus on the community.
12. Ibid., 87.
13. Ironically, this framing enacts a form of racial purity within race mixing by ignoring the Indian component.
14. Williamson, *New People*, 3.
15. Stephen Smith, *Myth, Media, and the Southern Mind*, 48.
16. Ibid., 154.
17. Ibid., 91, 60.
18. Ibid., 92–93.
19. As noted in footnote 108 of the introduction, the emergent configuration of the region as multiracial is poised to become the dominant within the academy, bifurcating southern discourse's dominant between its academic practice and other ones.

20. Of course, groups are minorities not because of their size but their social disadvantage and discrimination. In other words, minority status results from power differential, not size. Size, however, often plays a role in that social condition. Blacks in the United States qualify as a minority group based on both counts.

21. McPherson, *Reconstructing Dixie*, 7.

22. Ibid., 25–26.

23. Ibid., 7.

24. Baker Jr. and Nelson, "Preface: Violence, the Body and 'The South,'" 236. The recurring use by Houston Baker Jr. and Dana Nelson of quotation marks around "The South" reminds me of Michel Foucault's prior routine use of quotation marks around certain words to call their meaning into question. See footnote 22 of the introduction.

25. Fishkin, "Interrogating 'Whiteness,' Complicating 'Blackness,'" 428–29, 436–37.

26. In the wake of the emergence of multiculturalism in the 1990s and the greater public awareness of Latinos in the twenty-first century, the United States is rarely described as biracial today. One can argue that southern discourse is following a similar shift, only at a slower pace.

27. The issue of exceptionalism has routinely been debated both about the South as a region of the country and the United States as a nation of the world. In "The Power and the Glory: Myths of American Exceptionalism," Howard Zinn frames American exceptionalism as a rhetorical claim of divine ordination to justify exemption "from legal and moral standards accepted by other nations in the world." In contrast, Giorgio Agamben argues in *State of Exception* that legal situations of exceptions have become a common element of most Western states. Claims of southern exceptionalism typically function very differently than those for American exceptionalism, a position of deficiency for the former, superiority for the latter. Because the nation, unlike the region, has sustainable institutional structures it has sociocultural and geopolitical formations in addition to discursive formations upon which claims of exceptionalism can be based (and other nations compared). Because of this difference in underlying formations, regional exceptionalism depends on claims of distinctiveness which are always discursively mediated. Of course, because southern discourse is routinely incoherent and fragmentary, perpetually in formation, claims and denials of regional exceptionalism can exist simultaneously in various configurations of influence. I prefer to frame the discussion in terms of similarities and differences, which always exist simultaneously between social formations, institutional structures, and discursive practices. From such a perspective, an admission of difference is *not* a claim of regional exceptionalism based on distinctiveness.

28. Photographs in audiovisual media are experienced differently by viewers than those in print media (such as books and magazines) as well as in gallery displays. Because the audiovisual is a time-based medium, the viewer has a time constraint imposed on how long he or she can peruse the photograph, which in turn influences how much information can be obtained from it and the degree of contemplation achieved.

29. For example, see Bradbury, *Renaissance in the South*; Richard Gray, *Writing the South*; Richard King, *Southern Renaissance*; O'Brien, *Idea of the American South*; Rubin Jr. et al., *History of Southern Literature*; and Singal, *The War Within*. The Vanderbilt Agrarians, who

succeeded the Fugitives, are more often discussed in the literature than the Fugitives themselves; and, when the Agrarians are compared to another group from a southeastern state, typically it is Howard Odum and the movement of regional sociology associated with the University of North Carolina at Chapel Hill, not blues musicians.

30. I use the word "state" to refer to both the general apparatus of government and the specific geographical territories known as states in the United States. Hopefully, which meaning is intended will be clear from the context. When the word is included in a list such as "city, county, state, and federal" or the combination "southeastern state," I am referring specifically to government at the territorial state level and not to the overall apparatus. In contrast, when used in conjunction with the word "apparatus," I am referring to the overall structure of government.

31. Omi and Winant, *Racial Formation in the United States*, 84.

32. See Gramsci, *Pre-Prison Writings*, 313–37. Some comparative scholarship has been performed on southern Italy (the Italian Mezzogiorno) and the southeastern United States. For example, see Dal Lago and Halpern, *American South and the Italian Mezzogiorno*; Kreyling, "Italy and the United States"; Doyle, *Nations Divided*; and Dal Lago, *Agrarian Elites*. Although I admire Antonio Gramsci's work and find it useful, he views the region as a sociocultural, geopolitical, and economic formation rather than a discursive supplement as I do. The historical situations of the southeastern United States and southern Italy differ from a geopolitical perspective; the former attempted secession from a country, the latter unification into one.

33. Hall, "Gramsci's Relevance for the Study of Race and Ethnicity," 435.

34. This discussion is based on Bullock III and Gaddie, *Triumph of Voting Rights*; Black and Black, *Divided America*; and Browder, *The South's New Racial Politics*. Charles Bullock III and Ronald Gaddie note that in Alabama, at the time of their writing, though black state legislators were "elected roughly in proportion to the eligible electorate" (77), the state had "no African Americans elected to statewide constitutional offices" (70). As a result, the number of black officeholders as a percentage of total electoral positions shows underrepresentation of the electorate.

35. See Toby Miller, *Cultural Citizenship*.

36. Although this achievement has been under siege since the 2000 presidential election, as represented by the voting problems in Florida and Ohio over the years, the June 2013 Supreme Court decision declaring Section 4(b) of the Voting Rights Act of 1965 as unconstitutional has made continuance of this achievement questionable.

37. Toby Miller, *Technologies of Truth*, 5.

38. Ibid., 4, 265.

39. Brett, *Construction of Heritage*, 2.

40. The documentary *Maya Lin: A Strong Clear Vision* (Freida Lee Mock, 1994) contains a short section on the Civil Rights Memorial.

41. Valene Smith, "Introduction," 5.

42. Urry, *The Tourist Gaze*, 112.

43. Kirshenblatt-Gimblett, *Destination Culture*, 72.

44. "Birmingham Civil Rights Institute."

45. For a history of the Birmingham Civil Rights Institute from conception to opening, see Eskew, "Birmingham Civil Rights Institute and the New Ideology of Tolerance." In Glenn Eskew's assessment: "The chronology presented in the museum charts a particularly narrow trajectory. It defines the early 1960s as the key years of the struggle and events in Birmingham with the subsequent adoption of the 1964 Civil Rights Act as the climax of the civil rights movement all framed within the standard Montgomery to Memphis refrain. The victory over white supremacy presupposes the triumph of tolerance and the fulfillment of King's dream of assimilation, goals married to a master narrative of America's history that charts an ever-expanding democracy" (52–53). To have measured the success of the movement based on economic or social inequality "would not have fit the progressive theme of tolerance" (52).

46. A common criticism of the 1963 Birmingham civil rights campaign is that the movement provoked violence for the media to capture in order to show the ugliness of segregation and thereby win support for its cause and intervention by the federal government. Aldon Morris argues in "Birmingham Confrontation Reconsidered" against this view, countering that it was the "movement's efficient and skillful use of diverse tactics" combined with "the mobilization of extraordinarily large numbers of people" (623) which "generated the power that led to victory" (621) in Birmingham. He claims that the "intervention of the federal government was a response to the widespread breakdown of economic and social order in Birmingham rather than to mere violence against the protesters" (623). In the conclusion of his article, he notes that his analysis is "[b]ased on evidence and the historical record" (635). Yet he seems unaware that his analysis is ultimately only a social history of the events, a particular *narrative* of the events offered to the reader. The article is a theoretically engaged (as well as intellectually engaging) written history, but a history nonetheless and therefore subject to the same problems of narrativity associated with its writing, per Hayden White as discussed in the introduction.

47. Eskew, *But for Birmingham*, 260. The following analysis is based on a comparison of the history relayed in the exhibit to the one Eskew presents in his book. ACMHR stands for Alabama Christian Movement for Human Rights. It was formed in 1956 after Alabama banned the National Association for the Advancement of Colored People (NAACP) from operating in the state.

48. Ibid., 337.

49. Ibid., 268.

50. Kirshenblatt-Gimblett, *Destination Culture*, 149.

51. Brett, *Construction of Heritage*, 8.

52. In contrast, Spike Lee's 1997 documentary *4 Little Girls*, about the Sixteenth Street Baptist Church bombing, which also presents a general picture of race in Birmingham during 1963, does not ignore the conflicts that existed within the local black community at the time.

53. "Inspired by the Past."

The Birmingham Civil Rights Institute frames its permanent exhibit as not about race relations but confrontation of "the bigotry and racial discrimination of American society" ("Inspired by the Past"). Because of its academic legacy, I have chosen not to use the phrase "race relations" in this book except when it is included as part of a quotation. The intellectual framework of race relations, developed by sociologists Robert Ezra Frank in the 1910s at the University of Chicago, was the dominant academic racial paradigm through most of the twentieth century. Some scholars hold that this intellectual framework inhibited sociologists from perceiving the significance of the civil rights movement, both when it happened and for decades afterwards.

Although the concept "race relations" is meant to be value neutral, as Stephen Steinberg observes in *Race Relations: A Critique*, "its rhetorical function is to obfuscate the true nature of 'race relations,' which is a system of racial domination and exploitation based on violence, resulting in the suppression and dehumanization of an entire people over centuries of American history" (16). For Steinberg, unlike the alternative framework of racial oppression, race relations elides power differential by mapping the social terrain through a schematic of mutuality and attitudes; thereby, it assumes "racial prejudice arises out of a natural antipathy between groups on the basis of difference" and the solution is to "repair these fractured relationships" (17). In other words, race relations privileges personal prejudice over social structures and power differentials. In many ways, the concept of race relations fits neatly with that of color-blindness, as discussed in footnotes 2 and 11 of chapter two.

Unlike in the academy, when the phrase "race relations" was used within the civil rights movement it was not severed from the concept of racial oppression, which was perceived as needing to be changed in order to change race relations. This usage assumed not only that racial oppression was the problem, but that racial reconciliation was the solution. Unfortunately, the phrase "racial reconciliation" is too often personalized and evacuated of its civic dimension.

54. In her book, *Object Lessons*, Robyn Wiegman makes a similar observation about the use of screens in the Birmingham Civil Rights Institute. She argues that the BCRI thematizes the mass resistance of the movement "by installing its visitors in a space organized around issues and images of mobility" (160). Her observation about screens and mobility is also applicable to the Freedom Walk in Kelly Ingram Park across the street from the BCRI, which will be discussed shortly.

55. While the Birmingham Civil Right Institute's permanent exhibit begins with hands-on interactions, its organizing principle changes as it begins to relay the history of the civil rights movement, where projected audiovisual displays involving media news footage, often of a spectacular nature, dominate the galleries. The screen upon which this televisual material is projected is physically framed in many of these exhibits to place visitors in a particular position, such as inside a Freedom Rider bus or on the lawn of the Lincoln Memorial rather than in front of a television set. For a discussion of the issue of civil rights documentaries and the use of spectacular audiovisual media material, see Brasell, "From Evidentiary Presentation to Artful Re-Presentation." Jane Gaines's concept of political mimesis, discussed in the introduction, assists to explain the over-reliance on such material not only in documentaries on the civil rights movement and museum displays, such as those in the Birmingham Civil Rights Institute, but also provides the graphic basis for sculptural objects such as those installed in Kelly Ingram Park.

56. "The Civil Rights Memorial."

57. See "Freedom Walk Tour" and Cox, "From Centerpiece to Center Stage."

58. A combined university library and Rosa Parks museum has subsequently been built on the site.

59. Kirshenblatt-Gimblett, *Destination Culture*, 168.

60. Ibid., 155.

61. See Althusser, "Ideology and Ideological State Apparatuses."

62. The term "Bloody Sunday" refers to the first attempt by civil rights movement participants to march from Selma to Montgomery on 7 March 1965, which was aborted when, after crossing the Edmund Pettus Bridge, they were beaten and tear-gassed by law enforcement officers. Two other attempts occurred before marchers were finally able to cross the bridge on the third one.

63. Quoted in Tullos, *Alabama Getaway*, 147.

64. Wilson, *Baptized in Blood*, 13.

65. Ibid., 15.

66. To be racially progressive does not necessarily mean one is also sexually progressive in terms of women, lesbians (obviously not a separate category from "women"), gay men, and transgender people.

67. Brett, *Construction of Heritage*, 15.

68. See Williams, *Marxism and Literature*, 123.

69. The most commonly cited examples are the NuSouth flag created by Angel Quintero and Sherman Evans for their NuSouth Apparel clothing line and the *Captain Confederacy* comic book series created by Will Shetterly and Vince Stone. Both are discussed in McPherson, *Reconstructing Dixie*, 35–37 and 141–46, respectively.

70. Antonio Gramsci differentiates between a "war of manoeuvre" and a "war of position," the former condensed around one front where a breach enables a swift entry to victory, the latter across many fronts where no single opportunity exists for a decisive victory. A war of position is a protracted and uneven struggle by a social group for hegemonic control—not by coercion but through consent, as it tailors its ideas to be more acceptable to others while simultaneously incorporating elements from those others. A war of position can be economical, political, cultural, or discursive. See Gramsci, *Selections from the Prison Notebooks*, 233–39.

71. See "State's New License Plate Shoots for 'Star,'" *Birmingham News*, 23 September 2000, 1A, 9A; "Tag! You're It! Readers Take Artistic License on New Look for Vehicle IDS," *Birmingham News*, 22 October 2000, 1E, 14E; and Phillip Rawls, "'Heart of Dixie' Disappearing from More License Plates Yearly," *Birmingham News*, 14 December 2004, 4B.

72. The rap version of the song, recorded by Boyz after Money Always (B.A.M.A.), was released in 2005 and the movie that used the title, directed by Andy Trennant, was released in 2002.

73. See Bates, "Beyond Black and White"; Hill and Beaver, *Cultural Diversity in the U.S. South*; and Ray, *New Encyclopedia of Southern Culture: Volume 6: Ethnicity*.

Chapter 2

1. Martin Luther King Jr., *Testament of Hope*, 219.
2. Most race scholars today hold that racism changed in the post-civil rights era from being overt to covert, operating within a framework of professed color-blindness that avoids direct racial language. Eduardo Bonilla-Silva has labeled this new racism "color-blind racism." See Bonilla-Silva, *Racism without Racists*.

Charles Gallagher holds in "Color Blindness" that color-blind racism presupposes "an implied racist intent" (107) because it assumes that whites know racial disparity exists but choose to ignore it. He counters that research shows that, instead, many whites actually believe "the socioeconomic playing field *is* now level" (108) and that "they are part of a society where color no longer shapes life chances" (105). In other words, not only is society color-blind but that racial parity has already been achieved. Gallagher's critique, of course, does not invalidate the legitimacy of color-blind racism as an analytical framework but it does assist to illuminate why many whites are honestly perplexed by the charge that they are racist (for example, when they oppose government policies aimed at eliminating racial inequality or they deny the existence of white privilege).

3. One manifestation of this trend is the naïve "new abolitionist project" seeking to abolish whiteness, a trend critiqued by Howard Winant in "White Racial Projects." As Winant underscores, "[t]he abolition of whiteness is unthinkable without the eradication of the concept of race itself" (107), an act undesirable to many racial minorities because "race is not simply the product of racism" but also "of centuries of *resistance* to racism, . . . these undertakings in self-invention and resistance developed not only the peoples whom we now designate by the term 'of color,' but also in significant measures our general concepts of freedom and democracy" (111).

4. See Miles and Torres, "Does 'Race' Matter?"
5. Omi and Winant, *Racial Formation in the United States*, 60. Although Antonio Gramsci, like Raymond Williams, frames his theories in terms of sociocultural formations, his concept of common sense can easily be transferred to the discursive field as well. If synthesized with Michel Foucault, common sense as a form of knowledge emerges from the current régime of truth and is a mode of southern discourse.
6. Ibid., 12–13.
7. Ibid., 12.
8. Michael Omi and Howard Winant are not against the use of class analysis in relationship to race. Instead, the concern is with "assertions of the primacy of one category over the other" (Winant, *Racial Conditions*, 64) and approaches that "reduce race to class" (Winant, *Racial Conditions*, 34). For a discussion of the relationship between race and class from a cultural studies perspective, see Gilroy, *"There Ain't No Black in the Union Jack,"* 15–42.
9. Omi and Winant, *Racial Formation in the United States*, 5.
10. Ibid., 104.
11. In *The Silent Majority: Suburban Politics in the Sunbelt South* Matthew Lassiter challenges the common position that the southern strategy led to the success of the Republican Party in southeastern states. Rather than a top down southern strategy "inspired by the

Deep South and orchestrated from the White House," Lassiter attributes the Republican Party's success to "the suburban strategies developed in the Sunbelt South" (6). He holds that the Republican Party succeeded in southeastern states because of the emergence of segregated white suburbs underwritten by racist governmental (and corporate) mortgage policies combined with a color-blind discourse of individualism that denied such institutional advantages by whites. Per Lassiter: "The suburban politics of middle-class warfare charted a middle course between the open racism of the extreme right and the egalitarian agenda of the civil rights movement, based in an ethos of color-blind individualism that accepted the principle of equal opportunity under the law but refused to countenance affirmative action policies designed to overcome metropolitan structures of inequality" (4–5). He highlights that the very corporate leaders praised for "guiding local communities into compliance with [urban] desegregation, also played the most significant role in constructing a metropolitan landscape of spatial apartheid that first reoriented and then outlasted the arrangements of Jim Crow" (11). He claims that "[i]n affluent [white] suburbs . . . , color-blind ideology fused the naturalization of racial privilege with unapologetic enthusiasm for class exclusion," and in the process "displaced the burdens of racial integration onto working-class white neighborhoods" (10). I find Lassiter's historical argument compelling. Currently, however, the concept of the southern strategy has a secure grip in popular political discourse which, so far, has not engaged his counterargument.

12. With the 2010 midterm elections, twenty-four-hour news commentators like Rachel Maddow highlighted that the southern strategy no longer applies to just southeastern states, highlighting the fact that it was used in other areas of the country (such as Arizona) and expanded to include other racial and ethnic groups (such as Latinos).

13. Omi and Winant, *Racial Formation in the United States*, 11.

14. Gramsci, *Selections from the Prison Notebooks*, 419.

15. Ibid., 420.

16. Omi and Winant, *Racial Formation in the United States*, 63, 64.

17. Gramsci, *Selections from the Prison Notebooks*, 338, 337.

18. Ibid., 326.

19. See Mead, "Visual Anthropology in a Discipline of Words"; Lomax, "Cinema, Science and Cultural Renewal"; Heider, *Ethnographic Film*; and MacDougall, *Transcultural Cinema*.

20. Guillaumin, "'I Know it's Not Nice, But . . . ,'" 44.

21. Fuller, "Debating the Present through the Past," 168.

22. Ibid., 180, 171.

23. The historical narrativization of the civil rights movement within popular culture often presents the dispersed local activities now associated with the movement as though they were part of a national master plan. Although some events, such as the Freedom Rides and March on Washington, were broad in scope, most civil rights struggles emerged out of local initiatives, some of which then invited national black leaders to assist. Today, it is easy to lose sight of the uncertainty that surrounded the outcome of these struggles when they occurred; the successes of Birmingham and Selma are immortalized in popular culture, but the failure of Albany is not. Clayborne Carson, in "Civil Rights Reform and the Black Freedom Struggle," stresses: "Viewing the black struggle as a national civil rights reform effort

rather than a locally-based social movement has caused scholars to see Birmingham in the spring of 1963 and Selma in the winter and spring of 1965 as the prototypical black protest movements of the decade. In reality, however, hundreds of southern communities were disrupted by sustained protest movements that lasted, in some cases, for years. These local protest movements involved thousands of protesters, including large numbers of working class blacks, and local organizers who were more concerned with local issues, including employment opportunities and political power, than with achieving national legislation" (23–24). Carson's critique proceeds even further, claiming that "these local movements should not be viewed as protest activity designed to persuade and coerce the federal government to act on behalf of black civil rights. There was a constant tension between the national black leaders, who saw mass protest as an instrument for reform, and local leaders and organizers who were often more interested in building enduring local institutions rather than staging marches and rallies for a national audience" (27). A case can be made that it was this grassroots focus that provided the foundation for the eventual widespread transition during the 1970s and 1980s in many counties and municipalities from white-only political leaders, law enforcement officers, and civil servants to a significant number of blacks in such positions, at least in areas where blacks constituted a majority.

24. Dyer, *White*, 20.

25. Ibid., 45, 47.

26. Painter, "'Social Equality,' Miscegenation, Labor, and Power," 54.

27. Unlike eugenics in the 1930s, which used science for racist purposes, one can argue that today genetics is providing an anti-racist scientific argument that is essentialist. This secular anti-racist position shares affinity with the religious position expressed in *bro•ken/ ground*. In other words, both conceive human life (regardless of race) as originating from one common source, only science uses evolution by nature as that source while religion uses creation by God.

28. Fuss, *Essentially Speaking*, 119.

29. Omi and Winant, *Racial Formation in the United States*, 71.

30. Ibid., 54.

31. See Marx and Engels, *German Ideology*; Horkheimer and Adorno, "Culture Industry"; and Althusser, "Ideology and Ideological State Apparatuses."

32. See Foucault, *Archaeology of Knowledge*; Williams, *Marxism and Literature*; Deleuze and Guattari, *Anti-Oedipus* and *A Thousand Plateaus*; and Bourdieu, *Field of Cultural Production*.

33. Fulton, "Religion and Politics in Gramsci," 202.

34. Gramsci, *Selections from the Prison Notebooks*, 420.

35. David Chappell maintains in *A Stone of Hope: Prophetic Religion and the Death of Jim Crow* that in the struggle between segregationists and integrationists in the 1950s and 1960s, the latter more effectively used religion to justify their cause. He holds that, unlike their ardent defense of slavery, "white churches of the South" (5) were more likely to remain silent on the issue of segregation and segregationists were more likely to appeal to constitutional arguments like states' rights to defend their position instead of religion. As Chappell summarizes, "black southern activists got strength from old-time religion, and white

supremacists failed, at the same moment, to muster the cultural strength that conservatives traditionally get from religion" (8). Integrationists "succeeded in the great cultural battle over race and rights in the 1950s and early 1960s" because they were able to "use religion to inspire solidarity and self-sacrificial devotion to their cause" (8), a task which segregationists failed to achieve. In contrast, Jane Dailey frames the situation in "Sex, Segregation, and the Sacred after *Brown*" as a "titanic struggle waged by participants on both sides of the conflict to harness the immense power of the divine to their cause," with religion playing "a central role in articulating not only the challenge that the civil right movement offered Jim Crow but the *resistance* to that challenge" (122). Dailey labels these competing Christian orthodoxies "the theology of segregation" and "the integrationist Christian theology of liberation" (144). Regardless of which historical emplotment one accepts, most scholars would concede that today the theology associated with the civil rights movement is perceived within popular discourse as having won that struggle accompanying the elimination of segregation laws and discriminatory voting rules. This legacy helps to explain why religion can function so easily today within common sense related to racial formation in locales with a strong civil rights legacy.

36. Gramsci, *Selections from the Prison Notebooks*, 326.

37. See Charles Connerly, *"The Most Segregated City in America,"* 3–7. Connerly holds that "[t]he resulting conflict between blacks and whites over housing, and the violence that ensued, helped set the stage for the more nationally visible civil rights struggles of the 1960s" (6). The disproportionate impact on blacks caused by urban renewal and interstate projects was not unique to Birmingham and occurred all across the country in cities such as Chicago, Detroit, and Philadelphia. Also see Mohl, "Planned Destruction," and Scribner, *Renewing Birmingham*.

38. Ibid., 7. In 1950, Atlanta and Birmingham were roughly the same size. But while Atlanta experienced significant growth in the 1950s, Birmingham was hampered by its dependence on these declining industries.

39. Browder, *The South's New Racial Politics*, 32–33, 95. In the twenty-first century, a new partisan politics closely aligned with race has emerged in Alabama, one that is very different from the racial coalitions described by Browder which existed during the 1970s, '80s, and '90s and which enabled white Democrats to be elected to statewide and federal positions. While in the 1990s it may have appeared that this type of racial coalition politics would continue into the future, the twenty-first century demonstrated otherwise. In retrospect, *bro•ken/ground* can be seen as an attempt to strengthen this always-fragile racial coalition by providing a space where typical citizens who constitute it can explore the tensions that exist within it in order to reinforce its bonds.

40. The Birmingham Public Library has compiled the census materials for the various decades related to the city and race into a single chart. See http://www.bham.lib.al.us/resources/government/BirminghamPopulation.aspx (accessed 12 February 2011).

41. On the 1992 Alabama redistricting that created the black-majority federal congressional district, see Webster, "Congressional Redistricting and African-American Representation." According to Gerald Webster, such redistricting efforts were typically supported by the unusual alliance of racial minorities and Republicans. Per Webster, the GOP supported

such redistricting efforts because they believed "the greater packing of minorities in some districts will result in larger numbers of GOP-leaning white voters being left to compose neighboring districts" (552). Such was the case in Alabama, where the redistricting that created the new black-majority 7th U.S. congressional district resulted in switching the 6th U.S. congressional district from Democratic to Republican due to removing the city of Birmingham from the 6th district and placing it in the 7th district in order to create the black majority. As a result, the Alabama 6th U.S. district, in which the Birmingham suburbs are located, is predominately white and Republican, while the Alabama 7th U.S. district including the city is predominately black and Democratic.

42. This minority position for such whites is extremely mutable and transitory because of factors such as the degree of residential segregation present in the city neighborhoods within which they reside and the extent of their social interaction with family, friends, and colleagues in the predominately white suburbs.

43. By the twenty-first century, a white person could become positioned as a minority not only by living in the city but being a Democrat in a state where political parties and race were becoming associated with the axioms that Republicans are white and blacks are Democrats. Notice that these two axioms are not parallel constructions, which accounts for the precarious position in the state of white liberals who typically associate with the Democratic Party. In Alabama, blacks (in general) and white liberals share a common belief in the role of government, such as providing a social safety net, hence their affiliation with the Democratic Party, although on social issues (such as gay and lesbian civil rights and marriage) they are not as closely aligned due to the religious conservatism more prevalent in the former group. This precarious position assumed cultural expression in 2006, when automobile stickers began appearing across the city and surrounding suburbs of a large blue dot on a square red background; underneath the dot were the words "another bright blue dot in a really red state." The sticker (which I saw predominately on cars driven by whites) was developed by Birmingham residents Joellyn Beckham and Gina Williams as an antidote to their frustration and isolation of being liberal in a predominately conservative state. See Christina Crowe, "A Bright Blue Dot Brings Political Hope," *Black and White* (Birmingham, AL), 6 April 2006, 13. The stickers are sold by the Birmingham-based Brite Blue Dot Company at http://britebluedot.com.

44. This discussion is drawn from Haeberle, "Exploring the Effects of Single-Member Districts."

45. Alternatively, convoluted district gerrymandering can be used to accomplish the same result when residential segregation does not exist. Single-member districts (SMDs) work in the case of the Birmingham City Counsel because of segregation, not gerrymandering. Scholars agree that while SMDs work to eliminate racial underrepresentation, they do not work to eliminate sex underrepresentation. In 2010, women were proportionally represented on the city council.

46. Patricia Dedrick, "Watkins' Radio Ads Backing Arrington Draws Protests," *Birmingham News*, 9 October 1995, 2E. The Mark Fuhrman association operates from the principle that racists are a particular type of person. Michel Foucault contends in *The History of Sexuality, Volume I* that in the nineteenth century the homosexual became "a species" unlike the

earlier sodomite that was considered "a temporary aberration" (43). A shift occurred from homosexuality being perceived as a practice (a sin) to a type of person (a nature). Rather than a sexual act that anyone can perform, the performance of such acts came to designate this special type of person. Today, a similar shift is occurring in relationship to racism. Rather than viewing racism as an action capable of being performed by anyone, it has become associated with a special type of person. To call a person a racist today is perceived as a description of that person's being, not their behavior, as the racist has become "a species" rather than "a temporary aberration."

47. See Patricia Dedrick, "Black and White, Local Leaders Differ on Issues," *Birmingham News*, 26 February 1996, 1A, 2A. In 2012, Operation New Birmingham (ONB) merged with Main Street Birmingham to form REV Birmingham. While the new organization continued pursuing the economic development objective of ONB, it shed the ONB objective to promote racial harmony.

48. Bob Carlton, "The City Divided, Filmmakers Hope 'Broken Ground' Builds Racial Unity," *Birmingham News*, 11 April 1996, 6C.

49. See Geertz, *Interpretation of Cultures*, 3–30.

50. Foucault, "Technologies of the Self," 18. Michel Foucault identifies in "Technologies of the Self" four major types of technologies. Along with those of power and of the self, he also includes technologies of production and of sign systems. Per Foucault, technologies of production "permit us to produce, transform, or manipulate things," while technologies of sign systems "permit us to use signs, meanings, symbols, or signification" (18).

51. Butler, *Undoing Gender*, 7.

52. Davis, *Who Is Black?* 78.

53. See Snell, "Masked Men in the Magic City," 221.

54. Hale, *Making Whiteness*, 25.

55. While Jim Crow laws are associated with the eleven states of the former Confederate States of America (and often presumed to have only existed in those particular states), Jim Crow policies (especially in terms of housing) occurred across the country in cities including New York City, Detroit, Chicago, and Los Angeles. See Biondi, *To Stand and Fight*; Sugrue, *Origins of the Urban Crisis*; Hirsch, *Making the Second Ghetto*; and Sides, *L.A. City Limits*. For a critique of the de jure versus de facto distinction typically associated, respectively, with southeastern states versus the rest of the country, see Lassiter, "De Jure/De Facto Segregation."

56. Goffman, *Presentation of Self in Everyday Life*, 2.

57. Ibid., 4.

58. Ibid., 7.

59. Waugh, "Walking on Tippy Toes," 110.

60. In addition to Butler's *Gender Trouble*, two foundational articles on queer theory and performativity are Sedgwick, "Queer Performativity," and Butler, "Critically Queer." Butler's article originally appeared in the same 1993 issue of *GLQ* as Sedgwick's but she subsequently revised it for the 1997 Phelan anthology.

61. Butler, *Gender Trouble*, 141, 33.

62. Bill Nichols initially lays out four documentary modes of representation (expository, observational, interactive [later called participatory] and reflexive) in his 1991 book *Representing Reality*, 32–75, but then adds a fifth one when he includes a chapter on the performative mode in his 1994 book *Blurred Boundaries*, 92–106. Nichols's 2001 overview book on issues related to documentary film, *Introduction to Documentary*, includes a summary of the modes of documentary representation, now increased to six with the addition of the poetic mode (99–138). In *New Documentary*, Stella Bruzzi criticizes Nichols's "family tree" because "it imposes a false chronology onto what is essentially a theoretical paradigm" (3). I approach Nichols's categories as a useful taxonomy of documentary modes, not a historical progression, realizing that documentaries routinely combine modes.

63. Besides these dramatized and poetic performances, the documentary includes another type of performance that is common in performative documentaries: found footage inserts. Although the borrowed footage may not be original, much like dada modernist art it provides the raw material for a new expression. Archival photographic and moving image material is routinely used in participatory, reflexive, and performative mode documentaries for illustrative purposes, but performative documentaries also use such footage for impressionistic purposes. Edited into some of the talking heads of *bro•ken/ground* are such shots. The most jarring one appears when a black woman discusses the construction of whiteness and its association with power rather than ethnicity. During her remarks, a shot appears of white people walking on a landscape of snow followed by a shot of white particles flowing out of a pipe as a white man fills a bucket. In both shots, whiteness overwhelms the visual palette, aligning whiteness not only with color but territory and commoditization.

64. See hooks, *Black Looks*, 165–78.

65. Winant, *Racial Conditions*, 64.

66. This matter comes through most clearly in chapter four on consumer culture. See Hale, *Making Whiteness*, 121–97.

67. Fanon, *Black Skin, White Masks*, 112.

68. While the relationship between black and white residents dominates much of the city's history, it ignores the contemporary situation which includes the presence of multiple Asian American, Latino/a, and Muslim American communities within its metro area as well as recent African immigrants. Exclusion of these other racial and ethnic communities within the documentary is not completely unjustified given that they do not have a significant citywide presence. Besides maintaining a low-key presence, their size does not provide them with the local political clout of blacks. Therefore, their status as minorities functions locally very differently than blacks.

69. I cannot help but wonder if the reference to "green or blue" people may be a coded way to expand the discussion of civil rights beyond racial minorities to include sexual minorities. In other words, are the green and blue people gays, lesbians, and transgender people? If the concluding "Human Rights Gallery" of the Birmingham Civil Rights Institute, which attempts to position the civil rights movement as "part of an international human rights struggle," is any indication, the answer is a resounding "no" because the last time I visited it, gays, lesbians, and transgender people were not mentioned anywhere.

70. The quotation on the intertitle is from Martin Luther King Jr.'s short book *Why We Can't Wait*, 117, on the Birmingham campaign.

Chapter 3

1. I contemplated using the word "diasporic" instead of "expatriate" because of its greater academic esteem. "Expatriate" is, after all, a rather old-fashioned word, routinely used during the mid-twentieth century to refer not only to American writers living in Europe but also to writers living in New York City who grew up in southeastern states and who often wrote about locales in those states. Filmmakers are also cultural workers, just as novelists and playwrights are. I have chosen the latter word because of its resonances with this history, which during the mid-twentieth century was closely associated with such queer authors as Truman Capote, Carson McCullers, and Tennessee Williams, who seemed to epitomize the label "southern expatriate writer" during that time period.

2. I have chosen to refer to the southeastern expatriate road film as a cycle rather than a genre although an argument could easily be advanced that it is a subgenre of the road film. In *Film/Genre*, Rick Altman distinguishes between genres and cycles for Hollywood films. While genres are "broad *public* categories shared across the entire [film] industry," cycles are "identified with only a single studio" (59). The latter can be accomplished through parlay of contract actors or proprietary characters. But because cycles have other replicable characteristics, such as plot patterns and character types, they can eventually become genres available to any production company. The southeastern expatriate road film, besides being in a documentary form rather than a fictional form, is also made independently of the Hollywood studio system. Altman's distinction, which was based on a historical analysis of the Hollywood studio system, was not meant to be descriptive of either documentary or independent film. While the southeastern expatriate road film has clearly definable generic characteristics that are easily reproducible by other filmmakers with similar personal backgrounds, the filmmaker's presence (both physically and personality-wise) imparts a proprietary element to each documentary. Although I could make an analogy equating a region of the nation to a studio of the industry to justify use of the word "cycle" (one that I think would ultimately not hold), I have chosen to call the southeastern expatriate road film "a documentary cycle" on the pragmatic grounds that only a limited number of them were made.

3. See Ball, *Slaves in the Family*, and McCray, *Freedom's Child*.

4. On fiction film and miscegenation, see Marchetti, *Romance and the "Yellow Peril"*; Gaines, *Fire & Desire*; Courtney, *Hollywood Fantasies of Miscegenation*; and Beltrán and Fojas, *Mixed Race Hollywood*.

5. On the Thomas Jefferson and Sally Hemings controversy, see Walker, *Mongrel Nation*, and on Strom Thurmond, see Marilyn W. Thompson, "Woman Claims Thurmond as Father; Proof Is Forthcoming, Black Retiree Says," *Washington Post*, 14 December 2003, A1.

6. Renov, *Subject of Documentary*, 109.

7. Ibid., 110.

8. Lebow, *First Person Jewish*, xii.

9. Renov, *Subject of Documentary*, 110.

10. Lebow, *First Person Jewish*, xxi.

11. Russell, *Experimental Ethnography*, 276.

12. Pratt, *Imperial Eyes*, 7. Mary Louise Pratt describes autoethnography as "instances in which colonized subjects undertake to represent themselves in ways that *engage with* the colonizer's own terms," either "in response to or in dialogue with those metropolitan representations" (7).

13. For a discussion of the hick flick, see Richard Thompson, "What's Your 10-20?"; McDonough and Landis, "Hillbilly Heaven"; Kirby, *Media-Made Dixie*, 152–53; Ryan and Kellner, *Camera Politica*, 129–35; J. W. Williamson, *Hillbillyland*, 123–47; and Nystrom, *Hard Hats, Rednecks, and Macho Men*, 79–105.

14. Although Macky Alston did not personally choose to leave the southeastern United States, his parents did; they moved when he was a child.

15. Sedgwick, *Epistemology of the Closet*, 71. In recent years, the closet has played a significant role in two television series, *True Blood* on HBO and *Big Love* on Showtime; the trope is used as a metaphor for homosexuality while simultaneously being applied to the concrete situations of vampires in Louisiana and polygamous Mormons in Utah.

16. Foucault, *Power/Knowledge*, 215–16.

17. Foucault, *History of Sexuality, Volume 1*, 58, 59.

18. Ibid., 61–62.

19. Foucault, *Religion and Culture*, 168, 178.

20. Ibid., 141.

21. Butler, *Undoing Gender*, 164.

22. Quoted in Eaton, "Production of Cinematic Reality," 51.

23. Renov, *Subject of Documentary*, 200. Michael Renov specifically restricts his claim to only video, carving out other electronic/digital media. The "interactive mode" is the same as the "participatory mode." As noted in footnote 62 of chapter two, Bill Nichols first used the word "interactive" to describe the mode before changing it to "participatory."

24. Ibid., 264, 203.

25. Ibid., 203.

26. Because the term "cinematic apparatus" refers to only the reception process encompassing the interaction of the spectator, the text, and technology, I have invoked the Gilles Deleuze and Félix Guattari concept of assemblage so as to include the production process as well. Although the French word *agencement* is typically translated into English as "assemblage," which is the commonly accepted way to refer to this Deleuzian and Guattarian concept, Martin Joughin, translator of Deleuze's *Negotiations, 1972–1990*, holds that the English word "arrangement" comes closer to capturing their meaning. He believes the word "assemblage" "conveys neither the sense of preparation or orientation toward action nor that of reconfiguration" (196) associated with Deleuze's use of *agencement*. Therefore, I am using the word "arrangement" rather than the more commonly used English word "assemblage." The term "audiovisual arrangement" encompasses the various relationships and connections entailed in the production, distribution, and exhibition of audiovisual texts. It is meant as a means to integrate the concerns of industrial studies, textual studies, and reception studies.

27. Typical documentary filmmaking practices, such as pre-interviews with social actors and scripted voice-over narration by the filmmaker, means that in some situations the on-screen confessions are repeat performances, this time for the potential audience, contributing to the formation of subjectivity not through the originality of the confession but its repetition.

28. Lacan, *Écrits*, 19.

29. Silverman, *Subject of Semiotics*, 159.

30. See Metz, *Imaginary Signifier*, 42–57. For critiques of the application of Jacques Lacan's mirror phase to the cinematic apparatus, see Copjec, "The Orthopsychic Subject"; Allen, "Psychoanalytic Film Theory"; and Cowie, *Representing the Woman*.

31. Some scholars hold that the interlocutor in the psychoanalytical situation listens not only to assist the analysand but also him or herself, the process enacting a change in the analyst as well as the analysand. Although Michel Foucault does not specifically frame pastoral power as such, the addition of such a framework to the model does not invalidate it.

32. Judith Butler holds that "speaking is a bodily act" because vocalization requires use of "the larynx, the lungs, the lips, and the mouth" (*Undoing Gender*, 172). So while all spoken confessions may be bodily ones, not all bodily utterances are spoken ones.

33. Warner, *Trouble with Normal*, 57.

34. Butler, *Undoing Gender*, 42.

35. Gilles Deleuze holds that Michel Foucault was not interested in the subject per se but rather subjectification. Foucault's writings and interviews as translated into English, however, do mention the subject. Deleuze holds that "Foucault doesn't use the word *subject* as though he's talking about a person or a form of identity, but talks about 'subjectification' as a process and 'Self' as a relation (a relation to oneself)" (Deleuze, *Negotiations*, 92). Foucault's antagonism to identity is often attributed to why he never officially came out as gay (his sexual orientation was common knowledge, however, and he even gave interviews to a weekly gay and lesbian newspaper, *The Advocate*, and a monthly magazine, *Christopher Street*, toward the end of his life).

One can surmise Michel Foucault's animosity toward coming out accounts in part for his fascination with the early Christian pastoral because its hermeneutic of the self transpired through not just confession but also renunciation; it is a different conceptualization of the self than that offered by theories of identity. Gilles Deleuze views Foucault's turn to the matter of subjectification as "a practical search for another way of life, a new style" (Deleuze, *Negotiations*, 106), a means of "establishing different ways of existing," "existing not as a subject but as a work of art" (Deleuze, *Negotiations*, 92). Mark Vernon, in "'I am not what I am'—Foucault, Christian Asceticism and a 'way out' of Sexuality," argues that rather than "coming out," Foucault was concerned with finding a "way out" of "certain categories and forms of knowledge, including sexuality" that "shape, control and determine our pleasures" (202, 201). Per Vernon: "Foucault warns against 'coming out' becoming a programme that codifies relationships and prohibits inventiveness. Instead of 'coming out' Foucault suggests the term 'showing oneself' which, after the reading of the Christian texts, must be implicitly coupled to the act of renunciation, speaking of oneself only in order to find a 'way out' of one's self, the exact opposite of conformity to a predetermined way of being" (208).

36. In *Dirt and Desire*, Patricia Yaeger uses Mary Douglas's conceptualization of dirt to explore "southern women's writing." In contrast to Yeager, I focus on the relationship of dirt's boundary-crossing to another popular conceptual framework, the closet. I hold that *audiovisual* enunciations of southern discourse in film privilege water more often than dirt, a matter that deserves further exploration. While water is often associated with cleanliness and baptismal redemption, in film it is more likely to assume "dirty" characteristics through such presentations as swamps, bayous, and mud, thereby affirming Yaeger's overall conceptual approach to the region.

37. Mary Douglas, *Purity and Danger*, 35.

38. Ibid., 113.

39. Butler, *Undoing Gender*, 162.

40. Collins, "Like One of the Family," 15.

41. Bourdieu, "On the Family," 21, 22.

42. The so-called normal family is supposed to not only be composed of the same race but also one male husband and one female wife—in other words, not only the opposite sexes but one of each.

43. DaCosta, "All in the Family," 33.

44. Ibid., 32–33.

45. During the culture war, conservatives typically framed the issue as one about "homosexuals" and thereby "gays and lesbians." Although they sometimes used the latter phrase, the former phrase was more dominant. This is not surprising given the lingering traces of abnormal psychology that continues to accompany the word "homosexual." While transgendered people have historically been a part of most local gay and lesbian communities, and have sustained their own networks, during the 1990s a public transgender movement arose, as underscored by the appearance of books such as those by Leslie Feinberg, organizations such as the Transsexual Menace, and events such as those organized in reaction to the 1993 murder of teen transsexual Brandon Teena in Nebraska. Gay and lesbian politics since the Stonewall Riots has, at its best, been a coalition politics centering around issues of gender and sexuality (but realizing these are not separable from race and class) and during the 1990s attempts were made to not only be more sensitive to transgender and transsexual concerns but also to use more inclusive language as a social movement, hence the rise during that decade of the acronym "lgbt" (lesbian/gay/bisexual/transgender) as a label to replace "gay and lesbian." Of course, this was also the decade in which "queer" emerged as a sociopolitical-sexual label, and some activists expanded the lgbt acronym to lgbtq, adding queer, and others to lgbti, adding intersex. Although the word "transgender" implies an individual who changes gender and "transsexual" a change of sex, "transgender" is often used as an umbrella term for individuals who change their gender with an accompanying body change that runs on a continuum from none to complete, with those falling along the latter end of the spectrum being transsexuals.

46. On the Robert Mapplethorpe controversy, see Meyer, *Outlaw Representation*, 159–223, and on the Marlon Riggs controversy, see Bullert, *Public Television*, 91–122.

47. On the Oregon controversy, see the documentary *Ballot Measure 9* (Heather MacDonald, 1995).

48. Bérubé, "How Gay Stays White," 238.

49. Hobson, *But Now I See*, 4.

50. Michael Brown, *Closet Space*, 141.

51. Ibid., 145.

52. Although I normally refer to filmmakers and social actors by their last name, hereafter I will be using first names because so many social actors in the documentary have the same last name as the filmmaker. This use of the informal first name instead of the formal last name is not meant as a sign of disrespect but rather a practical solution to this problem.

53. Pierre Bourdieu argues in "On the Family as a Realized Category" that "the transmission of the *family name*" is a "basic element in the hereditary symbolic capital" (23). The legacy of slavery in the United States complicates this assertion because slaves (and thereby their descendants) typically assumed their master's family name. Even when heredity was involved in such situations, symbolic capital (much less financial capital) was rarely transmitted because the family was racialized as mono-racial, disinheriting such individuals (and thereby their descendants) from the family as kin due to racial difference. Exceptions, of course, do exist, such as Amanda America Dickson, whose life is documented in Kent Anderson Leslie's book, *Woman of Color, Daughter of Privilege*, which in turn provided the basis for the made-for-television movie, *A House Divided* (John Kent Harrison, 2000). In Macky's search for black relatives, the financial reinstatement of any black relatives disinherited from the family because of race was not broached.

54. Michael Taussig, "Secrecy" course syllabus, 1992, Department of Performance Studies, New York University. I would like to thank Jan Nathanson for pointing out Michael Taussig's definition of the public secret to me.

55. Sedgwick, *Epistemology of the Closet*, 3.

56. D. A. Miller, *Novel and the Police*, 206.

57. Fred Hobson's book is *Tell About the South: The Southern Rage to Explain*.

58. Gay and lesbian scholars are typically quick to point out that coming out is not *an* event but a process that never ends because every time a gay or lesbian person meets a new individual or group they have to decide whether to come out to that particular individual or group. In other words, coming out and the closet exist not only as either/or but also both/and.

59. Joel Williamson, *New People*, 96.

60. Spickard, "Illogic of American Racial Categories," 20.

Chapter 4

1. While some scholars use the terms "assimilation" and "acculturation" interchangeably, others differentiate between them through recourse to a distinction between the cultural and the social. In other words, acculturation refers to adoption of mainstream culture while assimilation refers to incorporation into mainstream social institutions. This means personal agency is the key component of the former while institutional structures are of the latter. As a result, Herbert Gans holds that "acculturation is always a faster process than

assimilation" (Gans, "Toward a Reconciliation of 'Assimilation' and 'Pluralism,'" 877). My qualification of the word "assimilation" with the word "cultural" in effect makes the resulting phrase synonymous with acculturation. As scholars are quick to point out, the straight-line theory of assimilation has numerous problems. Not only can some groups assimilate into a subordinate societal group rather than the mainstream (referred to as segmented assimilation in sociology literature) but a group could lose its culture yet retain its social ties. Along similar lines, given that culture is a dynamic ongoing process, a group may reconstruct its culture to make it palatable for retention. In other words, (cultural) assimilation and (subcultural) retention are not necessarily mutually exclusive processes.

2. Stuart Hall defines transcoding in "Spectacle of the 'Other'" as "taking an existing meaning and re-appropriating it for new meanings" (270). He outlines a number of different such strategies, the appropriate one here being "reversing the evaluation of popular stereotypes" (271). Just as the 1960s and 1970s saw such a move in terms of representations of blackness, one of the most popular being "black is beautiful," so too with those associated with the region through a discursive southern supplement. Here, however, the situation was reversed: images previously perceived as positive were now seen in a negative light because of the significant social changes that had occurred during the 1950s and 1960s.

3. While these two phrases are common, I appropriate them from the book titles of Bartley, *Rise of Massive Resistance*, and Brauer, *John F. Kennedy and the Second Reconstruction*.

4. As defined by Paul Gilroy in *"There Ain't No Black in the Union Jack,"* ethnic absolutism conceives "of black and white cultures, as fixed, mutually impermeable expressions of racial and national identity" (61).

5. On the terms "minoritizing" and "universalizing," see Sedgwick, *Epistemology of the Closet*, 85–86. The terms were proposed as a conceptual alternative to those of essentialism and constructionism.

6. Scott, "Evidence of Experience," 401.

7. Gilroy, *"There Ain't No Black in the Union Jack,"* 155.

8. Joyner, *Shared Traditions*, 207. This point is also made on page 23: "In the convergence of various African cultures and European cultures in the American South, white southerners had their old cultures Africanized by their black neighbors and black southerners had their old cultures Europeanized by their white neighbors."

While Charles Joyner operates from the dominate racial paradigm within southern discourse that the region is biracial, black and white, his work is a manifestation of the emergent trend within southern discourse discussed in the last chapter that redefines biraciality as mixture rather than separation. He holds that the two race-based cultures that compose the region are not separate but rather both contain elements of African and European influence.

9. See Philips, "African Heritage of White America."

10. On bluegrass music, see Rosenberg, *Bluegrass*.

11. The words "hybridity," "creolization," and "mestizaje" have also been used to describe such cross-cultural interaction. Paul Gilroy holds in "Cultural Studies and Ethnic Absolutism" that "theoretical terms like creolization and syncretism" are "manifestly inadequate" to describe the "fractal patterns of cultural and political exchange and transformation" that

scholars "try to specify" (192). Marcos Becquer and José Gatti have critiqued the concept of hybridity—which derives from biological husbandry—as heterosexist because it is based on the assumption of a hierarchical and linear heterosexual reproduction of cultural formations. They advocate use of the concept of syncretism instead, which they define as the "formal coexistence of components whose precarious identities are mutually modified in their encounter, yet whose distinguishing differences, as such, are not dissolved or elided in these modifications, but strategically reconstituted in an ongoing war of position" (Becquer and Gatti, "Elements of Vogue," 69).

12. On the societal level, individuals participate in numerous social and cultural formations, thereby contributing a syncretistic element to them that emerges from within.

13. While minority incorporation is not a new phenomenon, especially as related to music, its increase in intensity and range of types is. Particular incorporations can occur at the level of consumption, production, or both. When it entails production, the degree of institutional constraints and level of minority participation can vary significantly depending on the social, cultural, and economic capital of the minority parties involved. And, of course, today the situation has become more complex as individual minorities may be part of the mainstream institutions that are financing certain minority cultural expressions. From the perspective of consumption, while some minority cultural expressions consumed within the mainstream are also produced within it, others cross over from production in independent spaces. But, of course, independent spaces are not always minority-owned (or -controlled) spaces. In other words, minority cultural production outside of the mainstream typically entails constraints, as does production within it, even if they may be of a different kind.

Overview discussions of independent media as related to film are typically approached through the framework of how it differs from the mainstream in terms of economics and aesthetics. See for example Holmlund and Wyatt, *Contemporary American Independent Film*; Geoff King, *American Independent Cinema*; and Tzioumakis, *American Independent Cinema*.

14. Hall, "What is This 'Black' in Black Popular Culture?" 467.

15. Ibid., 468.

16. Theorizing the consumption of popular culture is another one of those areas where the issue of controlling structures versus individual agency routinely emerges. In general, the Frankfurt School privileges the former while the Birmingham School the latter. The classic Frankfurt School text on the issue is Horkheimer and Adorno, "Culture Industry." For an overview of the Birmingham School, see Turner, *British Cultural Studies*.

17. hooks, *Black Looks*, 21. While bell hooks is referring specifically to minority races and ethnicities, her statement is also applicable to minority genders and sexualities.

18. Ibid., 17.

19. From the reverse perspective of minority consumption of mainstream culture, the differentiation between cultural appropriation versus appreciation does not apply unless one assumes that minorities are not also part of the mainstream audience, which they typically are, consuming mainstream culture along with subcultural ones through multiple subject positions. But while sometimes minorities consume popular culture identically to dominant patterns, other times they do not; the situation is dependent upon the particular individual and specific cultural product. While anyone can identify with characters unlike

themselves, I hold that minorities are more apt at cross-identification and dis-identification than non-minorities because of their historical need for greater recourse to it when engaging with mainstream cultural products. On the concept of dis-identification, see Muñoz, *Disidentifications*.

20. For an historical overview of the philosophy of love, see Irving Singer's three-volume *The Nature of Love*, composed of *Volume 1: Plato to Luther*; *Volume 2: Courtly and Romantic*; and *Volume 3: The Modern World*.

21. hooks, *All About Love*, 165. For a detailed discussion of black feminism and love-politics, see Nash, "Practicing Love."

22. Singer, *Nature of Love, Volume 3: The Modern World*, 46.

23. Jenkins, *Textual Poachers*, 23–24.

24. Mercer, "'1968': Periodizing Politics and Identity," 436.

25. Gilroy, "One Nation under a Groove," 268.

26. My periodization of the 1970s should not be taken as literally the ten years that make up the decade. Cinema studies typically divide film history into periods of decades. Take, for example, the Scribner ten-volume History of American Cinema series. The last six volumes of the series, beginning with the 1930s, are periodized by decades. One way the 1960s has been periodized is from the 1963 death of President John F. Kennedy to the 1974 resignation of President Richard Nixon. I have not bound my periodization of the 1970s as precisely as this one of the 1960s, but I do include the early 1980s in it. Because film is not a live medium like radio and television, allowing for instant access, and because low-budget documentaries typically take years to develop, a time lag often exists between films and specific current events. But documentaries can manifest the overall fervor of their zeitgeist. For a discussion of issues related to periodizing the 1960s that can serve as a model for the periodization of other decades, see Jameson, "Periodizing the 60s."

27. While the debate, in general, divided along lines of arguing the region is either enduring or disappearing, the basic arguments were framed a number of different ways. Some writers on the enduring side include Rubin Jr. and Kilpatrick, *Lasting South*; Sellers Jr., *Southerner as American*; Simkins, *Everlasting South*; Killian, *White Southerners*; Reed, *Enduring South*; McWhiney, *Southerners and Other Americans*; Tindall, "Beyond the Mainstream"; Degler, *Place Over Time*; Fifteen Southerners, *Why the South Will Survive*; and Roland, "Ever-Vanishing South." Even when these writers admitted that the region is changing or acknowledged that the region and the nation shared similarities, they countered that this did not mean it was losing its distinctiveness.

Some writers on the disappearing side include Zinn, *Southern Mystique*; Cumming Jr., "Been Down Home So Long"; Egerton, *Americanization of Dixie*; and Current, *Northernizing the South*.

Rather than argue that the region *was* disappearing or enduring, some writers framed the debate in terms of the future. For example, see Ashmore, *Epitaph for Dixie*; Mayo, "Social Change, Social Movements and the Disappearing Sectional South"; Frank Smith, *Look Away from Dixie*; and Watters, *The South and the Nation*. Frank Smith approached the crisis as an opportunity for the region "to fully enter the mainstream of American life" (vi), while Pat Watters saw it as a lesson for "the nation as it enters a similar ordeal" (xv). In contrast, Selz

Mayo frames the matter within the older differentiation between sectionalism and regionalism derived from Howard Odum and the 1930s Chapel Hill regional sociology, arguing "a new potential regionalism has begun to show faintly on the horizon" as "the sectional south is disappearing" (1).

28. Rubin Jr., "An Image of the South," 13–14.

29. Zinn, *Southern Mystique*, 262.

30. Ibid., 13. Howard Zinn explicitly states that the purpose of the book is "to dispose of the myth of Southern exceptionalism" (239).

31. See Claude Sitton, "One Man's Prescription" [book review of *The Southern Mystique* by Howard Zinn], *New York Times Book Review*, 22 November 1964, 54, and T. Harry Williams, "All That Makes the Southerner" [book review of *Who Speaks for the South?* by James McBride Dabbs], *New York Times Book Review*, 22 November 1964, 3, 54.

32. See C. Vann Woodward, "Southern Mythology" [book review of *The Southern Mystique* by Howard Zinn], *Commentary* 39, no. 5 (May 1965): 60–63.

33. See Molly Ivins, "Are the South and the Nation Exchanging Their Strengths or Their Sins?" [book review of *The Deep South States of America* by Neal R. Peirce and *The Americanization of Dixie: The Southernization of America* by John Egerton], *New York Times Book Review*, 21 April 1974, 7.

34. Egerton, *Americanization of Dixie*, xx.

35. In *Finding Purple America*, Jon Smith holds that this question is constitutive of "old southern studies" and was not challenged until the emergence in the twenty-first century of a "new southern studies" that disrupted its underlying assumptions.

36. See Campbell Jr., *Celluloid South*, 14, 20. When the genre reappeared briefly during the 1970s, with films such as *Mandingo* (Richard Fleischer, 1975), it had been reconfigured for the change in racial politics that had transpired during the interim but never achieved the popularity or longevity of its earlier incarnation.

37. One might also add the 1965 murders of white civil rights supporters Reverend James J. Reeb in Selma and Viola Liuzzo on the highway between Selma and Montgomery as she transported marchers home after the march. Although these acts of violence were against whites, it was because they were, in the language of the time, "nigger lovers," a rather telling phrase within the context of hooks's contention that the distinction between cultural appropriation and appreciation is whether one loves blackness.

38. Torres, *Black, White, and In Color*, 17, 18.

39. Ibid., 19.

40. As a discursive practice, the region will remain an object of knowledge as long as it is used as one because it is not dependent on a circular interaction with a social formation for reproduction to exist, such as with the family as argued by Pierre Bourdieu in "On the Family." As a result, the very discussion of the region disappearing only ensures its endurance by contributing to its formation, even if in terms of a negation. Because the debate typically assumed a physical sociocultural region rather than a discursive region, social anxiety routinely accompanied the crisis of legitimacy at its peak.

41. The distinction between mass culture, popular culture, and folk culture is not always easy to draw. Folk culture is typically placed in opposition to high culture, with high culture

associated with the ruling class, requiring formal training, and artists monetarily compensated, and folk culture associated with the poor, requiring no formal training, and enacted by nonprofessionals. Popular culture is typically conceived as between these two poles, aligning initially with folk culture until the advent of mass communication technologies made it synonymous with mass culture. Folk culture and mass culture are commonly differentiated by the former being a culture *of* the people and the latter a culture *for* the masses. While both cultures may be anonymous, mass culture is typically perceived as produced by a culture industry seeking a profit in contrast to folk culture's emergence from a particular collective community. But folk cultures are not the only cultures to emerge from a collective community. Subcultures do too, although their cultural expressions often take the form of low-end mass media. But folk culture is not naturally bound to popular culture. Sometimes it aligns with high culture. Today, folk culture easily circulates in such institutions of high culture as museums and art galleries, where its practitioners are celebrated as individual artists creating original works in a primitive mode (for example, the women quilt makers of Gee's Bend captured in the documentary *The Quiltmakers of Gee's Bend* [Celia Carey, 2004]). Many of the 1970s documentaries sought to capture noncommercial cultural practices of rural working-class people whose artifacts were not mass-produced—in other words, what was thought of at the time as folk culture.

42. The Southern Circuit is an annual program of independent films that tours "communities across the South." It was founded by the South Carolina Arts Commission in 1975 but is now managed by Southern Arts. See www.southarts.org/southerncircuit (accessed 4 September 2013).

43. Sharon Sherman discusses the documentaries by Les Blank, Tom Davenport, Bill Ferris, and Judy Peiser in her book *Documenting Ourselves: Film, Video, and Culture* as examples of folkloric documentaries, which she defines as focused "primarily on traditions, those expressive forms of human behavior which are communicated by interactions and whose formal features mark them as traditional" (63). Alternately, folklore could be framed through the concept of vernacular rather than tradition. She approaches folklore (and folkloric documentaries) through the framework of "people as communicators" rather than "texts as communications" (68). In terms of film, while the former approach works as a production strategy when making a documentary (the element complementary to fieldwork), in terms of audience reception it does not make sense because the film is the communicator, not the people captured on the screen. The concept of enunciation within cinema studies emerged to address this particular occurrence, approaching film texts as utterances. In contrast, I approach these documentaries through the rubric of redemptive ethnographies as will be discussed shortly. For a general overview of folklore studies, see Georges and Jones, *Folkloristic*, and for a theoretical analysis of folklore studies, see Bendix, *In Search of Authenticity*.

44. The segments include *Jazz Parade: Feet Don't Fail Me Now* (Alan Lomax, 1990), *Cajun Country: Don't Drop the Potato* (Alan Lomax, 1990), *The Land Where the Blues Began* (Alan Lomax, 1990), *Appalachian Journey* (Mark Dibb, Mark Kidel, and Alan Lomax, 1990), and *Dreams and Songs of the Noble Old* (Mark Dibb, Mark Kidel, and Alan Lomax, 1990).

45. See Gruber, "Ethnographic Salvage."

46. By the 1980s, the news coverage of blacks had drastically changed from the 1960s. Rather than victims of brutalization by whites, blacks were presented primarily as perpetuators of urban crime. See Herman Gray, "Television, Black Americans, and the American Dream."

47. Martin Luther King Jr., *Testament of Hope*, 219. The concept of redemption has a secular meaning as well as a religious one and, per David Bobbitt, King's rhetoric synthesized both senses. See Bobbitt, *Rhetoric of Redemption*, 31.

48. Martin Luther King Jr., *Why We Can't Wait*, 117.

49. For a religious definition of redemption, see Marcoulesco, "Redemption."

50. For a discussion of Martin Luther King Jr. and redemptive suffering, see West, "Religious Foundations of the Thought of Martin Luther King Jr.," 127–29; Baldwin, *There is a Balm in Gilead*, 230–52; and Keith D. Miller, *Voice of Deliverance*, 150–58.

51. Martin Luther King Jr., *Testament of Hope*, 19.

52. Ibid., 20. Although this chapter touches briefly on the concept of community through the invocation of Martin Luther King Jr.'s "beloved community," I will not be exploring the concept of community itself, which appears in political science, sociology, and anthropology. The concept of community has been used to refer to particular geographical locales (the community of Harlem, the community of Greenwich Village, etc.) and to identity-based groups not necessarily bounded by geography (the black community, the gay community, the Christian community, etc.). While community is not identical to the neighborhood, much less the local, it does often have a spatial component that, while not synonymous with it, does traverse it. The concept has been routinely critiqued for its romanticism of an innocent lost past and/or idealization of a utopian unity (as well as a cohesion dependent upon coercion). Part of the difficulty with defining the term is, as Gerald Creed observes in "Reconsidering Community," it "includes at least three component meanings: a group of people, a quality of relationship (usually with a positive normative value), and a place/location" (4). Scholars such as Jean-Luc Nancy, in *The Inoperative Community*, and Giorgio Agamben, in *The Coming Community*, argue that, because of the impossibility of constituting community, we should—for lack of a better phrase to describe their position—live in being, a response that promotes passivity per Miranda Joseph. In *Against the Romance of Community*, she notes that "they seem to miss the whole reason that community is interesting at all, which is to say the fact that community generates not an attitude of 'whatever' but rather the strongest of passions. . . . Community is one of the most motivating discourses and practices circulating in contemporary society" (xxx).

53. Martin Luther King Jr. disliked the phrase "Black Power" and he critiqued it as a conceptual framework in chapter two of *Where Do We Go from Here*, 23–66.

54. Burrow Jr., *God and Human Dignity*, 160. Agapé (family love) is one of the three types of love differentiated by Greek philosophers, along with eros (sexual love) and philia (friendship). The term was appropriated by early Christians to mean "love of God." An engagement with peace and justice raises the specter of power and, in this particular context, its relationship to love. Martin Luther King Jr. acknowledges in *Where Do We Go from Here* that "love and power are usually contrasted as polar opposites. Love is identified with a resignation of power and power with a denial of love" but "[p]ower at its best is love

implementing the demands of justice. Justice at its best is love correcting everything that stands against love" (37).

55. Ellul, *Presence of the Kingdom*, 47.

56. Ibid., 50.

57. Burrow Jr., *God and Human Dignity*, 155. In chapter six of his book, Rufus Burrow Jr. explores the concept of beloved community and the philosophy of personalism as they were adopted by King. Personalism, he maintains, "stresses not merely the individual *or* the communal, but *persons-in-community*" (155).

58. Robinson, *Gospel of Jesus*, x, xi. The sayings Gospels, non-narrativized collections of Jesus's sayings, were the earliest forms of the Gospels, providing the source material for the later narrative Gospels of Matthew, Luke, and John in today's Bible. Two such collections existed, one the Gospel of Mark, also in today's Bible, and a lost text that has been reconstructed from various sources by biblical scholars that is referred to as the "Sayings Gospel Q." Matthew and Luke share similar sayings not in Mark which are attributed by scholars to this lost-sayings Gospel. Two sayings Gospels existed because of the nature of the early Christian communities, with Mark intended for Christian Gentiles and the Sayings Gospel Q for Christian Jews. As James Robinson highlights, in the saying Gospels, unlike the narrativized Gospels, "Jesus himself made no claim to lofty titles or even to divinity" (xi), he "did not point to himself to understand what he was doing or to explain himself to others" but rather "pointed to God: what he was doing was actually God reigning through human action" (220), an example worth following.

59. Ibid., viii.

60. Jon Smith offers a provocative analysis of white conservative Christianity and mourning (in this case over the loss of white supremacy) in *Finding Purple America*, 50–64.

61. While popular culture continues to closely associate the civil rights movements with the southeastern states, academic scholars no longer do so, as represented by works such as Countryman, *Up South*; Jones, *The Selma of the North*; and Lassiter and Crespino, *The Myth of Southern Exceptionalism*. Although the former two books are about cities in the northeastern and Midwestern United States, respectively, the comparative associations in their titles allude to the earlier presumption linking the movement with the southeastern United States.

62. One of the popular (and now-classic) books from this period was Frantz Fanon's *The Wretched of the Earth*. Martin Luther King Jr. critiqued Fanon's advocacy of violence in *Where Do We Go from Here?* 55, 65–66.

63. The term "Third World" has historically been used a number of ways. The most common was as a general reference to underdeveloped countries (now typically referred to as "developing countries") but it was also used in the more specific way of a space between American capitalism and Soviet socialism. For an interrogation of the concept, see "Three Worlds Theory: End of a Debate" in Ahmad, *In Theory*, 287–318.

64. See Marcus, *Ethnography through Thick and Thin*, 161–77. Although George Marcus allows for working-class and middle-class eccentrics in explicitly class-bound societies, in less explicitly class-bound societies like the United States, he claims that "eccentricity is predominantly associated with the lavishly powerful, wealthy, and famous, and when it is not . . . its class associations are much more muted and masked" (167).

65. Ibid., 166.

66. For a detailed analysis of the concept of cultural imperialism, see Tomlinson, *Cultural Imperialism*. Cultural imperialism is commonly equated with media imperialism, although this is only one way to define the term. Earlier incarnations of media imperialism assumed media users were passive consumers. But as John Tomlinson argues, the way audiences interpret media texts cannot be predetermined or guaranteed. From an economic perspective, the exportation of American media around the globe has hurt mass cultural production in some parts of the world but not others. For example, when Hollywood films account for 90 percent of what is shown on the theater screens in a country, sustained local film production becomes very difficult without governmental economic subsidiaries or screen quotas for locally made films.

67. Kirby, *Media-Made Dixie*, 162.

68. Besides the extensive catalogue of documentaries made by Les Blank since the early 1970s, some other documentaries on Louisiana Cajuns include *Les Blues de Balfa* (Yasha and Carrie Aginsky, 1983), *Cajun Visits (Visites Cajuns)* (Yasha and Carrie Aginsky, 1983), *Gumbo: The Mysteries of Creole and Cajun Cooking* (Stephen Duplantier and Marc Porter, n.d.), *D.L. Menard: Cajun Musician* (Stephen Duplantier and Marc Porter, n.d.), *Cajun Crossroads* (Karen Snyder, 1987), *Cajun Country* (Mike Alexander, 1988), *Cajun Country: Don't Drop the Potato* (Alan Lomax, 1990), *Anything I Catch: The Handfishing Story* (Pat Mire, 1990), *Dance for a Chicken: The Cajun Country Mardi Gras* (Pat Mire, 1993), and *Against the Tide: The Story of the Cajun People of Louisiana* (Pat Mire, 2000).

Besides the extensive catalogue of documentaries made by Appalshop since its founding in 1969, some other documentaries on the Appalachian Mountains include *The High Lonesome Sound: Kentucky Mountain Music* (John Cohen, 1962), *Chase the Devil: Religious Music of the Appalachian Mountains* (Jeremy Marre, 1982), *Music In the Old Time Way: Traditional Music and Musicians from the Southern Appalachians* (Philip S. Morgan, 1986), *Talking Feet: Solo Southern Dance: Buck, Flatfoot and Tap* (Mike Seeger with Ruth Pershing, 1987), *Ballad of a Mountain Man: The Story of Bascom Lamar Lunsford* (David Hoffman, 1989), *Appalachian Journey* (Mark Dibb, Mark Kidel, and Alan Lomax, 1990), and *High Lonesome: The Story of Bluegrass Music* (Rachel Liebling, 1991).

69. The terms "Cajun" and "Creole" can be confusing at times. Cajuns are descendants of the Acadian colonial settlers in southwestern Louisiana who were French-speaking. In contrast, "Creole" is used in two irreconcilable ways: to refer to white descendants of French and Spanish settlers from the colonial era, and to refer to people of mixed-race ancestry, typically assumed to be black and white but historically often American Indian too. Cajuns who have African ancestry are commonly referred to as Creoles, although they may speak French. So, as a group, Cajuns are not internally immune to the problem of racism as many Creoles will attest. Black Cajuns (aka Creoles) developed their own musical style, zydeco. The fleeting popularity of the music in the 1980s, along with documentaries about it, slowly brought the issue of racial difference among Cajuns to the surface. But in the 1970s Cajun was often assumed to be a white French-speaking ethnicity. Documentaries on zydeco include *Zydeco: Creole Music and Culture in Rural Louisiana* (Nicholas R. Spitzer, 1986), *Zarico* (Andre Gladu, 1984), *Zydeco Gumbo* (Daniel Hildenbrandt, 1988), and

J'ai ete au bal/I Went to the Dance (Les Blank with Chris Strachwitz and Maureen Gosling, 1989). Spitzer's *Zydeco* explicitly addresses the position of Creoles as an in-between racial group, a concept that will be discussed further in chapters five and six. One interviewee in the documentary defines Creoles as a mixture of French, Indian, African, and sometimes even Spanish blood. Although he does not include the speaking of French in his definition, this characteristic operates as a given within the documentary, with older participants often speaking the language. Another interviewee relays how, while growing up, Creoles were considered inferior by both blacks and whites. Yet even as an intermediary group between blacks and whites that has experienced prejudice, Creoles have also discriminated themselves. This same interviewee further recounts how old people told him that some Creole dance clubs hung a comb in their doorway and patrons who could not walk through it were not admitted. The documentary argues that despite recent pressures for Creoles to identify as black, they have maintained their separate identity through family ties, church affiliations, and social clubs.

70. See Susan Douglas, *Listening In*, 105–116.
71. See John Thompson, "Screen Acting and the Commutation Test."
72. Gaines, *Fire and Desire*, 131.
73. Of course, in practice the musicians participating in these styles are not so racially exclusive. For example, Bill Monroe, who is considered the founder of bluegrass, in his early days before the style associated with him congealed, played with black fiddler Arnold Shultz. While blues had a major impact on certain styles of rock music in the 1960s and '70s such as the Rolling Stones to the Allman Brothers, the past few decades have seen an explosion of white blues groups.

Chapter 5

1. Chion, *Audio-Vision*, 5.
2. *Birmingfind 1981* calendar.
3. The booklets were published by Birmingfind in 1981 and 1982 and are not identified by author. They were written, however, by Jeff Norrell or under his supervision and include *Elyton-West End: Birmingham's First Neighborhood*; *The Best People in the World Live in Wylam*; *The Italians: From Bisacquino to Birmingham*; *Birmingham's Lebanese: "The Earth Turned to Gold"*; *The New Patrida: The Story of Birmingham's Greeks*; and *The Other Side: The Story of Birmingham's Black Community*.
4. This discussion on Italians in Birmingham is based on Birmingfind's *The Italians* as well as Fede, *Italians in the Deep South*, and McKiven Jr., *Iron & Steel*.
5. Roediger, *Working Toward Whiteness*, 12.
6. Ibid., 13.
7. Ibid., 121.
8. Roediger, *Towards the Abolition of Whiteness*, 191.
9. See Banton, *Racial Theories*, 198–99.
10. See Moberg and Thomas, "Indochinese Resettlement."

11. The benefits and disadvantages of mainstreaming have been at various historical times a hot topic of debate among many racial and sexual minorities. Although there has been a significant increase in mainstream representations of transgender people in comparison to the dearth that existed twenty years ago, the pull of the mainstream has been slower for transgender people than gays and lesbians, just as the pull of the mainstream for gays and lesbians, especially on television, was slower than for blacks. For example, most mainstream teen films now typically have a best friend or sidekick who is either black or gay. In many ways, in relationship to mainstreaming, Asian Americans are in a similar position today to transgender people. And Native Americans continue to fall off the radar.

12. Alba, "Immigration and the American Realities of Assimilation and Multiculturalism," 7.

13. Ibid., 21.

14. Ibid., 8.

15. See Gans, "Symbolic Ethnicity." Per Herbert Gans, symbolic ethnicity is "characterized by a nostalgic allegiance to the culture of the immigrant generation . . . that can be felt without having to be incorporated in everyday behavior" (9).

16. Alba and Nee, *Remaking the American Mainstream*, 287. Richard Alba and Victor Nee differentiate between boundary-crossing and boundary-blurring in terms of how the social distance between a minority group and the mainstream can be narrowed. While boundary-crossing describes how assimilation has been traditionally conceptualized as the dissolution of the minority group as a result of its adoption of the mainstream, thereby crossing into the mainstream by shedding its difference, boundary-blurring refers to the incorporation of the minority group into the mainstream by shifting the boundary of what is considered the mainstream to include it. Alba and Nee use an example from religion to demonstrate how "the mainstream expands to accommodate cultural alternatives" (282). As a result of Jewish and Catholic immigrants, the boundaries of the American mainstream that were initially defined as Protestant "moved to include these alternative models of religious belief and practice" (283).

17. On Los Isleños, see Din, *Canary Islanders of Louisiana*, and Samantha Perez, *Isleños of Louisiana*. Also see the website for the Los Islenos Heritage and Cultural Society at www.LosIslenos.org and the documentary *Louisiana's Lost Treasure: The Isleños* (Samantha Perez and Joshua Robin, 2009).

18. Irvan Perez performed at numerous folk festivals and, at the time of his death in 2008, was known as the best décimas performer in Louisiana. He was a major champion of the documentation and preservation of Los Isleños history and culture. For one of his presentations, see Irvan Perez, "Isleños of St. Bernard Parish."

19. Some writers claim the first Filipinos arrived in North America during 1763 in Louisiana. They were deserters from Spanish ships, locally called Manilamen, who settled in the swamps outside of New Orleans. On Filipinos in Louisiana, see Marina Espina, *Filipinos in Louisiana*, and the documentary *Dancing the Shrimp* (Isabel and Jim Kenny, 1992). Malcolm Churchill, in "Louisiana History and Early Filipino Settlement," disputes the 1763 date, claiming it was much later.

20. On Ybor City, see Mormino and Pozzetta, *Immigrant World of Ybor City*.

21. A significant body of work is emerging on Latinos in southeastern states. Some of that work includes Murphy, Blanchard, and Hill, *Latino Workers in the Contemporary South*; Heather Smith and Furuseth, *Latinos in the New South*; Odem and Lacy, *Latino Immigrants and the Transformation of the U.S. South*; and Lippard and Gallagher, *Being Brown in Dixie*. Given that the first two chapters of this book focus on the city of Birmingham, Alabama, I was unable to find a documentary on Latinos in that particular city or state. However, Raymond Mohl has written extensively on the topic.

22. Foley, "Partly Colored or Other White," 135.

23. Marrow, "New Immigrant Destinations," 1053. Helen Marrow provides a book-length study of these two eastern North Carolina counties in *New Destination Dreaming*. Her book contains one chapter on how the Latinos in the two counties view whites and another on how they view blacks. On the latter issue as it relates to another locale in a southeastern state, see McClain et al., "Racial Distancing in a Southern City." The results of the McClain et al. study align with that of Marrow.

24. On the Spanish spoken by Los Isleños, see Lipski, *Language of the Isleños*, and Lestrade, "Continuing Decline of Isleño Spanish in Louisiana."

25. The trifecta territorialization, deterritorialization, and reterritorialization are from Gilles Deleuze and Félix Guattari in *Anti-Oedipus* and *A Thousand Plateaus*. The concept, per Núria Vilanova in "Deterritorialization," is a "metaphor about capitalism as a voracious machine that would progressively absorb a diversity of 'territories,' such as agriculture, culture, education, and industry, to the point of 'deterritorializing' them and leaving the proletariat (in the Marxist sense) without territory. . . . Capitalism is a system in a state of ongoing reterritorialization since it constantly attempts to take over—deterritorialize—multiple forms of interaction within a community, a group, or a family" (120). While territory is used metaphorically by Deleuze and Guattari similar to the way the closet is often used as discussed in chapter three, this does not negate it as also related to concrete space. In other words, deterritorialization can also be approached as the uncoupling of culture from space, both geographical and social. For a discussion of deterritorialization, see Canclini, *Hybrid Cultures*, 228–41; Appadurai, *Modernity at Large*, 27–47; and Tomlinson, *Globalization and Culture*, 106–149.

26. See Greenbaum, "Marketing Ybor City." Susan Greenbaum argues that in the revitalization of the neighborhood, city planners and urban developers have rewritten the history of the neighborhood. Not only has there been a tendency to conceive of the neighborhood as historically white, minimizing the presence of Afro-Cubans among the Spaniards and Italians, but also to rewrite the radicalism associated with its ethnic white residents. As Greenbaum concludes: "Many of the influential Latins and some of the academics have been linked in an unspoken conspiracy to recast the immigrant experience in Ybor City into a gentler, less disturbing image. Following a broader trend in the United States, ethnic history is celebrated as affirming, rather than challenging, basic tenets of the American political system. Radicalism in Ybor City is not disguised, but rather is portrayed as a kind of adolescent rebellion which, under the stern tutelage of Tampa's city fathers, the descendants have now outgrown. Assimilation and individualism, not resistance and collectivism, finally won them opportunity and prosperity" (74). Although made prior to revitalization of the

neighborhood, Jamison's documentary does not fall prey to either of these two tendencies. The documentary incorporates both of them as factors that shaped the fabric of what was the neighborhood.

27. Mormino and Pozzetta, *Immigrant World of Ybor City*, 10.

Chapter 6

1. I use the word "Chinese" here as a reference to race, not ethnicity or nationality. Therefore, no need exists to accompany it with the word "American" because, as with the use of the terms "black" and "white" to designate race, it also assumes citizenship. I borrow this usage of the word from the interviewees in the documentary, in which all three racial groups in the Mississippi Delta unanimously use the word as a racial designator (albeit referring to race with a strong cultural association).

For a general history of the Mississippi Delta, see Cobb, *Most Southern Place on Earth*. Numerous documentaries exist on the Mississippi Delta. Some of them include *Blues Maker* (Christian Garrison, 1969), *Give My Poor Heart Ease: Mississippi Delta Bluesmen* (William Ferris, 1975), *Good Mornin' Blues* (Walt Lowe, 1978), *Mississippi Blues* (Bertrand Tavernier and Yannick Bernard, 1983), *Mississippi Delta Blues* (Anthony Herrera, 1984), *The Land Where the Blues Began* (Alan Lomax, 1990), *Deep Blues* (Robert Mugge, 1991), and *Delta Blues* (Gary R. Thieman, 1994). As the titles in this list suggest, documentaries on the Mississippi Delta tend to focus in general on black culture and in particular on blues music. Although not its focus, *Mississippi Triangle* begins with a nod to this close association of the Mississippi Delta with black music; immediately after the title credits, a black man plays a gospel song on a piano and then another plays a blues song on a guitar.

2. For a general history of Chinese in southeastern states, see Cohen, *Chinese in the Post-Civil War South*. On the Mississippi Chinese, see Quan, *Lotus Among the Magnolias*; Schneider and Schneider, "Structural Analysis of the Chinese Grocery Store"; and Loewen, *Mississippi Chinese*. The Mississippi Chinese have been discussed in numerous articles and book chapters, but Loewen's book is typically used as the source material for those discussions, just as it is here.

3. This chapter is based on an earlier article, "'So that we have our own color': *Mississippi Triangle*, Textual Posturing, and Racial Negotiation," *Film Criticism* 26, no. 3 (Spring 2002): 31–51. Although Leslie Bow does not engage these prior claims in *Partly Colored: Asian Americans and Racial Anomaly in the Segregated South* when discussing the documentary, she assumes a similar position, that it enunciates a critique of the Mississippi Chinese. While my focus is restricted to issues related to the film proper, Bow positions the documentary within the broader context of an analysis of Asian Americans in the "American South" (3) as an "interstitial population" (11) that makes "visible social structure" (17). Her concept of "racial interstitiality" is offered as a way to move beyond the limitations of older frameworks, such as "honorary white" and "partially colored," used to describe Asian Americans within the context of a discourse dominated by biraciality. Although my concern is with how biraciality circulates as a denial of other races within the region during the so-called

post-segregation era, her warning deserves reiteration: "Looking at the 'partly colored races' under segregation does not fundamentally challenge the South's historically embedded investment in a black-white binary, nor does it simply offer a pluralist corrective that prefigures the emergence of a more multicultural South" (20).

4. Dittus, "*Mississippi Triangle*," 40.

5. Xing, *Asian America through the Lens*, 100.

6. Marchetti, "Ethnicity, the Cinema, and Cultural Studies," 298, 302. Gina Marchetti's position is actually much more complex than this quotation reveals because she also concedes that the documentary "tacitly sides with certain groups over others" (298), that of the black-Chinese, who she asserts "represent the synthetic moment of understanding created by the film's dialectical representation of race and ethnicity" (302). She does not reconcile, however, why this synthesis is not a textual point of view or conclusion.

7. Bonitzer, "Silences of the Voice," 321.

8. Dittus, "*Mississippi Triangle*," 39.

9. The documentary contains numerous talking heads with subtitles at the bottom of the screen to identify them. None of the individuals in these three scenes are identified by subtitles, although one orally identifies herself by name in a voice-over narration that substitutes for a talking-head interview.

10. The documentary does not officially state that the couple is married. It has to be inferred from the quick shot of his hand wearing a wedding ring. Extra-textual material surrounding the documentary identifies the young white man as Lawrence King and the young Chinese woman as Mai King. Extra-textual material also identifies the Chinese girl at the swimming pool as Mai's sister. While Mai's marriage to a white man necessitates no justification, her younger sister's playing with black girls does.

11. See Bernardi, "Heat in the Delta."

12. Dittus, "*Mississippi Triangle*," 39.

13. Ibid., 39–40.

14. Ibid., 40.

15. Ibid., 39.

16. All of this information is gleaned from Loewen, *Mississippi Chinese*.

17. Bernardi, "Heat in the Delta," 22, 23.

18. Shohat and Stam, *Unthinking Eurocentrism*, 204.

19. Marchetti, "Ethnicity, the Cinema, and Cultural Studies," 305.

20. On ethnographic film, see Crawford and Turton, *Film as Ethnography*; Hockings, *Principles of Visual Anthropology*; Loizos, *Innovation in Ethnographic Film*; MacDougall, *Transcultural Cinema*; and Ruby, *Picturing Culture*.

21. Dittus, "*Mississippi Triangle*," 40.

22. Loewen, *Mississippi Chinese*, 64.

23. Ibid., 2, 5.

24. Roediger, *Working Toward Whiteness*, 13.

25. The documentary contains numerous examples of blatant racism by Chinese toward blacks; they say things they most likely would not if the interviews had transpired in a mixed-race environment. For example, an unidentified elderly Chinese man uses the word

"nigger" to refer to blacks, and a young Chinese man expounds, "Blacks in the South have such a low social status that you simply can't be seen in public with them and still expect to have any respect."

26. Although counterintuitive, the continued acceptance of the one-drop rule in terms of who is black also contributes to this situation. (Although blacks accept the rule as much as whites, that fact does not eliminate it from being a manifestation of white supremacy that shapes social relations.)

27. Some scholars maintain that a not-black stance is inherently racist because it presumes that association with blackness is negative. While on an abstract level I find the critique persuasive, when historically situated within a white supremacy society that perceives itself as biracial, such a position would mean that non-black-or-white groups have no option but blackness rather than have their "own color."

28. See Morrison, "On the Backs of Blacks."

29. Although important differences exist in how they conceive the specifics of the situation, many racial theorists and social scientists hold that at the beginning of the twenty-first century a new racial hierarchy is emerging in the United States; an intermediary group is being incorporated between black and white. In other words, the dominant configuration of race as biracial (black and white) is being replaced by a tri-racial configuration with a middle group; this new multilayered arrangement is still a hierarchy, however, similar to the binary configuration with blacks continuing to be confined to the bottom. In this new alignment, Asian Americans and Latinos are predicted to be in all three categories depending on their color gradation, assimilation attainment, and ethnic affiliation. For example, see Gans, "Possibility of a New Racial Hierarchy," and Bonilla-Silva, "From Bi-racial to Tri-Racial." Herbert Gans assumes this intermediary group is temporary, a way station before members can be assigned to one of the other two categories, while Eduardo Bonilla-Silva conceives of it as a permanent new racial category. Many scholars hold that another change is also occurring, the dominant divide for classification shifting from a white/nonwhite divide to a black/nonblack one. The emergence of a black/nonblack divide is supported by a number of studies showing that Latinos and Asian Americans generally hold attitudes closer to those of whites than blacks. See Yancey, *Who Is White?* One alternative proposed to racial hierarchy is racial triangulation. Of course, the components of a triangulation process can also have unequal value judgments (and social rewards) attached to them similar to the linear hierarchical approach. See Kim, "Racial Triangulation of Asian Americans."

Although the region was framed discursively as white during the segregation era and subsequently biracial, the lived experiences of race at the local level ranged from mono-racial to multiracial regardless of how the region was racialized. Of course, the more appropriate descriptor of this earlier configuration is "white supremacy." The distinction is important because it allowed for the reconciliation of the region as mono-racial when lived experience at the local level was not. As a result, blacks and other races were positioned as outsiders, not southerners, and therefore disenfranchisement—regardless of type—was legitimized.

While *Mississippi Triangle* includes segments on the history of the Mississippi Chinese during segregation, in particular the legal battle over whether they could attend white schools (which they lost), the documentary was made in the desegregated era and most of the interviewees' comments about race in the Delta are about the present (the early 1980s, when the documentary was made). The distinction between these two eras becomes muddled in many discussions of the documentary. As a result, I wonder how much of the ability of the Mississippi Chinese to change their status within Delta society was derived from the racial and social instabilities that existed during the transition between these two eras.

The transition from a segregated society to a desegregated society is often framed as a historical rupture. Although significant change occurred in the aftermath of the civil rights movement, on certain levels continuity persists between the two eras. I am beginning to wonder if a discourse of biraciality during an era claimed to be desegregated (with the persistent occurrence of segregation) functions similarly to a discourse of white supremacy during an era of segregation (with the routine occurrence of sanctioned interaction). In other words, can the recourse to a discourse of biraciality function similarly to color-blind racisim?

30. Bernardi, "Heat in the Delta," 23.

31. An aggregation of the 1980 census data for the Mississippi counties typically aligned as constituting the Mississippi Delta shows that while the percentage of blacks in the lowest-income bracket was significantly higher than the percentage of whites, blacks appeared in all of the income brackets, just at a significantly lower percentage than whites. In other words, the income spread for blacks was greater at the poverty end than for whites and its tail of the upper-income brackets much narrower.

32. Although the documentary contains a few old photographs of Mississippi Chinese, it contains no archival film footage of them.

Chapter 7

1. Subsequent to the release of the documentary, Malinda Maynor's name changed to Malinda Maynor Lowery. Because the documentary is under the name Malinda Maynor, I will be referring to her by that last name when discussing the documentary.

Although I am very interested in film aesthetics, as indicated by some of the documentaries I selected to focus on in this book, my concern with Maynor's documentary is not with its aesthetics per se. In *Indigenous Aesthetics: Native Art, Media, and Identity*, Steven Leuthold explores the issue of whether a distinct aesthetic exists for Native Americans. I will not be concerned with whether Maynor's documentary inhabits a native aesthetic, not even if that native aesthetic is qualified with the descriptor "southern" or "southeastern." The form of her film, however, is typical of autobiographical diariestic documentaries. The aesthetics can be considered indicative of the institutional production context out of which it emerged, that of a student film project.

2. Sider, *Lumbee Indian Histories*, 214.

3. Ethridge and Hudson, "Early Historic Transformation of the Southeastern Indians," 38, 39.

4. Sider, *Lumbee Indian Histories*, 243.

5. Porter III, "Nonrecognized American Indian Tribes," 20.

6. The conclusions I draw about the tri-racial isolate school of thought is based on a review of the following literature: Gilbert Jr., "Memorandum Concerning the Characteristics of the Larger Mixed-Blood Racial Islands"; Price, "Geographic Analysis of White-Negro-Indian Racial Mixtures"; Berry, *Almost White*; Beale, "Overview of the Phenomenon of Mixed Racial Isolates"; Pollitzer, "Physical Anthropology and Genetics of Marginal People"; and Edgar Thompson, "Little Races."

7. Although most of these writers deal with the eastern United States, their samples often disproportionately come from southeastern states or they differentiate that area from the rest of the United States.

8. For a detailed discussion of the tri-racial isolate literature in relationship to the misidentification of native communities, see Greenbaum, "What's In a Label?"

9. See Quinn Jr., "Southeast Syndrome: Notes on Indian Descendant Recruitment Organizations." For a rebuttal to Quinn Jr., see Starna, "Southeast Syndrome: A Prior Restraint of a Non-Event."

10. Christopher Arris Oakley contends in "Native South in the Post-World War II Era" that "if a Cherokee woman married a white man and gave birth to his son, that child was considered Cherokee, not 'one-half' Cherokee" because "Indian peoples in the South, most of whom were matrilineal, based identity on clan [derived from one's mother] and community, not race" (74). He concludes: "In the twentieth century, though, race became an additional component of Indianness in the South" (75).

11. Ward Churchill, "Crucible of American Indian Identity," 43.

12. Forbes, "Manipulation of Race, Caste and Identity," 14.

13. Historically, Native Americans were also enslaved, so they have the precarious history of having been both slaves and slaveholders.

14. The term "five-civilized tribes" has been critiqued as racist. It is Eurocentric because these five Indian groups are considered "civilized" by the United States government since they adopted institutional structures and/or customs similar to United States whites. The term implies that Indian social structures and cultures were not civilized, thereby invoking the stereotype of the savage Indian.

15. Perdue, "Southern Indians and Jim Crow," 78.

16. The term is derived not from the large number of African Americans that live in the area but rather the quality of the soil. Because of its rich, dark soil, the portion of the Black Belt in Alabama and Mississippi was predominately agricultural and, therefore, between Indian removal in the early 1830s and the Civil War in the early 1860s, the home of many farms and plantations that used slave labor.

17. The community adopted the formal designation MOWA Band of Choctaw Indians in the 1970s when they began to seek federal recognition. The prefix "MOWA" is derived from the two counties in which the group resides (Mobile County and Washington County). The tribe was recognized by the state of Alabama in 1981 but denied recognition by the federal government in 1997. On the MOWA Band of Choctaw Indians, see Matte, *They Say the Wind is Red*; Cramer, *Cash, Color, and Colonialism*, 113–36; and Matte, "Extinction by Reclassification." In addition, the *Mobile Press Register* ran a special four-part series by Bill Finch on the MOWA Choctaws called "The Forgotten Tribe" from 24–27 November 1994. Although

historian Jacqueline Matte and anthropologist Susan Greenbaum have worked with the MOWA Choctaws, limited academic research has been published on them.

The main ethnographer of the Poarch Band of Creek Indians has been Anthony Paredes. On the Poarch Band of Creek Indians, see Paredes, "Emergence of Contemporary Eastern Creek Indian Identity"; Paredes, "Back from Disappearance"; Paredes, "Kinship and Descent in the Ethnic Reassertion of the Eastern Creek Indians"; and Paredes, "Federal Recognition and the Poarch Creek Indians." On the popular front, the *Mobile Register* ran a special week-long series on the group's history, culture, and economic development from 22–26 November 1992.

18. On the United Houma Nation, see Stanton, "Southern Louisiana Survivors"; Duthu, "Houma Indians of Louisiana"; Mark Edwin Miller, *Forgotten Tribes*, 156–208; and D'Oney, "Houma Nation." The documentary *Hidden Nation* (Barbara Sillery and Oak Lea, 1994) provides a general overview of the tribe and its history.

19. Snipp, "Some Observations about Racial Boundaries," 677.

20. The main ethnographers of the Lumbee Tribe of North Carolina have been Karen Blu and Gerald Sider. On the Lumbee Tribe of North Carolina, see Evans, "North Carolina Lumbees"; Blu, *Lumbee Problem*; Sider, *Lumbee Indian Histories*; Blu, "Lumbee Ethnohistory"; Blu, "Homeplace and Community Among the Lumbee"; Dial and Eliades, *Only Land I Know*; and Lowery, *Lumbee Indians in the Jim Crow South*.

21. Lowery, *Lumbee Indians in the Jim Crow South*, 263.

22. Perdue, "Legacy of Indian Removal," 36.

23. Historically, the entangled relationships between whites, blacks, and native peoples have not been uniform or simple. For example, some native tribes owned black slaves while others incorporated runaway slaves into their tribe. Similarly, some native tribes fought with the Confederacy while others with the Union. In the face of such historical complexity, my pronouncements ring rather simplistic and reductionary.

24. Taylor, *Reconstructing the Native South*, 96.

25. Bataille and Silet, "Entertaining Anachronism," 40.

26. Ward Churchill, *Fantasies of the Master Race*, 233.

27. Forbes, "Manipulation of Race, Caste and Identity," 23.

28. Ibid., 41.

29. Porter III, "Nonrecognized American Indian Tribes," 19. Frank Porter III lists four factors which are "responsible for holding these Indian groups together during the nineteenth century." They are: (1) "maintenance of family unity," (2) "the transition from an aboriginal to a Euro-American concept of land tenure," (3) "the adoption of specific [Euro-] American core institutions," and (4) "the effect of racial discrimination" and prejudice.

30. This grounding of Indianness in kinship rather than the body or culture led the Lumbee, per Malinda Maynor Lowery in *Lumbee Indians in the Jim Crow South*, to practice historically a diffused form of leadership rather than the centralized form required by the United States government for federal recognition. As she highlights: "Indians only embraced the idea of a 'tribe' with a single name and a central government when external forces demanded they conform to those identity definitions in order to affirm their Indianness" (261).

31. On the Poarch Band of Creek Indians, see footnote 17. On the Eastern Band of Cherokee Indians, see Finger, *Eastern Band of Cherokees*; Neely, "Acculturation and Persistence among North Carolina's Eastern Band of Cherokee Indians"; Neely, "Snowbird Cherokees:

Adaptation and Ethnic Preservation in the Southern Appalachians"; Finger, *Cherokee Americans*; Neely, *Snowbird Cherokees*; Neely, "Adaptation and the Contemporary North Carolina Cherokee Indians."

32. On the Hollywood Indian, see Stedman, *Shadows of the Indian*; Bataille and Silet, *Pretend Indians*; Rollins and Connor, *Hollywood's Indian*; and Kilpatrick, *Celluloid Indians*.

33. Neely, "Adaptation and the Contemporary North Carolina Cherokee Indians," 29.

34. Neely, "Acculturation and Persistence among North Carolina's Eastern Band of Cherokee Indians," 156.

35. Paredes, "Federal Recognition and the Poarch Creek Indians," 125.

36. Paredes, "Back from Disappearance," 137.

37. See Berg, *Latino Images in Film*.

38. Bhabha, *Location of Culture*, 89.

39. Neale, "Same Old Story," 43.

40. Social reality obviously encompasses not only interpersonal interaction but interaction with the media as well. As noted in the introduction, our interaction with people influences our experience with the media, just as our interaction with the media influences our experience with people. To avoid implying that the media is not part of lived experience, I am using the awkward phrase "non-media-based social reality." One could argue that in our media-saturated society the two have become so intertwined that any separation is an artificial one.

41. See Hall, "Spectacle of the 'Other.'"

42. Butler, *Bodies That Matter*, 129.

43. Romine, *The Real South*, 9.

Conclusion

1. Kennedy, *Melungeons*, 15, 12. On the Melungeons, also see Schrift, "Melungeons and the Politics of Heritage." A significant body of literature has emerged on the Melungeons in the wake of the initial publication of Kennedy's book in 1994, ranging from C. S. Everett's historical inquiry, "Melungeon History and Myth," to Katherine Vande Brake's literary analysis, *How They Shine: Melungeon Characters in the Fiction of Appalachia*, part of Mercer University Press's book series on Melungeons.

2. Kennedy, *Melungeons*, 139.

3. Several DNA studies have been performed on Melungeons. The two most recent ones draw—as one might expect, given that they use different methodologies and populations—different conclusions. See Yates and Hirschman, "Toward a Genetic Profile of Melungeons in Southern Appalachia," and Estes, Goins, Ferguson, and Crain, "Melungeons, A Multi-Ethnic Population." While the former study found the heritage of the Melungeons to contain a wide variety of ethnicities similar to those discussed by Kennedy and others in the documentary *Melungeon Voices*, the latter study did not. Both studies, however, acknowledge that not all families have the same configuration of heritages.

Bibliography

Abu-Lughod, Lila. "Writing against Culture." In *Recapturing Anthropology: Working in the Present*, ed. Richard G. Fox, 137–62. Santa Fe, NM: School of American Research Press, 1991.
Agamben, Giorgio. *The Coming Community*. Trans. Michael Hardt. Minneapolis: University of Minnesota Press, 1993.
———. *Potentialities: Collected Essays in Philosophy*. Ed. and trans. Daniel Heller-Roazen. Stanford, CA: Stanford University Press, 1999.
———. *State of Exception*. Trans. Kevin Attell. Chicago: University of Chicago Press, 2005.
Ahmad, Aijaz. *In Theory: Classes, Nations, Literatures*. London: Verso, 1992.
Alba, Richard. "Immigration and the American Realities of Assimilation and Multiculturalism" [annual presidential address to the Eastern Sociological Society]. *Sociological Forum* 14, no. 1 (March 1999): 3–25.
Alba, Richard, and Victor Nee. *Remaking the American Mainstream: Assimilation and Contemporary Immigration*. Cambridge, MA: Harvard University Press, 2003.
Allen, Richard. "Psychoanalytic Film Theory." In *A Companion to Film Theory*, eds. Toby Miller and Robert Stam, 123–45. Malden, MA: Blackwell, 1999.
Althusser, Louis. "Ideology and Ideological State Apparatuses (Notes toward an Investigation)." In *Lenin and Philosophy, and Other Essays*, trans. Ben Brewster, 127–86. New York: Monthly Review Press, 1971.
Altman, Rick. *Film/Genre*. London: British Film Institute, 1999.
Anderson, Benedict. *Imagined Communities: Reflections on the Origin and Spread of Nationalism*. Revised edition. London: Verso, 1991.
Appadurai, Arjun. *Modernity at Large: Cultural Dimensions of Globalization*. Minneapolis: University of Minnesota Press, 1996.
Ashmore, Harry S. *An Epitaph for Dixie*. New York: Norton, 1958.
Ayers, Edward L. "What We Talk about When We Talk about the South." In *All Over the Map: Rethinking American Regions*, eds. Edward L. Ayers, Patricia Nelson Limerick, Stephen Nissenbaum, and Peter S. Onuf, 62–82. Baltimore: Johns Hopkins University Press, 1996.
Baker, Houston A., Jr., and Dana D. Nelson. "Preface: Violence, the Body and 'The South.'" *American Literature* 73, no. 2 (June 2001): 231–44.
Baldwin, Lewis V. *There is a Balm in Gilead: The Cultural Roots of Martin Luther King Jr.* Minneapolis: Fortress Press, 1991.
Ball, Edward. *Slaves in the Family*. New York: Farrar, Straus and Giroux, 1998.
Banton, Michael. *Racial Theories*. Second edition. Cambridge, England: Cambridge University Press, 1998.

Bartley, Numan V. *The Rise of Massive Resistance: Race and Politics in the South during the 1950s.* Baton Rouge: Louisiana State University Press, 1969.

Bataille, Gretchen M., and Charles L. P. Silet. "The Entertaining Anachronism: Indians in American Film." In *The Kaleidoscopic Lens: How Hollywood Views Ethnic Groups*, ed. Randall M. Miller, 36–53. Englewood, NJ: Jerome S. Ozer, 1980.

———, eds. *The Pretend Indians: Images of Native Americans in the Movies.* Ames: Iowa State University Press, 1980.

Bates, Eric. "Beyond Black and White." *Southern Exposure* 22, no. 3 (Fall 1994): 11–15.

Beale, Calvin L. "An Overview of the Phenomenon of Mixed Racial Isolates in the United States." *American Anthropologists* 74, no. 3 (June 1972): 704–710.

Becquer, Marcos, and José Gatti. "Elements of Vogue." *Third Text*, no. 16 (1991): 65–81.

Beltrán, Mary, and Camilla Fojas, eds. *Mixed Race Hollywood.* New York: New York University Press, 2008.

Bendix, Regina. *In Search of Authenticity: The Formation of Folklore Studies.* Madison: University of Wisconsin Press, 1997.

Berg, Charles Ramírez. *Latino Images in Film: Stereotypes, Subversion, Resistance.* Austin: University of Texas Press, 2002.

Bernardi, Adria. "Heat in the Delta: Reactions to the Triangle." *Southern Exposure* 12, no. 4 (July/August 1984): 22–23.

Berry, Brewton. *Almost White.* New York: Macmillan, 1963.

Bérubé, Allan. "How Gay Stays White and What Kind of White It Stays." In *The Making and Unmaking of Whiteness*, eds. Birgit Brander Rasmussen, Eric Klinenberg, Irene J. Nexica, and Matt Wray, 234–65. Durham: Duke University Press, 2001.

Bhabha, Homi K. "Introduction: Narrating the Nation." In *Nation and Narration*, ed. Homi K. Bhabha, 1–7. London: Routledge, 1990.

———. *The Location of Culture.* London: Routledge, 1994.

Biondi, Martha. *To Stand and Fight: The Struggle for Civil Rights in Postwar New York City.* Cambridge, MA: Harvard University Press, 2003.

"Birmingham Civil Rights Institute: Inspired by the Past, a Vision for the Future." Birmingham Civil Rights Institute, Birmingham, Alabama, n.d. Brochure.

Black, Earl, and Merle Black. *Divided America: The Ferocious Power Struggle in American Politics.* New York: Simon & Schuster, 2007.

Blu, Karen L. *The Lumbee Problem: The Making of an American Indian People.* Cambridge, England: Cambridge University Press, 1980.

———. "'Reading Back' to Find Community: Lumbee Ethnohistory." In *North American Indian Anthropology: Essays on Society and Culture*, eds. Raymond J. DeMallie and Alfonso Ortez, 278–95. Norman: University of Oklahoma Press, 1994.

———. "'Where Do You Stay At?': Homeplace and Community among the Lumbee." In *Senses of Place*, eds. Steven Feld and Keith H. Basso, 197–227. Santa Fe, NM: School of American Research Press, 1996.

Bobbitt, David A. *The Rhetoric of Redemption: Kenneth Burke's Redemption Drama and Martin Luther King Jr.'s "I Have a Dream" Speech.* Lanham, MD: Rowman & Littlefield, 2004.

Bogue, Ronald. *Deleuze on Music, Painting, and the Arts.* New York: Routledge, 2003.

Bone, Martyn. *The Postsouthern Sense of Place in Contemporary Fiction*. Baton Rouge: Louisiana State University Press, 2005.

Bonilla-Silva, Eduardo. *Racism without Racists: Color-Blind Racism and the Persistence of Racial Inequality in the United States*. Lanham, MD: Rowman & Littlefield, 2003.

———. "From Bi-racial to Tri-Racial: Towards a New System of Racial Stratification in the USA." *Ethnic and Racial Studies* 27, no. 6 (November 2004): 931–50.

Bonitzer, Pascal. "The Silences of the Voice: (*A propos* of *Mai 68* by Gudie Lawaetz)." In *Narrative, Apparatus, Ideology: A Film Theory Reader*, ed. Philip Rosen, 319–34. New York: Columbia University Press, 1986.

Bourdieu, Pierre. *The Field of Cultural Production: Essays on Art and Literature*. Ed. Randal Johnson. New York: Columbia University Press, 1993.

———. "On the Family as a Realized Category." *Theory, Culture & Society* 13, no. 3 (1996): 19–26.

Bow, Leslie. *Partly Colored: Asian Americans and Racial Anomaly in the Segregated South*. New York: New York University Press, 2010.

Bradbury, John M. *Renaissance in the South: A Critical History of the Literature, 1920–1960*. Chapel Hill: University of North Carolina Press, 1963.

Bradshaw, Michael. *Regions and Regionalism in the Unites States*. Jackson: University Press of Mississippi, 1988.

Brasell, R. Bruce. "From Evidentiary Presentation to Artful Re-Presentation: Media Images, Civil Rights Documentaries, and the Audiovisual Writing of History." *Journal of Film and Video* 56, no. 1 (Spring 2004): 3–16.

Brauer, Carl M. *John F. Kennedy and the Second Reconstruction*. New York: Columbia University Press, 1977.

Brennan, Timothy. "The National Longing for Form." In *Nation and Narration*, ed. Homi K. Bhabha, 44–70. London: Routledge, 1990.

Brett, David. *The Construction of Heritage*. Cork, Ireland: Cork University Press, 1996.

Browder, Glen. *The South's New Racial Politics: Inside the Race Game of Southern History*. Montgomery, AL: NewSouth Books, 2009.

Brown, Michael P. *Closet Space: Geographies of Metaphor from the Body to the Globe*. London: Routledge, 2000.

Brown, Richard Maxwell. "The New Regionalism in America, 1970–1981." In *Regionalism and the Pacific Northwest*, eds. William G. Robbins, Robert J. Frank, and Richard E. Ross, 37–96. Corvallis: Oregon State University Press, 1983.

Bruzzi, Stella. *New Documentary*. Second edition. London: Routledge, 2006.

Bullert, B. J. *Public Television: Politics and the Battle over Documentary Film*. New Brunswick, NJ: Rutgers University Press, 1997.

Bullock, Charles S., III. and Ronald Keith Gaddie. *The Triumph of Voting Rights in the South*. Norman: University of Oklahoma Press, 2009.

Burrow, Rufus, Jr. *God and Human Dignity: The Personalism, Theology, and Ethics of Martin Luther King Jr.* Notre Dame, IN: University of Notre Dame Press, 2006.

Butler, Judith. *Gender Trouble: Feminism and the Subversion of Identity*. New York: Routledge, 1990.

———. *Bodies That Matter: On the Discursive Limits of "Sex"*. New York: Routledge, 1993.
———. "Critically Queer." In *Playing with Fire: Queer Politics, Queer Theories*, ed. Shane Phelan, 11–29. New York: Routledge, 1997.
———. *Undoing Gender*. New York: Routledge, 2004.
Campbell, Edward D. C., Jr. *The Celluloid South: Hollywood and the Southern Myth*. Knoxville: University of Tennessee Press, 1981.
Canclini, Néstor García. *Hybrid Cultures: Strategies for Entering and Leaving Modernity*. Trans. Christopher L. Chiappari and Silvia L. López. Minneapolis: University of Minnesota Press, 1995.
Carson, Clayborne. "Civil Rights Reform and the Black Freedom Struggle." In *The Civil Rights Movement in America*, ed. Charles W. Eagles, 19–32. Jackson: University Press of Mississippi, 1986.
Caserio, Robert L., Lee Edelman, Judith Halberstam, José Esteban Muñoz, and Tim Dean. "Forum: The Antisocial Thesis in Queer Theory." *PMLA* 121, no. 3 (May 2006): 819–28.
Casetti, Francesco. *Theories of Cinema, 1945–1995*. Trans. Francesca Chiostri and Elizabeth Gard Bartolini-Salimbeni. Austin: University of Texas Press, 1999.
"Central Alabama's Black Heritage Trail: Your Places in History: Selma, Montgomery, Tuskegee." Unidentified, n.d. Brochure.
Chappell, David L. *A Stone of Hope: Prophetic Religion and the Death of Jim Crow*. Chapel Hill: University of North Carolina, 2004.
Chatterjee, Partha. "Beyond the Nation? Or Within?" *Social Text*, no. 56 (Fall 1998): 57–69.
Chion, Michel. *Audio-Vision: Sound on Screen*. Trans. Claudia Gorbman. New York: Columbia University Press, 1994.
Churchill, Malcolm. "Louisiana History and Early Filipino Settlement: Searching for the Story." *Bulletin of the American Historical Collection Foundation* 27, no. 2 (1992): 25–48.
Churchill, Ward. *Fantasies of the Master Race: Literature, Cinema, and the Colonization of American Indians*. Ed. M. Annette Jaimes. Monroe, ME: Common Courage Press, 1992.
———. "The Crucible of American Indian Identity: Native Tradition versus Colonial Imposition in Postconquest North America." *American Indian Culture and Research Journal* 23, no. 1 (1999): 39–67.
"The Civil Rights Memorial: Forty Lives for Freedom." Southern Poverty Law Center, Montgomery, Alabama, n.d. Brochure.
Claval, Paul. "The Region as a Geographical, Economic and Cultural Concept." *International Social Science Journal* 39, no. 2 (May 1987): 159–72.
Clifford, James. *The Predicament of Culture: Twentieth-Century Ethnography, Literature, and Art*. Cambridge, MA: Harvard University Press, 1988.
Cobb, James C. *The Most Southern Place on Earth: The Mississippi Delta and the Roots of Regional Identity*. New York: Oxford University Press, 1992.
———. *Redefining Southern Culture: Mind and Identity in the Modern South*. Athens: University of Georgia Press, 1999.
Cohen, Lucy M. *Chinese in the Post–Civil War South: A People Without a History*. Baton Rouge: Louisiana State University Press, 1984.
Colebrook, Claire. *Gilles Deleuze*. London: Routledge, 2002.

Collins, Patricia Hill. "Like One of the Family: Race, Ethnicity, and the Paradox of US National Identity." *Ethnic and Racial Studies* 24, no. 1 (January 2001): 3–28.
Connerly, Charles E. *"The Most Segregated City in America": City Planning and Civil Rights in Birmingham, 1920–1980*. Charlottesville: University of Virginia Press, 2005.
Copjec, Joan. "The Orthopsychic Subject: Film Theory and the Reception of Lacan." *October*, no. 49 (Summer 1989): 53–71.
Countryman, Matthew J. *Up South: Civil Rights and Black Power in Philadelphia*. Philadelphia: University of Pennsylvania Press, 2006.
Courtney, Susan. *Hollywood Fantasies of Miscegenation: Spectacular Narratives of Gender and Race, 1903–1967*. Princeton: Princeton University Press, 2005.
Cowie, Elizabeth. *Representing the Woman: Cinema and Psychoanalysis*. Minneapolis: University of Minnesota Press, 1997.
———. *Recording Reality, Desiring the Real*. Minneapolis: University of Minnesota Press, 2011.
Cox, Thomas H. "From Centerpiece to Center Stage: Kelly Ingram Park, Segregation, and Civil Rights in Birmingham, Alabama." *Southern Historian*, vol. 18 (1997): 5–28.
Cramer, Renée Ann. *Cash, Color, and Colonialism: The Politics of Tribal Acknowledgment*. Norman: University of Oklahoma Press, 2005.
Crawford, Peter Ian, and David Turton, eds. *Film as Ethnography*. Manchester, England: Manchester University Press, 1992.
Creed, Gerald W. "Reconsidering Community." In *The Seductions of Community: Emancipations, Oppressions, Quandaries*, ed. Gerald W. Creed, 3–22. Santa Fe, NM: School of American Research Press, 2006.
Culler, Jonathan. *On Deconstruction: Theory and Criticism after Structuralism*. Ithaca, NY: Cornell University Press, 1982.
Cumming, Joseph B., Jr. "Been Down Home So Long it Looks Like Up To Me: The Americanization of Dixie." *Esquire* 76, no. 2 (August 1971): 84–90, 110, 114.
Current, Richard N. *Northernizing the South*. Athens: University of Georgia Press, 1983.
DaCosta, Kimberly McClain. "All in the Family: The Familial Roots of Racial Division." In *The Politics of Multiracialism: Challenging Racial Thinking*, ed. Heather M. Dalmage, 19–41. Albany: State University of New York Press, 2004.
Dailey, Jane. "Sex, Segregation, and the Sacred after *Brown*." *Journal of American History* 91, no. 1 (June 2004): 119–44.
Dal Lago, Enrico. *Agrarian Elites: American Slaveholders and Southern Italian Landowners, 1815–1861*. Baton Rouge: Louisiana State University Press, 2005.
Dal Lago, Enrico, and Rick Halpern, eds. *The American South and the Italian Mezzogiorno: Essays in Comparative History*. New York: Palgrave, 2002.
Davis, F. James. *Who Is Black?: One Nation's Definition*. University Park, PA: Pennsylvania State University Press, 1991.
Degler, Carl N. *Place over Time: The Continuity of Southern Distinctiveness*. Baton Rouge: Louisiana State University Press, 1977. Reprint, Athens: University of Georgia Press, 1997.
DeLanda, Manuel. *A New Philosophy of Society: Assemblage Theory and Social Complexity*. London: Continuum, 2006.

Deleuze, Gilles. *Bergsonism*. Trans. Hugh Tomlinson and Barbara Habberjam. New York: Zone Books, 1988.
———. *Negotiations, 1972–1990*. Trans. Martin Joughin. New York: Columbia University Press, 1995.
———. *Two Regimes of Madness: Texts and Interviews, 1975–1995*. Ed. David Lapoujade. Trans. Ames Hodges and Mike Taormina. New York: Semiotext(e), 2007.
Deleuze, Gilles, and Félix Guattari. *Anti-Oedipus: Capitalism and Schizophernia*. Trans. Robert Hurley, Mark Seem, and Helen R. Lane. Minneapolis: University of Minnesota Press, 1983.
———. *A Thousand Plateaus: Capitalism and Schizophrenia*. Trans. Brian Massumi. Minneapolis: University of Minnesota Press, 1987.
———. *What is Philosophy?* Trans. Hugh Tomlinson and Graham Burchell. New York: Columbia University Press, 1994.
Derrida, Jacques. *Of Grammatology*. Trans. Gayatri Chakravorty Spivak. Baltimore: Johns Hopkins University Press, 1976.
Dial, Adolph L., and David K. Eliades. *The Only Land I Know: A History of the Lumbee Indians*. San Fransciso: Indian Historian Press, 1975. Reprint, Syracuse, NY: Syracuse University Press, 1996.
Din, Gilbert C. *The Canary Islanders of Louisiana*. Baton Rouge: Louisiana State University Press, 1988.
Dittus, Erick. "*Mississippi Triangle*: An Interview with Christine Choy, Worth Long and Allan Siegel." *Cineaste* 14, no. 2 (September 1985): 38–40.
Dollimore, Jonathan. *Sexual Dissidence: Augustine to Wilde, Freud to Foucault*. New York: Oxford University Press, 1991.
D'Oney, J. Daniel. "The Houma Nation: A Historiographical Overview." *Louisiana History* 47, no. 1 (Winter 2006): 63–90.
Douglas, Mary. *Purity and Danger: An Analysis of the Concepts of Pollution and Taboo*. London: Routledge, 1991. Originally published 1966.
Douglas, Susan J. *Listening In: Radio and the American Imagination*. New York: Times Books, 1999.
Doyle, Don H. *Nations Divided: America, Italy, and the Southern Question*. Athens: University of Georgia Press, 2002.
Duck, Leigh Anne. *The Nation's Region: Southern Modernism, Segregation, and U.S. Nationalism*. Athens: University of Georgia Press, 2006.
———. "Southern Nonidentity." *Safundi* 9, no. 3 (Summer 2008): 319–30.
Duthu, N. Bruce. "The Houma Indians of Louisiana: The Intersection of Law and History in the Federal Acknowledgment Process." *Louisiana History* 38, no. 4 (Fall 1997): 409–436.
Dyer, Richard. *White*. London: Routledge, 1997.
Eaton, Mick. "The Production of Cinematic Reality." In *Anthropology—Reality—Cinema: The Films of Jean Rouch*, ed. Mick Eaton, 40–53. London: British Film Institute, 1979.
Edelman, Lee. *No Future: Queer Theory and the Death Drive*. Durham: Duke University Press, 2004.

Egerton, John. *The Americanization of Dixie: The Southernization of America.* New York: Harper's Magazine Press, 1974.
Elias, Amy J. "Postmodern Southern Vacation: Vacation Advertising, Globalization, and Southern Regionalism." In *South to a New Place: Region, Literature, Culture*, eds. Suzanne W. Jones and Sharon Monteith, 253–82. Baton Rouge: Louisiana State University Press, 2002.
Ellul, Jacques. *The Presence of the Kingdom.* Trans. Olive Wyon. New York: Seabury Press, 1967.
Eskew, Glenn. *But for Birmingham: The Local and National Movements in the Civil Rights Struggle.* Chapel Hill: University of North Carolina Press, 1997.
———. "The Birmingham Civil Rights Institute and the New Ideology of Tolerance." In *The Civil Rights Movement in American Memory*, eds. Renee C. Romano and Leigh Raiford, 28–66. Athens: University of Georgia Press, 2006.
Espina, Marina. *Filipinos in Louisiana.* New Orleans: A. F. Laborde & Sons, 1988.
Estes, Roberta J., Jack H. Goins, Penny Ferguson, and Janet Lewis Crain. "Melungeons, A Multi-Ethnic Population." *Journal of Genetic Genealogy*, no. 7 (Fall 2011). http://www.jogg.info/72/files/Estes.pdf (accessed 26 June 2014).
Ethridge, Robbie, and Charles Hudson. "The Early Historic Transformation of the Southeastern Indians." In *Cultural Diversity in the U.S. South: Anthropological Contributions to a Region in Transition, Southern Anthropological Society Proceedings, No. 31*, eds. Carole E. Hill and Patricia D. Beaver, 34–50. Athens: University of Georgia Press, 1998.
Evans, W. McKee. "The North Carolina Lumbees: From Assimilation to Revitalization." In *Southeastern Indians Since the Removal Era*, ed. Walter L. Williams, 49–71. Athens: University of Georgia Press, 1979.
Everett, C. S. "Melungeon History and Myth." *Appalachian Journal* 26, no. 4 (Summer 1999): 358–409.
Fairclough, Norman. *Discourse and Social Change.* Cambridge, England: Polity Press, 1992.
Fanon, Frantz. *The Wretched of the Earth.* Trans. Constance Farrington. New York: Grove Press, 1963.
———. *Black Skin, White Masks.* Trans. Charles Lam Markmann. New York: Grove Press, 1967.
Fede, Frank Joseph. *Italians in the Deep South: Their Impact on Birmingham and the American Heritage.* Montgomery, AL: Black Belt Press, 1994.
Fifteen Southerners. *Why the South Will Survive.* Athens: University of Georgia Press, 1981.
Finger, John R. *The Eastern Band of Cherokees, 1819–1900.* Knoxville: University of Tennessee Press, 1984.
———. *Cherokee Americans: The Eastern Band of Cherokees in the Twentieth Century.* Lincoln: University of Nebraska Press, 1991.
Fishkin, Shelley Fisher. "Interrogating 'Whiteness,' Complicating 'Blackness': Remapping American Culture." *American Quarterly* 47, no. 3 (September 1995): 428–66.
Foley, Neil. "Partly Colored or Other White: Mexican Americans and Their Problem with the Color Line." In *Beyond Black & White: Race, Ethnicity, and Gender in the U.S. South*

and Southwest, eds. Stephanie Cole and Alison M. Parker, 123–44. College Station: Texas A&M University Press, 2004.

Forbes, Jack D. "The Manipulation of Race, Caste and Identity: Classifying AfroAmericans, Native Americans and Red-Black People." *Journal of Ethnic Studies* 17, no. 4 (Winter 1990): 1–51.

Foucault, Michel. *The Archaeology of Knowledge, and, The Discourse on Language*. Trans. A. M. Sheridan Smith. New York: Pantheon Books, 1972.

———. *Power/Knowledge: Selected Interviews and Other Writings, 1972-1977*. Ed. Colin Gordon. Trans. Colin Gordon, Leo Marshall, John Mepham, and Kate Soper. New York: Pantheon Books, 1980.

———. *The History of Sexuality, Volume 1: An Introduction*. Trans. Robert Hurley. New York: Vintage Books, 1980.

———. "Technologies of the Self." In *Technologies of the Self: A Seminar with Michel Foucault*, eds. Luther H. Martin, Huck Gutman, and Patrick H. Hutton, 16–49. Amherst: University of Massachusetts Press, 1988.

———. "Governmentality." In *The Foucault Effect: Studies in Governmentality: with Two Lectures by and an Interview with Michel Foucault*, eds. Graham Burchell, Colin Gordon, and Peter Miller, 87–104. Chicago: University of Chicago Press, 1991.

———. "Politics and the Study of Discourse." In *The Foucault Effect: Studies in Governmentality: with Two Lectures by and an Interview with Michel Foucault*, eds. Graham Burchell, Colin Gordon, and Peter Miller, 53–72. Chicago: University of Chicago Press, 1991.

———. *Foucault Live: Interviews, 1961-1984*. Ed. Sylvère Lotringer. Trans. Lysa Hochroth and John Johnston. New York: Semiotext(e), 1996.

———. *Religion and Culture*. Ed. Jeremy R. Carrette. New York: Routledge, 1999.

"A Freedom Walk Tour of the Historical Kelly Ingram Park: A Place of Revolution & Reconciliation." Urban Impact, Birmingham, Alabama, n.d. Brochure.

Fuller, Jennifer. "Debating the Present through the Past: Representations of the Civil Rights Movement in the 1990s." In *The Civil Rights Movement in American Memory*, eds. Renee C. Romano and Leigh Raiford, 167–96. Athens: University of Georgia Press, 2006.

Fulton, John. "Religion and Politics in Gramsci: An Introduction." *Sociological Analysis* 48, no. 3 (1987): 197–216.

Fuss, Diana. *Essentially Speaking: Feminism, Nature & Difference*. New York: Routledge, 1989.

Gaines, Jane M. "Political Mimesis." In *Collecting Visible Evidence*, eds. Jane M. Gaines and Michael Renov, 84–102. Minneapolis: University of Minnesota Press, 1999.

———. *Fire and Desire: Mixed-Race Movies in the Silent Era*. Chicago: University of Chicago Press, 2001.

Gallagher, Charles A. "Color Blindness: An Obstacle to Racial Justice?" In *Mixed Messages: Multiracial Identities in the "Color-Blind" Era*, ed. David L. Brunsma, 103–116. Boulder, CO: Lynne Rienner, 2006.

Gans, Herbert J. "Symbolic Ethnicity: The Future of Ethnic Groups and Cultures in America." *Ethnic and Racial Studies* 2, no. 1 (January 1979): 1–20.

———. "Toward a Reconciliation of 'Assimilation' and 'Pluralism': The Interplay of Acculturation and Ethnic Retention." *International Migration Review* 31, no. 4 (Winter 1997): 875–92.

———. "The Possibility of a New Racial Hierarchy in the Twenty-First-Century United States." In *The Cultural Territories of Race: Black and White Boundaries*, ed. Michèle Lamont, 371–90. Chicago: University of Chicago Press, 1999.

Geertz, Clifford. *The Interpretation of Cultures: Selected Essays*. New York: Basic Books, 1973.

Georges, Robert A., and Michael Owen Jones. *Folkloristic: An Introduction*. Bloomington: Indiana University Press, 1995.

Gilbert, William Harlen, Jr. "Memorandum Concerning the Characteristics of the Larger Mixed-Blood Racial Islands of the Eastern United States." *Social Forces* 24, no. 4 (May 1946): 438–47.

Gilroy, Paul. "One Nation under a Groove: The Cultural Politics of 'Race' and Racism in Britain." In *Anatomy of Racism*, ed. David Theo Goldberg, 263–82. Minneapolis: University of Minnesota Press, 1990.

———. *"There Ain't No Black in the Union Jack": The Cultural Politics of Race and Nation*. Chicago: University of Chicago Press, 1991.

———. "Cultural Studies and Ethnic Absolutism." In *Cultural Studies*, eds. Lawrence Grossberg, Cary Nelson, and Paula A. Treichler, 187–98. New York: Routledge, 1992.

Goffman, Erving. *The Presentation of Self in Everyday Life*. New York: Anchor Books, 1959.

Goldfield, David R. *Black, White, and Southern: Race Relations and Southern Culture, 1940 to the Present*. Baton Rouge: Louisiana State University Press, 1990.

Gramsci, Antonio. *Selections from the Prison Notebooks*. Ed. and trans. Quintin Hoare and Geoffrey Nowell Smith. New York: International Publishers, 1971.

———. *Pre-Prison Writings*. Ed. Richard Bellamy. Trans. Virginia Cox. Cambridge, England: Cambridge University Press, 1994.

Gray, Herman. "Television, Black Americans, and the American Dream." *Critical Studies in Mass Communication* 6, no. 4 (December 1989): 376–86.

Gray, Richard. *Writing the South: Ideas of an American Region*. Cambridge, England: Cambridge University Press, 1986.

———. "Foreword: Inventing Communities, Imagining Places: Some Thoughts on Southern Self-Fashioning." In *South to a New Place: Region, Literature, Culture*, eds. Suzanne W. Jones and Sharon Monteith, xiii–xxiii. Baton Rouge: Louisiana State University Press, 2002.

Greenbaum, Susan. "Marketing Ybor City: Race, Ethnicity, and Historic Preservation in the Sunbelt." *City & Society* 4, no. 1 (June 1990): 58–76.

———. "What's In a Label? Identity Problems of Southern Indian Tribes." *Journal of Ethnic Studies* 19, no. 2 (1991): 107–126.

Greenblatt, Stephen. *Renaissance Self-Fashioning: From More to Shakespeare*. Chicago: University of Chicago Press, 1980.

Greeson, Jennifer Rae. *Our South: Geographic Fantasy and the Rise of National Literature*. Cambridge, MA: Harvard University Press, 2010.

Grossberg, Lawrence. *Cultural Studies in the Future Tense*. Durham: Duke University Press, 2010.

Gruber, Jacob W. "Ethnographic Salvage and the Shaping of Anthropology." *American Anthropologist* 72, no. 6 (December 1970): 1289–99.

Guattari, Félix. *Chaosmosis: An Ethico-Aesthetic Paradigm*. Trans. Paul Bains and Julian Pefanis. Bloomington: Indiana University Press, 1995.

Guillaumin, Colette. "'I Know it's Not Nice, But . . .': The Changing Face of 'Race.'" In *Race, Identity, and Citizenship: A Reader*, eds. Rodolfo D. Torres, Louis F. Mirón, and Jonathan Xavier Inda, 39–46. Malden, MA: Blackwell Publishers, 1999.

Gupta, Akhil, and James Ferguson. "Beyond 'Culture': Space, Identity, and the Politics of Difference." In *Culture, Power, Place: Explorations in Critical Anthropology*, eds. Akhil Gupta and James Ferguson, 33–51. Durham: Duke University Press, 1997.

Haeberle, Steven H. "Exploring the Effects of Single-Member Districts on an Urban Political System: A Case Study of Birmingham, Alabama." *Urban Affairs Review* 33, no. 2 (November 1997): 287–97.

Hale, Grace Elizabeth. *Making Whiteness: The Culture of Segregation in the South, 1890–1940*. New York: Vintage Books, 1998.

Hall, Stuart. "Race, Articulation, and Societies Structured in Dominance." In *Black British Cultural Studies: A Reader*, eds. Houston A. Baker Jr., Manthia Diawara, and Ruth H. Lindeborg, 16–60. Chicago: University of Chicago Press, 1996.

———. "Gramsci's Relevance for the Study of Race and Ethnicity." In *Stuart Hall: Critical Dialogues in Cultural Studies*, eds. David Morley and Kuan-Hsing Chen, 411–40. London: Routledge, 1996.

———. "What is This 'Black' in Black Popular Culture?" In *Stuart Hall: Critical Dialogues in Cultural Studies*, eds. David Morley and Kuan-Hsing Chen, 465–75. London: Routledge, 1996.

———. "The Spectacle of the 'Other.'" In *Representation: Cultural Representations and Signifying Practices*, ed. Stuart Hall, 223–79. London: Sage Publications, 1997.

Haraway, Donna J. *Simians, Cyborgs, and Women: The Reinvention of Nature*. New York: Routledge, 1991.

Hardt, Michael. *Gilles Deleuze: An Apprenticeship in Philosophy*. Minneapolis: University of Minnesota Press, 1993.

Hebdige, Dick. *Subculture: The Meaning of Style*. London: Routledge, 1979.

Heider, Karl G. *Ethnographic Film*. Austin: University of Texas Press, 1976.

Henninger, Katherine. *Ordering the Façade: Photography and Contemporary Southern Women's Writing*. Chapel Hill: University of North Carolina Press, 2007.

Hill, Carole E., and Patricia D. Beaver, eds. *Cultural Diversity in the U.S. South: Anthropological Contributions to a Region in Transition, Southern Anthropological Society Proceedings, No. 31*. Athens: University of Georgia Press, 1998.

Hirsch, Arnold R. *Making the Second Ghetto: Race and Housing in Chicago, 1940–1960*. Cambridge, England: Cambridge University Press, 1983.

Hobsbawm, Eric. "Introduction: Inventing Traditions." In *The Invention of Tradition*, eds. Eric Hobsbawm and Terence Ranger, 1–14. Cambridge, England: Cambridge University Press, 1983.

Hobson, Fred. *Tell About the South: The Southern Rage to Explain*. Baton Rouge: Louisiana State University Press, 1983.

———. *But Now I See: The White Southern Racial Conversion Narrative*. Baton Rouge: Louisiana State University Press, 1999.

Hockings, Paul, ed. *Principles of Visual Anthropology*. Second edition. Berlin: Mouton De Gruyter, 1995.

Holmlund, Chris, and Justin Wyatt, eds. *Contemporary American Independent Film: From the Margins to the Mainstream*. New York: Routledge, 2005.
hooks, bell. *Black Looks: Race and Representation*. Boston: South End Press, 1992.
———. *All About Love: New Visions*. New York: William Morrow, 2000.
Horkheimer, Max, and Theodor W. Adorno. "The Culture Industry: Enlightenment as Mass Deception." In *Dialectic of Enlightenment*, trans. John Cumming, 120–67. New York: Continuum, 1991. Originally published 1944.
Humphries, Jefferson. "The Discourse of Southernness: Or How We Can Know There Will Still Be Such a Thing as the South and Southern Literary Culture in the Twenty-First Century." In *The Future of Southern Letters*, eds. Jefferson Humphries and John Lowe, 119–33. New York: Oxford University Press, 1996.
"Inspired by the Past, A Vision for the Future: Footsteps: Birmingham Civil Rights Institute." Birmingham Civil Rights Institute, Birmingham, AL, n.d. Brochure.
Jameson, Fredric. "Periodizing the 60s." In *The 60s Without Apology*, eds. Sohnya Sayres, Anders Stephanson, Stanley Aronowitz, and Fredric Jameson, 178–209. Minneapolis: University of Minnesota Press, 1985.
Jenkins, Henry. *Textual Poachers: Television Fans & Participatory Culture*. New York: Routledge, 1992.
Jones, Patrick D. *The Selma of the North: Civil Rights Insurgency in Milwaukee*. Cambridge, MA: Harvard University Press, 2009.
Joseph, Miranda. *Against the Romance of Community*. Minneapolis: University of Minnesota Press, 2002.
Joyner, Charles. *Shared Traditions: Southern History and Folk Culture*. Urbana: University of Illinois Press, 1999.
Kennedy, N. Brent. *The Melungeons: The Resurrection of a Proud People*. Revised edition. Macon, GA: Mercer University Press, 1997.
Killian, Lewis M. *White Southerners*. New York: Random House, 1970.
Kilpatrick, Jacquelyn. *Celluloid Indians: Native Americans and Film*. Lincoln: University of Nebraska Press, 1999.
Kim, Claire Jean. "The Racial Triangulation of Asian Americans." *Politics and Society* 27, no. 1 (March 1999): 105–138.
King, Geoff. *American Independent Cinema*. Bloomington: Indiana University Press, 2005.
King, Martin Luther, Jr. *Why We Can't Wait*. New York: Harper & Row, 1964.
———. *Where Do We Go from Here: Chaos or Community?* Boston: Beacon Press, 1968.
———. *A Testament of Hope: The Essential Writings and Speeches of Martin Luther King Jr.* Ed. James M. Washington. San Francisco: HarperSanFrancisco, 1991.
King, Richard H. *A Southern Renaissance: The Cultural Awakening of the American South, 1930–1955*. New York: Oxford University Press, 1980.
Kirby, Jack Temple. *Media-Made Dixie: The South in the American Imagination*. Revised edition. Athens: University of Georgia Press, 1986. Originally published 1978.
Kirshenblatt-Gimblett, Barbara. *Destination Culture: Tourism, Museums, and Heritage*. Berkeley: University of California Press, 1998.

Kreyling, Michael. "*The Fathers*: A Postsouthern Narrative Reading." In *Southern Literature and Literary Theory*, ed. Jefferson Humphries, 186–205. Athens: University of Georgia Press, 1990.

———. *Inventing Southern Literature*. Jackson: University Press of Mississippi, 1998.

———. "Italy and the United States: The Politics and Poetics of the 'Southern Problem.'" In *South to a New Place: Region, Literature, Culture*, eds. Suzanne W. Jones and Sharon Monteith, 285–302. Baton Rouge: Louisiana State University Press, 2002.

Lacan, Jacques. *Écrits: A Selection*. Trans. Alan Sheridan. New York: Norton, 1977.

Ladd, Barbara. *Nationalism and the Color Line in George W. Cable, Mark Twain, and William Faulkner*. Baton Rouge: Louisiana State University Press, 1996.

Lassiter, Matthew D. *The Silent Majority: Suburban Politics in the Sunbelt South*. Princeton: Princeton University Press, 2006.

———. "De Jure/De Facto Segregation: The Long Shadow of a National Myth." In *The Myth of Southern Exceptionalism*, eds. Matthew D. Lassiter and Joseph Crespino, 25–48. New York: Oxford University Press, 2010.

Lassiter, Matthew D., and Joseph Crespino, eds. *The Myth of Southern Exceptionalism*. New York: Oxford University Press, 2010.

Lebow, Alisa. "Faking What? Making a Mockery of Documentary." In *F Is for Phony: Fake Documentary and Truth's Undoing*, eds. Alexandra Juhasz and Jesse Lerner, 223–37. Minneapolis: University of Minnesota Press, 2006.

———. *First Person Jewish*. Minneapolis: University of Minnesota Press, 2008.

Leslie, Kent Anderson. *Woman of Color, Daughter of Privilege: Amanda America Dickson, 1849–1893*. Athens: University of Georgia Press, 1995.

Lestrade, Patricia M. "The Continuing Decline of Isleño Spanish in Louisiana." *Southwest Journal of Linguistics* 21, no. 1 (June 2002): 99–117.

Leuthold, Steven. *Indigenous Aesthetics: Native Art, Media, and Identity*. Austin: University of Texas Press, 1998.

Lippard, Cameron D., and Charles A. Gallagher, eds. *Being Brown in Dixie: Race, Ethnicity, and Latino Immigration in the New South*. Boulder, CO: FirstForumPress, 2011.

Lipski, John M. *The Language of the Isleños: Vestigial Spanish in Louisiana*. Baton Rouge: Louisiana State University Press, 1990.

Loewen, James W. *The Mississippi Chinese: Between Black and White*. Second edition. Prospect Heights, IL: Waveland Press, 1988.

Loizos, Peter. *Innovation in Ethnographic Film: From Innocence to Self-Consciousness, 1955–1985*. Chicago: University of Chicago Press, 1993.

Lomax, Alan. "Cinema, Science, and Cultural Renewal." *Current Anthropology* 14, no. 4 (October 1973): 474–80.

Lowery, Malinda Maynor. *Lumbee Indians in the Jim Crow South: Race, Identity, and the Making of a Nation*. Chapel Hill: University of North Carolina Press, 2010.

MacDougall, David. *Transcultural Cinema*. Ed. Lucien Taylor. Princeton: Princeton University Press, 1998.

Marchetti, Gina. "Ethnicity, the Cinema, and Cultural Studies." In *Unspeakable Images: Ethnicity and the American Cinema*, ed. Lester D. Friedman, 277–307. Urbana: University of Illinois Press, 1991.

———. *Romance and the "Yellow Peril": Race, Sex, and Discursive Strategies in Hollywood Fiction*. Berkeley: University of California Press, 1993.

Marcoulesco, Ileana. "Redemption." In *Encyclopedia of Religion, Volume 11: Pius IX-Rivers*, second edition, editor in chief Lindsay Jones, 7640–42. Detroit: Macmillan Reference USA, 2005.

Marcus, George E. *Ethnography through Thick and Thin*. Princeton: Princeton University Press, 1998.

Marrow, Helen B. "New Immigrant Destinations and the American Colour Line." *Ethnic and Racial Studies* 32, no. 6 (July 2009): 1037–57.

———. *New Destination Dreaming: Immigration, Race, and Legal Status in the Rural American South*. Stanford, CA: Stanford University Press, 2011.

Marx, Karl, and Frederick Engels. *The German Ideology, Part One: with selections from Parts Two and Three, together with Marx's "Introduction to a Critique of Political Economy"*. Ed. C. J. Arthur. New York: International Publishers, 1970.

Matte, Jacqueline Anderson. *They Say the Wind is Red: The Alabama Choctaw: Lost in Their Own Land*. Revised edition. Montgomery, AL: NewSouth Books, 2002.

———. "Extinction by Reclassification: The MOWA Choctaws of South Alabama and Their Struggle for Federal Recognition." *Alabama Review* 59, no. 3 (July 2006): 163–204.

Mayo, Selz C. "Social Change, Social Movements and the Disappearing Sectional South" [annual presidential address to the Southern Sociological Society]. *Social Forces* 43, no. 1 (October 1964): 1–10.

McClain, Paula D., et al. "Racial Distancing in a Southern City: Latino Immigrants' Views of Black Americans." *Journal of Politics* 68, no. 3 (August 2006): 571–84.

McCray, Carrie Allen. *Freedom's Child: The Life of a Confederate General's Black Daughter*. Chapel Hill, NC: Algonquin Books of Chapel Hill, 1998.

McDonough, Jimmy, and Bill Landis. "Hillbilly Heaven." *Film Comment* 21, no. 6 (November/December 1985): 55–59.

McKiven, Henry M., Jr. *Iron and Steel: Class, Race, and Community in Birmingham, Alabama, 1875–1920*. Chapel Hill: University of North Carolina Press, 1995.

McPherson, Tara. *Reconstructing Dixie: Race, Gender, and Nostalgia in the Imagined South*. Durham: Duke University Press, 2003.

McWhiney, Grady. *Southerners and Other Americans*. New York: Basic Books, 1973.

Mead, Margaret. "Visual Anthropology in a Discipline of Words." In *Principles of Visual Anthropology*, second edition, ed. Paul Hockings, 3–10. Berlin: Mouton de Gruyter, 1995.

Mercer, Kobena. "'1968': Periodizing Politics and Identity." In *Cultural Studies*, eds. Lawrence Grossberg, Cary Nelson, and Paula A. Treichler, 424–49. New York: Routledge, 1992.

Metz, Christian. *Film Language: A Semiotics of the Cinema*. Trans. Michael Taylor. New York: Oxford University Press, 1974.

———. *The Imaginary Signifier: Psychoanalysis and the Cinema*. Trans. Celia Britton, Annwyl Williams, Ben Brewster, and Alfred Guzzetti. Bloomington: Indiana University Press, 1982.

Meyer, Richard. *Outlaw Representation: Censorship and Homosexuality in Twentieth-Century American Art*. Oxford: Oxford University Press, 2002.

Miles, Robert, and Rodolfo D. Torres. "Does 'Race' Matter? Transatlantic Perspectives on Racism after 'Race Relations.'" In *Race, Identity, and Citizenship: A Reader*, eds. Rodolfo D. Torres, Louis F. Mirón, and Jonathan Xavier Inda, 19–38. Malden, MA: Blackwell Publishers, 1999.

Milian, Claudia. *Latining America: Black-Brown Passages and the Coloring of Latino/a Studies*. Athens: University of Georgia Press, 2013.

Miller, D. A. *The Novel and the Police*. Berkeley: University of California Press, 1988.

Miller, Keith D. *Voice of Deliverance: The Language of Martin Luther King Jr. and Its Sources*. New York: Free Press, 1992.

Miller, Mark Edwin. *Forgotten Tribes: Unrecognized Indians and the Federal Acknowledgment Process*. Lincoln: University of Nebraska Press, 2004.

Miller, Toby. *Technologies of Truth: Cultural Citizenship and the Popular Media*. Minneapolis: University of Minnesota Press, 1998.

——. *Cultural Citizenship: Cosmopolitanism, Consumerism, and Television in a Neoliberal Age*. Philadelphia: Temple University Press, 2007.

Mills, Gary B. *The Forgotten People: Cane River's Creoles of Color*. Baton Rouge: Louisiana State University Press, 1977.

Mills, Sara. *Discourse*. London: Routledge, 1997.

Mitchell, Don. "There's No Such Thing as Culture: Towards a Reconceptualization of the Idea of Culture in Geography." *Transactions of the Institute of British Geographers* 20, no. 1 (1995): 102–116.

Moberg, Mark, and J. Stephen Thomas. "Indochinese Resettlement and the Transformation of Identities along the Alabama Gulf Coast." In *Cultural Diversity in the U.S. South: Anthropological Contributions to a Region in Transition, Southern Anthropological Society Proceedings, No. 31*, eds. Carole E. Hill and Patricia D. Beaver, 115–28. Athens: University of Georgia Press, 1998.

Mohl, Raymond A. "Planned Destruction: The Interstates and Central City Housing." In *From Tenements to the Taylor Homes: In Search of an Urban Housing Policy in Twentieth-Century America*, eds. John F. Bauman, Roger Biles, and Kristin M. Szylvian, 226–45. University Park, PA: Pennsylvania State University Press, 2000.

Mormino, Gary R., and George E. Pozzetta. *The Immigrant World of Ybor City: Italians and their Latin Neighbors in Tampa, 1885–1985*. Urbana: University of Illinois Press, 1987. Reprint, Gainesville: University Press of Florida, 1998.

Morris, Aldon D. "Birmingham Confrontation Reconsidered: An Analysis of the Dynamics and Tactics of Mobilization." *American Sociological Review* 58, no. 5 (October 1993): 621–36.

Morrison, Toni. "On the Backs of Blacks." In *Arguing Immigration: The Debate Over the Changing Face of America*, ed. Nicolaus Mills, 97–100. New York: Simon & Schuster, 1994.

Muñoz, José Esteban. *Disidentifications: Queers of Color and the Performance of Politics*. Minneapolis: University of Minnesota Press, 1999.

——. *Cruising Utopia: The Then and There of Queer Futurity*. New York: New York University Press, 2009.

Munslow, Alun. *Deconstructing History*. London: Routledge, 1997.

Murphy, Arthur D., Colleen Blanchard, and Jennifer A. Hill, eds. *Latino Workers in the Contemporary South, Southern Anthropological Society Proceedings, No. 34*. Athens: University of Georgia Press, 2001.

Nancy, Jean-Luc. *The Inoperative Community.* Trans. Peter Connor, Lisa Garbus, Michael Holland, and Simona Sawhney. Minneapolis: University of Minnesota Press, 1991.

Nash, Jennifer C. "Practicing Love: Black Feminism, Love-Politics, and Post-Intersectionality." *Meridians: Feminism, Race, Transnationalism* 11, no. 2 (2013): 1–24.

Neale, Steve. "The Same Old Story: Stereotypes and Difference." In *The Screen Education Reader: Cinema, Television, Culture,* eds. Manuel Alvarado, Edward Buscombe, and Richard Collins, 41–47. New York: Columbia University Press, 1993.

Neely, Sharlotte. "Acculturation and Persistence among North Carolina's Eastern Band of Cherokee Indians." In *Southeastern Indians Since the Removal Era,* ed. Walter L. Williams, 154–73. Athens: University of Georgia Press, 1979.

———. "Snowbird Cherokees: Adaptation and Ethnic Preservation in the Southern Appalachians." In *Cultural Adaptation to Mountain Environments, Southern Anthropological Society Proceedings, No. 17,* eds. Patricia D. Beaver and Burton L. Purrington, 107–121. Athens: University of Georgia Press, 1984.

———. *Snowbird Cherokees: People of Persistence.* Athens: University of Georgia Press, 1991.

———. "Adaptation and the Contemporary North Carolina Cherokee Indians." In *Indians of the Southeastern United States in the Late 20th Century,* ed. J. Anthony Paredes, 29–43. Tuscaloosa: University of Alabama Press, 1992.

Nichols, Bill. *Representing Reality: Issues and Concepts in Documentary.* Bloomington: Indiana University Press, 1991.

———. *Blurred Boundaries: Questions of Meaning in Contemporary Culture.* Bloomington: Indiana University Press, 1994.

———. *Introduction to Documentary.* Bloomington: Indiana University Press, 2001.

Nystrom, Derek. *Hard Hats, Rednecks, and Macho Men: Class in 1970s American Cinema.* Oxford: Oxford University Press, 2009.

Oakley, Christopher Arris. "The Native South in the Post-World War II Era." *Native South,* no. 1 (2008): 61–79.

O'Brien, Michael. *The Idea of the American South, 1920–1941.* Baltimore: Johns Hopkins University Press, 1979.

Odem, Mary E., and Elaine Lacy, eds. *Latino Immigrants and the Transformation of the U.S. South.* Athens: University of Georgia Press, 2009.

Omi, Michael, and Howard Winant. *Racial Formation in the United States: From the 1960s to the 1990s.* Second edition. New York: Routledge, 1994.

Painter, Nell Irvin. "'Social Equality,' Miscegenation, Labor, and Power." In *The Evolution of Southern Culture,* ed. Numan V. Bartley, 47–67. Athens: University of Georgia Press, 1988.

Paredes, J. Anthony. "The Emergence of Contemporary Eastern Creek Indian Identity." In *Social and Cultural Identity: Problems of Persistence and Change, Southern Anthropological Society Proceedings, No. 8,* ed. Thomas K. Fitzgerald, 63–80. Athens: University of Georgia Press, 1974.

———. "Back from Disappearance: The Alabama Creek Indian Community." In *Southeastern Indians Since the Removal Era,* ed. Walter L. Williams, 123–41. Athens: University of Georgia Press, 1979.

———. "Kinship and Descent in the Ethnic Reassertion of the Eastern Creek Indians." In *The Versatility of Kinship*, eds. Linda S. Cordell and Stephen Beckerman, 165–94. New York: Academic Press, 1980.

———. "Federal Recognition and the Poarch Creek Indians." In *Indians of the Southeastern United States in the Late 20th Century*, ed. J. Anthony Paredes, 120–39. Tuscaloosa: University of Alabama Press, 1992.

Parker, Andrew, Mary Russo, Doris Sommer, and Patricia Yaeger. "Introduction." In *Nationalisms & Sexualities*, eds. Andrew Parker, Mary Russo, Doris Sommer, and Patricia Yaeger, 1–18. New York: Routledge, 1992.

Perdue, Theda. "The Legacy of Indian Removal" [annual presidential address to the Southern Historical Association]. *Journal of Southern History* 78, no. 1 (February 2012): 3–36.

———. "Southern Indians and Jim Crow." In *The Folly of Jim Crow: Rethinking the Segregated South*, eds. Stephanie Cole and Natalie J. Ring, 54–90. College Station: Texas A&M University Press, 2012.

Perez, Irvan. "Isleños of St. Bernard Parish." In *Documenting Cultural Diversity in the Resurgent American South: Collectors, Collecting, and Collections*, eds. Margaret R. Dittemore and Fred J. Hay, 90–99. Chicago: Association of College and Research Libraries, 1997.

Perez, Samantha. *The Isleños of Louisiana: On the Water's Edge*. Charleston, SC: History Press, 2011.

Philips, John Edward. "The African Heritage of White America." In *Africanisms in American Culture*, second edition, ed. Joseph E. Holloway, 372–96. Bloomington: Indiana University Press, 2005.

Phillips, Ulrich B. "The Central Theme of Southern History." *American Historical Review* 34, no. 1 (October 1928): 30–43.

Pollitzer, William S. "The Physical Anthropology and Genetics of Marginal People of the Southeastern United States." *American Anthropologist* 74, no. 3 (June 1972): 719–34.

Porter, Frank W., III. "Nonrecognized American Indian Tribes in the Eastern United States: An Historical Overview." In *Strategies for Survival: American Indians in the Eastern United States*, ed. Frank W. Porter III, 1–42. New York: Greenwood Press, 1986.

Pratt, Mary Louise. *Imperial Eyes: Travel Writing and Transculturation*. London: Routledge, 1992.

Price, Edward T. "A Geographic Analysis of White-Negro-Indian Racial Mixtures in Eastern United States." *Annals of the Association of American Geographers* 43, no. 2 (June 1953): 138–55.

Quan, Robert Seto. *Lotus Among the Magnolias: The Mississippi Chinese*. Jackson: University Press of Mississippi, 1982.

Quinn, William W., Jr. "The Southeast Syndrome: Notes on Indian Descendant Recruitment Organizations and Their Perceptions of Native American Culture." *American Indian Quarterly* 14, no. 2 (Spring 1990): 147–54.

Ray, Celeste, ed. *The New Encyclopedia of Southern Culture: Volume 6: Ethnicity*. Chapel Hill: University of North Carolina Press, 2007.

Reed, John Shelton. *One South: An Ethnic Approach to Regional Culture*. Baton Rouge: Louisiana State University Press, 1982.

———. *The Enduring South: Subcultural Persistence in Mass Society*. Revised edition. Chapel Hill: University of North Carolina Press, 1986. Originally published 1972.
Renov, Michael. *The Subject of Documentary*. Minneapolis: University of Minnesota Press, 2004.
Robinson, James M. *The Gospel of Jesus: A Historical Search for the Original Good News*. San Francisco: HarperSanFrancisco, 2005.
Rodowick, D. N. *Gilles Deleuze's Time Machine*. Durham: Duke University Press, 1997.
Roediger, David R. *Towards the Abolition of Whiteness: Essays on Race, Politics, and Working Class History*. London: Verso, 1994.
———. *Working Toward Whiteness: How America's Immigrants Became White*. New York: Basic Books, 2005.
Roland, Charles P. "The Ever-Vanishing South" [annual presidential address to the Southern Historical Association]. *Journal of Southern History* 48, no. 1 (February 1982): 3–20.
Rollins, Peter C., and John E. O'Connor, eds. *Hollywood's Indian: The Portrayal of the Native American in Film*. Lexington: University Press of Kentucky, 1998.
Romine, Scott. "Where Is Southern Literature? The Practice of Place in a Postsouthern Age." In *South to a New Place: Region, Literature, Culture*, eds. Suzanne W. Jones and Sharon Monteith, 23–43. Baton Rouge: Louisiana State University Press, 2002.
———. *The Real South: Southern Narrative in the Age of Cultural Reproduction*. Baton Rouge: Louisiana State University Press, 2008.
Rosenberg, Neil V. *Bluegrass: A History*. Revised edition. Urbana: University of Illinois Press, 2005.
Rubin, Louis D., Jr. "An Image of the South." In *The Lasting South: Fourteen Southerners Look at Their Home*, eds. Louis D. Rubin Jr. and James Jackson Kilpatrick, 1–15. Chicago: Henry Regnery, 1957.
Rubin, Louis D., Jr., and James Jackson Kilpatrick, eds. *The Lasting South: Fourteen Southerners Look at Their Home*. Chicago: Henry Regnery, 1957.
Rubin, Louis D., Jr., et al., eds. *The History of Southern Literature*. Baton Rouge: Louisiana State University Press, 1985.
Ruby, Jay. *Picturing Culture: Explorations of Film and Anthropology*. Chicago: University of Chicago Press, 2000.
Russell, Catherine. *Experimental Ethnography: The Work of Film in the Age of Video*. Durham: Duke University Press, 1999.
Ryan, Michael, and Douglas Kellner. *Camera Politica: The Politics and Ideology of Contemporary Hollywood Film*. Bloomington: Indiana University Press, 1988.
Said, Edward W. *Orientalism*. New York: Pantheon Books, 1978.
Schneider, Mary Jo, and William M. Schneider. "A Structural Analysis of the Chinese Grocery Store in the Mississippi Delta." In *Visions and Revisions: Ethnohistoric Perspectives on Southern Cultures, Southern Anthropological Society Proceedings, No. 20*, eds. George Sabo III and William M. Schneider, 83–97. Athens: University of Georgia Press, 1987.
Schrift, Melissa. "Melungeons and the Politics of Heritage." In *Southern Heritage on Display: Public Ritual and Ethnic Diversity within Southern Regionalism*, ed. Celeste Ray, 106–129. Tuscaloosa: University of Alabama Press, 2003.

Scott, Joan W. "The Evidence of Experience." In *The Lesbian and Gay Studies Reader*, eds. Henry Abelove, Michèle Aina Barale, and David M. Halperin, 397–415. New York: Routledge, 1993.

Scribner, Christopher MacGregor. *Renewing Birmingham: Federal Funding and the Promise of Change, 1929–1979*. Athens: University of Georgia Press, 2002.

Sedgwick, Eve Kosofsky. *Epistemology of the Closet*. Berkeley: University of California Press, 1990.

———. "Queer Performativity: Henry James's *The Art of the Novel*." *GLQ* 1, no. 1 (1993): 1–16.

Sellers, Charles Grier, Jr., ed. *The Southerner as American*. Chapel Hill: University of North Carolina Press, 1960.

Sherman, Sharon R. *Documenting Ourselves: Film, Video, and Culture*. Lexington: University Press of Kentucky, 1998.

Shohat, Ella, and Robert Stam. *Unthinking Eurocentrism: Multiculturalism and the Media*. London: Routledge, 1994.

Sider, Gerald M. *Lumbee Indian Histories: Race, Ethnicity, and Indian Identity in the Southern United States*. Cambridge, England: Cambridge University Press, 1993.

Sides, Josh. *L.A. City Limits: African American Los Angeles from the Great Depression to the Present*. Berkeley: University of California Press, 2003.

Silverman, Kaja. *The Subject of Semiotics*. New York: Oxford University Press, 1983.

Simkins, Francis Butler. *The Everlasting South*. Baton Rouge: Louisiana State University Press, 1963.

Simpson, Lewis P. *The Brazen Face of History: Studies in the Literary Consciousness in America*. Baton Rouge: Louisiana State University Press, 1980.

Singal, Daniel Joseph. *The War Within: From Victorian to Modernist Thought in the South, 1919–1945*. Chapel Hill: University of North Carolina Press, 1982.

Singer, Irving. *The Nature of Love, Volume 1: Plato to Luther*. Second edition. Chicago: University of Chicago Press, 1984.

———. *The Nature of Love, Volume 2: Courtly and Romantic*. Chicago: University of Chicago Press, 1984.

———. *The Nature of Love, Volume 3: The Modern World*. Chicago: University of Chicago Press, 1987.

Smiley, David L. "The Quest for the Central Theme in Southern History." *South Atlantic Quarterly* 71, no. 3 (Summer 1972): 307–325.

Smith, Frank E. *Look Away from Dixie*. Baton Rouge: Louisiana State University Press, 1965.

Smith, Heather A., and Owen J. Furuseth, eds. *Latinos in the New South: Transformations of Place*. Aldershot, England: Ashgate, 2006.

Smith, Jon. Review of *Reconstructing Dixie: Race, Gender, and Nostalgia in the Imagined South* by Tara McPherson. *Mississippi Quarterly* 57, no. 4 (Fall 2004): 666–71.

———. *Finding Purple America: The South and the Future of American Cultural Studies*. Athens: University of Georgia Press, 2013.

Smith, Stephen A. *Myth, Media, and the Southern Mind*. Fayetteville: University of Arkansas Press, 1985.

Smith, Valene L. "Introduction." In *Hosts and Guests: The Anthropology of Tourism*, second edition, ed. Valene L. Smith, 1–17. Philadelphia: University of Pennsylvania Press, 1989.

Snell, William R. "Masked Men in the Magic City: Activities of the Revised Klan in Birmingham, 1916–1940." *Alabama Historical Quarterly* 34, nos. 3–4 (Fall–Winter 1972): 206–227.

Snipp, C. Matthew. "Some Observations about Racial Boundaries and the Experiences of American Indians." *Ethnic and Racial Studies* 20, no. 4 (October 1997): 667–89.

Spickard, Paul R. "The Illogic of American Racial Categories." In *Racially Mixed People in America*, ed. Maria P. P. Root, 12–23. Newbury Park, CA: Sage Publications, 1992.

Stanton, Max E. "Southern Louisiana Survivors: The Houma Indians." In *Southeastern Indians Since the Removal Era*, ed. Walter L. Williams, 90–109. Athens: University of Georgia Press, 1979.

Starna, William A. "The Southeast Syndrome: A Prior Restraint of a Non-Event." *American Indian Quarterly* 15, no. 4 (Fall 1991): 493–502.

Stedman, Raymond William. *Shadows of the Indian: Stereotypes in American Culture*. Norman: University of Oklahoma Press, 1982.

Steinberg, Stephen. *Race Relations: A Critique*. Stanford, CA: Stanford Social Science, 2007.

Sugrue, Thomas J. *The Origins of the Urban Crisis: Race and Inequality in Postwar Detroit*. Princeton: Princeton University Press, 1996.

Taylor, Melanie Benson. *Reconstructing the Native South: American Indian Literature and the Lost Cause*. Athens: University of Georgia Press, 2011.

Thompson, Edgar T. "The Little Races." *American Anthropologist* 74, no. 5 (October 1972): 1295–1306.

Thompson, John O. "Screen Acting and the Commutation Test." *Screen* 19, no. 2 (Summer 1978): 55–69.

Thompson, Richard. "What's Your 10-20?" *Film Comment* 16, no. 4 (July/August 1980): 34–42.

Tindall, George B. "The Central Theme Revisited." In *The Southerner as American*, ed. Charles Grier Sellers Jr., 104–129. Chapel Hill: University of North Carolina Press, 1960.

———. "Mythology: A New Frontier in Southern History." In *The Idea of the South: Pursuit of a Central Theme*, ed. Frank E. Vandiver, 1–15. Chicago: University of Chicago Press, 1964.

———. "Beyond the Mainstream: The Ethnic Southerners" [annual presidential address to the Southern Historical Association]. *Journal of Southern History* 40, no. 1 (February 1974): 3–18.

Tomlinson, John. *Cultural Imperialism*. Baltimore: Johns Hopkins University Press, 1991.

———. *Globalization and Culture*. Chicago: University of Chicago Press, 1999.

Torres, Sasha. *Black, White, and In Color: Television and Black Civil Rights*. Princeton: Princeton University Press, 2003.

Tullos, Allen. *Alabama Getaway: The Political Imaginary and the Heart of Dixie*. Athens: University of Georgia Press, 2011.

Turner, Graeme. *British Cultural Studies: An Introduction*. Third edition. London: Routledge, 2003.

Tzioumakis, Yannis. *American Independent Cinema: An Introduction*. New Brunswick, NJ: Rutgers University Press, 2006.

Urry, John. *The Tourist Gaze: Leisure and Travel in Contemporary Societies*. London: Sage Publications, 1990.

Vande Brake, Katherine. *How They Shine: Melungeon Characters in the Fiction of Appalachia*. Macon, GA: Mercer University Press, 2001.

Vandiver, Frank E. "Introduction." In *The Idea of the South: Pursuit of a Central Theme*, ed. Frank E. Vandiver, vii–ix. Chicago: University of Chicago Press, 1964.

Vernon, Mark. "Postscript: 'I am not what I am'—Foucault, Christian Asceticism and a 'way out' of Sexuality." In Michel Foucault, *Religion and Culture*, ed. Jeremy R. Carrette, 199–209. New York: Routledge, 1999.

Vilanova, Núria. "Deterritorialization." In *Dictionary of Latin American Cultural Studies*, eds. Robert McKee Irwin and Mónica Szurmuk, 120–25. Gainesville: University Press of Florida, 2012.

Visker, Rudi. *Michel Foucault: Genealogy as Critique*. Trans. Chris Turner. London: Verso, 1995.

Walker, Clarence E. *Mongrel Nation: The America Begotten by Thomas Jefferson and Sally Hemings*. Charlottesville: University of Virginia Press, 2009.

Wallerstein, Immanuel. "What Can One Mean by Southern Culture?" In *The Evolution of Southern Culture*, ed. Numan V. Bartley, 1–13. Athens: University of Georgia Press, 1988.

Warner, Michael. *The Trouble with Normal: Sex, Politics, and the Ethics of Queer Life*. Cambridge, MA: Harvard University Press, 2000.

Watters, Pat. *The South and the Nation*. New York: Pantheon Books, 1969.

Waugh, Thomas. "Walking on Tippy Toes: Lesbian and Gay Liberation Documentary of the Post-Stonewall Period 1969–84." In *Between the Sheets, In the Streets: Queer, Lesbian, Gay Documentary*, eds. Chris Holmlund and Cynthia Fuchs, 107–124. Minneapolis: University of Minnesota Press, 1997.

Webster, Gerald R. "Congressional Redistricting and African-American Representation in the 1990s: An Example from Alabama." *Political Geography* 12, no. 6 (November 1993): 549–64.

West, Cornel. "The Religious Foundations of the Thought of Martin Luther King Jr." In *We Shall Overcome: Martin Luther King Jr. and the Black Freedom Struggle*, eds. Peter J. Albert and Ronald Hoffman, 113–29. New York: Pantheon, 1990. Reprint, New York: Da Capo, 1993.

White, Hayden. *Tropics of Discourse: Essays in Cultural Criticism*. Baltimore: Johns Hopkins University Press, 1978.

Wiegman, Robyn. *Object Lessons*. Durham: Duke University Press, 2012.

Williams, Raymond. *Marxism and Literature*. Oxford: Oxford University Press, 1977.

———. *Keywords: A Vocabulary of Culture and Society*. Revised edition. New York: Oxford University Press, 1985.

Williamson, J. W. *Hillbillyland: What the Movies Did to the Mountains and What the Mountains Did to the Movies*. Chapel Hill: University of North Carolina Press, 1995.

Williamson, Joel. *The Crucible of Race: Black-White Relations in the American South since Emancipation*. New York: Oxford University Press, 1984.

———. *New People: Miscegenation and Mulattoes in the United States*. New York: Free Press, 1980. Reprint, Baton Rouge: Louisiana State University Press, 1995.

Wilson, Charles Reagan. *Baptized in Blood: The Religion of the Lost Cause, 1865–1920*. Athens: University of Georgia Press, 1980.

Winant, Howard. *Racial Conditions: Politics, Theory, Comparisons.* Minneapolis: University of Minnesota Press, 1994.

———. "White Racial Projects." In *The Making and Unmaking of Whiteness*, eds. Birgit Brander Rasmussen, Eric Klinenberg, Irene J. Nexica, and Matt Wray, 97–112. Durham: Duke University Press, 2001.

Winston, Brian. *Claiming the Real II: Documentary: Grierson and Beyond.* London: British Film Institute, 2008.

Wright, Susan. "The Politicization of 'Culture.'" *Anthropology Today* 14, no. 1 (February 1998): 7–15.

Xing, Jun. *Asian America through the Lens: History, Representations, and Identity.* Walnut Creek, CA: AltaMira Press, 1998.

Yaeger, Patricia. *Dirt and Desire: Reconstructing Southern Women's Writing, 1930–1990.* Chicago: University of Chicago Press, 2000.

Yancey, George. *Who Is White?: Latinos, Asians, and the New Black/Nonblack Divide.* Boulder, CO: Lynne Rienner, 2003.

Yates, Donald N., and Elizabeth C. Hirschman. "Toward a Genetic Profile of Melungeons in Southern Appalachia." *Appalachian Journal* 38, no. 1 (Fall 2010): 92–111.

Zinn, Howard. *The Southern Mystique.* New York: Alfred A. Knopf, 1964.

———. "The Power and the Glory: Myths of American Exceptionalism." *Boston Review* 30, nos. 3–4 (Summer 2005). http://bostonreview.net/zinn-power-glory (accessed 30 August 2013).

Index

Absolutism, cultural, and race, 126–27, 200, 253n4
Acculturation. *See* Assimilation
Adams, Jessica, 19
Affinity, racial, 64, 221. *See also* Coalition politics
Agamben, Giorgio, 21, 24, 236n27, 258n52
Agee, 137
AIDS, 116–17
Alba, Richard, 161, 262n16
Alston, Macky, 27, 99, 103–4, 114–15, 118–23, 249n14, 252n53
Althusser, Louis, 61, 83, 148
Altman, Rick, 248n2
Alvarez, Louis, 17, 34, 155, 162–63
American Indians. *See* Native Americans
American Tongues, 162
Anderson, Benedict, 4–6, 20, 226n26
Appalachian Mountains, 126, 128, 137, 145, 146, 217–18, 220–21, 260n68
Appalshop Media Center (Whitesburg, Kentucky), 137, 260n68
Appreciation, cultural, 125, 129–30, 254n19, 256n37
Appropriation, cultural, 125, 127–31, 133, 146, 150, 254n19, 256n7
Articulation: definition of, 234n107; of ethnicity within southern discourse, 177–78; of race in *bro•ken/ground*, 78–83, 91–92; of race in *Tell About the South*, 47; of race to culture, 64, 66, 126–29, 130–31, 146, 149–50, 159–60, 162; of race through religion, 80–82, 148; of race within southern discourse, 33, 41–43, 45, 50, 67, 100, 132, 137, 142, 145, 148, 162, 179

Asian Americans, 30, 31, 33, 35, 159, 160, 179, 192–93, 206, 220, 234n108, 247n68, 262n11, 264n3, 266n29. *See also* Mississippi Chinese
Assimilation, 158, 160, 266n29; definition of, 161–62, 262n16; cultural (acculturation), 35, 127–29, 133, 177; and Latino/as, 263n26; and *Mississippi Triangle*, 184, 193; and Native Americans, 199; social vs. cultural, 252n1
Atmore, Alabama, 202
Audience, 76, 175, 254n19, 260n66; and documentary film, 25–26, 233n94, 257n43. *See also* Possible
Audiovisual arrangement, 106–8, 249n26
Autoethnography. *See* Ethnographic film
Ayers, Edward, 35

Baker, Houston A., Jr., 236n24
Ball, Edward, 100
Band of Angels, 100, 133
Banton, Michael, 159
Bayou La Batre, Alabama, 33, 159
Berg, Charles Ramírez, 214
Bernardi, Adria, 185
Bérubé, Allan, 112
Bhabha, Homi K., 5, 214–15
Bi-civic heritage. *See* Heritage
Biracialism, 31, 32–35, 39, 63, 65–66, 67–68, 110, 125, 128, 162, 177, 179, 196, 217, 221, 236n26, 253n8; as barrier for other races and ethnicities, 155, 174, 179, 180, 190, 192–93, 197–98, 199, 200, 201, 206, 210, 219, 220, 264n3, 266n27, 266n29; and *bro•ken/ground*, 91, 93–95; definition

of, 43–44, 159; emergence in southern discourse of, 41–46; as incorporation of blackness into southern discourse, 126, 132, 145, 150; and *Nuestra Communidad,* 171, 174; redefined as mixed, 100–101, 111, 123–24; and *Tell About the South,* 40, 46–51

Birmingfind, 156–57, 261n3

Birmingham, Alabama, 53, 54–55, 56, 68, 70, 74–76, 77, 80, 82, 84–86, 87, 94–95, 123, 125, 134, 138, 156–60, 166, 201, 238n46, 238n52, 242n23, 244nn37–38, 244n40, 245n41, 245n43, 245n45

Birmingham Civil Rights Institute (BCRI), 40, 53–58, 60, 69–70, 94, 238n45, 238n53, 239n54–55, 247n69

Birth of a Nation, The, 133, 146

Black, Merle, 41

Black Belt, 84, 201–2, 268n16

Black Delta Religion, 149

Blackness, suffering as redemptive of America, 138, 140–41, 143. *See also* Biracialism; Civil rights movement; Electoral politics; Race; Racism; Third Worldism

Blank, Les, 136, 142, 257n43, 260n68

Blood, 118, 120; good vs. bad for Native Americans, 203, 205, 208; many, 48, 50; mixed, 78, 185, 211; quantum for Native Americans, 200, 216; Spanish, 164, 165, 261n69

Bloody Sunday, 61, 240n62

Bluegrass music, 128, 136, 145, 149, 260n68, 261n73

Blues music, 47, 50, 128, 136, 142, 145, 149, 237n29, 261n73, 264n1

Bogue, Ronald, 23, 231n74

Bonilla-Silva, Eduardo, 266n29

Bonitzer, Pascal, 183

Born for Hard Luck: Peg Leg Sam Jackson, 141, 142

Bourdieu, Pierre, 16, 83, 110, 233n87, 252n53, 256n40

Bow, Leslie, 234n108, 264n3

Bradshaw, Michael, 3

Brett, David, 53, 55, 64

bro•ken/ground, 27, 33, 68, 70, 74–86, 89–95, 121, 125, 138, 243n27, 244n39, 247n63

Browder, Glen, 84, 244n39

Brown, Michael, 115

Brown, Richard Maxwell, 3, 223n3

Bruzzi, Stella, 247n62

Butler, Judith, 87, 88–89, 105, 109, 216, 246n60, 250n32

Cajuns, 126, 136, 142, 145–46, 165, 217, 260nn68–69; music, 149, 150

Carson, Clayborne, 242n23

Center for New American Media, 162

Center for Southern Folklore (Memphis, Tennessee), 136, 148

Chappell, David, 243n35

Chatterjee, Partha, 3

Chief: Calvin McGhee and the Forgotten Creeks, The, 198, 209–10, 212–13, 215

Children's March (sculpture), 60

Chion, Michel, 156

Choy, Christine, 35, 179, 180, 183, 187–91, 194, 196

Christianity, 63, 111–12, 122, 148, 180, 211, 243n35, 250n35, 258n54, 259n58, 259n60, 262n16; and community, 138–40; and race, 82, 101. *See also* God-created difference

Churchill, Ward, 200, 207

Cinéma Vérité, 106

Cinematic apparatus, 107–8, 249n26

Citizenship, 52–53, 158, 171, 264n1; cultural, 39, 52–53, 64, 65–66, 67; political, 56, 60–61, 67; racial, 39–40, 61, 64–66, 67, 201

Civil Rights Act of 1964, 57, 238n45

Civil Rights Memorial (Montgomery, Alabama), 53, 57, 237n40

Civil rights movement, 72, 83, 100, 101, 126, 132, 189, 195, 201, 235n2, 238n46, 239n53, 242n11, 242n23, 243n35, 244n37, 259n61; and television, 134–35, 146. *See also* Heritage

Index

Civil War. *See* Heritage
Closet, 99, 104, 117, 123, 218, 249n15, 251n36, 263n25; and AIDS, 116–17; and coming out, 109–10; and politics, 117; and race, 100, 110–11, 118, 121–22, 124; and sexuality, 104, 112–16, 252n58
Coalition politics, 190, 194, 201, 206, 221. *See also* Racial affinity
Colebrook, Claire, 226n30
Collins, Patricia Hill, 110
Color: color line, 124, 173–74, 191–92; have own, 180, 185, 194, 196, 266n27; as metaphor for race, 69–70, 82, 94, 220, 247n63; of photographs in *Tell About the South*, 46, 50; on posted signs, 56, 91. *See also* Color-blindness
Color-blindness, 52, 69, 82; as racism, 85, 239n53, 241n2, 242n11, 267n29
Coming out. *See* Closet
Common sense: definition of, 73–74, 241n5; and race, 71, 73–74, 80, 82, 86, 124; and religion, 82, 83, 244n35. *See also* Religion of the people
Community: beloved, 138–40, 259n57; coming, 24; critique of, 258n52; imagined, 4–7, 226n26
Commutation test, 148; and race, 149
Confederate States of America, 16, 52, 63, 224n10, 232n80, 246n55
Confessional, 114, 117, 250n32; and disciplinary power, 105; and documentary film, 106–9, 250n27; interlocutor, 105–8, 250n31; and pastoral power, 105–6, 148, 250n35
Connerly, Charles, 83–84, 244n37
Cowie, Elizabeth, 24–25, 232n86, 233n94, 250n30
Creed, Gerald, 258n52
Creoles, 164, 217, 235n11, 260n69
Crisis of legitimacy, 126, 131–35, 137, 141, 144–45, 256n40. *See also* Disappearing South; Enduring South
Culler, Jonathan, 14

Culture, 8–9, 25, 225n20, 254n13, 256n41; definition of, 6; and imagined community, 5–6; and region, 3, 7, 13, 14, 224n18, 232n80. *See also* Absolutism; Appreciation; Appropriation; Articulation; Assimilation; Citizenship; Culture war; Imperialism; Miscegenation; Ownership; Poaching; Preservation
Culture war, 111–12, 251n45

DaCosta, Kimberly McClain, 110
Dailey, Jane, 244n35
Daughter from Danang, 30
Davenport, Tom, 136, 141, 142, 257n43
Davis, F. James, 87
Davis, Jefferson, 63
de Certeau, Michel, 130
Dear Jesse, 34, 99, 103–4, 112–13, 115, 117
Degler, Carl, 12, 32–33, 47, 72, 234n105, 255n27
Deleuze, Gilles, 16, 21–26, 83, 226n30, 228n37, 230n56, 231nn66–67, 231n74, 232n77, 232n80, 232n87, 233nn94–95, 249n26, 250n35, 263n25
Democrats, 66, 112, 244n39, 245n41, 245n43
Derrida, Jacques, 13–14, 229n44, 230n56
Deterritorialization, 5, 176, 228n40, 263n25
Direct cinema, 89
Disappearing South, 12, 132–33, 137, 144, 145, 255n27, 256n40
Discourse, definition of, 8–10. *See also* Southern discourse
Discursive practice: region as, 4, 7–14, 17–21, 27, 33, 35–36, 177, 217, 228n41, 229n44, 256n40; film as, 24–25, 26–27, 232n84. *See also* Discourse; Southern discourse
Displaced in the New South, 179
Distinctiveness: regional, 12, 32–33, 35–36, 63, 72–73, 132–33, 144, 217, 234n105, 246n55, 255n26; ethnic, 156, 161–62; of ethnicity in *Mosquitoes and High Water*, 164, 166; of region in redemptive ethnographies, 126, 137; of region in *Tell*

About the South, 46–47. *See also* Mediated distinctiveness
Dixon, Julie Williams, 217, 218
DNA studies, 100, 219–20, 270n3
Dolgin, Gail, 30
Dollimore, Jonathan, 36
Douglas, Mary, 109, 251n36
Douglas, Susan, 146
Drake, James, 58–60
Duck, Leigh Anne, 4, 13, 15, 228n41
Dyer, Richard, 79

Eastern Band of Cherokee Indians (North Carolina), 209–12, 269n31
Eccentricity, 8, 30, 32, 142, 143–44, 259n64
Editing: and *bro•ken/ground*, 74–76, 78, 80, 247n63; and documentary film, 26, 106; and ethnographic film, 74; and *Mississippi Triangle*, 180–83, 186–89, 196; and redemptive ethnographies, 142
Edmund Pettus Bridge (Selma, Alabama), 61, 62, 134, 240n62
Egerton, John, 133, 255n27
Electoral politics, 112, 117, 242n12, 244n39; and blacks, 44, 51–52, 53, 64, 237n3; and race, 72, 84–85, 201, 237n34. *See also* Politics
Ellul, Jacque, 138–39
Ends of the Earth, The, 162
Enduring South, 12, 132–33, 255n27, 256n40
Enunciation: definition of, 234n97, 257n43; of Latino/as in *Nuestra Communidad*, 174; of race in *Tell About the South*, 46–51; of race in *bro•ken/ground*, 80–82; of race in *Mississippi Triangle*, 182, 195; of region, 8, 13, 14, 251n36; of region in documentaries, 27–28; of self in documentary film, 106
Eskew, Glenn, 54–55, 238n45, 238n47
Essentialism: racial (as anti-racist), 80–82, 94, 125, 206, 243n27; and region, 4, 7, 35
Ethnicity, 35, 127, 155, 156–59, 160–62, 177, 193, 242n12, 260n69, 263n26, 266n29; and *bro•ken/ground*, 78–80, 247n63, 247n68; ethnic paradigm, 71–72; and *Living in America*, 166–68, 170; and *Mississippi Triangle*, 190; and *Mosquitoes and High Water*, 162, 164–66; and *Nuestra Communidad*, 171–74; symbolic, 161, 262n15; vs. race, 159
Ethnography: and film, 136, 145, 173, 203, 265n20; autoethnography, 102, 249n12; and *bro•ken/ground*, 70, 74; and *Mississippi Triangle*, 180, 186–90; redemptive, 126, 137–45, 150, 155, 160, 165, 168, 221, 257n43; salvage, 82, 137–38, 165, 170
Ethridge, Robbie, 198
Etiquette, racial, 87–88, 92, 189–90, 191
Event, 22–23, 25–26, 29, 54, 89, 106, 123, 138, 139, 183, 231n74, 232n80, 252n58, 255n26; and writing history, 17–18
Exceptionalism: American, 236n27; cultural, 128; local, 94; regional, 14; southern, 14, 32, 45, 72–73, 94, 132–33, 226n25, 232n80, 235n5, 256n30. *See also* Distinctiveness

Fairclough, Norman, 27–28
Family, 13, 251n42; and creole identity, 261n69; in *Family Name*, 118, 120–21; and Indian identity, 208–9, 269n29; in *Melungeon Voices*, 218, 219, 221; as metaphor (brothers and sisters), 101, 111, 123–24; and race, 100, 110–11, 124, 252n53; in *Real Indian*, 203, 205, 208; as social and discursive formation, 16; in southeastern expatriate road film, 103, 115
Family Name, 27, 34, 99–100, 101, 114–15, 118–23, 127, 252n53
Fannie Bell Chapman: Gospel Singer, 144
Fanon, Frantz, 92, 143, 259n62
Faulkner, William, 47–50
Ferris, William (Bill), 34, 136, 144, 147–49, 257n43, 264n1
Fire Hosing of Demonstrators (sculpture), 59–60

Fishkin, Shelley Fisher, 45
Foley, Neil, 173
Forbes, Jack, 200, 209
Forrest, Nathan Bedford, 61–62
Foucault, Michel, 8–11, 15–16, 17, 20–21, 24, 51, 83, 86, 105–6, 109, 148, 225n22, 230n56, 231n66, 236n24, 241n5, 245n46, 246n50, 250n31, 250n35
Franco, Vicente, 30
Freedom Riders, 134, 239n55, 242n23
Freedom Walk (Birmingham, Alabama), 40, 57–61, 239n54
Fugitives, 47, 50, 236n29
Fuller, Jennifer, 77
Fuss, Diana, 81

Gaines, Jane, 25, 108, 123, 148–49, 239n55, 248n4
Gallagher, Charles, 241n2
Gans, Herbert, 161, 252n1, 262n15, 266n29
Gays, lesbians, and transgender people, 83, 99, 103–4, 111–17, 160, 240n66, 245n43, 247n69, 250n35, 251n45, 252n58, 262n11
Geertz, Clifford, 29, 86
Gilroy, Paul, 128, 131, 241n8, 253n4, 253n11
God-created difference, race as, 80–82, 243n27
Goffman, Erving, 87–89
Governmentality, 15–16
Gramsci, Antonio, 51, 65, 71, 73–74, 82–83, 134, 237n32, 240n70, 241n5
Gravel Springs Fife and Drum, 149
Greenbaum, Susan, 263n26, 268n8, 269n17
Greeson, Jennifer, 4
Greetings from Out Here, 27, 34, 99, 103, 112–13, 115–17
Guattari, Félix, 21–26, 227n30, 228n37, 231n67, 232n77, 231n80, 233nn94–95, 249n26, 263n25

Hale, Grace Elizabeth, 19, 87, 91, 224n6
Hall, Stuart, 51, 129, 215, 234n107, 253n2
Heart of Dixie, 66–67

Hegemony, 129, 134; of race in southern discourse, 65, 66, 67, 162; in southern studies, 18–19, 36. *See also* War of position
Heider, Karl, 74
Helms, Jesse, 103, 104, 112, 117–18
Henninger, Katherine, 229n55
Heritage, 128, 160, 165–66, 167, 209, 219; definition of, 53–54, 55; bi-civic, 61–67; civil rights, 33, 39–40, 50, 52–67, 69–70, 123, 140, 165, 221; civil war, 19, 33, 39, 46, 61–65, 104, 126, 224n10
Hershfield, Joanne, 34, 155, 179
Hick flick, 102–3, 249n13
Hierarchies, racial, 81, 174, 194, 199, 266n29
HIV, 104, 116–17
Hobson, Fred, 114, 122
hooks, bell, 91, 129–30, 146, 254n17, 256n37
Hudson, Charles, 198
Humphries, Jefferson, 223n5
Hurston, Zora Neale, 47, 49–50
Hush Hoggies Hush: Tom Johnston's Praying Pigs, 34, 147–49
Hybridity, 45; critique of, 254n11

Identity, southern, 15
Imagined community. *See* Community
Imagined South, 4, 7, 8, 19–20, 24, 223n6, 225n22, 226n26
Imperialism, cultural, 144–45, 260n66
In-betweenness, racial, 35, 42, 158–59, 160, 192–93; and *Living in America*, 167; and creoles, 261n69
Indian Removal (Trail of Tears), 201, 210, 211, 268n16
Invented South, 4, 7, 223n6, 225n22
Isleños, Los, 156, 162–66, 175–77, 262nn17–18, 263n24
It Ain't City Music, 136

Jamison, Gayla, 34, 155, 166–69, 176, 264n26
Jenkins, Henry, 130
Jim Crow, 72, 87, 170, 242n11, 243n35, 246n55

Joseph, Miranda, 258n52
Joyner, Charles, 128, 197, 253n8

Kelly Ingram Park (Birmingham, Alabama), 40, 53, 55, 57–59, 134, 239nn54–55
Kennedy, Brent, 217–20, 270n3
King, Martin Luther, Jr., 54, 62, 63, 69, 95, 112, 138–39, 143, 238n45, 258n47, 258nn52–54, 259n57, 259n62
Kirby, Jack Temple, 144–45
Kirkman, Tim, 34, 99, 103–4, 115, 117
Kirshenblatt-Gimblett, Barbara, 54, 55, 57, 58
Kolker, Andrew, 17, 34, 155, 162–63
Ku Klux Klan, 62, 87, 90–91, 172

Lacan, Jacques, 20, 21, 107–8, 229n44, 230n59, 231n65, 231n67, 250n30
Lassiter, Mathew, 241n11
Latino/as, 42, 156, 159, 179, 209, 220, 234n108, 236n26, 242n12, 263n21, 266n29; civil rights movement, 173; and *Living in America*, 169; and *Mosquitoes and High Water*, 164; and *Nuestra Communidad*, 170–74
Lawson, Chris, 27, 68, 70, 74–75, 90, 125
Lebow, Alisa, 101–2, 230n59
Lee, Robert E., 63
Lenticular logic, 19–20, 44–45, 65, 150
Living in America: One Hundred Years of Ybor City, 34, 155, 160, 166–70, 173, 175–77
Local: definition of, 227n37, 234n99, 258n52; and documentary film, 26–28, 34; and race, 33, 43–44, 52, 61, 67, 83, 94, 155, 217, 242n23, 266n29; relation to regional, 6, 7, 10, 12–14, 17, 32, 36, 39, 45, 63, 73, 77, 94, 116, 137, 145, 148, 156, 177, 228n34, 228nn40–41, 229n44; trans-local, 73, 94, 177, 228n37
Loewen, James, 191–92, 193, 264n2
Lomax, Alan, 74, 137, 257n44, 260n68, 264n1
Long, Worth, 35, 179, 183

Long take: and *bro•ken/ground*, 74–76; and ethnographic film, 74
Lost cause, 43, 63–64
Love, 99, 103, 105, 256n37; ethics of, 129–30, 131, 139–40; and Christian community, 138–40; and power, 258n54
Lowery, Malinda Maynor, 35, 196, 198, 202–5, 207–8, 267n1, 269n30
Lumbee Indians (North Carolina), 35, 166, 198, 202–8, 216, 269n20, 269n30

MacDougall, David, 74
Made in Mississippi: Black Folk Arts and Crafts, 149
Mai's America, 29–32, 137, 234n100
March from Selma to Montgomery (1965), 61–62, 69–70, 94, 235n2, 240n62, 256n37
March on Washington (1963), 62, 69, 242n23
Marchetti, Gina, 180–81, 190, 248n4, 265n6
Marcus, George, 143–44, 259n64
Marrow, Helen, 174, 263n23
Maynor, Malinda. *See* Lowery, Malinda Maynor
McElwee, Ross, 99, 102–4, 117, 137
McGhee, Calvin, 213–16
McIntosh, Alabama, 33, 202
McPherson, Tara, 4, 19, 44–45, 65, 150, 240n69
Mead, Margaret, 74
Mediated distinctiveness, 11–12, 17, 33, 35–36, 217, 236n27
Melungeon Voices, 217–21, 270n3
Mercer, Kobena, 131
Metz, Christian, 108, 229n53
Miles, Robert, 71
Miller, D. A., 122
Miller, Toby, 52–53
Mills, Sara, 8
Mimesis, 25, 215–16, 233n89; political, 25, 108, 239n55
Mimicry, 25, 64, 214–16, 233n89

Mirror phase, and documentary film, 107–8, 250n30
Miscegenation, 34, 42; bodily, 100–101, 109–11, 124, 197; cultural, 109, 128–29, 131–32, 150, 175, 197, 253n8, 254n12; and *Family Name*, 104, 118, 120–22
Mise-en-scène: and Birmingham Civil Rights Institute, 56–57; and *bro•ken/ground*, 74, 76, 80; and documentary film, 26; and Freedom Walk sculptures, 59; and *Mississippi Triangle*, 180, 184, 196
Mississippi Chinese, 33, 35, 158–59, 160, 190–93, 206, 264n2, 264n3; and *Mississippi Triangle*, 179–90, 194–96, 264n1, 265n25, 266n29
Mississippi Delta, 33, 35, 47, 87, 158–60, 190–92, 228n37, 264n1, 267n31; and *Mississippi Triangle*, 179–80, 184–87, 189–90, 194–96, 267n29
Mississippi Delta Blues, 136
Mississippi Triangle, 35, 179–96, 264n1, 266n29
Mixed race, 44, 100–101, 109–11, 123–24, 164, 260n69; and *Family Name*, 120; and *Melungeon Voices*, 217–21; and *Mississippi Triangle*, 182; and *Real Indian*, 204–5, 211; and Native Americans, 199–200, 202, 214, 216. *See also* Blood
Mobile, Alabama, 33, 159, 202, 268n17
Mofford, Eric, 179
Mono-racial, 33, 110, 124, 150, 217, 252n53, 266n29
Mormino, Gary, 158, 178
Morris, Aldon, 238n46
Morris, Errol, 142
Morrison, Toni, 193
Mosquitoes and High Water, 34, 155, 160, 162–66, 173, 175–76
MOWA Band of Choctaw Indians (Alabama), 202, 268n17
Multiracialism, 33, 50, 67, 95, 123, 179–80, 194, 217, 220, 235n19, 266n29
Munslow, Alan, 17

Mutability, racial, 61, 124, 142, 149, 168, 245
Myth, 3, 43, 171, 223n5, 228n40, 236n27, 256n30

Native Americans, 33, 35, 42, 127–28, 160, 165–66, 191, 192–93, 197–202, 217, 218–19, 234n108, 262n11, 267n1, 268nn13–14, 269n23; Hollywood stereotype of, 203, 205, 207–9, 212–16, 268n14; and powwow, 206, 208, 210–11, 214; and *Real Indian*, 203–9; and representational strategies, 209–16; and segregation, 166, 206. *See also* Blood; Family; Indian Removal; Southeast syndrome; Sovereignty
Neale, Stephen, 215
Neely, Sharlotte, 211, 269n31
New Criticism, 28–29
New York City, 10, 45, 99, 103–4, 115–16, 135, 167, 170, 172, 246n55, 248n1
Nichols, Bill, 26, 89, 233n92, 247n62, 249n23
Normal, 9, 109; and family, 110–11, 251n42
Norrell, Jeff, 157–58
Nuestra Communidad: Latinos in North Carolina, 34, 155, 160, 170–74, 177, 179
Omi, Michael, 71–73, 81, 94, 170, 241n8
One-drop rule, 42, 78, 110, 201, 205, 266n26. *See also* Blood
Open Secret, 120, 121–22, 123
Operation New Birmingham, 85–86, 246n47
Ownership, cultural, 130–31

Painter, Nell Irvin, 79
Panter, Rich, 198, 209
Paredes, Anthony, 214, 269n17
Paris Is Burning, 215
Peiser, Judy, 34, 136, 144, 147–49, 257n43
Perdue, Theda, 206
Performance: of Indianness, 212–16; racial performance in *bro•ken/ground*, 89–92;

in *Real Indian*, 208; in redemptive ethnographies, 142–43, 146
Performative documentary, 74, 89, 143, 203, 247nn62–63
Performativity: definition of, 87–89, 246n60; racial, 146, 188, 192, 216; racial, in bro•ken/ground, 92–94
Philadelphia, Mississippi, 33
Philips, John Edward, 128
Phillips, Ulrich B., 41
Photographs, 9, 46, 52, 62, 74, 111, 158, 166, 208, 218, 229n44, 229n55, 236n28, 247n63, 267n32
Place, 103, 176, 258n52; sense of, 8, 109, 208; out of, 109, 115
Poaching: cultural, 130–31; racial, 124, 131, 146, 149–50; southern supplement as, 7, 13–14, 15–16, 27, 32, 228n41, 232n86
Poarch Band of Creek Indians (Alabama), 166, 202, 209–14, 233n89, 269n17
Police Attack Dog (sculpture), 58–60
Political mimesis. *See* Mimesis
Politics: gerrymandering, 84, 245n45; majority-minority political districts, 44, 52, 83–84, 244n41; single-member political districts (SMD), 84–85, 245n45. *See also* Coalition politics; Electoral politics
Poras, Marlo, 29, 31
Porter, Frank W., III, 199, 209, 269n29
Possible: audience, 25, 28, 106–8, 177, 250n27; and Christianity, 139; concept of, 20–24, 231n65, 231n74, 232nn76–77; and documentary film, 24–26, 233n95; South, 4, 19–20, 24, 36, 95, 111, 140, 155, 177, 221, 231n67, 232n82
Post-raciality, 52
Postsouthern (term), 226n25
Potentiality. *See* Possible
Pozzetta, George, 158, 178
Pratt, Mary Louise, 102, 249n12
Preservation, cultural, 137–38, 156, 160, 162, 175–77

Pro-filmic, and documentary film, 25–29, 106, 142–43, 186, 233n95
Psychoanalysis, 20, 21, 231n65, 250n31. *See also* Mirror phase
Public secret. *See* Open secret

Race: black/nonblack divide, 174, 193, 266n29; black/white binary, 34, 174, 191–92; brown race, 159, 171, 174; vs. ethnicity, 71–72, 159; vs. ethnicity in *Mosquitoes and High Water*, 165; vs. ethnicity in *Living in America*, 167–68; vs. ethnicity in *Melungeon Voices*, 220; vs. ethnicity in *Nuestra Communidad*, 171–74; white/nonwhite divide, 158, 172, 174, 192, 193, 205, 266n29
Race relations, 73, 95, 178, 183, 188, 194, 235n9, 239n53
Racial divide, 50, 77–78
Racism, 51, 60–61, 72, 81, 88, 103, 129, 130, 132–33, 146, 241n3, 242n11, 243n27, 246n46, 268n14; anti-black, 72, 117, 193, 206, 266n27; and bro•ken/ground, 76, 82, 90–91, 93; and creoles, 260n69; and *Greetings from Out Here*, 113; and in-betweenness, 158; and *Living in America*, 167; and *Melungeon Voices*, 218; and *Mississippi Triangle*, 181, 183, 188, 193, 265n25; New Racism, 132, 241n2; and *Nuestra Communidad*, 172; personal vs. institutional, 80, 131–32; and *Real Indian*, 205–6. *See also* Color-blindness
Rape, 120, 122
Real Indian, 35, 196, 202–9, 216, 218
Reconciliation, racial, 55, 77–78, 92, 123, 239n53
Redemptive ethnography. *See* Ethnography
Reed, John Shelton, 13, 41, 223n5, 224n6, 255n27
Regionalism. *See* Culture; Discursive practice; Distinctiveness; Enunciation; Essentialism; Exceptionalism; Local; Sound

Religion of the people, 73–74, 83, 86. *See also* Articulation; Christianity; Common sense
Renov, Michael, 101–2, 106, 249n23
Republicans, 72, 224n10, 241n11, 244n41, 245n43
Reynolds, Burt, 102–3
Richardson, Riché, 19
Riggs, Marlon, 89, 111, 251n46
Robinson, James, 140, 259n58
Roediger, David, 158, 160, 174, 192
Romine, Scott, 4, 6, 19–20, 216, 226n25, 226n30, 228n40
Rouch, Jean, 106, 107
Rubin, Louis D., Jr., 132, 133
Russell, Catherine, 102

Said, Edward, 226n26
Sectionalism, 4–5, 224n10, 256n27
Sedgwick, Eve, 104, 246n60, 253n5
Segregation, racial, 32, 44, 50–51, 56–57, 65–66, 82, 85, 87, 91, 93, 132, 238n46, 243n35, 245n42, 245n45, 266n29. *See also* Native Americans
Selma, Alabama, 40, 53, 61–63, 134, 202, 243n23, 256n37
Sherman, Sharon, 257n43
Sherman's March, 99, 101–4, 114
Shohat, Ella, 18, 189
Shores, Max, 198, 209
Sider, Gerald, 198–99, 269n20
Siegel, Allan, 35, 179, 183, 187
Siegelman, Don, 63
Simpson, Penny, 34, 155, 179
Simulacrum, 226n30
Single-member political districts. *See* Politics
Smith, Jon, 4, 19–20, 230n57, 256n35, 259n60
Smith, Stephen, 43
Smith, Valene, 53–54
Snowbird Cherokees, 198, 209–12
Sound (including aural), 18, 26, 88, 156, 165; and *bro•ken/ground*, 76–77; and *Living*

in America, 176; and *Mosquitoes and High Water*, 164–65, 175; and *Nuestra Communidad*, 171; and *Real Indian*, 208; and redemptive ethnographies, 142–43; and region, 8, 16–17, 28; and *Tell About the South*, 47
South. *See* Southern discourse
Southeast syndrome, 200, 202
Southeastern expatriate road film (SERF), 34, 99, 102–4, 106–7, 122, 218, 248n2; and closet, 109, 115–18; and culture war, 111–14
Southern Circuit, 136, 257n42
Southern discourse: definition of, 4, 7–12, 226n26, 227n30, 236n27, 241n5; and disciplinary boundaries, 3–4, 18–19, 225n22, 233n94, 234n99; emergent, dominant, and residual strains of, 41, 45, 64–65, 100–101, 123–24; and history, 17–19; and race, 33–35, 41, 43, 45, 67, 72, 111, 123–24, 125, 146, 155, 219, 221, 235n19, 236n26, 253n8; and reception, 11, 28–29, 137–38, 140. *See also* Articulation; Biracialism; Crisis of legitimacy; Disappearing South; Enduring South; Exceptionalism; Hegemony; Possible; Subjectivity; Supplement
Southern Poverty Law Center (Montgomery, Alabama), 13, 57
Sovereignty: and imagined community, 4–5; and Native Americans, 201, 203, 206, 208. *See also* Sectionalism
Spears, Ross, 27, 40, 46, 49, 137
Spiro, Ellen, 27, 99, 103–4, 115–16
Spitzer, Nicholas, 260n69
St. Bernard Parish, Louisiana, 34, 156, 160, 164–66, 176
Stam, Robert, 18, 189
"Stars Fell on Alabama," 66–67
State apparatus, 51–52; vs. governmental unit, 237n30
Steinberg, Stephen, 239n53
Strategy, southern, 72–73, 94, 241n11, 242n12

Subjectivity, 10; and confessional, 109, 250n27, 250n35; ethnic, 159; filmmaker's, 101–2; and *Hush Hoggies Hush*, 148; southern, 15–17, 27, 36, 232n80; trans-racial, 56–61, 221

Supplement: southern, 6, 7, 12–14, 32 (*see also* Poaching); thick vs. thin, 29–30; thin, 170, 178

"Sweet Home Alabama," 66–67

Syncretism, 65, 133, 253n11. *See* Miscegenation

Tampa, Florida, 34, 156, 158, 166–69, 178, 263n26

Taussig, Michael, 122

Taylor, Melanie Benson, 206, 234n108

Tell About the South, 27, 33, 40, 46–51

Third Worldism, 141, 143–45, 259n63

Thompson, John, 148–49

Tindall, George, 41, 223n5, 255n27

Tomlinson, John, 9, 260n66, 263n25

Tongues Untied, 89, 111

Toomer, Jean, 47–50

Torres, Rodolfo D., 71

Torres, Sasha, 134

Trail of Tears. *See* Indian Removal

Trans-local. *See* Local

Trans-racial subjectivity. *See* Subjectivity

Tri-racial isolate, 199–200, 202, 218, 268n8

Tri-racialism, 33, 42, 174, 266n29; and *Mississippi Triangle*, 179–80, 194–95. *See also* In-betweenness, racial

United Houma Nation in Louisiana, 165, 202, 269n18

Urry, John, 54

Vernon, Florida, 142–43

Virtual South, 231n67, 232n82

Visker, Rudi, 20, 225n22

Voting Rights Act of 1965, 53, 62, 237n36

Wallerstein, Immanuel, 224n18

War of position, 65, 134, 240n70, 254n11

Warner, Michael, 109

Webster, Gerald, 244n41

White, Hayden, 17–18, 219

White supremacy, 32–33, 41, 43, 51, 64, 66, 78, 90–92, 93, 124, 132, 133–35, 140–41, 145, 146, 150, 193, 194, 205–6, 217, 238n45, 259n60, 266nn26–27, 266n29

Whites, as minority, 84–85, 245nn42–43

Williams, Raymond, 41, 64–65, 83, 225n20, 241n5

Williamson, Joel, 42, 45, 197, 235n9

Wilson, Charles Reagan, 63–64

Winant, Howard, 71–73, 81, 94, 170, 241n3, 241n8

Winston, Brian, 25–26, 233n94

Wolfe, Thomas, 47, 49–50

Woodward, C. Vann, 133

Wrinkle, Margaret, 27, 68, 70, 74–75, 90, 125

Xing, Jun, 180

Yaeger, Patricia, 251n36

Ybor City (Tampa, Florida), 34, 156, 158, 162, 166–70, 175–76, 263n26

Yeah You Rite! The Way They Talk in New Orleans, 17, 162

Zeiger, David, 179

Zinn, Howard, 132–33, 236n27, 255n27, 256n30

Zydeco, 149, 150, 217, 260n69

Zydeco: Creole Music and Culture in Rural Louisiana, 260n69

www.ingramcontent.com/pod-product-compliance
Lightning Source LLC
Chambersburg PA
CBHW030608230426
43661CB00053B/1897